Depositions

Depositions

Scenes from the Late Medieval Church and the Modern Museum

Amy Knight Powell

ZONE BOOKS · NEW YORK

2012

ZONE BOOKS
1226 Prospect Avenue
Brooklyn, NY 11218

Printed in the United States of America.

Distributed by The MIT Press,
Cambridge, Massachusetts, and London, England

Library of Congress Cataloging-in-Publication Data

Powell, Amy (Amy Knight), 1973-
Depositions : scenes from the late medieval church and the modern museum / Amy Powell.
p. cm.
Includes bibliographical references and index.
ISBN 978-1-935408-20-8 (alk. paper)
1. Jesus Christ—Burial—Art. 2. Weyden, Rogier van der, 1399 or 1400–1464—Criticism and interpretation. 3. Christian art and symbolism—Medieval, 500–1500. 4. Art—Exhibition techniques—Social aspects. 5. Art museums—Social aspects. I. Title. II. Title: Scenes from the late medieval church and the modern museum.

N8053.2.P69 2012
704.9'4853—DC23

2011037203

Contents

In memory of my father, Gerald Powell

Preface

Despite its chronologically organized galleries, the institution of the modern museum gives rise to formal comparisons between works of art from different times and places. This is one of the reasons why artists, art historians, and others have found the museum so hard to live with. The museum, in the words of one art historian, is a "machine for formalist looking."[1] Here objects of the past are severed from their original contexts and brought under the same roof as objects of the present, which are no less stripped of the historical conditions of their making. According to the traditional and long-discredited logic of the museum, this loss of context is humanity's gain: the work finds a new home—so the story goes—in the universal category of Art embodied in the museum.

But there is a better logic by which the decontextualizing space of the museum can be seen to do justice to objects transposed from distant times and places. While every object in the museum has been subject to historical deracination, not every museum object is the *unsuspecting* victim of this process. Even some objects made before the era of the museum and the "autonomous" work of art anticipate it. This book is about a group of late medieval paintings and sculptures of the deposition of Christ from the cross that quite knowingly foretell the process by which they will eventually find their way into the confines of the museum, where the old image inevitably becomes apple to some new orange—which is to say, begins to look like something it is not.

By the late Middle Ages, the deposition from the cross had begun to be represented on a scale and with a frequency that rivaled that of the crucifixion, to which it had earlier been a mere accessory (plate 1).[2] As the iconography of the Deposition grew in importance over the course of the fifteenth century, picturing the deposition of Christ—the *imago Dei*, "the image of the invisible God" (Colossians 1.15)—became an occasion to imagine the deposition of the *image as such.*[3] By exploiting the auto-iconoclastic implications of the deposition scene, artists gave measured form to late medieval iconophobia. In so doing, they prefigured the imminent iconoclasms of the Protestant Reformation. Wanting to put an end to the Catholic cult of images, Protestant reformers would find themselves performing a well-rehearsed gesture: the deposition of what they liked to call dead images.

The late medieval Deposition's prefiguration of Reformation iconoclasm prefigures, in turn, the repeated "deaths" of art since the invention of the camera. This is the premise of the vignettes devoted to twentieth-century works of art that conclude each chapter of this book.[4] These vignettes are based on formal comparisons that bridge but do not collapse the historical distance separating the early modern world from the more recent past. Indeed, difference is the condition of possibility for the surreal prefiguration or *pseudomorphic resemblance*—as I will call it here—that aligns the book's chapters with the vignettes that close them.[5]

"Pseudomorphosis" is a term of abuse. Having appropriated it from mineralogy, Oswald Spengler first used it as such in *The Decline of the West* (1917–1920) to "designate those cases in which an older alien Culture lies so massively over the land that a young Culture, born in this land, cannot get its breath and fails not only to achieve pure and specific expression-forms, but even to develop fully its own self-consciousness."[6] Although Spengler provides examples of artistic pseudomorphosis, it is Erwin Panofsky who brings the term squarely into the discipline of art history, shifting its meaning slightly in the process—"pseudomorphosis: the emergence of a form

A, morphologically analogous to, or even identical with, a form B, yet entirely unrelated to it from a genetic point of view."[7] And it is Donald Judd who perhaps puts the idea best when he says: "A lot of things look alike, but they're not necessarily very much alike."[8] Art historians now use the term pseudomorphosis as Judd does, that is, to dismiss misleading comparisons based on formal similarities where there is no similarity of artistic intent.[9]

It is precisely the pseudomorph's capacity to mislead that has moved surrealists, in contrast to art historians, to celebrate it. The image that joins conceptually incomparable things can derive "from itself a ridiculous *formal* justification," explains Breton in the first *Manifesto of Surrealism*.[10] In Bataille's *Story of the Eye*, pseudomorphosis is *the* unconscious mechanism that keeps both desire and the narrative moving. The protagonist of Bataille's *Story* is not an eye per se but rather a white orb whose guises include but are not limited to the organ of sight. The unfolding of the story's pseudomorphic logic sees this object through a series of transformations sanctioned by a shared whiteness and rotundity: from a pussycat's saucer of milk, to a soft-boiled egg, to the decorticated testicles of a bull and, finally, the enucleated eye of a dirty priest. With each of these transformations comes the frisson of discovering, via formal resemblance, a kinship where it was least expected.[11]

With or without authorial permission, works of art—just like eyes and eggs—enter into liaisons with other works from distant times and places, licensed to associate with them by nothing more than their structure, shape, color, or texture. Each particular liaison may be accidental but that there will be such liaisons, one way or another, seems to be inevitable. In its promiscuity, form has a way of detaching works of art from the people who worked them and from the time and place in which they were made, not by transcending history—that would be the metaphysical understanding of form as "idea" or "essence"—but rather by transgressing history, at least, our linear conception of it.[12] The art historian who discreetly overlooks these transgressions (insisting that although certain historically distant objects may look alike, they cannot *mean* alike) risks consigning meaning to a space beyond the contours of the object and beyond the rhythms of discourse, that is, to a realm of ideas unencumbered by what Bataille calls concrete forms.[13] The art historian who, on the contrary, takes pseudomorphosis seriously follows Bataille in pursuing a meaning inseparable from the shapes it inhabits.

For Bataille, each thing is monstrously singular; it can do no more than *resemble* other things.[14] Resemblance counts a great deal for Bataille for just this reason, particularly where it joins what we expect to be incommensurable. That God and shit (the sacred and the excremental) share the formal characteristic of being heterogeneous to the social body is the very root of Bataille's heterology.[15] To call this kind of resemblance *merely formal*—as does the person who uses the term pseudomorphosis in its now conventional, dismissive sense—is to posit an opposition between form and content that Bataille's "base materialism" systematically deconstructs.[16] The objects in the pseudomorphic sequences of the *Story of the Eye* do not owe their significance to some cryptic primal scene; they do not owe their meaning to history. Rather, they carry it with them in their very whiteness and rotundity.[17] This is not to say that they are autonomous—on the contrary. Isolated and misconstrued, they are anything but self-governing. Dislodged from the (context of the) human face, the seemingly autonomous eye (or work of art) discovers its heteronomy in its subjection to other objects.

I take this subjection to be the subject of Louise Lawler's *Pictures That May or May Not Go Together, 1997–98*, a photograph of paintings lying dormant on the racks of a museum storeroom (figure 1). Few situations show better what paintings have in common: rectilinearity, flatness, stillness, a frame. Nor is this a bad situation for suggesting that what they *do not have in common* is of greater interest than what they do. In the museum, we cannot see the painting for the frame, the object for the institution, the difference for the sameness. This is what has been described and more often decried as the homogenizing effect of the modern museum.[18] While they describe

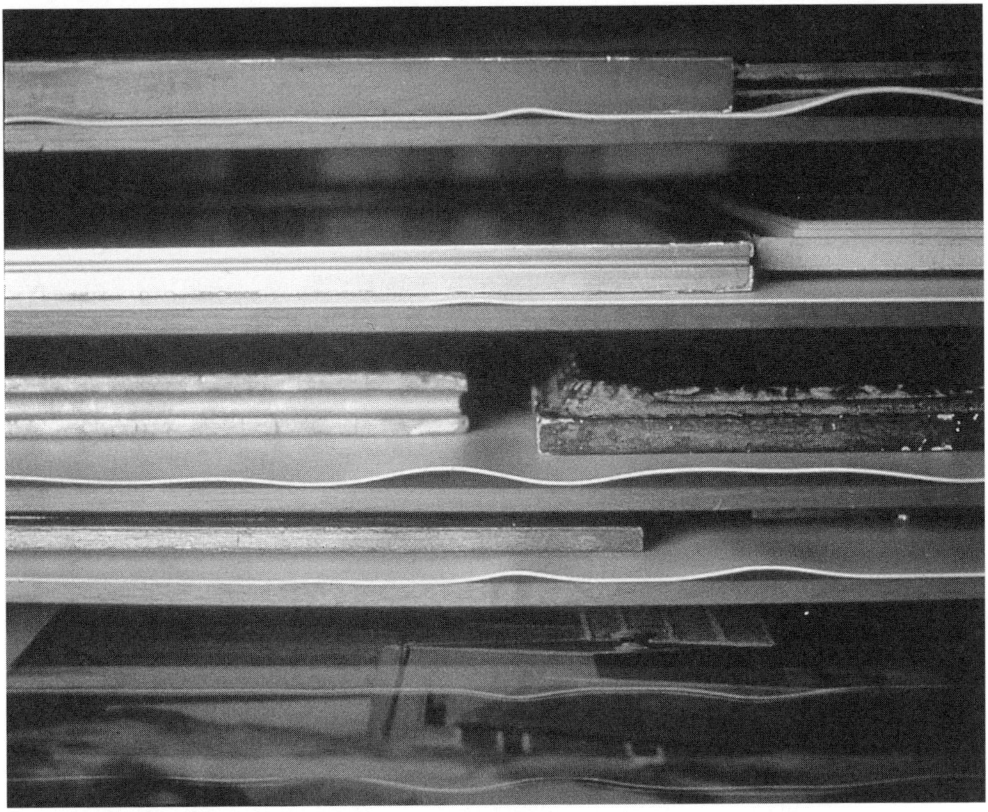

Figure 1. Louise Lawler, *Pictures That May or May Not Go Together, 1997–98*, cibachrome, 61 × 76.2 cm. The History of Art and Architecture Department, Harvard University, Cambridge. (Photo: Louise Lawler and Metro Pictures.)

and decry the flattening of difference, Lawler's photographs also delight in the formal rhymes set up by the museum, discovering in those rhymes a figure for the peculiar contingency of the work of art, whose meaning is dependent upon its context but never definitively determined by any one context—least of all its original context.

If there is little nostalgia for lost origins in Lawler's pictures of museums, there is even less in her photographs of private collections. In *Pollock and Tureen, Arranged by Mr. and Mrs. Burton Tremaine, Connecticut, 1984*, Lawler lets one red, white, black, yellow, and green tangle play against the other, tracing the collectors' meaning-making and meaning-robbing decorative juxtapositions (plate 2). "Both photographs are taken in homes," Lawler once explained in reference to a pair of her photographs, "so it seemed interesting to juxtapose them; meaning is also made through juxtaposition."[19] Indeed, with some strategic cropping, a Pollock becomes a soup tureen as easily as Bataille's eye becomes a cat's milk dish. Lawler's camera capitalizes on the logic of pseudomorphism without denying its distortions. Equal measures truth and distortion, Lawler's story of objects makes much of their promiscuity—which is precisely what most art historians would rather overlook.

Art historians are not alone in trying to ignore and even prevent the promiscuous straying and intermingling of works of art. Modernists, including Marinetti—here writing in the Futurist Manifesto (1909)—condemn the museum as a place where such mixing occurs: "Museums: cemeteries! Identical, really, in the horrible promiscuity of so many bodies scarcely known to one another."[20] Most post-studio practices, including performance art and site-specific installation, stem from a related belief, namely, that the movement of the work of art from its site of production to its place of exhibition is the first in a series of (bad) displacements that permit the work to become an instrument of others.[21]

To protect against such instrumentalization, artist Daniel Buren drafted in 1968 what he called an *Avertissement*, a contract between artist and owner, the breach of which entails the annulment of

Buren's authorship: "Using the *Avertissement* is not so much to control, as to clarify that the work can be totally spoiled by misuse. You have to be clear about that. If you spoil my work, I have at least the modest opportunity to say through my *Avertissement*, 'OK, you can spoil it, it's your right. But it's not my work anymore.'"[22] In 1971, critic Seth Siegelaub and lawyer Robert Projansky wrote and circulated a similar contract (The Artist's Reserved Rights Transfer and Sale Agreement) guaranteeing the artist aesthetic control over and financial rights to his or her work until the death of the artist—the *physical* death of the artist. The "death of the author" theorized around the same time is difficult to reconcile with a contract of this sort, which for all its progressive intentions reinforces capitalism's equation of art and personal property.[23]

This book begins from the premise that works of art *do not belong* to their makers, which is not to say that those makers should not be adequately remunerated but simply that form is too promiscuous to remain faithful to its author's intentions. As far as art history is concerned, improprieties of form are particularly disorienting where they blur the line separating old from new, which is what happens so often when the historical object takes its place in the museum—and the museum is where one meets most of the late medieval paintings and sculptures of the deposition from the cross that are the subject of this book. That one finds these Depositions displa(y)ced in the museum—or in a church that has itself become an exhibition space with admission fees, wall text, and so on—is anything but incidental to their subject matter. This is particularly clear when it comes to crucifixes with movable arms, strange puppet-like sculptures whose shoulders are hinged because they were used in the late Middle Ages to reenact Christ's burial each year on Good Friday, when they were deposed from the cross, wrapped in linens, and, with arms lowered to their sides, placed in structures built to resemble sepulchers (figure 2, plate 3). Equipped with the means of their own removal, crucifixes with movable arms are ready and waiting to be put away and to be taken out again by anyone who wants to do so.

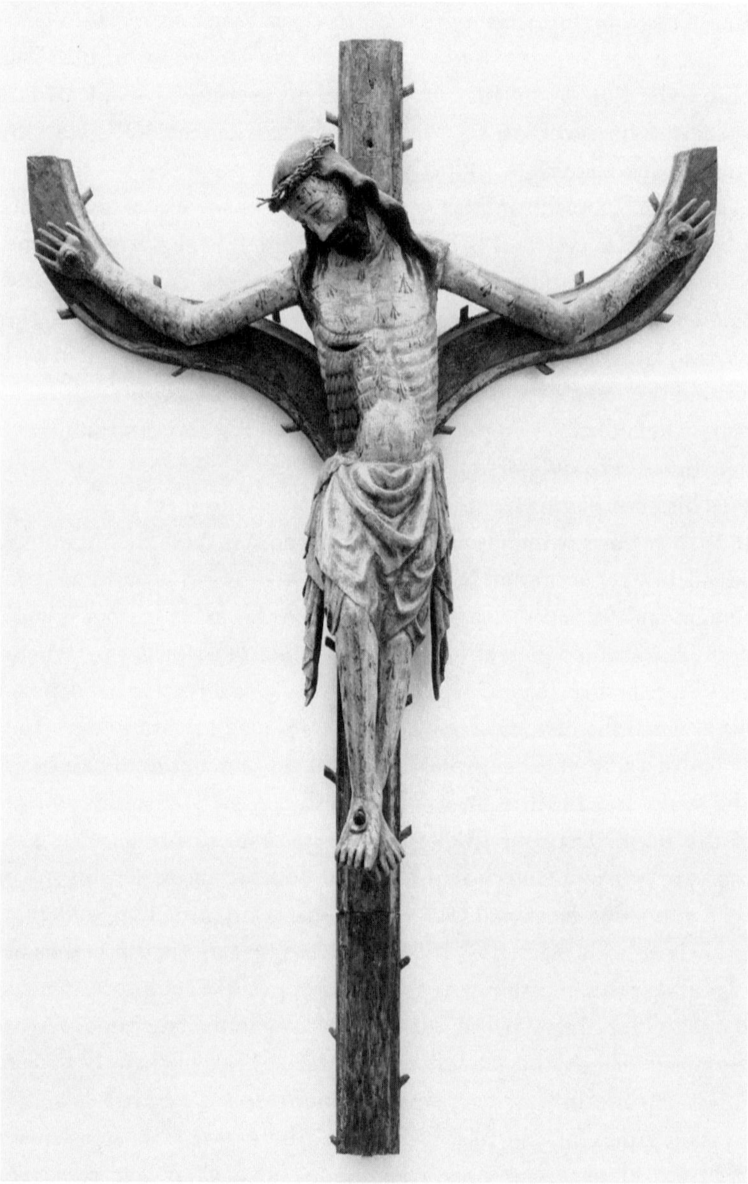

Figure 2. Swabian, *Crucifix with Movable Arms* (ca. 1350) from the Basilica of St. Lorenz in Kempten, Germany, polychromed wood, height 166 cm. (Photo: Kunstverlag Peda.)

The Deposition rite for which these puppets were made inaugurated a forty-hour period of the crucifix's occultation, which came to an end on Easter Sunday with the celebration of Christ's resurrection, when the crucifix was restored to visibility. In the sixteenth century, iconoclastic reformers would depose all but a handful of these objects, inaugurating, in turn, a much longer period of the movable crucifix's invisibility, which came to an end only in the 1960s, when art historians interested in late medieval liturgical culture began to bring these surprising objects to light—again. When the deposed image relegated to a church attic or museum storeroom is re-elevated, it finds itself in a new context and in that new context it makes new "friends." These new affinities reveal it to be the promiscuous thing it always was. The decontextualizing and recontextualizing space of the museum merely facilitates what was, one way or another, bound to happen. I certainly do not want to suggest that the modern museum is blameless; but its shortcomings do not result from the fact that it removes objects from their original contexts and places them in new relations.[24]

More problematic than this decontextualization and recontextualization is the pretense museum curators and art historians sometimes make to being agents of *resurrection*, capable of resuscitating past life. For, neither institution nor individual can restore life to an object that never had it. The promiscuity of the work of art—its return, reiteration, and perpetuation beyond its original moment—is the surest sign it never lived. The late medieval paintings and sculptures considered here are the first to admit this. Allegories of their own "deadness" and knowing harbingers of their future reappearances, these objects look forward to their existence in places far from the ones for which they were made, in the company of strangers, and in times exceeding the short lifespans of their makers. We might, therefore, think of their sojourn in the modern museum less as a regrettable loss of their original context and "life" than as a perfectly appropriate expression of their carefully engineered capacity to be taken down and to be put up again.

What follows is an introduction that sets the stage for the remainder of the book. The body of the book is then divided into two parts, each of whose chapters ends with a vignette of the perverse kind I describe above. Part One focuses on the popular medieval reenactment of the deposition from the cross. What was deposed and buried in the annual Deposition rite was an effigy of Christ, but attention to the form of the rite and the special movable crucifixes made for it reveals that effigy to have also represented something else. I will argue that the Good Friday effigy played in fact two roles: it was at once an image of Christ and an image of the images that had come to represent him. It was not only Christ, then, who was deposed and buried each year but also the *image as such*.

In Part Two, I leave behind the liturgy and its movable sculptures to address the still art of painting—to begin with, an influential altarpiece painted around 1435 by Rogier van der Weyden for the chapel of the Crossbowmen's Guild of Louvain. This painting brings together within a single frame the ostension and occultation of the image that the liturgy spread out in time. Joseph of Arimathea and Nicodemus perform the ostension as they pause in their efforts to remove Christ's body from the cross, while the occultation is implied by the movement of that body toward the obscurity of the grave *and* by the repetition of forms that begins in the center of the composition, where the Virgin collapses into a posture parallel to her son's. With this repetition of forms, Rogier lowers the image of God into a series, depriving it of the singularity and centrality that would make it authoritative and, thereby, reinforcing the essentially iconoclastic structure of the deposition scene.

Judging from its afterlife in copies and pastiches, Rogier's painting had more of an impact on northern European representations of the deposition than any other contemporary painting; it has been said that it was "*the* most influential painting of Northern fifteenth-century art."[25] The remainder of Part Two is devoted to three paintings that recapitulate Rogier's composition, two by the anonymous Master of the St. Bartholomew Altar and one by Jan Mostaert. While all three paintings adopt significant aspects of Rogier's composition, each recreates in its own *distinctive* way the tension that gave Rogier's painting its particular force on the eve of the Reformation: the deposed body's suspension between apparition and waning.

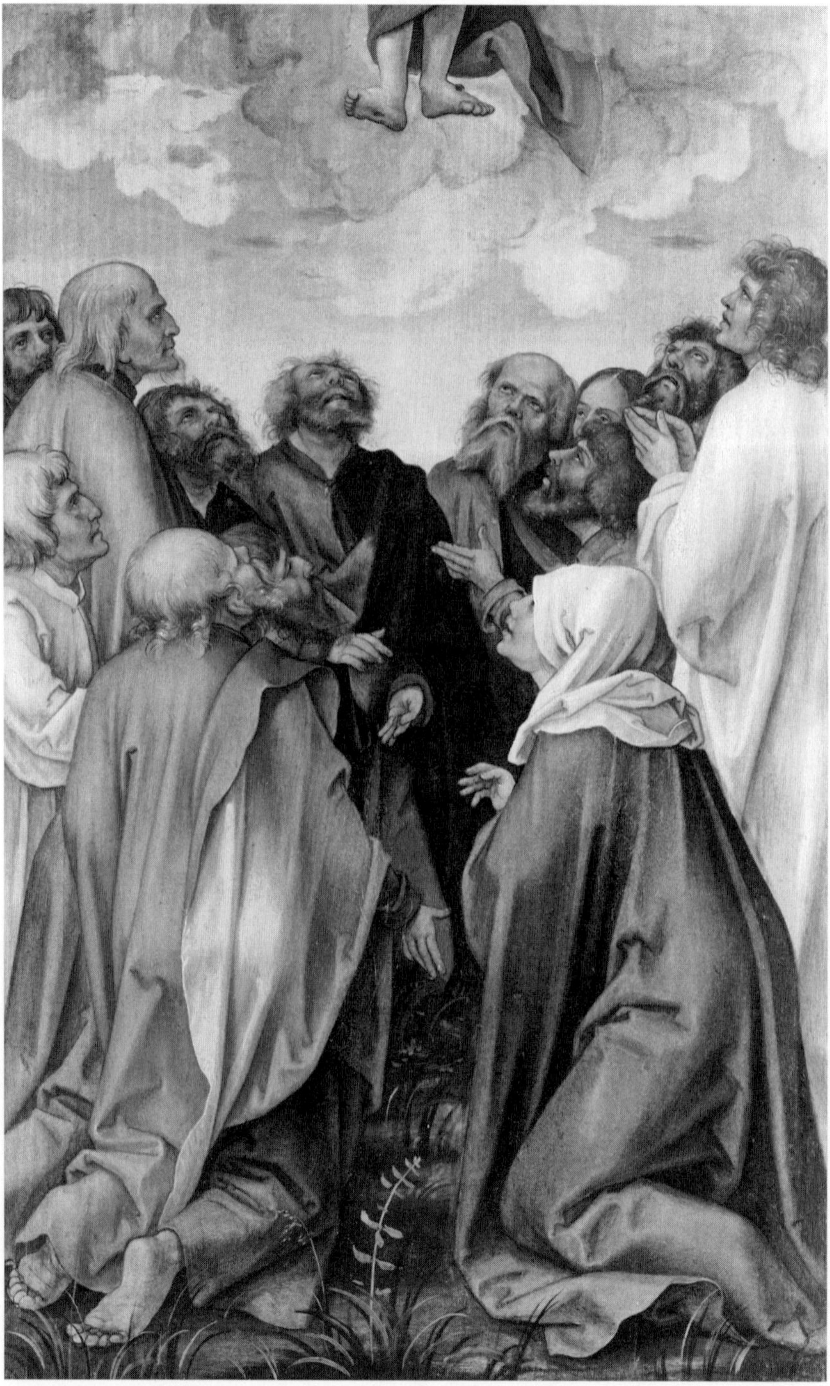

Figure 3. Hans Suess von Kulmbach, *The Ascension of Christ* (ca. 1510), oil on panel, 61.5 × 35.9 cm. Metropolitan Museum of Art, New York, Rogers Fund, 1921 (21.84). (Photo: The Metropolitan Museum of Art.)

INTRODUCTION

The Suspended Figure

Two feet and the hem of a red robe disappearing into the clouds are all that remain visible as the body moves up and out of view (figure 3). Lowered to earth at the incarnation, Christ now returns from whence he came—the *deus ex machina* played backwards. His ascent draws the gaze of the apostles up along with it, until they lose sight of the body—as we are about to do. The picture of a Christ who has all but exited the top of the frame, the so-called Disappearing Christ, is not an end in itself but rather a stepping-stone to another world.[1] Marking the distance between the apostles and that world is a bank of clouds into which the body disappears—a metaphor for God's invisibility, like the clouds in Deuteronomy 4.11–12, where Moses says: "you approached and stood at the foot of the mountain while the mountain was blazing up to the very heavens, shrouded in dark clouds. Then the Lord spoke to you out of the fire. You heard the sound of words but saw no form." Seeing no form or *almost* no form is what the Disappearing Christ illustrates with its strategic deployment of the frame.

After the Byzantine Empire's extended Iconoclastic Controversy (ca. 726–843), the sacred image enjoyed a relatively stable position both there and in the Roman Catholic world, until the Protestant Reformation.[2] In the Eastern Church, it played a quasi-sacramental role as an embodiment of the deity.[3] Officially, the Western Church denied the image this metaphysical power, allowing for its use primarily in the unthreatening form of storyteller. What image-veneration the Western Church openly permitted was understood to pass directly to the prototype—Christ, the Virgin, or the saints—without accruing to the image itself.[4] Theologians in the West maintained that sacred images were useful tools of instruction and aids to pious reflection that could do no more than *guide* viewers to "the invisible by means of the visible." The phrase derives from an eighth-century addition to Gregory the Great's letter to Secundinus of 599: "We do no harm in wishing to show the invisible by means of the visible.... We do not, in truth, bow down before this image as before the divinity, but we adore him whose birth, passion or enthronement in glory the image recalls."[5] Gregorian images are signposts directing viewers toward a divinity that cannot be apprehended with the eyes. They define the path from the visible to the invisible as a one-way street. Corporeal seeing is the precursor to spiritual seeing, and once the latter is attained—within time by a precious few, but at the end of time by all who have been saved—images will cease to be necessary. Pictures of the Disappearing Christ do their best to move the viewer closer to this final imageless destination.

Pictures of the deposition from the cross made in northern Europe on the eve of the Protestant Reformation do something different.[6] Rather than establishing a limited area of competence for sacred pictures as aids to spiritual vision, they simultaneously present and withdraw an image that is much more than a provisional means. Two competing movements structure the iconography of the Deposition in this period: Joseph and Nicodemus display the deposed body to the viewer; and they lower it toward the grave. With these two gestures, they present Christ, while announcing his imminent disappearance.[7]

Paul de Man sees this kind of tension between appearance and disappearance as the engine of all figuration. In an essay on Shelley's unfinished last poem, *The Triumph of Life*, de Man describes the appearance of a rainbow: "The entire scene of the shape's apparition and subsequent waning is structured as a near-miraculous suspension between these two different forces whose interaction gives to the figure the hovering motion which may well be the mode of being of all figures."[8] De Man discovers the same trope of suspension in Wordsworth: "A full-fledged theory of metaphor as suspended meaning... can be elaborated on the basis of Wordsworth's use of 'hangs.'... But then 'hangs' is, by Wordsworth's own avowal, *the* exemplary metaphor for metaphor, for figuration in general."[9] Shelley's hovering motion and Wordsworth's suspended meaning are not only metaphors for metaphor but also figures for the duplicity of their texts: "A literary text simultaneously asserts and denies the authority of its own rhetorical mode."[10] Elsewhere, de Man explains that the text "turns back upon itself in a manner that puts the authority of its own affirmations in doubt, especially when these affirmations refer to the modes of writing that it advocates."[11] For de Man, reading is accordingly a matter of finding where the text changes tack, moving from assertion to denial and back again.

Tension between assertion (apparition) and denial (waning) is more vivid in images of the deposition than in the Disappearing Christ. The Disappearing Christ tells us very little about the incarnate God's appearance, which is almost entirely sublimated into the invisibility above the frame. By contrast, the Deposition shows us that body, boldly asserting its visibility even as it is carried to the grave. Moreover, the sepulchral obscurity toward which the deposed body is being lowered will render it invisible without transmuting it into something more elevated in the process. This difference in direction, then, captures the essential difference between these two pictures of a body moving out of view. While the movement upward is sublimatory, leaving nothing but the hem of a garment for the viewer to cling to in its wake, the movement downward is iconoclastic and perpetually incomplete, never ceasing to be freighted with a body.

Deposing the Image

Religious images were used in the West in many ways, of course, beyond those officially sanctioned by the church. This was especially true in the late Middle Ages, when they were produced in ever-greater numbers. Miraculous images, indulgenced images, and the cults that developed around them are all evidence that, in the time leading up to the Reformation, the Western Church was accommodating and even promoting the very same practices it professed, in Gregory's name, to condemn. Stressing the Reformation's epochal break with what came before, modern scholars have tended to take these phenomena as evidence that an iconophilic if not outright idolatrous popular culture flourished on the eve of the Reformation. Not so long ago, Jeffrey Hamburger could still write: "If anything, the expressions of skepticism regarding images, let alone outright hostility, running right through the fifteenth century, even within the religious mainstream, have been underplayed, as if the period were one of unabashed and unopposed iconophilia."[12]

Early in the twentieth century, Johan Huizinga argued that the defining characteristic of the fourteenth and fifteenth centuries was the popular will to move "living thought from the abstract in the direction of the pictorial."[13] Huizinga's account of the prodigious production of real and mental images in the time before the humanism of Erasmus and the iconoclasm of the Reformation belongs to a story of modernity's transcendence of medieval magic and superstition. Although few scholars would now endorse Huizinga's pejorative assessment of late medieval iconophilia, the narrative of secularization that structures his argument continues to exert a powerful influence over the discipline of art history.[14]

Integral to Hans Belting's formulation of this narrative is the belief that medieval viewers treated icons as if they were alive: "The viewer and the person depicted in the image were related to one another mimetically. The viewer tried to assimilate himself to the depicted person and demanded back from the latter the quality of aliveness which he himself possessed."[15] The Reformation and the emergence of Art during the Renaissance changed this relationship, according to Belting. The immediacy and specularity of the icon were lost, replaced by the mediation of metaphor. Belting's distinction between the medieval image and the modern work of art has helped move the study of pre-modern visual culture beyond strictly aesthetic concerns, but it has also made it more difficult to see how images modulated their claims to presence and liveliness well before the Reformation. And it has led us to underestimate the depths of late medieval iconophobia.

Seemingly at odds with Belting's emphasis on the presence and liveliness of medieval images is Herbert Kessler's account of how those images—including the Disappearing Christ—used inscriptions or pictorial devices to remind viewers that what they "saw on the walls of the churches were images perceived with human eyes and not the divine presences that could be apprehended through the spirit alone."[16] But Kessler's discussion, which grants images an important limited role in medieval piety, can be reconciled with Belting's. The two arguments are complementary, together comprising a single world split between official moderation and popular excess.[17]

What slips through this shared hermeneutic grid is the image *split from within* between moderation and excess. Suspended or oscillating between the assertion and denial of its own rhetorical modes, the late medieval Deposition from the Cross is this. Just as boldly as it presents a vision of Christ, it undermines its own claim to offer the viewer any such thing.[18] It does so by capitalizing on the iconoclasm written into the biblical narrative it depicts. The Deposition from the Cross tells the story of the deposition of an image—indeed, *the* Christian image. Christ is not just one image of God among others. According to Paul, he is the most perfect image of God among men and, as such, the image upon which salvation depends. For, in his capacity as the *imago Dei recreans*, Christ can restore to man the lost perfection of his prelapsarian state. Christ is also the image that justifies all other images of God, as far as the Christian iconophile is concerned: when the Word became flesh, the picturing of God became possible.[19]

Insofar as Christ is the *imago Dei*, the Deposition is a tale of iconoclasm—not in the literal sense of image-*breaking* but in the sense of the lowering of the image from visibility. Employing familiar iconoclastic strategies, including marginalization, mortification, fragmentation, and veiling, late medieval representations of the Deposition (both in painted and ritual forms) emphasized the iconoclasm built into the biblical story. In so doing, they gave viewers and participants in the liturgy a chance to rehearse the disappearance of the image without having it disappear for good. Before any iconoclasts attacked them, these images and rituals were already self-reflexive allegories of their own *suspended undoing*.

I will argue in this book that late medieval pictures and ritual reenactments of the deposition reflect a desire to see the image put away. Even the suspension of the iconoclasm they picture will turn out to answer to this want. In order to understand what the disappearance of the image seemed to offer at the time these Depositions were made, it will help to first sketch the contours of late medieval iconophobia—the iconophobia that scholars who draw a strict line between the medieval and the modern have been inclined to overlook. Only with some feeling for the distrust that images aroused in the late Middle Ages can one begin to assess what was then at stake in picturing the quintessential image being lowered from view.[20]

Late Medieval Iconophobia

In *The Gothic Idol: Ideology and Image-Making in Medieval Art*, Michael Camille shows just how widespread and multifaceted iconophobia in fact was in the later Middle Ages. This iconophobia involved criticism of images made by "Others"—pagans, Saracens, and Jews—but also distrust of images made by Christians.[21] While mainstream theologians certainly expressed this distrust, by the later Middle Ages religious and political dissidents, many of whom the Church labeled heretics, had become the sharpest critics of religious images and the uses to which they were being put.[22]

One of the things driving this dissent and its attendant disdain for images was an enthusiasm for poverty and community associated with the apostles.[23] Christian iconophobia had not always been as closely linked to concerns about wealth as it would come to be in the later Middle Ages. Before this time, it had been more a theological than an economic matter. When, at the end of the sixth century, Gregory defended images in a letter to Bishop Serenus of Marseille, he did not so much as breathe a word about money: "Word has since reached us that you, gripped by blind fury, have broken the images of the saints with the excuse that they should not be adored. And indeed we heartily applaud you for keeping them from being adored, but for breaking them we reproach you.... To adore images is one thing; to teach with their help what should be adored is another. What scripture is to the educated, images are to the ignorant."[24]

Gregory's voice of moderation and defense of images as bibles of the illiterate would reverberate down through the centuries. The Carolingians, for example, adopted his *via media* in response to the restoration of icons in Byzantium following the Second Council of Nicaea in 787. This meant that even while opposing Byzantine iconoclasm, the Carolingians nonetheless condemned the Nicaean Council's iconodule position as idolatrous, endorsing only the didactic and rememorative use of images that Gregory recommended.[25] Although opposition to images on economic grounds had always been part of the Christian debate about images—Jerome criticized the economy of religious images already in the fourth century—it was central to neither the Byzantine image controversy nor the Carolingian response to it.[26]

By contrast, economic, ascetic, and anti-materialist opposition to images were among the most consistent features of the heresies that began to flourish around the year 1000, after centuries of dormancy.[27] The Cathars, who spread through Lombardy and Languedoc in the twelfth and thirteenth centuries, provoking the Albigensian Crusade of 1209–1229, rejected images on Manichaean and ascetic grounds.[28] Waldensians were likewise unable to reconcile images with the asceticism exemplified by their founder, Peter Waldes, a wealthy merchant who, according to legend, had a conversion experience around 1173 that inspired him to give away all his possessions. Although Waldes tried to obtain papal sanction for his life of apostolic poverty, he was eventually cast out of the Church as a heretic. By the thirteenth century, his followers—the itinerant, preaching Waldensians—could be found throughout western and central Europe declaring cemeteries, churches, and all the rituals and objects associated with them, including, of course, the Church's many images, to be no more sacred than the open fields.[29]

The late fourteenth and early fifteenth centuries saw the rise of the last great heresies of the Middle Ages, the Lollards of England and the Hussites of Bohemia. Pilgrimages, endowed masses, and the veneration of relics and images were regularly censured in the sermons of both these groups. While different in their political aspirations, Lollards and Hussites alike affirmed the laity's power to pursue a relationship with God unmediated by the Church, and many agreed that such a pursuit obviated the need for prayers to intercessory images of the Virgin and saints. Both groups were also deeply critical of the *economy* of sacred images, maintaining that the wealth bound up in that economy should be redistributed to the poor.[30] These criticisms were part of larger political and economic agendas. The Lollards advocated voluntary tithes and the disendowment of the Church. In Bohemia, where the Church owned something on the order of half the land, Jan Hus condemned the clergy for charging fees to administer the sacraments and for other forms of simony.[31]

By 1419, the Hussite movement had given rise to a radical faction, the Taborites, whose communalism and iconoclasm divided them not only from Rome but also from the more conservative members of their own church. Inspired by the belief that the earthly social order could be transformed into an image of heaven, the Taborites established communities without private property: "Henceforth at Hradiště and Tábor there is nothing that is mine or thine. Rather, all things in the community shall be held in common for all time and no one is permitted to hold private property. The one who does commits sins mortally.... No longer shall there be a reigning king or a ruling lord; for there shall be servitude no longer. All taxes and exactions shall cease and no one shall compel another to subjection."[32] Taborites held the Church's images to be part and parcel of a godforsaken economy of private ownership, inequality, and greed. Not content to merely polemicize, they took the abolition of idols into their own hands, burning down monasteries and sacking churches in August 1420, for which mainstream Hussites condemned them.[33]

The Taborites' iconoclasm is a relatively rare example of late medieval iconophobia spilling over into outright image-breaking, but many of the lay religious movements that emerged toward the end of the Middle Ages exhibited the same disdain for ecclesiastical wealth that fueled the violence in Bohemia.[34] Although they did not always criticize images directly, many Beguines, Beghards, Free Spirits, and followers of the *devotio moderna* chose a life of poverty that precluded the production and ownership of lavish images. Shunning not only the Church's ritual and wealth but also its hierarchy, they lived alone or in self-governing communities sworn to simplicity and poverty.[35] Images played a role in the devotional life of some of these ascetics, but that role was circumscribed by what they could afford. Few of these dissidents were full-fledged iconoclasts. Few were adherents of a strictly imageless devotion. They simply felt that the sacred exceeded the objects, spaces, and times to which the Church confined it.[36] Like all Christians, they were oriented toward redemption, but theirs was not reserved for the future.[37] They believed proximity to God was attainable in the present and renounced possessions, including images, in order to enter already that time in which earthly attachments would no longer bind them.

To draw a sharp line between an iconophilic late Middle Ages and an iconophobic Reformation is to overestimate the medieval belief in the magical power of images and to underestimate the political and economic concerns of medieval viewers.[38] While those late medieval dissidents who openly disdained the Church's cult of images may not have represented a large percentage of the Christian population, their attitude toward images reveals a shift in the Western image-debate that involved more than their relatively small circles. Well before Reformation iconoclasm erupted in the sixteenth century, that debate had ceased to be confined to a small sphere of theologians and had instead become a matter of broad social significance.[39]

Reformation Iconoclasm

The Protestant Reformation gave rise to iconoclasm on a scale not seen in the Christian world since the Byzantine image controversy of the eighth and ninth centuries.[40] Significant iconoclastic movements began in the 1520s and 1530s in Germany and Switzerland, before spreading over the next decades into England and Scotland and then into France and the Netherlands. The nature and extent of iconoclasm were different in each of these places and in each of the monasteries, villages, towns, and cities within them. Some iconoclasms were violent and illegal; others were planned and carried out in an orderly fashion by ecclesiastic or civic officials.[41] But the whole of northern Europe saw serious challenges to the legitimacy of sacred images.

The form and tenor of a given iconoclastic event depended in large measure on whether it was initiated by so-called magisterial or radical reformers. Although most Protestant reformers found fault with the Catholic cult of images, magisterial reformers tended to condemn the breaking of images as well. Martin Luther not only spoke out against the destruction of images but also defended the continued use of certain images in churches. Ulrich Zwingli and Jean Calvin likewise sought to avert image-breaking, which they viewed as a threat to law and order.[42] Luther, Zwingli, and Calvin countenanced reforming political action only on the part of magistrates, that is, princes and city councils. They wished to see the churches cleansed of their Catholic images, but they wanted it done peacefully and under the strict supervision of the appropriate authorities.

If magisterial reformers attempted to leave existing social hierarchies intact, radical reformers sought to either escape or destroy them.[43] For radicals, iconoclasm was part of an effort to bring the equality of heaven down to earth. Collectively known as Anabaptists, Libertines, or simply fanatics—to both Catholics and Protestants, who opposed them with equal ferocity—radicals were anything but a unified group. But whether "communitarian, mystical, millennialist, Sabbatarian, synodal, immersionist, egalitarian, separatist from the magistracy, separatist from the congregationally banned"—to use George Huntston Williams' words—radicals tended to organize voluntary communities with the aim of changing political and economic relations along with religious life.[44] Like Lollards and Hussites before them, some Reformation radicals refused to pay secular taxes and sacred tithes.[45] And many radicals fought on the side of the peasants in the German Peasants' War of 1524–1526, among them Thomas Müntzer, who is famous for saying: "In the face of usury, interest, and taxes, no one can come to faith."[46]

In his "Sermon Before the Princes" (1524), this same Müntzer quotes the call for the destruction of images in Deuteronomy 7.5: "You should show no mercy to the idolatrous. Break down their altars! Destroy and burn their images."[47] Because his aim was to bring down all the "pomp and affluence of this world" along with its sacred images, Müntzer did not restrict his attacks on idolatry to the churches.[48] As recounted in the *Muehlhausen Chronicle*, he also called for an end to the idol of personal property: "You have removed the idolatry of images and altars from the churches; if you now want to be blessed, so you must also get rid of the idols in the houses and chests, especially the beautiful tin dishes on the walls, the jewelry, silver, and money from the chests."[49]

In his *Territorial Constitution for Tyrol* (1526), Michael Gaismair's exhortation to remove images follows fast on the heels of his demand for social leveling: "*Fifth (decree)*: all the encircling walls around cities, castles, and fortifications in the territory should be torn down . . . so that there are no differences among people in the sense that one is higher than another or able to do wrong to another. . . . Rather, there should be complete equality in the territory. *Sixth (decree)*: all images, statues, and chapels which are not parish churches should be abolished together with the Mass."[50] The anonymous author who addressed the Assembly of the Common Peasantry in May 1525 makes explicit the association between images and inequality implied by Gaismair's sequence of decrees: "The fundamental and true root of all idolatry is the unlimited power of hereditary rulers, which had its origins in Babylon under the first established king."[51] Rejecting civic, noble, and clerical privilege as well as the ostentatious display of those privileges in the form of costly images, the radicals won over a good deal of reforming energy to their cause. Extreme as their iconoclasm and egalitarian communalism were, they had widespread appeal.[52]

Magisterial reformers vehemently opposed utopian aspirations of the radical kind. Luther maintained that the Fall of Man made social inequality inevitable and coercive government a necessity. Secular authority must always be obeyed, he argued, because tyranny is preferable to the anarchy of rebellion: "The mob neither has any moderation nor even knows what moderation is. And every person in it has more than five tyrants hiding in him."[53] Convinced that the life of salvation was reserved for heaven, Luther believed that all attempts to achieve equality in this life were doomed to breed violence. To safeguard against the tyranny of the mob, he insisted, religious reform should be pursued within the existing political orders rather than through the founding of a radically new one.[54]

Luther held up the notorious 1534-1535 Anabaptist experiment in Münster as a cautionary tale of where radical reform could lead. In Münster, iconoclasm was part of a social and religious revolution aimed at abolishing hierarchical government and private property in all its forms.[55] The Münsterites not only attacked images but also eliminated the guild system, prohibited locks and fences, required that all work be committed to the commune without remuneration, forbade the purchase or sale of goods, and made the possession of money a capital offense.[56] The Münster experiment failed both practically and ethically. Despite having attracted thousands of supporters from Westphalia and the Netherlands, it was suppressed within less than two years—but not before its leaders had assumed the role of kings and resorted to violence, threatening to kill dissenters, instituting a polygymy that numbered women among the goods to be held in common, and calling for the expulsion of Jews, whom they regarded as inextricably bound up with the outlawed money economy.[57]

Imagining the Future

Both the Catholic who affirmed images and the magisterial reformer who rejected them had something authoritative in mind: the Catholic a face, the Protestant a white wall—"In Zürich we have churches which are positively luminous; the walls are beautiful white," writes

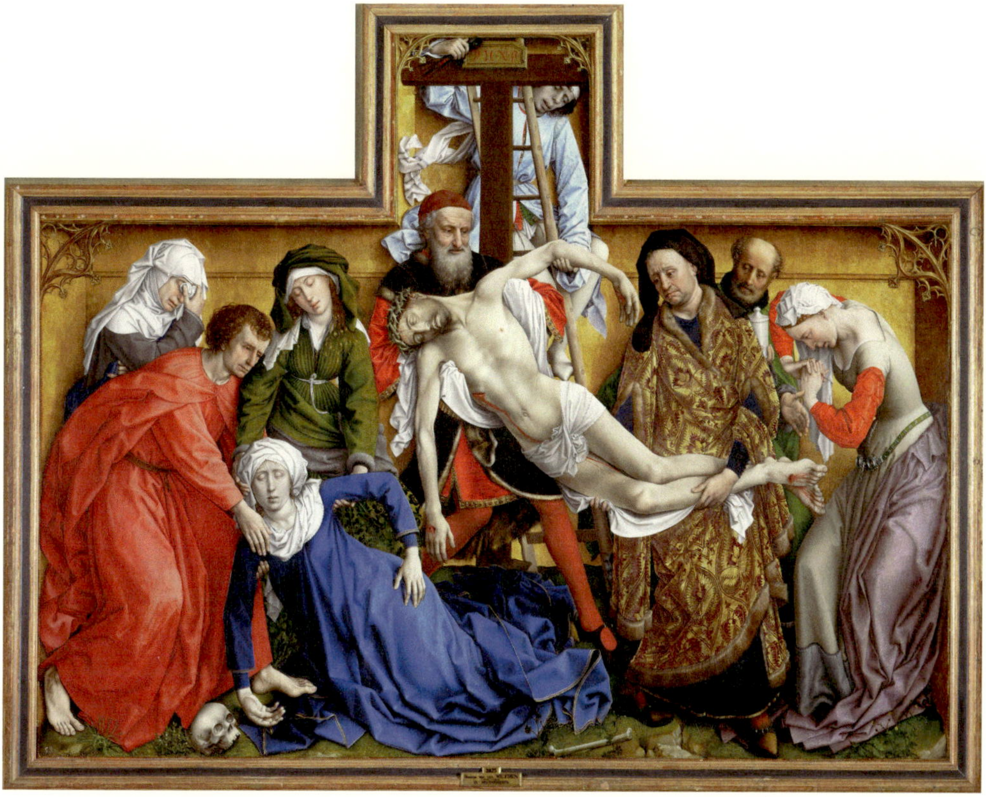

Plate 1. Rogier van der Weyden, *Deposition from the Cross* (ca. 1435), oil on panel, 220 × 262 cm. Museo Nacional del Prado, Madrid. (Photo: Erich Lessing/Art Resource, New York.)

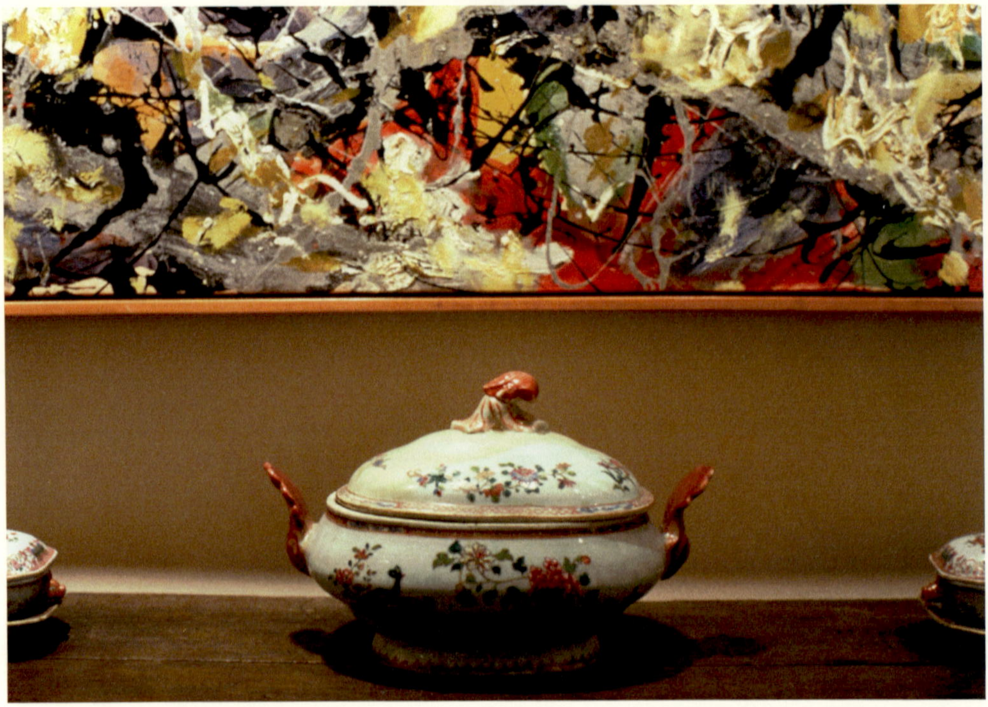

Plate 2. Louise Lawler, *Pollock and Tureen, Arranged by Mr. and Mrs. Burton Tremaine, Connecticut*, 1984, cibachrome, 71.5×99.6 cm. (Photo: Louise Lawler and Metro Pictures.)

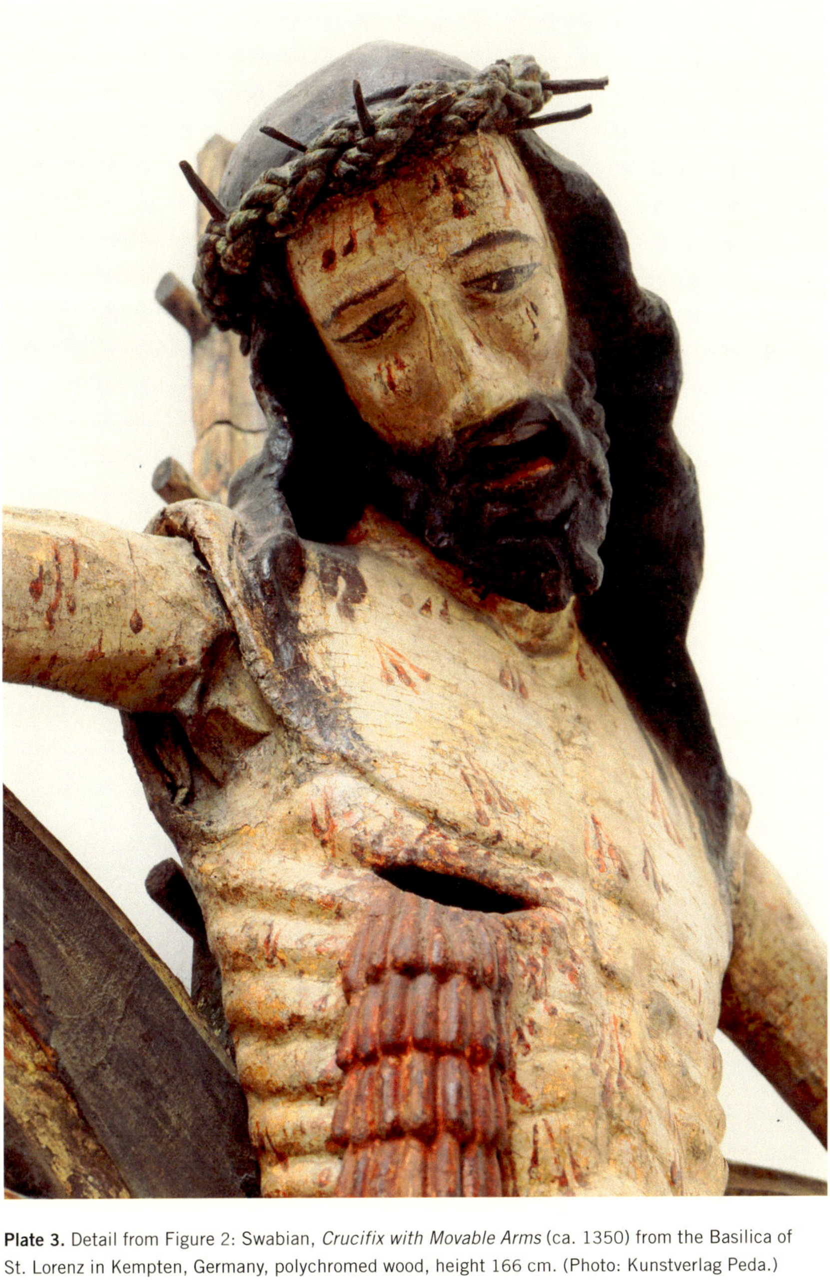

Plate 3. Detail from Figure 2: Swabian, *Crucifix with Movable Arms* (ca. 1350) from the Basilica of St. Lorenz in Kempten, Germany, polychromed wood, height 166 cm. (Photo: Kunstverlag Peda.)

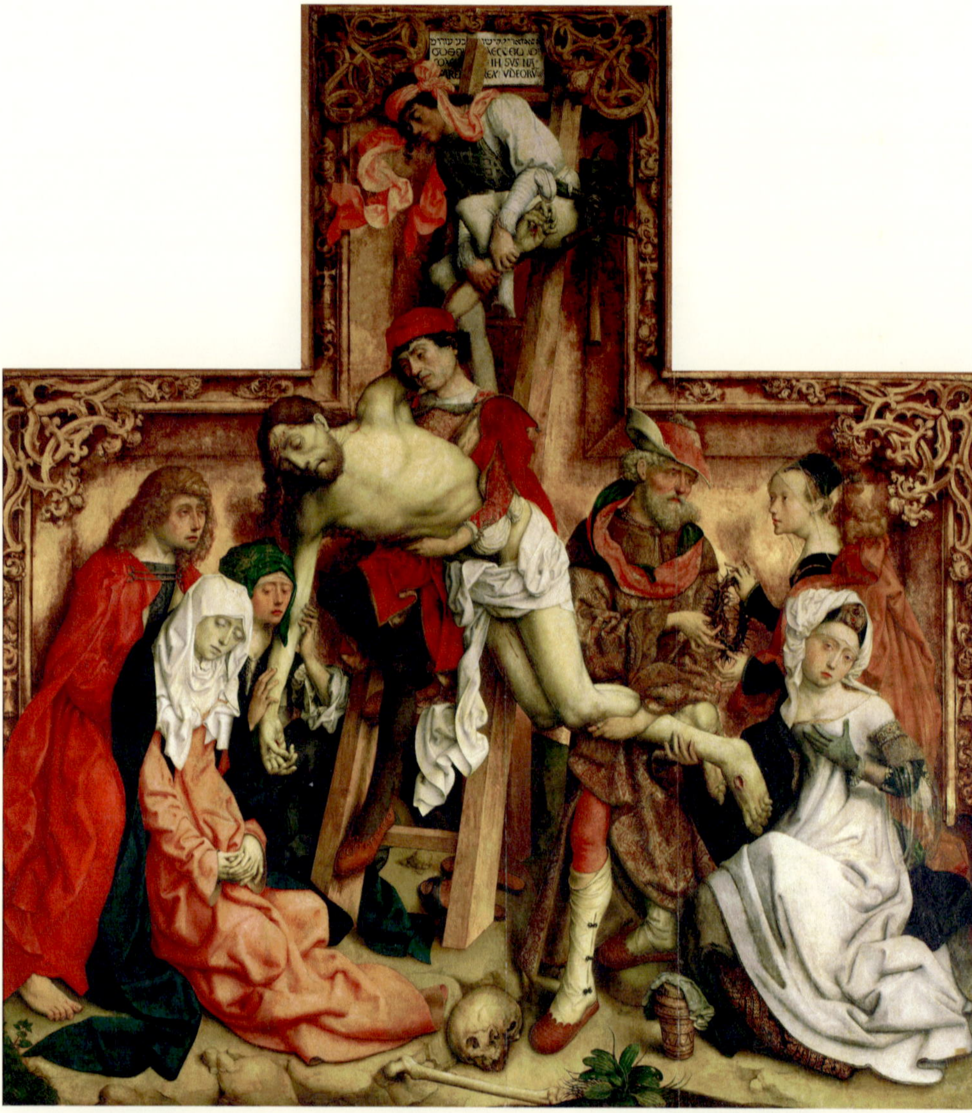

Plate 4. Master of the St. Bartholomew Altar, *Deposition from the Cross* (ca. 1490), oil on panel, 227 × 210 cm. Musée du Louvre, Paris. (Photo: Erich Lessing/Art Resource, New York.)

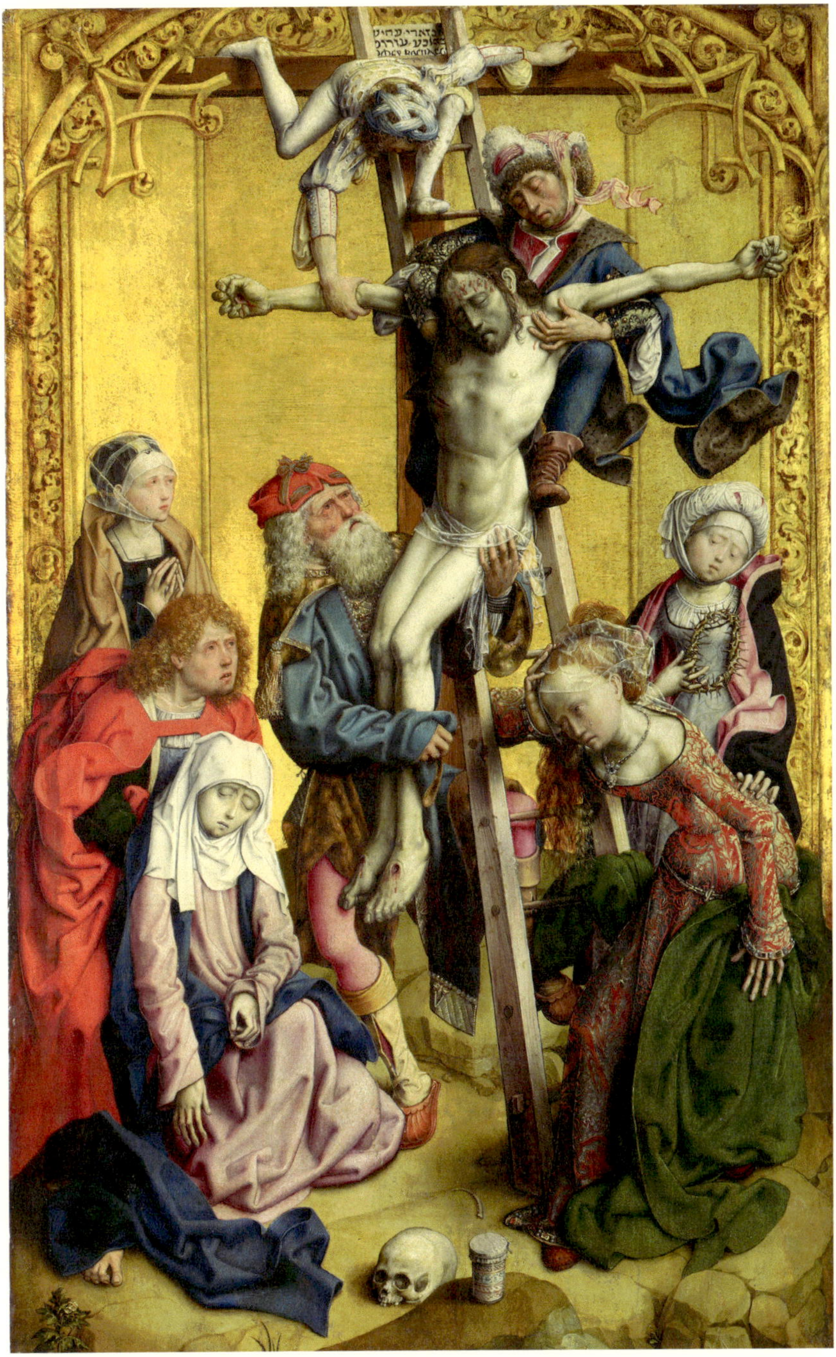

Plate 5. Master of the St. Bartholomew Altar, *Deposition from the Cross* (ca. 1500), oil on panel, 74.9 × 47.3 cm. National Gallery of Art, London. (Photo: The National Gallery.)

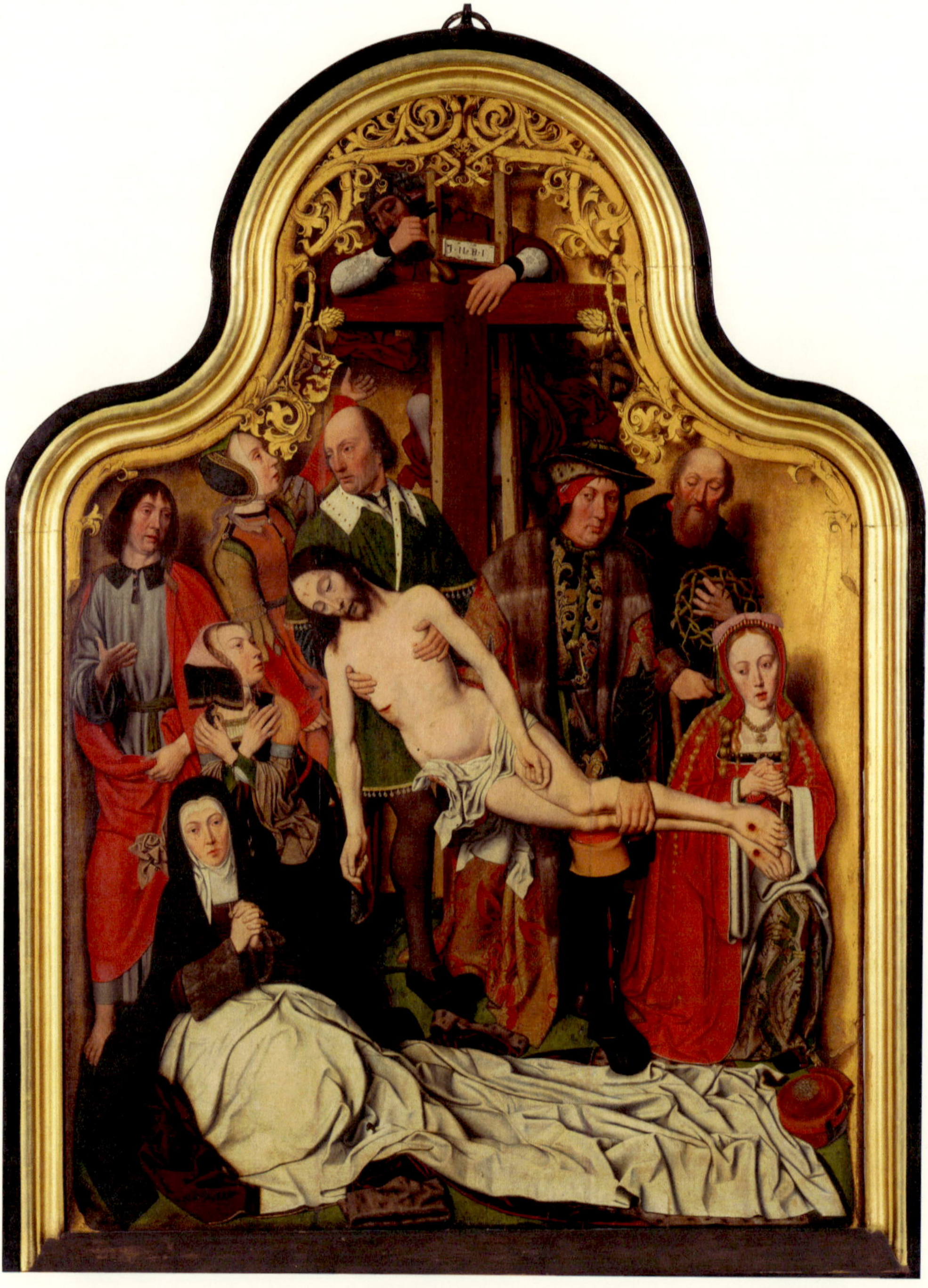

Plate 6. Jan Mostaert, *Deposition from the Cross* (ca. 1520), oil on panel. Musées Royaux des Beaux-Arts de Belgique, Brussels. (Photo: Musée Royaux des Beaux-Arts de Belgique.)

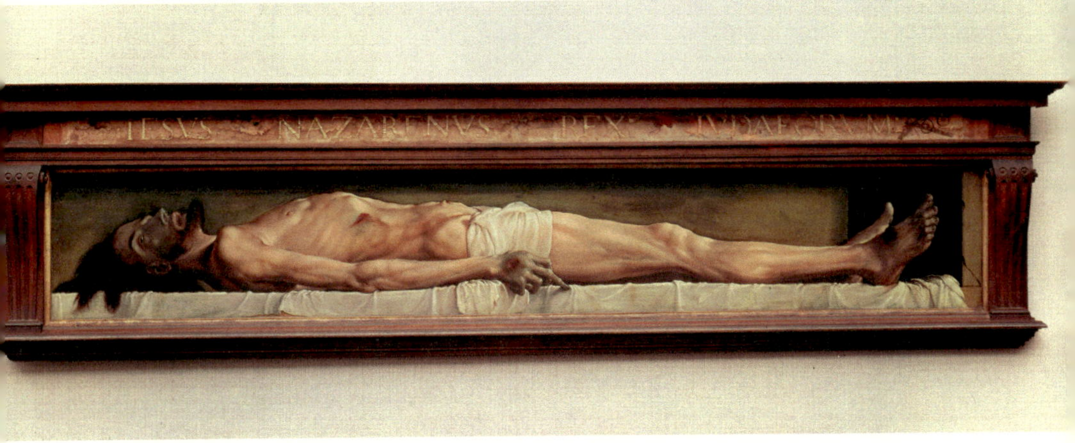

Plate 7. Hans Holbein the Younger, *Dead Christ in the Tomb* (1521–1522), oil on panel, 30.5 × 200 cm. Kunstmuseum, Basel. (Photo: Erich Lessing/Art Resource, New York.)

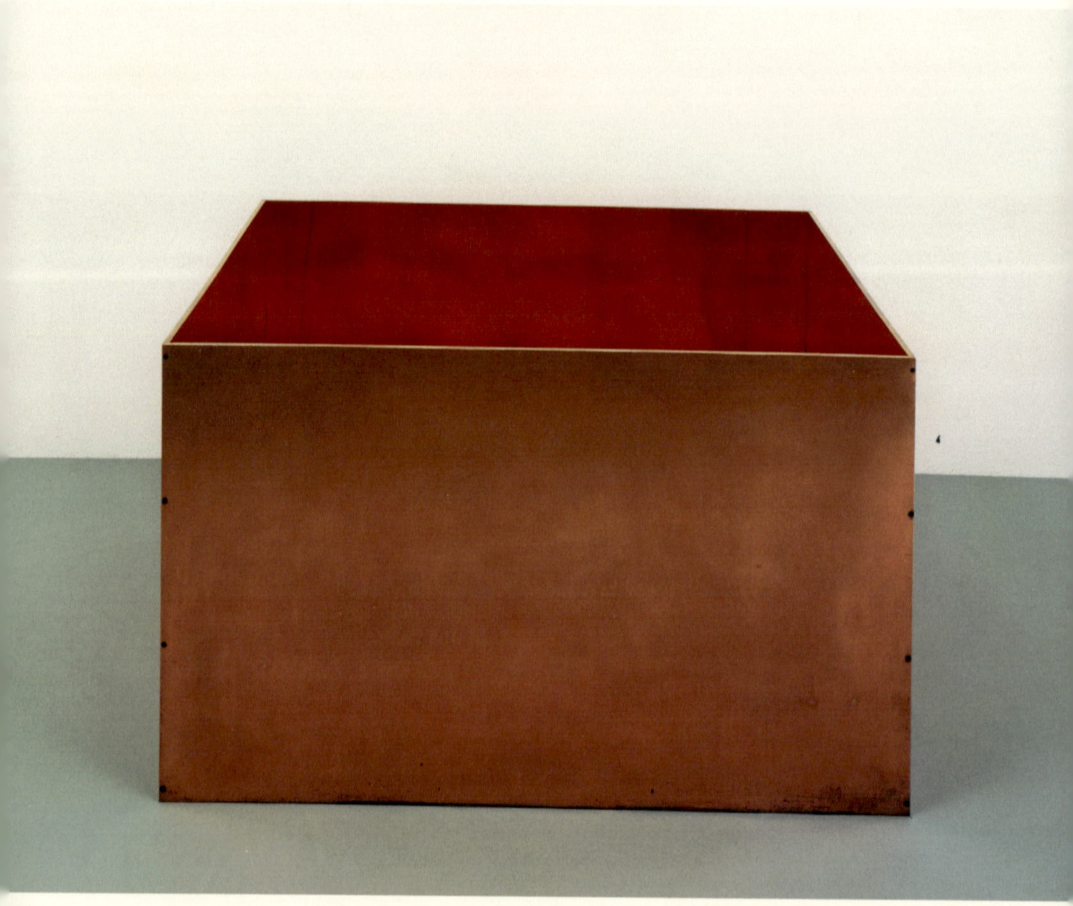

Plate 8. Donald Judd, *Untitled* (1972), copper, enamel, and aluminum, 91.6 × 155.5 × 178.2 cm. Tate Modern, London. © Judd Foundation. Licensed by VAGA, New York. (Photo: Tate, London 2009.)

Zwingli.[58] For the magisterial reformer, part of the beauty of the white wall was that its blankness empowered the prince to act on behalf of the invisible God until the revelation of His face: because He does not show himself in this world, argued the magisterial reformer, God needs a secular authority as his proxy here on earth.

When they did not succumb to megalomaniacal fantasies of their own election as they did in Münster, radicals attempted to steer a course clear of both Catholic idols *and* the white walls magisterial reformers substituted for them. Radicals were interested in the negating gesture itself and the space it opened up, before that gesture hardened into an "image" of imagelessness—the white wall—that the prince could point to as the justification of his power. Following the twists and turns whereby Reformation image-breakers unwittingly participated in the empowerment of images and themselves became the makers of new images, Joseph Koerner has shown just how difficult this "holding open" would prove to be.[59] According to Koerner, the iconoclast who felt compelled to attack the image did so because he mistook its representation for fact: "Imagining that iconophiles know the wood falsely (as God, not wood), they hit the wood but instead strike *representation*—of a deity, of an institution, of a social body. No wonder the critical gesture rebounds. Representation from the start, the wood becomes, in its 'specious' (as Emser put it) exposure, representation once again."[60]

Not only does the iconoclast misunderstand what the image means to the iconophile; he also fails to see that it is already a dialectical clash between making and unmaking, as Koerner shows: "Religious imagery has iconoclasm built into it. Charged with portraying God's miserable, human death, church pictures were engineered both to save appearances and to reject them."[61] The success of the image of the broken body of Christ is a function of its blatant inadequacy to the task of representing an all-powerful God. Glossing Luther's "Heidelberg Disputation," Koerner explains: "Before any attempt to paint it, the crucifix was already an image and an iconoclasm, a face and its defacement, the epiphany as total eclipse."[62] According to Koerner, the eclipse of the image that takes place in time looks forward to the final dialectical overcoming of the image at the end of time—when we will no longer have to content ourselves with representation: "The aesthetics of the ugly, whether Christian or modern, are a provisional, deceptive stage in a larger movement at the end of which truth, beauty, and power stand revealed."[63]

While some of the images I consider here are gruesome, others represent a body not made ugly by its torture and death. These depict a Christ who, having shed the most disfiguring marks of the passion, is sadly beautiful as he moves toward (without ever reaching) the obscurity of the grave. These images are not ugly enough to be sublimated into a beautiful truth to come. Nor does even the most abject image make way for the end of images at the end of time when it is held perpetually suspended between the visibility of the cross and the invisibility of the grave. The body pictured in the late medieval Deposition is both too capable of beauty and too tenacious in its suspension to be swept up in the dialectic Koerner describes. Under the pretext of picturing an historical event—the lowering of Christ from the cross—late medieval painters and participants in the Deposition rite described the *interminable* co-presence of the image and its eclipse.[64]

In the late Middle Ages, the newly popular iconography of the Deposition took shape amidst occasionally open but more often latent aggression toward images. Late medieval dissidents gave up images in order to have already the proximity to God that the Church reserved for heaven. Radical reformers would likewise attempt to pull the utopian political possibilities of the future into the present, countering the self-serving ideology of the princes who wanted them to wait.[65] These late medieval and Reformation iconoclasts *set out* to strike representation—of a God but even more so of an institution and a social body: they wanted neither the face of the Catholic icon nor the facelessness of an invisible God whose absence sanctions the authority of the prince.

Late medieval Deposition iconography *politicizes* the image-question—just as dissidents and radicals did. With its perpetual suspension, it lowers the image proffered by the Catholic Church, without forcing that image to yield its place to a white wall that is an "image" of an invisible God who promises to reveal himself at the end of time; the deposed body which never finally disappears never makes way for that end. But the Deposition's suspended movement does not simply illustrate the utopian politics of dissidents and radicals who were unwilling to have their salvation deferred. In fact, when it comes to the future, the Deposition tells a very different story. Although it lays claim to the future by stubbornly refusing to go away, it does not pretend that the future can be had at no cost. The loss of the *present* is the price to be paid for having tomorrow already today. The body pictured in the Deposition never stops falling away from its own presence, center, and authority. Only in this state of perpetual self-absenting, can it have what the future holds.

The Politics of Iconoclasm

It comes as no surprise that modern assessments of late medieval and Reformation iconoclasm have been politically charged. In 1975, Horst Bredekamp laid his cards on the table: "Whoever considers the fight against the spiritual-social relations of the Middle Ages an 'epochal step forward,' will therefore also not be able to underestimate or denigrate the iconoclasm that was an instrument of one of the movements that waged this battle."[66] Only a few years earlier, Martin Warnke had assembled a collection of essays on iconoclasm, including his own study of the Münsterites. He published the volume under the auspices of the Ulmer Verein für Kunstwissenschaft, an organization founded in 1968.[67] The political tenor of '68 permeates this collection. Warnke's introduction lifts the categorical stigma attached to iconoclasm as a form of political action: "Those acts of destruction that balanced destruction with new construction are counted among the great events of art history. Those acts of destruction that undertook the transgression against symbols of power from a position of powerlessness, without being able to establish new symbols of power"—or without *wanting* to establish new symbols of power, which is how I would describe the radical project at its best—"are lamented and denounced as senseless iconoclasms."[68] Warnke's recuperation of the political meaningfulness of iconoclastic acts and his dialectical treatment of creation and destruction continue to be influential, but in the time that has elapsed since the publication of Warnke's groundbreaking work, the *violence* of iconoclasm has lost much of the luster it had in '68.[69]

Although no one has contributed more to our understanding of iconoclasm nor better demonstrated that its study exposes the inadequacies of formalist art history, David Freedberg is far less persuaded than Warnke of iconoclasm's legitimacy.[70] Freedberg argues that the seemingly aberrant iconoclastic act is the expression of a perfectly ordinary human emotion: "We too may be disturbed and troubled by specific images; but can it be that such feelings . . . are somehow akin to the over-demonstrative, violent, and ultimately damaging behavior of the image breakers?"[71] Freedberg is not defending the destruction of images here. He simply wants us to recognize the kinship between our own responses to images and the fearful reaction of the iconoclast.[72] According to Freedberg, it was this fear masquerading as sophistication that fueled mid-twentieth-century efforts to make paintings about nothing.[73] Fear of the power of images, Freedberg argues, motivated American abstraction and paralyzed the higher-stakes image-making that goes "in search of the world beyond painting for its subject matter."[74]

Freedberg stops short of privileging the old masters, but more than one recent study of iconoclasm suggests that modern art has erred in its iconoclastic rejection of earlier modes of picturing. Although markedly different in their politics, these studies share a common skepticism about the negative aspects of modernism. Culminating in a conservative endorsement of the image along with "law, property, and other institutions," Alain Besançon's *The Forbidden Image: An Intellectual History of Iconoclasm* weaves together the history of the denigration of images and the history of Western art.[75] The central argument of the book's final chapters is that the "iconoclasm" of abstract art was born of mystical rather than political aspirations.[76] Besançon discovers in modernist abstraction a noble, if ultimately misguided, recapitulation of the problem of the divine image, which allows him to take *postmodern* art to task, in suitably ominous tones, for its nihilism and even, implicitly, for its godlessness.[77]

From an altogether different political standpoint, Bruno Latour and Peter Weibel have described the negative consequences of the "enlightened" idol-smashing that they find rampant in modern life. In the exhibition and catalog *Iconoclash*, they uncouple iconoclasm and progressive politics, casting a pall in the process over modernist and postmodernist negations. Latour describes twentieth-century art with more than a little regret: "Generations of iconoclasts smashing each other's faces and works. A fabulous large-scale experiment in nihilism. A maniacal joy in self-destruction. A hilarious sacrilege. A sort of deleterious aniconic inferno."[78] The utopian belief that the power of images can be released into less mediated forms is the very definition of intolerance, according to Latour: "fundamentalism is the conviction that mediations may be bypassed."[79]

Latour makes a plea for saving images: "Images do count; they are not mere tokens, and not because they are prototypes of something away, above, beneath; they count because they allow one to move to *another* image, exactly as frail and modest as the former one—but *different*."[80] In a world of free-flowing cascades of images, we would indeed have no more need of iconoclasts. But does this scenario not forget that behind any given image there is bound to be someone invested in *its* preservation and that the body of that image—"frail" as it may be—makes demands not unlike those of a corpse? What do we do with the obsolete image? Do we put it in the museum, in the grave, in the trash? Only in a virtual world or a world of virtual images can objects be so easily removed from view. In the material world, images continue to take up space long after they have ceased to be useful or desirable, and their removal requires an act of violence—even if only the muted violence of consigning them to museum storage.

Latour sees aggression toward images as the avoidable product of a misunderstanding: "what is it that contemporary art has so forcefully tried to escape? To what target was so much iconoclasm directed, so much asceticism, so much violent and sometimes frenetic energy? To religious icons and their obsession for real presence? But they have never been about presenting something other than absence."[81] As true as this may often be, images—including religious icons—are always also the brokers of political power. Modernism's iconoclasms have not been as naïve as Latour here makes them out to be. For, the negativity of modernism—in its most important forms—has been more political than theological. "What the enemies of modern art, with a better instinct than its anxious apologists, call its negativity," writes Adorno, "is the epitome of what established culture has repressed and that toward which art is drawn."[82]

That negativity has fueled labors of love just as much as it has stoked what Latour calls experiments in nihilism. When Roland Barthes identifies modernism with the knowledge of impossibility—"To be modern is to know *what is no longer possible*"—he is referring to the painstaking undoing from within of the very thing the artist "knew and *knew how to make*."[83] While modernism's sacrificial process has been the most intimate of self-examinations, its inwardness has opened again and again onto the shared field of what "established culture has repressed," that is, onto politics. Insofar as modernism has been the enacting of this politicized self-sacrifice, its iconoclasms have been neither simply obedient responses to the Second Commandment nor empty rehearsals of Enlightenment critique. Rather, these iconoclasms have been politically necessary—if not always successful—purgings of painting's means of repression.

God and the Camera

By concluding each chapter of this book about the early modern image of Christ with a vignette devoted to a twentieth-century work of art, the last thing I want to do is suggest that all of modernism is a crypto-mysticism. Modernism is not everywhere haunted by a hidden God, as Besançon would have it. But insofar as the early modern images I am concerned with address themselves to the future, we should not relegate them exclusively to the past, as a strictly historicist account would have us do. Countering the authority of the image in the present in order to lay claim to the mythic future that the Church and the prince place out of reach, the late medieval Deposition from the Cross makes holes in time through which the image slips free of its original moment. In the temporally impure space of the museum, the deposed body perpetually suspended over the abyss of its own disappearance opens the "present" to the untimeliness of images.

Late medieval images of the body being deposed from the cross cannot, of course, really know the future they address. But they share with the objects they meet there an auto-iconoclasm, that is, a politicized self-negation. Although *modernist* iconoclasm is inseparable from the recent history of capitalism, industrialization, and ready-made images mass-produced by the camera, to say that this iconoclasm is uniquely modern is to believe too readily in the avant-garde's rhetoric of historical rupture and to forget how thoroughly *theological* all myths of beginnings and endings are bound to be, including the modernist myth of the "death of painting"—that "hackneyed issue of the death of painting," as Thierry de Duve has called it.[84]

It did not take long for Paul Delaroche's response to seeing a daguerreotype for the first time—"From today, painting is dead!"—to find its way into Flaubert's *Dictionary of Received Ideas*: "*Art*: What good is it, since it is being replaced by mechanical processes that do the job better and faster?"[85] In the 1930s, Walter Benjamin began to elaborate this *idée reçue* into a history of modern painting's "flight from photography," as Adorno calls it.[86] De Duve and others have since argued that, in an effort to stake out a territory distinct from the mimetic field of the photographic image, painting gave up what had since the Renaissance constituted its mimetic arsenal—chiaroscuro, linear perspective, figuration, and so on.[87] Conceding these illusionistic devices to the mass-produced photograph, painters from Courbet to Pollock have cultivated an aesthetics of touch as one strategy for marking painting's difference from the camera's industry of instantaneous resemblance.[88]

But this holding of painting apart from the mass production of the camera has been complicated all along the way by what critics describe as a defensive assimilation of the machine: painters "sought to give their craft a reprieve by 'internalizing' some of the features and processes of the technology threatening it," de Duve explains.[89] Assimilation of the machine has also been an *offensive* strategy, an assault on the demands of the bourgeois consumer who expects painting to console him by being everything the alienated commodity is not. This defense / assault has played out in endless ambiguous identifications with capitalism's modes of production and consumption: "To survive reality at its most extreme and grim," Adorno writes, "artworks that do not want to sell themselves as consolation must equate themselves with that reality."[90] In the nineteenth century, this equation found its most thoroughgoing formulation in the "divisionism" of Georges Seurat, who subjected painting itself to mechanization.[91]

In the twentieth century, the "death of painting" at the hands of the machine underwrote the optimism of Suprematism, Constructivism, Futurism, and the Bauhaus, the parodic anti-aesthetics of Dada and Surrealism, the mass-culture appropriations of Pop, the art-workers ethos of minimalism, and the aesthetics of administration and indifference governing one strain of conceptual, performance, site-specific, and video art. In all of this, the value conferred on the machine has varied, as have the politics associated with it.[92] At moments the figure for a collectivity that holds the means of artistic production in common, the machine in other instances figures everything hard and alienated.[93] But whether utopian or dystopian, the machine is a figure for the inexorable: it plays the part of what could not be otherwise.

The discourse of the death of painting is fundamental to the politicized negativity of modern art. But where it leans too heavily on the claim that the death of painting is *inevitable*, that discourse can have a depoliticizing effect. Through an ideological slight of hand, talk of the death of painting can turn technology into that death's natural cause. Despite being manmade, the machine then becomes something more "alive," less constrained by convention, and more real than what we find in the museum. It is but a short step from this to the deification or demonization of the camera. Once that move is made, the camera enters into a pseudomorphic relation with the creator / destroyer God, whose images are always truer than anything humans make. Naturalizing the end of painting, the discourse of the death of painting thereby trades in the political efficacy of an *intentional* self-sacrifice for a rhetoric of the foregone conclusion.

The "death of painting" at the hands of the camera is, in fact, no more inevitable, no more God-given, than its birth. De Duve describes the painter's position after the fateful invention: "The fact that industrialization has bereft painters of their traditional social function as purveyors of images—the fact, for example, that photography has taken over the market for portraits and other representations—does not in the slightest make the practice of painting objectively impossible. It makes it useless in regard to this traditional function."[94] The modern painter experiences his task as impossible because industry does it better—but it is, in fact, merely superfluous. The task of the late medieval maker of images of God (and perhaps all image-makers) was just as possible yet superfluous—possible as demonstrated by the long history of such images, superfluous because God did it better when he created Adam in his own image and again when he descended into the flesh.

"Here we encounter the law of the surrealist image," to quote Barthes quoting Breton quoting Reverdy: "*the more distant and accurate the relations of two realities, the stronger the image*."[95] Distant but accurate is the pseudomorphic relation between God and the Camera, both jealous makers of the perfect image, whose making is effortlessly superior to that of the human hand and whose images embarrass human endeavors to match them. Human images are made, often with a good deal of purposiveness, but they never *need to be*. While this "purposiveness without purpose" is for Kant the very essence of the autonomous work of art, it is a thorn in the side of pre and post-Enlightenment image-makers. It dogs every late medieval attempt to fashion an image of God; and it thwarts all those avant-garde aspirations to erase the line between art and life, to open the "mausoleum" of the museum to the living. But this superfluity is also the source of the image's political efficacy, since it alone makes room for things humanly created (and destroyed) among all those things that are said to be divinely given (and taken away).

In the late medieval Deposition, the suspended figure figures this condition of politically charged superfluity by turning back upon itself and putting its own claims to authority in doubt without yielding its place to a mythic future, when the gap between the image and its necessity would finally, mercifully, be closed—be that either the end of time or the end of Art. The suspended figure being lowered from the cross scrambles not only the Christian teleology that looks forward to the end of images but also the art-historical teleology that fixes the beginning of Art somewhere in the Renaissance and its redemptive end—its merging with life—somewhere around now. In the Deposition, the image never disappears and Art never makes way for something less contrived.

PART ONE

The Deposition Rite

CHAPTER ONE

Ritualized Hostility

The crucifix—the most important image in the church or, as iconoclasts in Maastricht put it in 1566, "the greatest idol (*affgoederije*) that was in the church"—was displayed throughout the year.[1] Crucifixes adorned altars and roodscreens; portable crucifixes were carried in processions; and on Good Friday of each year crucifixes were ceremonially interred in a ritual commemorating Christ's deposition from the cross and entombment.

The Deposition rite is one of several quasi-dramatic embellishments of the liturgy that had taken shape by the tenth century.[2] Although the Deposition rite, like the other rites associated with the sepulcher—the Elevation and the Visit to the Sepulcher (*Visitatio sepulchri*)—was never included in the Roman liturgy, from which the liturgies of most of Western Christianity derived, textual and material artifacts attest to its regular performance throughout most of Europe, especially in German-speaking areas and in England, from about the thirteenth century until the Council of Trent (1545–1563).[3] While the Deposition rite is recorded as early as the tenth century and has never completely disappeared—it is still performed in some places today—the thirteenth to the sixteenth century was the time of its greatest popularity.[4]

Orchestrated at a local level, paraliturgical rites reflected the interests of audiences not usually involved in the liturgy. In some cases, they afforded laypeople an opportunity to participate directly in the ceremonies of the Church, for example, in the form of processions.[5] Although they were a far cry from the vernacular religious plays, which were being staged outside the Church with elaborate sets and costumes by the thirteenth century, these rites made the liturgy more theatrical.[6] By many accounts, they also undermined the sobriety of the officially sanctioned ceremony.

The description of the Deposition rite that follows is intended to uncover the social and imaginative functions it served beyond those explicitly identified in the official documents. Modern historians have generally described the paraliturgical rites as a response to the laity's desire for vivid and realistic images of biblical history. Although most were probably just that, I will suggest that the Deposition rite in particular responded to a diametrically opposed longing—namely, *to have done with images*. The Deposition rite, whose central gesture of putting away the image is hardly conducive to sensuous gratification, served as an antidote to the veneration of images at other times of year. It served, we might say, as a ritual disavowal of the image under the guise of burial.[7]

A Description of the Rite

The earliest extant record of a Deposition rite belongs to the *Monastic Agreement of the Monks and Nuns of England*, a compilation of continental and English monastic practices assembled in the tenth century in conjunction with the reform of the Benedictine monasteries of England. From the monastic context, the Deposition would spread to non-monastic churches. But already within the monasteries, the rite was justified in terms of the edifying effect it might have on those not fully versed in the liturgy. Instructions are first given for the Adoration of the Cross, a ceremony in which the crucifix is processed to the altar and unveiled while the clergy sing psalms and penitents who have crept barefoot to the cross prostrate themselves before it. Then follow instructions for the Deposition:

> Now since on that day we solemnize the burial of the Body of our Saviour, if anyone should care or think fit to follow in a becoming manner certain religious men in a practice worthy to be imitated for the strengthening of the faith of unlearned common persons and

> neophytes, we have decreed this only: on that part of the altar where there is space for it there shall be a representation as it were of a sepulchre, hung about with a curtain, in which the holy Cross, when it has been venerated, shall be placed in the following manner: the deacons who carried the Cross before shall come forward and, having wrapped the Cross in a napkin there where it was venerated, they shall bear it thence, singing the antiphons *In peace, in the selfsame; He shall dwell*; and *My flesh shall rest in hope*, to the place of the sepulchre. When they have laid the Cross therein, in imitation as it were of the burial of the Body of our Lord Jesus Christ, they shall sing the antiphon *After the Lord was buried*.[8]

In the *Monastic Agreement*, the words "representation" and "imitation" indicate the mimetic nature of the Deposition rite. Here and elsewhere, the rite was staged more or less as a funeral, with some combination of candles, mourning robes, aspersion, censing, and a shroud.[9] During the Deposition rite in the All Saints Church of Wittenberg, "the four chaplains climb the ladder, and remove the image in an orderly manner, and lay the image in the bier," before candles are placed around the body, "as one is accustomed to doing for princely funerals."[10] The fourteen men who assist the four chaplains and who walk in the procession that follows the Deposition wear mourning clothing suitable for the occasion.[11]

The sepulcher took different forms, the simplest of which was an altar outfitted with curtains, like the one described in the *Monastic Agreement*. Other accounts refer to temporary wooden and cloth constructions set up separately from the altar. Independent coffer-shaped sepulchers with and without shrine structures built around them have survived, some still containing effigies of the dead Christ (figures 4–5). More elaborate sepulchers took the form of freestanding chapels—either temporary wooden structures or permanent stone buildings, like the one erected around 1260 in the Cathedral of Our Lady in Constance, which is modeled on the Holy Sepulcher in Jerusalem (figure 6). In France and England, the sepulcher tended to be in or near the chancel.[12] In Germany, it was usually on the west side of the nave, though it could be found next to the choir screen

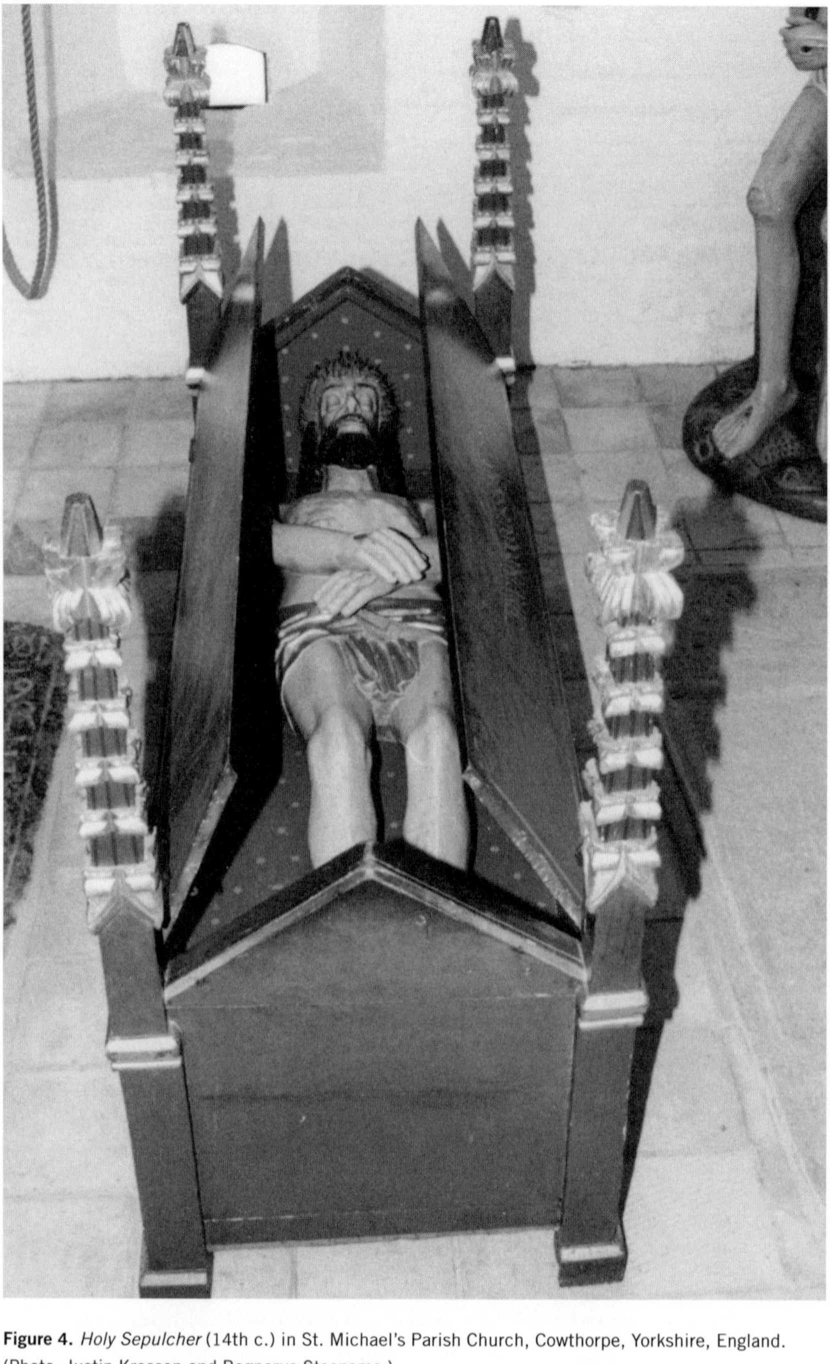

Figure 4. *Holy Sepulcher* (14th c.) in St. Michael's Parish Church, Cowthorpe, Yorkshire, England. (Photo: Justin Kroesen and Regnerus Steensma.)

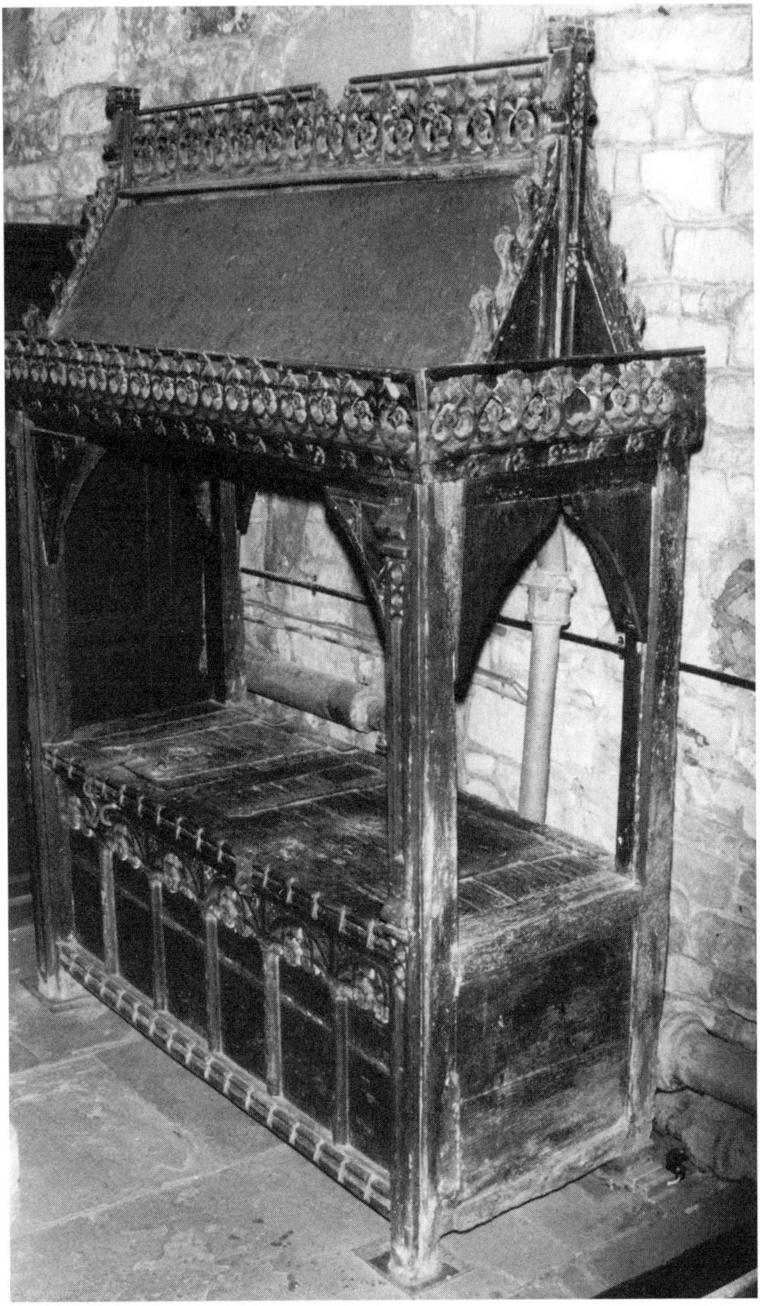

Figure 5. *Holy Sepulcher with Effigy* (ca. 1500) in the Bridgettine convent church, Mariager, North Jutland, Denmark. (Photo: Justin Kroesen and Regnerus Steensma.)

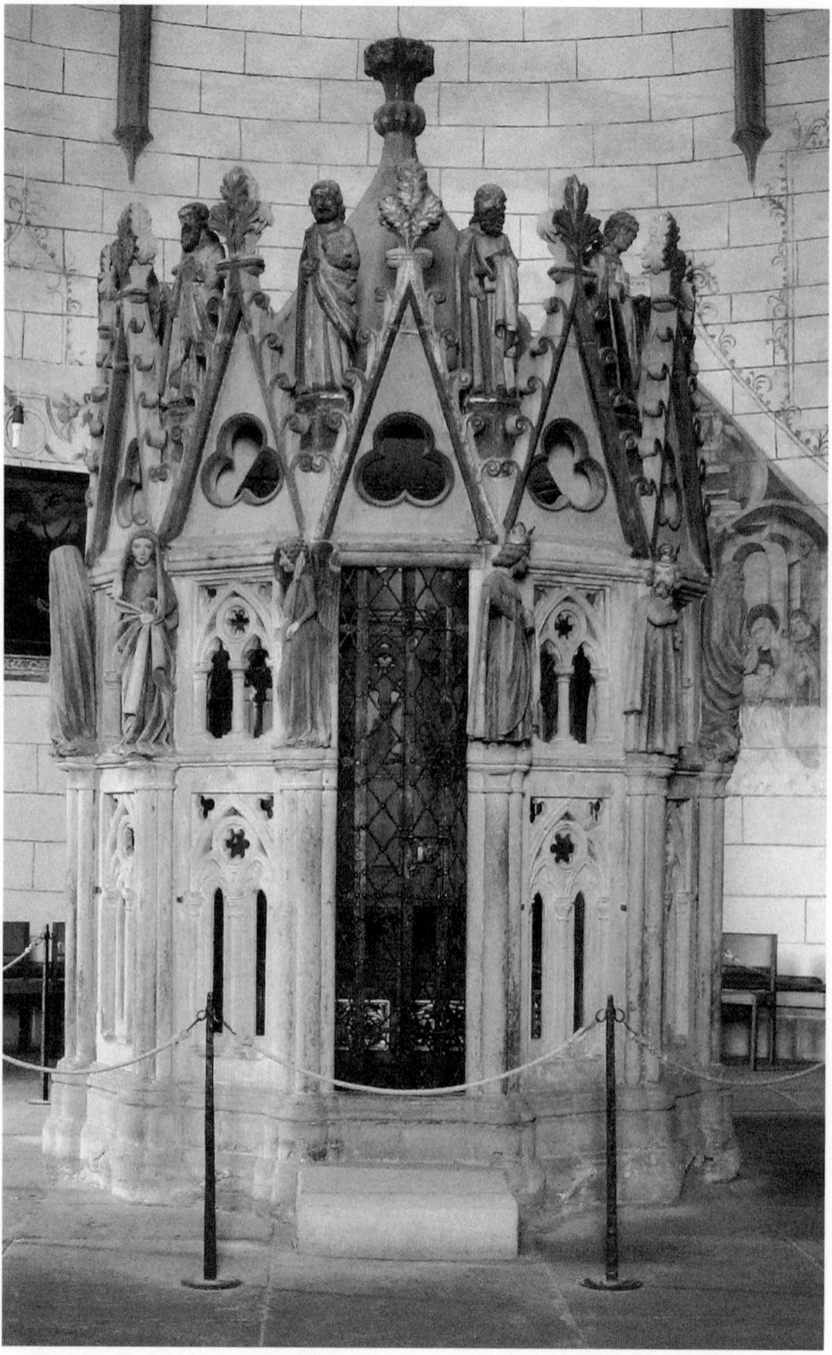

Figure 6. *Holy Sepulcher* (ca. 1260) in the Mauritius Chapel, Cathedral of Our Lady, Constance, Switzerland. (Photo: Wikimedia Commons.)

or in the choir itself. Many churches, especially in England but also elsewhere, still have niches or vaulted enclosures built into the wall that once served as sepulchers (figure 7). These now bare architectural frames would have been decorated with lights and draperies and "all fitting furniture thereto," as the 1531 will of Lord Dacre says.[13]

After being deposited in the sepulcher, the crucifix remained hidden there for the roughly forty-hour period of the grave rest. Candles were burned, psalms sung, and prayers said continuously during the vigil: "In that same place the holy Cross shall be guarded," the *Monastic Agreement* mandates, "with all reverence until the night of the Lord's Resurrection. And during the night let brethren be chosen by twos and threes, if the community be large enough, who shall keep faithful watch, chanting psalms."[14] The guarding of the sepulcher was a practical matter. At the Church of St. Stephen's Walbrook in London payments were made in 1485 "to the Clerks for coals, water, and ale, and candle when they watched the sepolker."[15] Clerics like these were employed to prevent theft of the candles and the Eucharistic Host that was sometimes buried, sometimes in an expensive pyx, along with the crucifix. A Bamberger ritual of 1514 requires that the grave be locked so that "neither impious people, nor heretics, nor Jews can steal or desecrate the Host."[16]

The grave watch also served the symbolic function of representing the devotion of the community. Those who had the means could participate indirectly by making bequests for payment of the guards and for candles to burn during the night. In 1453, Bishop Petrus von Augsburg made a donation of "stipends for scholars, who to honor the suffering and death of our Savior should recite the psalms uninterruptedly by the Holy Sepulcher from Good Friday until Easter"[17]; in 1543, Goodman of Bradden gave "unto the sepulker lyght a browne cow"; in 1519, Sir John Pollard bequeathed "ten bee hyvys to meynteyn the sepulture light."[18]

Sometimes laypeople other than the paid guards were allowed to take part in the forty-hour vigil—a rare opportunity to participate directly in church ceremony. Judging from the sacristy manual

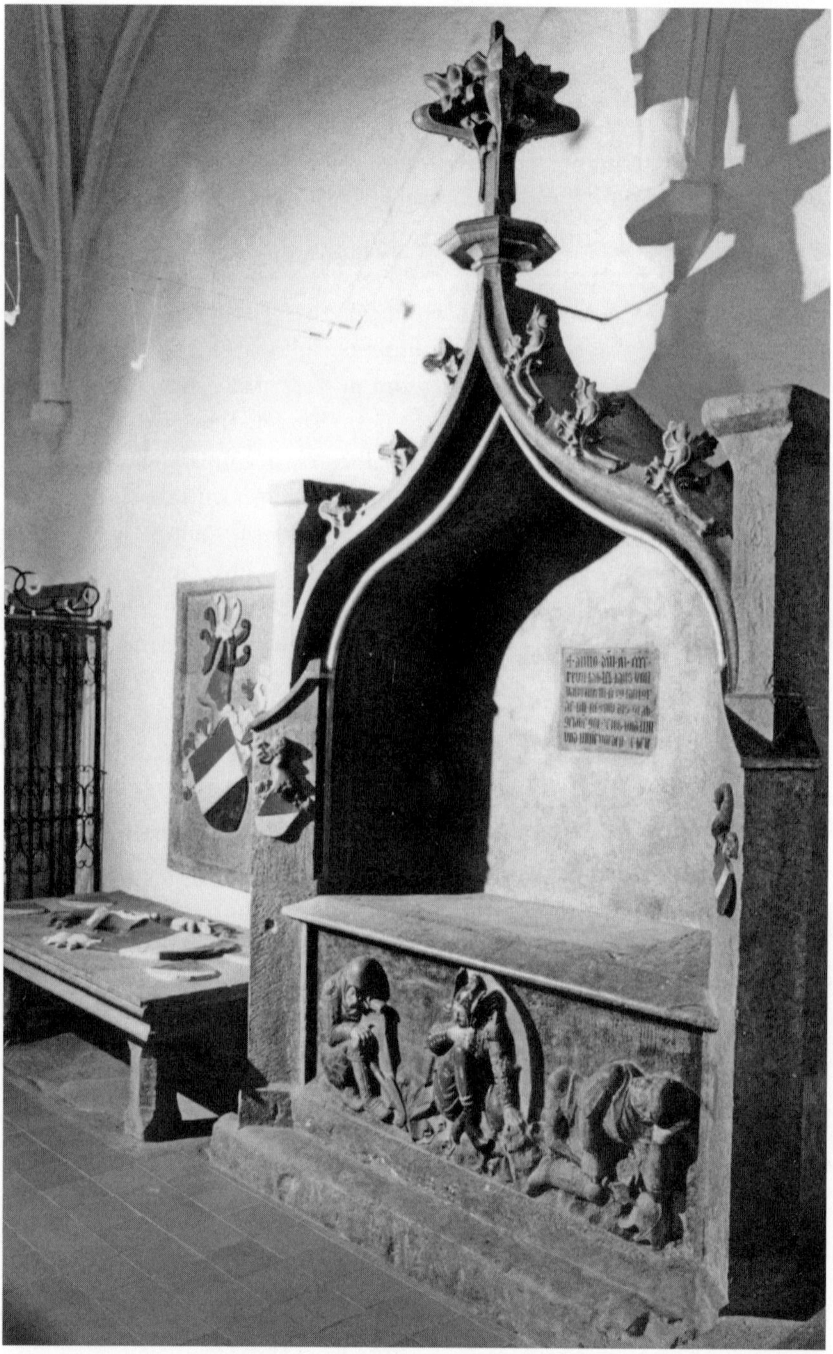

Figure 7. *Holy Sepulcher and Founder's Tomb* in the former monastery church, Schönenwerd, Switzerland. (Photo: Justin Kroesen and Regnerus Steensma.)

of the Cathedral of Brixen, this opportunity was enthusiastically embraced: "After matins . . . you [the officiate] must remain in the church for a while and watch over the candles by the grave, since you cannot close the church before nine or ten [at night], because the people are still in the church. After that, when everyone is out, the students or the choirmaster may stop singing the psalms, but they must return at four [in the morning] to sing the psalms, because the people also normally come at that hour."[19] The Brixen manual suggests that "the people" were eager to stay late and return again before dawn to worship at the sepulcher. But a number of German idioms related to the sepulcher suggest that not everyone was so enthusiastic: the phrase *'s heilige grab hüete* (to watch the Holy Sepulcher) means to be bored.[20] Various official complaints document the use of alcohol to alleviate this boredom. In 1552, the canon of the Cathedral of Constance reported that "the students at the grave consume a great deal each year, get completely drunk, and then become ridiculous."[21]

Lay participation in the liturgy opened a space not only for popular piety but also for spontaneous displays of indifference and irreverence.[22] The legendary prankster Til Eulenspiegel took advantage of lay participation in the *Visitatio sepulchri*—the paraliturgical rite representing the visit of the three women to the empty grave on Easter morning—to orchestrate things such that the rite would devolve into a brawl among the actors, who included local farmers and the minister's maidservant.[23] The Deposition rite's relation to these popular displays of irreverence is unique among the paraliturgical rites. For, even when it was conducted soberly, the Deposition rite involved the laying aside of the crucifix and the inversion of norms of ocular veneration. The songs that accompany the Deposition rite in the form of antiphons and responsories build toward a *negation of vision* that formalizes the more spontaneous expressions of irreverence associated with lay participation in the paraliturgy.

Although the songs included in the Deposition rite vary, some feature regularly enough to establish two themes: the removal of Christ from visibility and his repose in a cloistered space apart.[24]

The sequence of songs mandated in 1489 for the Benedictine monastery at Prüfening is typical.[25] The first responsory functions as the verbal equivalent of an ostension, celebrating the beholding of Christ with the eyes: "*Ecce quomodo moritur iustus*—Behold how the just man dies and nobody feels it in his heart; just men are carried away and nobody looks. The just man has been taken from the face of iniquity, and the memory of him will be in peace."[26] This is an exhortation to *see* Christ, as if to compensate for the blindness of those who failed to recognize him at his death. But signaling his retreat from the world and from a visibility associated with the light of the sun, the responsory that follows quickly terminates this ocular recognition: "*Recessit pastor noster*—Our shepherd, the fount of living water, has departed, at whose passing the sun was obscured. For he who held the first man captive has himself been captured."[27] The antiphon that follows confirms this withdrawal from visibility by describing the burial: "*Joseph ab Arimathia*—Joseph of Arimathea embraced the body of Jesus, and buried him in his sepulcher."[28] And the final responsory reinforces the theme of Christ's retirement from the world by celebrating the inviolability of the tomb: "*Sepulto Domino*—At the burial of the Lord, the tomb was sealed by rolling a stone to the mouth of the grave. Soldiers were stationed who would guard it."[29] To emphasize the inaccessibility of the buried body, some versions of the Deposition rite visualized this sealing: in Brixen, two planks were carefully laid over the grave; in Salzburg, cloth wrappings and a stone secured the tomb; in Strasbourg, the sepulcher was bound with cords.[30]

The antiphon *In peace, in the selfsame*, which takes its text from Psalms 4.8, was sometimes also included in the Deposition rite.[31] In his meditation on that psalm, Augustine links the rest found *in idipsum* (in the selfsame) to a cessation of worldly vision: "And that is why the person of faith rejoices and says, *In peace, in the selfsame, I will rest and sleep*, leaving aside those many people who are completely fragmented by their desire for temporal things, and asks, *Who has anything good to show us?* when all the time these things are to be sought on the inside, in simplicity of heart, rather than on the outside, by using the eyes."[32] When the words "In peace, in the selfsame, I will rest and sleep" were sung during the Deposition rite, what Augustine here calls the inside became associated with the enclosure of the tomb. In the quiet and darkness of the grave—the antiphon suggests—worldly vision ceases.

Darkness played an accordingly important role in the liturgy of the *Triduum sacrum*, the period extending from Thursday evening through Sunday of Holy Week. During the *Triduum*, matins and lauds took the name *Tenebrae* (Darkness) from the responsory *Tenebrae factae sunt* (There was darkness). During matins, candles were lit and then extinguished one by one as the antiphons and responsories were sung. This continued through lauds until, at the end of the last psalm, darkness enveloped the church.[33] In some cases, churches remained darkened for all of Good Friday. Rabanus Maurus (d. 856) explains that on this day "the candles are not lit in the church, because when our Redeemer himself was crucified the stars were hidden."[34] The darkening of churches on Good Friday reinforced the withdrawal of the *imago Dei* recounted in the gestures and song sequences of the Deposition rite.

In his satirical account of *Tenebrae*, the reformer Thomas Kirchmair tells us what, according to him, *really* happened under cover of this darkness. Kirchmair is particularly interested in the laity, who customarily made noise during the *Tenebrae* service by banging a variety of objects, including devices known as clappers. This banging replaced the ringing of the church bells while they were silenced in recognition of Christ's time in the grave. The noise of the clappers was also timed to punctuate the reading of the Gospel at the moments of Christ's betrayal, arrest, and death. As Kirchmair recounts it, the noisy service devolves into chaos:

> From Thurseday then till Easter come...
> First three dayes space the belles are wilde, in silence for to lie,
> When from the toppes of hawtie towres, with clappers lowd they crie.
> The boyes in euery streat doe runne, and noyses great they make,
> While as in calling men to Church their wooden clappers shake.

> Thre nightes at midnight vp they rise, their Mattens for to heare,
> Appoynted well with clubbes and staues, and stones in order theare:
> The Sexten straightwayes putteth out the candles speedely,
> And straight the Priest with rustie throte, alowde begins to cry.
> Then furious rage begins to spring, and hurlyburly rise,
> On pewes and desks and seates they bounce, and beate in dredfullwise:
> Thou woudst suppose they were possest, with sprightes and deuills all,
> Or fury such as forceth them, that vpon Baccus call.
> Some beaten downe with clubbes and staues, amongst the pewes do ly
> And others almost brainde with stones, or wounded mortally.
> Well serues the darckenesse for these deedes, and thereto doth agree,
> The fashions like of euery one, that thus enraged bee.[35]

According to Kirchmair, the excesses of Holy Week tend more in the direction of destructive rage than loving veneration and *Tenebrae* is cover more for iconoclastic riot than idol worship. Although Kirchmair does not mention any images being struck, it is not hard to imagine them receiving a blow or two along with the furniture and the unfortunate people "beaten downe with clubbes and staues."

The grave rest came to an end on Easter, when an image of Christ was brought forth from the sepulcher in celebration of his resurrection. The *Monastic Agreement* describes an unceremonious Elevation conducted before the people were allowed to return to the church: "Before the bells are rung for Matins, the sacrists shall take the Cross and set it in its proper place."[36] The rite performed in Durham Cathedral before the suppression of the monasteries was a more splendid and public affair. Here the crucifix deposed on Good Friday, which was not well suited to the Easter celebration, was replaced during the grave rest with an image of the triumphant Christ equipped with a container for the Host:

> Then they both risinge came to the Sepulchre, out of the which, with great reverence, they tooke a maruelous beautifull Image of our Sauiour, representinge the Resurrection, with a crosse in his hand, in the breast whereof was enclosed in bright christall the Holy Sacrament of the altar, throughe the which christall the Blessed Host was

> conspicuous to the behoulders. Then, after the eleuation of the said picture, carryed by the said 2 monkes uppon a faire ueluett cushion, all embrodered, singinge the anthem of *Christ is risen,* they brought [it] to the high altar, settinge that on the midst therof, whereon it stood, the two monkes kneelinge on theire knees before the altar, and senceing it all the time that the rest of the whole quire was in singinge the foresaid anthem of *Christ is risen*.[37]

The ceremonial display of an image of the living Christ thus brought to an end the forty-hour period of the crucifix's occultation and the mourning that accompanied it.

Shutters, Veils, and Sepulchers

Burial rituals are structurally ambivalent, implying an admixture of goodwill and horror. Participants in these rituals generally announce the goodwill, speaking words of love, respect, and sorrow, leaving it to their actions to express the horror. So it was in the annual reenactment of the burial of Christ. The mournful participants gathered to pay homage to the image during the burial and vigil—"the holy cross should be kept watch over with *all reverence*" (my emphasis), insists the *Monastic Agreement*—while the gesture of removing the image from view represented whatever more negative feelings toward it these participants had. To read the Deposition rite as a (horrified) disavowal of the image is both to read it against the grain and to take its movements at face value. Nowhere does the medieval Church *declare* that the Deposition rite was intended to express hostility toward the image; it simply leaves it to the participants in the rite *to act* as if that were the case.

Periodic removal of images from view played a major role in late medieval religious life. It was particularly important in the visual regime of central and northern European churches, where winged polyptych altarpieces were popular from about the thirteenth to the sixteenth century. The imagery on the exterior of these altarpieces tended to be austere relative to what was inside: it was usually flatter, less monumental, and less colorful. The images on the exterior of Rogier van der Weyden's *Altarpiece of the Last Judgment*, for example, are painted in muted colors (figure 8). Only the red of the face and wings of the angel to the far left hints at the vibrant colors and abundant gold of the interior (figure 9).[38] And nothing in the shallow niches of the exterior, which are ostensibly contiguous with our own space, prepares us for the expansive and colorful vision of the end of time that opening the wings reveals. The exteriors of some winged altarpieces had only non-figurative decorations or no painting at all.[39]

Modern scholars have tended to describe the shuttering of altarpieces as a deprivation imposed by church officials on a populace hungry for images.[40] On this account, the Church strategically limited access to images that the laity had an unqualified desire to see. In fact, not a great deal is known about the opening and closing of altarpiece wings. It seems that most were opened on Sundays and on the saints' feast days and closed the rest of the year. Although this means that they were closed more days than not, a glimpse of their interiors would not have been the rare and coveted experience that modern historians have often made it out to be. Lynn Jacobs points out that in late medieval Utrecht the number of Sundays and feast days totaled about one hundred per year.[41] If altarpieces spent one out of every three or four days open, their interiors were visible often enough to be a familiar part of church-going life. Instead of being a long-awaited revelation, the display of these interiors was part of a steady rhythm of hiding and revealing—less epiphany than clockwork.[42] Like the reliable automatons of a cuckoo clock whose figures emerge through trap doors to mark the hours, the appearance and disappearance of images in late medieval churches registered the passage of time and the cyclical structure of the liturgical year.

The liturgical calendar's longest period for hiding images were the forty days of Lent, when it was customary to strip altars of ornament and to cover paintings and sculptures. (This period of abstinence was, in fact, cut short when, during the final week of Lent, images were used in the paraliturgical rites of Holy Week.) A fifteenth-century miracle legend describes a statue in the church of Daventry outfitted with Lenten shutters: "In a pillar of the

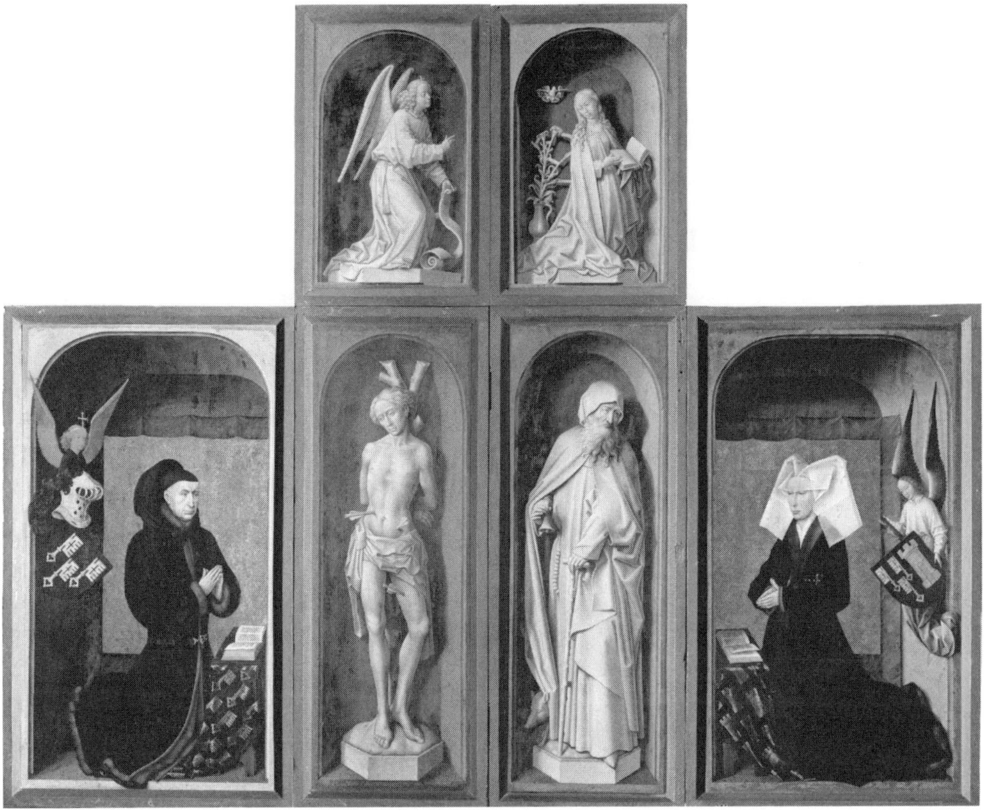

Figure 8. Rogier van der Weyden, *Altarpiece of the Last Judgment* (ca. 1443–1451), exterior, oil on panel partly transferred to canvas. Musée de Hotel-Dieu, Beaune. (Photo: Erich Lessing/Art Resource, New York.)

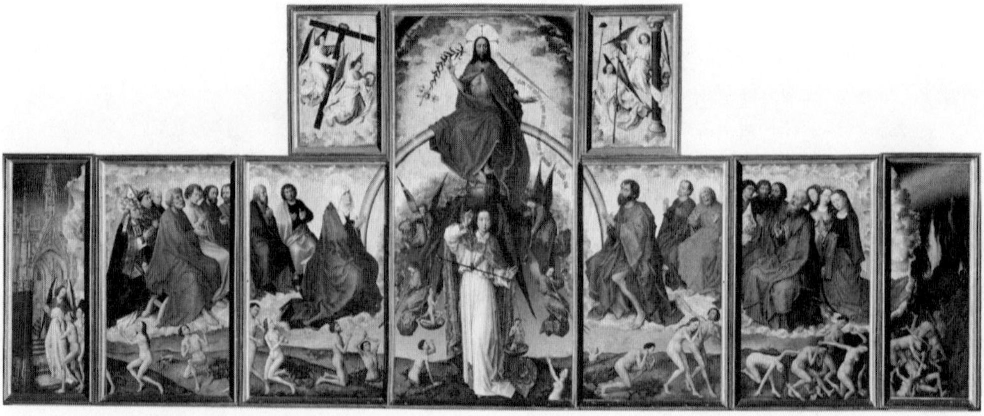

Figure 9. Rogier van der Weyden, *Altarpiece of the Last Judgment* (ca. 1443–1451), interior, oil on panel partly transferred to canvas, 220 × 547.6 cm. Musée de Hotel-Dieu, Beaune. (Photo: Erich Lessing/Art Resource, New York.)

churche . . . was a lytle ymage of Seint Anne, made of alleblaster, standynge fixed to the pillar, closed and clasped togethars with four bordes, small, payntyd, and gowynge rownd abowt the ymage, in manar of a compas, lyke as it is to see comonly and all abowt . . . And this ymage was thus shett closed and clasped, accordynge to the rulles that, in all churchis of England, be observyd, all ymages to be hid from Ash Wednesday to Estarday in the mornynge."[43] Statues and paintings not equipped with their own shutters were veiled during Lent, while cloths were hung on rods to conceal altars or the entire space of the choir.[44] A late-fifteenth-century Book of Hours from the southern Netherlands pictures a church interior with figures in prayer, one before an altar whose retable and sculpted crucifix are draped in white sheets marked with red crosses (figure 10).[45]

Many Lenten cloths were white or monochromatic, but others were much less plain. In 1472, a wealthy merchant named Jacob Gürtler donated an historiated Lenten cloth to the Church of St. John in Zittau (figure 11). Measuring approximately twenty-seven feet by twenty-two feet, the cloth is decorated with forty-five scenes from the Old Testament above forty-five from the New, arranged in ten rows and nine columns beginning in the upper left corner with the creation of heaven and earth and ending with the Last Judgment at lower right.[46] Although anything but simple, historiated Lenten cloths like this one replaced the monumental, iconic, and often three-dimensional forms of altarpieces and sculptures with rows of small, flat images. These sequences of images formed a visual sermon of sorts, which would seem to tally with Gregory's justification of images as bibles of the illiterate. Indeed, below each row of images in the Zittau cloth runs a line of rhymed verse in Gothic minuscule, which would have told viewers in words what the images show, if only it had been legible to them. At 1.7 inches, these letters were in fact too small to decipher unless one was very close to the cloth—even for those few congregants who were able to read. The images the words describe would also have been hard to make out from any distance because of their small size.

Thus, for only a few people would the experience of the Zittau

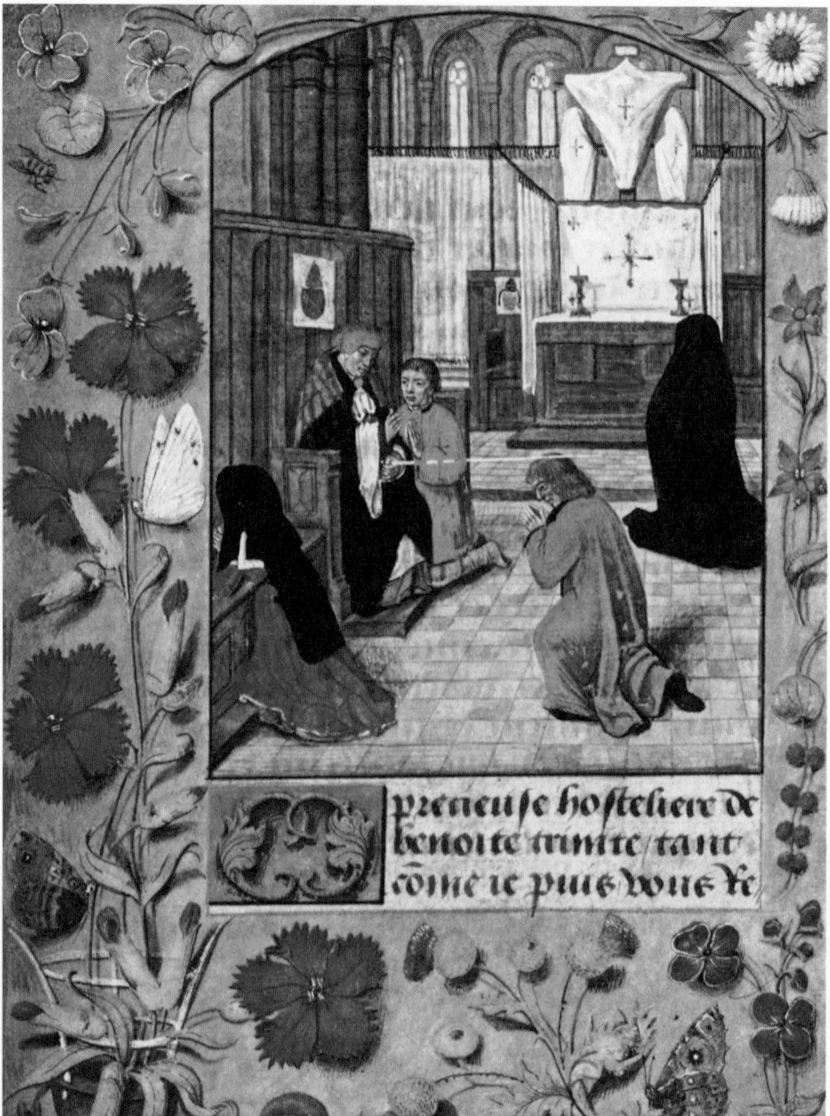

Figure 10. Southern Netherlandish, *Office of Penance* (ca. 1492) from a Book of Hours, miniature 11.5 × 15.5 cm, British Library, London, ms. 25,698, fol. 9r. (Photo: The British Library Board.)

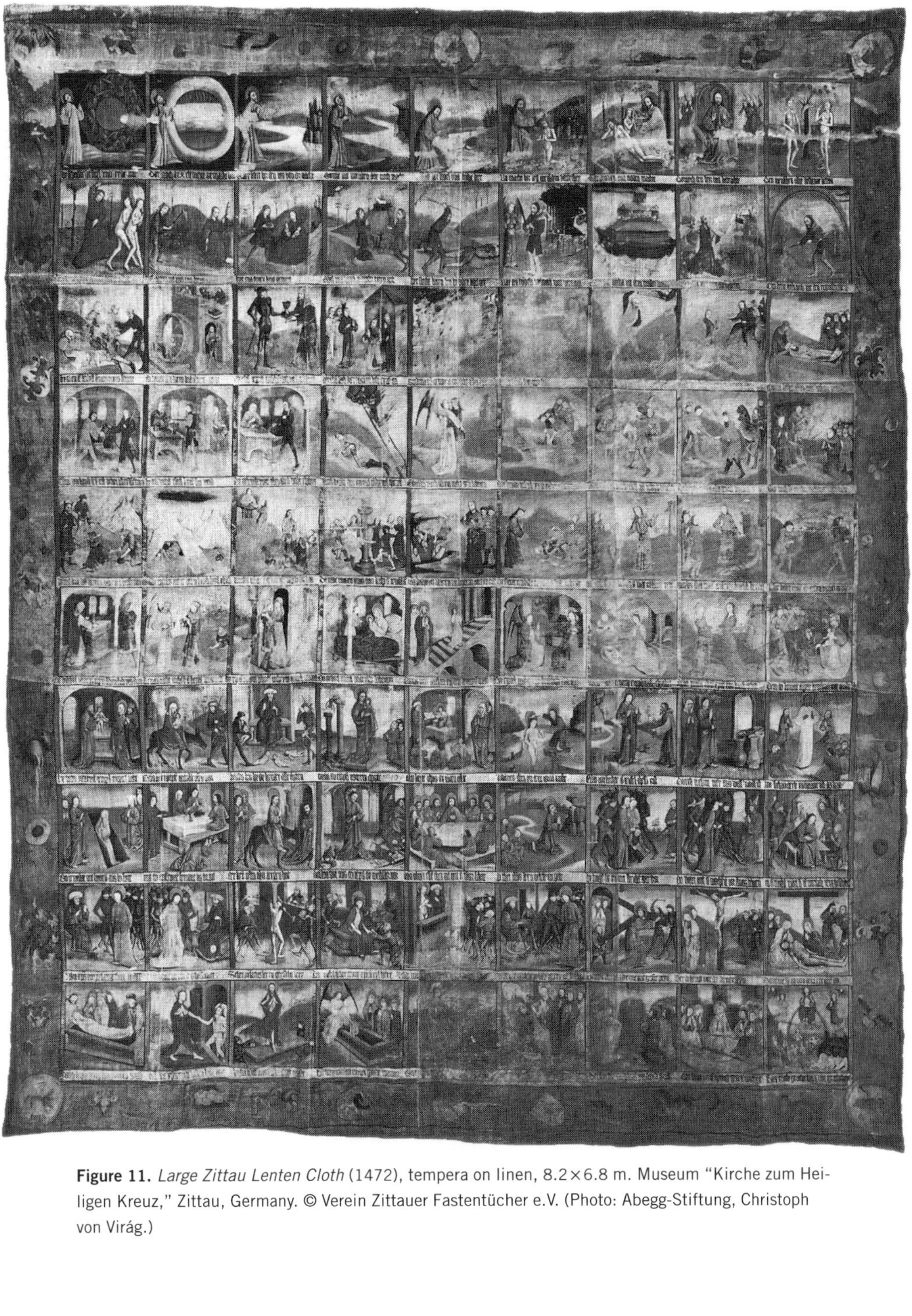

Figure 11. *Large Zittau Lenten Cloth* (1472), tempera on linen, 8.2×6.8 m. Museum "Kirche zum Heiligen Kreuz," Zittau, Germany. © Verein Zittauer Fastentücher e.V. (Photo: Abegg-Stiftung, Christoph von Virág.)

cloth have been one of reading, and for only a few more would the cloth have provided the visual sermon that Gregory recommends. For most, the Lenten cloth would have had a still more censorious effect. For this majority, the cloth appeared as a grid with a repetition and variation of abstract forms within its squares. Breaking up the visual field into units too small and numerous to be "read" much less worshipped, the cloth was a powerful *deflector* of the venerating gaze. While historiated Lenten cloths like the one in Zittau cannot be said to abstain from images in any absolute sense—indeed, they could be said to revel in them—they nonetheless negated the object of veneration even more thoroughly than Gregory's visual sermon by fragmenting and miniaturizing the pictorial field.[47]

For the forty hours Christ's effigy was hidden in a sepulcher, this sepulcher functioned much like contemporary altarpiece shutters and Lenten veils. In fact, some sepulchers were decorated with narrative scenes similar in format to those found on shutters and veils. The sepulcher in the formerly Cistercian cloister at Wienhausen is decorated with thirty scenes from the life of Christ, arranged in the same manner as the Zittau cloth (figure 12).[48] When the rear lid of this sepulcher is closed and the front open, the scenes can be read from upper left to lower right, beginning with the Annunciation and ending with an image of the Heavenly Jerusalem that fills two squares.

When both lids of the Wienhausen sepulcher are closed, the pictorial field is divided into eight squares depicting the men guarding the tomb. This divided field is what the people who came to pray at the sepulcher during the grave rest would have seen while the crucifix remained hidden from their view. When sepulchers were closed, the relatively small narrative scenes or figures decorating their exteriors formed a screen between the viewer and the three-dimensional, often life-size, effigy of Christ within. Like the intermittent shuttering of altarpieces throughout the year and the temporary veiling of images during Lent, the sepulchering of the crucifix hid the object of veneration from view. When sepulchers were entirely devoid of imagery, which they (like altarpiece shutters and Lenten veils) sometimes were, their negation of the image was even more severe.

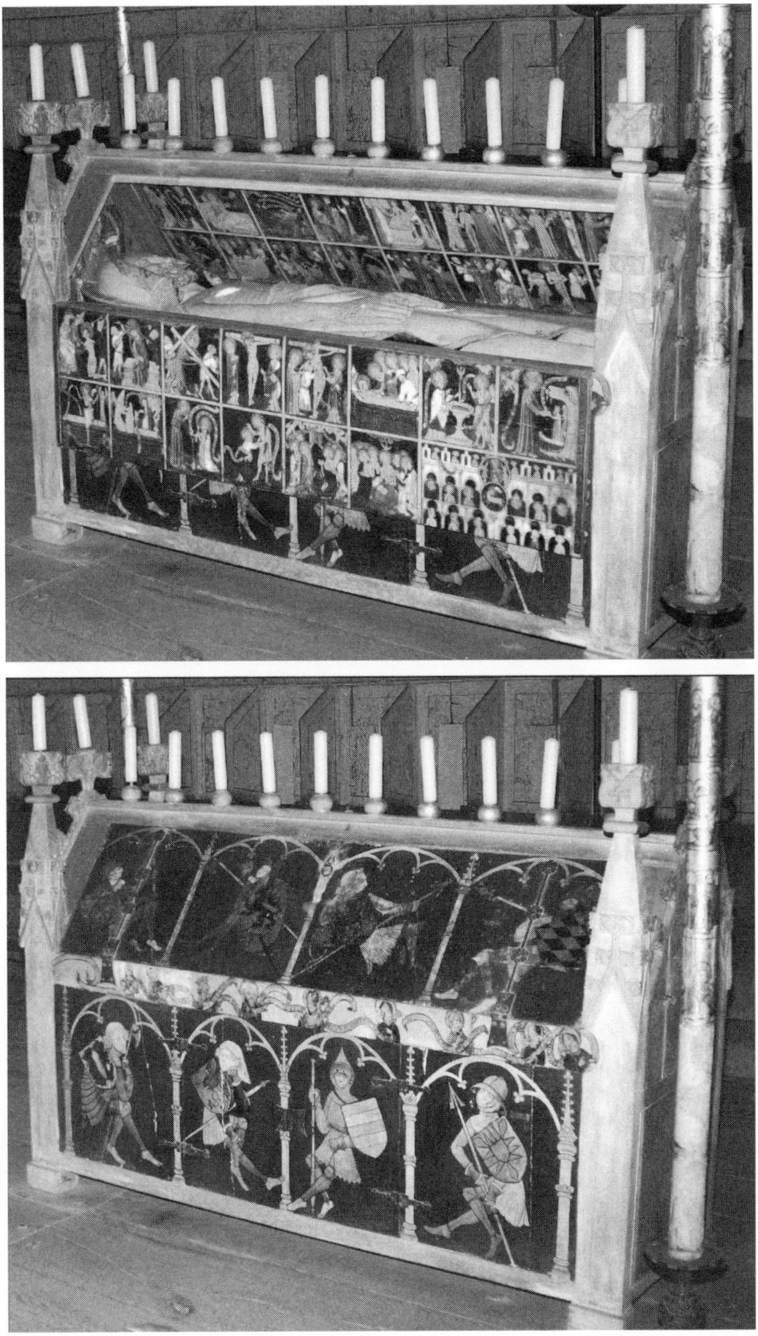

Figure 12. *Holy Sepulcher with Effigy* (effigy ca. 1290 and sepulcher ca. 1450), polychromed wood, sepulcher dimensions 252 × 80.5 × 172 cm. The upper photograph shows the rear lid closed and the front open; the lower photograph shows both lids closed. Former Cistercian Abbey of Wienhausen, Germany. (Photo: Kloster Wienhausen.)

In his liturgical treatise of 1286, Guillaume Durand describes the Lenten practice of hiding images as an allegory of the concealedness of Christ's divinity during the passion: "It is fitting that everything that pertains to the decoration of the church ought to be removed or covered during the season of Lent, which is done, according to some, on Passion Sunday, since from that point, the Divinity was hidden or veiled in Christ; for He handed Himself over to be seized and flogged as a man, as if He no longer had the power of the Divinity in Himself."[49] The annual re-creation of this hiddenness belongs to the liturgical reenactment of Christ's story and the commemoration of his suffering. It also serves, according to Durand, as a salutary reminder of how it was to live before the era of grace: "The covering of the sanctuary and the cross signify the letter of the Law, that is, its carnal observance, or what was in the Old Testament, before the Passion of Christ, when the understanding of sacred Scripture was veiled, covered, and obscure, and those who lived during that time always had a veil before their eyes, that is, a shady knowledge."[50]

But scripture was not simply unveiled in the era of grace, according to Durand, who goes on to say that Lenten cloths also denote the incapacity of *all humans* to behold God, even after the incarnation. The original sin that necessitated Christ's sacrifice carries the blindness of the old era into the new. Because of this chronic sightlessness, Durand adds to his list of explanations for Lenten cloths our unworthiness: "Three types of veils are hung in church . . . The first signifies the letter of the Law; the second denotes our unworthiness, since we are unworthy or rather powerless to enter Heaven; the third, the restraint of our carnal pleasure."[51] Veils are hung in churches, then, not only to remind congregants of a blindness overcome but also to represent the blindness with which they themselves are afflicted and to warn against seeking with carnal vision what can only be known spiritually.[52] Durand's account of the Lenten observance is split between irreconcilable positions: the blindness represented by the Lenten cloth both does and does not persist in the present era of grace, for spiritual blindness both was and was not overcome by the incarnation. Bracketed by the Adoration of the

Cross and the Elevation, the Deposition rite partakes of this same duplicity, wherein the assertion and denial (or the acceptance and rejection) of the sacred image are made to coexist.

The Deposition rite's temporary occultation of the crucifix is different on two counts from Gregorian moderation. While Gregorian images are intended to move the viewer in only one direction, the hiding of the image on Good Friday is reversible. All burials are provisional according to Christian dogma, but the burial of Christ was particularly short-lived. Bound as it is to the narrative wherein Christ is resurrected only forty hours after his body is laid in the grave, the Deposition rite's disavowal of the image came to an end on Easter Sunday. Yet while it lasted, that disavowal was more absolute than anything Gregory, in his moderation, had thought necessary. If Gregorian images are sublimated into the blinding light of heaven, as they lift the viewer from an ocular experience of the *imago Dei* to an inward experience of the invisible God, the Good Friday effigy is brought low and shrouded in darkness—but only temporarily.

Well-Rehearsed Gestures

Some Protestant reformers pointed to the periodic hiding of images in Catholic churches as a model for their own iconoclastic activity. In an anonymous play written in Amsterdam in 1558, not long before iconoclasm swept the Netherlands, allegorical personifications speak for different religious confessions. Representing the Protestant position, *Godly Wise Man* debates the merits and demerits of sacred images with a Catholic character by the name of *Worldly Scholar*. In laying out his views against images, *Godly Wise Man* asks why it has been customary to cover them during Lent if they are in fact as innocent as his interlocutor makes them out to be. He then proceeds to answer his own question, explaining that the Lenten practice betrays a bad conscience about images.[53] In much the same manner, Zwingli discovers in the old practice of closing altarpiece shutters a first step toward a more definitive end to images. On 10 December 1523, he advised the Zurich city council: "First it is our opinion that the paintings should be immediately closed and not opened again until further notice. They are, after all, closed during periods of fasting and the other images are covered over."[54]

In 1529, the city council of Nuremberg likewise declared that Veit Stoss's recently installed *Virgin of the Rosary*, which was normally veiled on non-feast days, should remain indefinitely covered.[55] And in 1556, Polish and Bohemian Calvinists agreed on a gradual phasing out of images: first closing altarpieces, then veiling them with sheets, before finally removing them altogether.[56] In the words and deeds of iconoclasts like the fictional *Godly Wise Man*, Zwingli, the Nuremberg city council, and the Polish and Bohemian Calvinists, we find sixteenth-century reformers expressing their hostility toward images in a manner that was inherited from the very objects and practices they sought to get rid of.

Protestant reformers who invoked Lenten traditions as they committed acts of iconoclasm had an explanation for those traditions different from Durand's. According to Durand, images were covered during Lent because of the viewer's unworthiness to look at them; according to the iconoclasts, images were covered because of their unworthiness to be seen. Reformation iconoclasts covered images and suggested that observers of Lent did the same because there was something wrong with those images—not the people who looked at them. I have suggested here that participants in the Deposition rite buried the image for the same reason. But where the long-standing Lenten and Good Friday practices were part of a steady oscillation between acceptance and rejection, the reformers' *permanent* shuttering, veiling, and sepulchering arrested the cuckcoo-clock-like movement of the late medieval (para)liturgy by favoring one of its two extremes.

Vignette: Sol LeWitt's **Buried Cube** *(1968)*

In 1968, Sol LeWitt buried a cube containing an object known only to himself and to the collectors on whose property he buried it.[57] Just a couple of years earlier, he had announced that "the serial artist does not attempt to produce a beautiful or mysterious object but functions merely as a clerk cataloging the results of the premise."[58]

Although mystery is exactly what the burial of an unknown object would seem to produce, the deadpan documentation of *Buried Cube Containing an Object of Importance but Little Value* dispels the curiosity upon which mystery depends. When the "certificate" for *Buried Cube* appeared in the catalogue of a 1970 exhibition at the Haagse Gemeentemuseum, the artist supplied the following captions (figure 13): The Visser Family and the cube; Dick v. d. Net, maker of the cube; The artist and the cube; The shovel; The artist digging; The hole; The cube in the hole; The hole filled in."[59] The banality of everything that is known in this parody of art's last rites—a small group of bored participants, a shovel, dirt—assures us that what is unknown cannot be that interesting.

In his commentary on *Buried Cube* in the MoMA catalog of 1978, LeWitt gives his reasons for withdrawing the (art) object from the art system: "Gertrude Stein said a work of art was either priceless or worthless. The art system trivializes art by assigning monetary values to it, thus turning art into a commodity."[60] LeWitt buries the cube ostensibly in an effort to put to rest the "whole mystery of commodities, all the magic and necromancy," as Marx calls it, that surrounds the commodified work of art.[61]

LeWitt had been using partially closed cubes for hiding things since the early sixties. Like *Buried Cube*, these earlier cubes contain something of importance. *Wall Structure in Nine Parts, Each Containing a Work of Art by Other Artists* is assembled out of nine painted wooden cubes with slatted sides. *Cube with Random Holes Containing an Object* holds a sculpture by Grace Wapner. Then appear the cubes that do not contain a work of art but only another cube. Cubes hidden within other cubes first appear in sets C and D of LeWitt's *Serial Project No. 1 (ABCD)*, a work that elaborates "all major variations in two and three dimensions" of placing one form within another (figure 14).[62] It is in reference to this work that LeWitt insists that serial art does not produce mystery. He explains: "if the viewer cannot see the interior form, one may believe it is there or not, but one knows which form one believes is there or not there. The evidence given him or her by the other pieces in the set and by

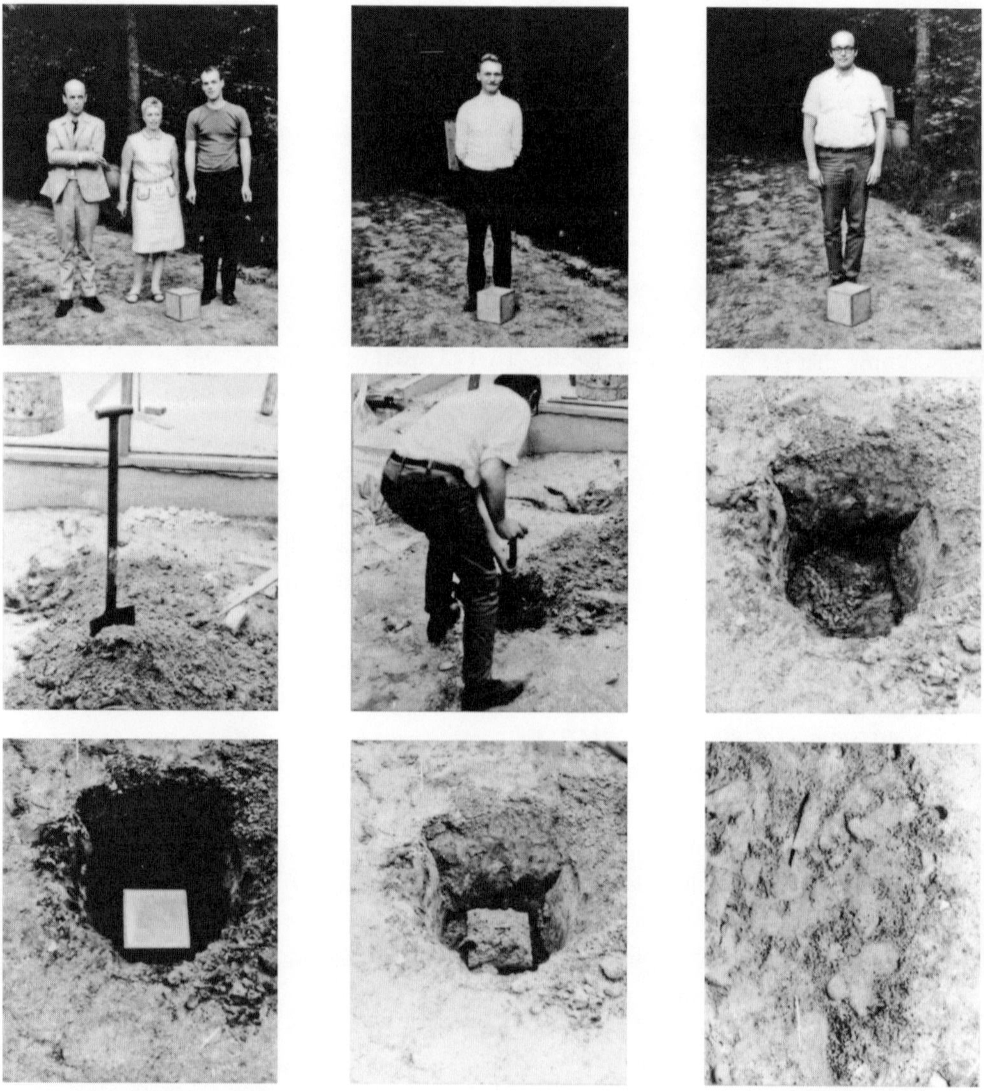

Figure 13. Sol LeWitt, *Buried Cube Containing an Object of Importance but Little Value* (1968), black-and-white photographs mounted on paper, 31.8 × 25.4 cm. LeWitt Collection, Chester, CT. © 2010 The LeWitt Estate/ARS, New York. (Photo: The LeWitt Collection and PaceWildenstein, New York.)

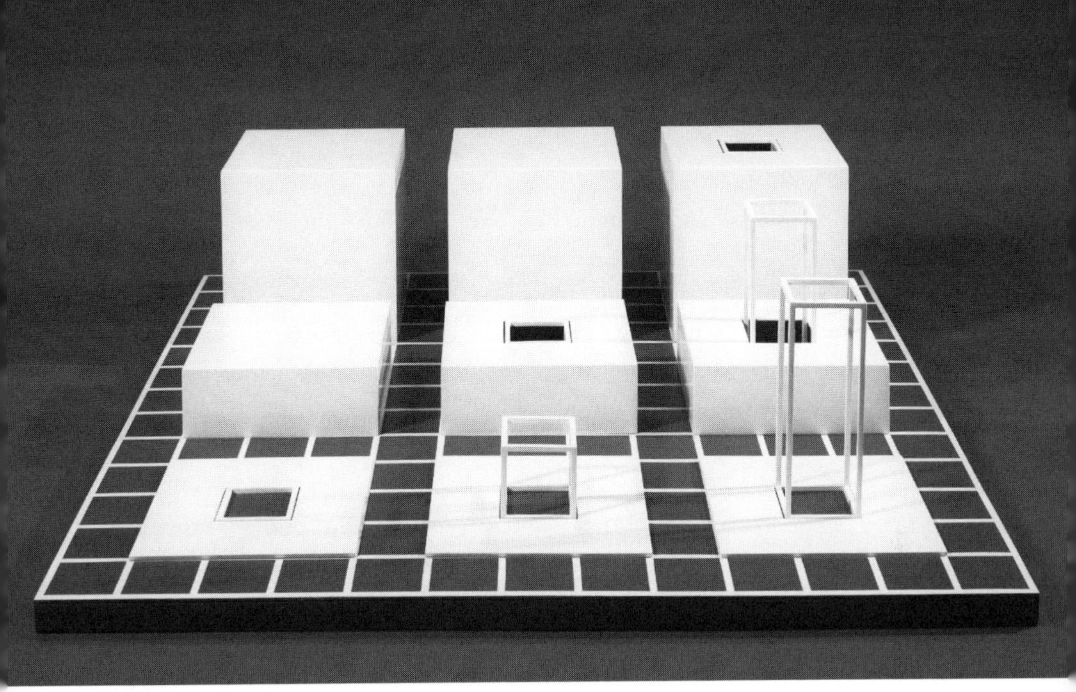

Figure 14. Sol LeWitt, *Serial Project #1 Set C* (1966–1969), baked enamel on aluminum, 22.9×83.8 cm. (Photo: Ellen Page Wilson. Courtesy of The LeWitt Collection and PaceWildenstein, New York.)

reference to the other sets will inform the viewer as to what should be there."[63]

In *Cubes with Hidden Cubes*, LeWitt isolates and elaborates the hiding of objects that occurs in certain sets of *Serial Project No. 1*: "When *Serial Project No. 1 (ABCD)* was done, some of the pieces in parts C & D (outside closed) contained elements not seen but implied by the logic of the piece. *Cubes with Hidden Cubes* was a further investigation of the idea.... It proposed that one needn't actually see things to understand their form and placement (figures 15–16)."[64] According to LeWitt, the hidden elements are unmysterious because we fill in what we cannot see in accordance with what we have seen elsewhere. Whether we can see it or not, there is only ever more of the same. Whether or not we believe there is something there is a matter of indifference since, in either case, the object of our (dis)belief is known to us.

The buried and hidden pieces would drop out of LeWitt's work. The cube that became a lasting part of his sculptural idiom did not allow for hiding because it had no walls; LeWitt called it open. But the artist's early interest in hiding things persisted through his later work, being brought to bear on the containing cube itself. In *Incomplete Open Cube*, the missing elements of the cube are implied by the cube's simple and predictable shape (figure 17): "Because it is standard and universally recognized, no intention is required of the viewer. It is immediately understood that the cube represents the cube, a geometric figure that is uncontestably itself."[65] The ghostly but unmysterious presence of what is absent in *Incomplete Open Cube* is indicated in the drawing *Four- and Eight-Part Incomplete Open Cubes (Numerical)* (figure 18). Here, complete open cubes are sketched in pencil. Superimposed over the pencil lines, ink lines delineate the structure's "incomplete" form. What remains visible of the pencil after the superimposition of ink indicates what will *not* be visible in the sculpture: the missing or "hidden" but not-unknown elements.

LeWitt's "hiding" of objects or elements in such a way that they do not give rise to curiosity parodies religious and art-world rituals designed to create mystery and (art-market) value. One would

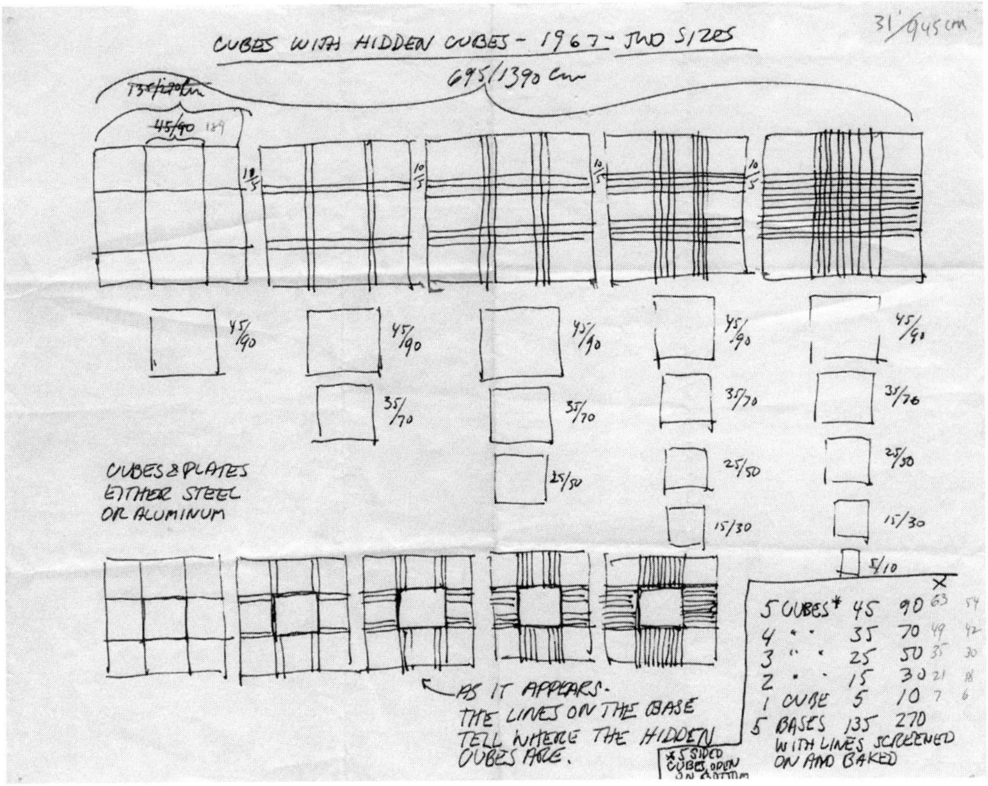

Figure 15. Sol LeWitt, *Working Drawing for Cubes with Hidden Cubes* (1967), ink on paper, 21.6 × 27.9 cm. The LeWitt Collection, Chester, CT. © 2010 The LeWitt Estate/ARS, New York. (Photo: R. J. Phil. Courtesy of The LeWitt Collection and PaceWildenstein, New York.)

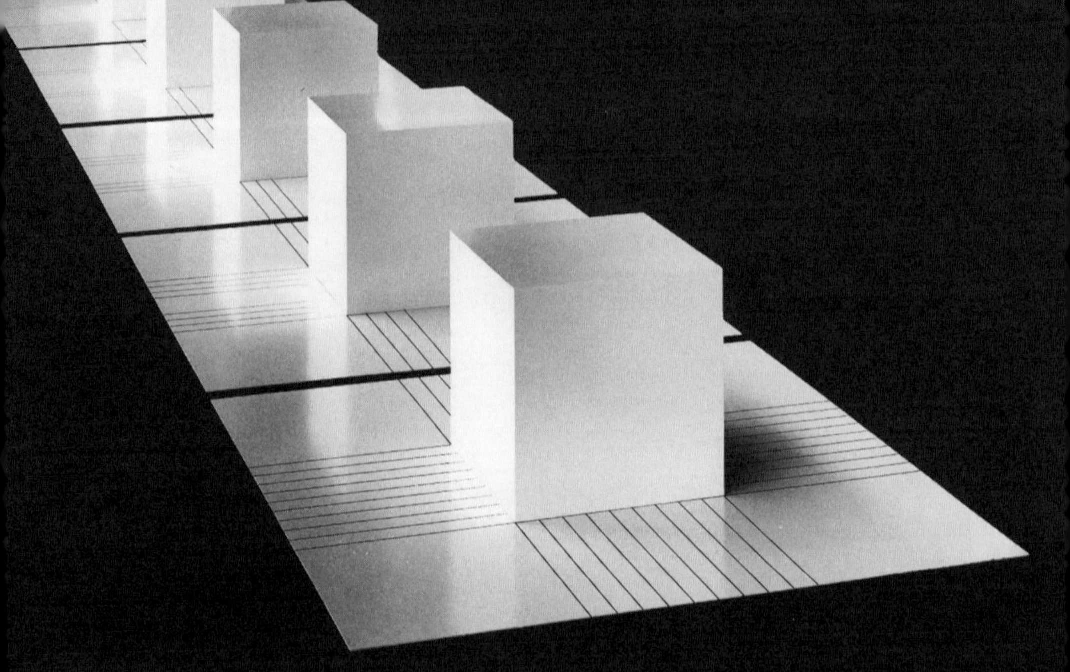

Figure 16. Sol LeWitt, *Cubes with Hidden Cubes* (1967/1977), baked enamel on aluminum, 63 × 63 × 63 cm. The FER Collection, Ulm. © 2010 The LeWitt Estate/ARS, New York. (Photo: Archive FER Collection.)

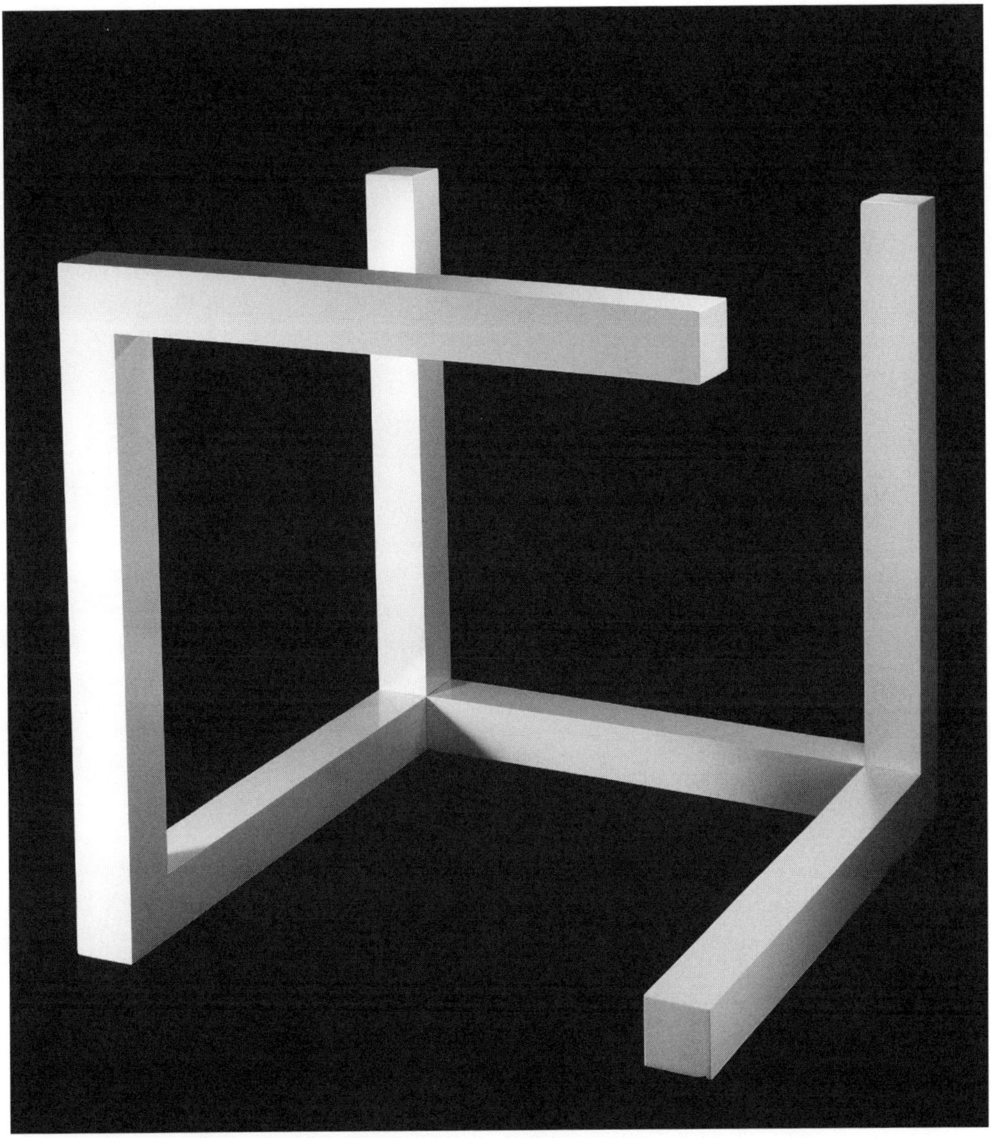

Figure 17. Sol LeWitt, *Incomplete Open Cube* (1968), painted aluminum, 105 × 105 × 105 cm. Nationalgalerie, Staatliche Museen zu Berlin, Sammlung Marzona 0341. © 2010 The LeWitt Estate/ARS, New York. (Photo: Peter Neumann. Bildarchiv Preussischer Kulturbesitz/Art Resource, New York.)

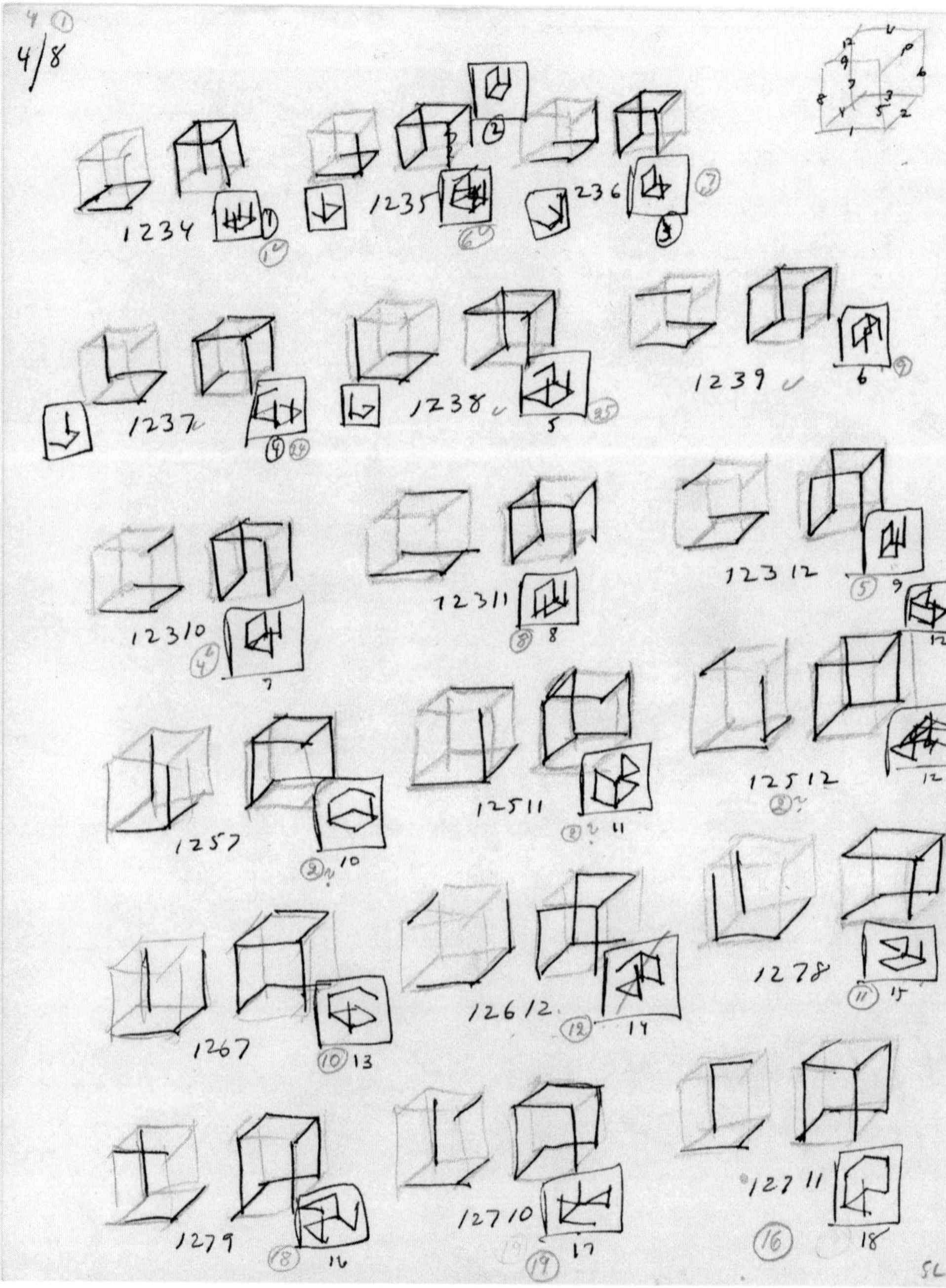

Figure 18. Sol LeWitt, *Working Drawing for Four- and Eight-Part Incomplete Open Cubes* (Numerical) (1973–1974), ink and pencil on paper, 27.9 × 21.6 cm. Wadsworth Atheneum Museum of Art, Hartford, CT, The Douglas Tracy Smith and Dorothy Potter Smith Fund, and partial gift of Carol and Sol LeWitt. (Photo: Wadsworth Atheneum Museum of Art.)

think that the late medieval Deposition rite and the veiling of images during Lent could be counted among such rituals. But when we compare these old religious practices to LeWitt's *Buried Cube*, the parody cuts both ways: LeWitt's parodic gesture is less sober and the parodied rites less mystifying than each at first may seem.

Compare the certificate LeWitt issued for *Buried Cube* to the story that begins with God's creation of the world in the upper left and ends with the Disappearing Christ in the lower right corner of a Lenten cloth from the village church of Haimburg (figure 19).[66] Though not a veil, LeWitt's certificate intervenes between the viewing subject and an object of importance just as the Lenten cloth does. With their grids of small repeated forms, both the photographic certificate and the linen cloth block the possessive gaze that seeks a valuable object.[67] God's nonchalance as he coolly calls into existence the world, the beasts, and Adam and Eve is not so different from LeWitt's feigned gravity as he stands prepared to bury his cube in the dirt (figure 20). The Lenten cloth's emotional litotes meets the *Buried Cube*'s hyperbolic solemnity half-way—the Lenten cloth is more deadpan and its latter-day parody less flat than one is at first prepared to see.[68]

The medieval Deposition rite is likewise closer to LeWitt's parody than a reading that relies on the predictable distinction between a credulous Middle Ages and a disenchanted modernity allows. The words that accompany the Deposition rite progress from the responsory *Behold how the just man dies* to the responsory *At the burial of the Lord*, celebrating the movement of the *imago Dei* from the openness of the cross to the obscurity of the grave, where the crucifix was kept out of sight. While it reposed in the grave, this crucifix could have been perfectly well *imagined* by anyone who had seen one before—which would have been anyone who had ever set foot in a church or, for that matter, had ever walked Europe's country roads. Around 1500—to say nothing of other times—the crucifix was hardly less "universally recognized" than LeWitt's cube was in 1968.

Because the crucifix came to mind in certain contexts whether it was before the eyes or not, Luther saw no real sense in banishing it from the church: "whether I will or not, when I hear of Christ, an

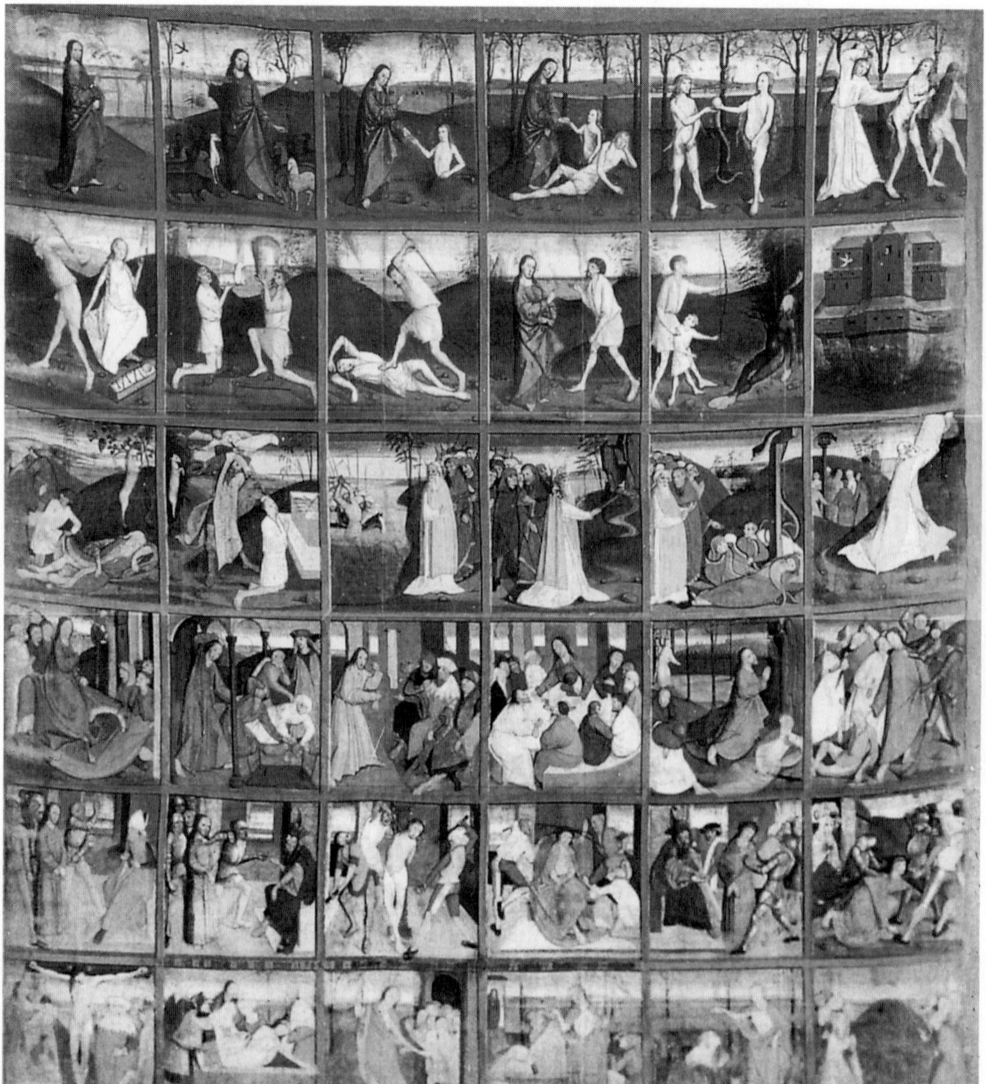

Figure 19. *Lenten Cloth* (1504) from the parish church in Haimburg bei Völkermarkt, Austria, distemper on linen, 420×380 cm. (Photo: Professor Heinz Ellersdorfer. Courtesy of the Katholische Kirche in Kärnten — Diözese Gurk.)

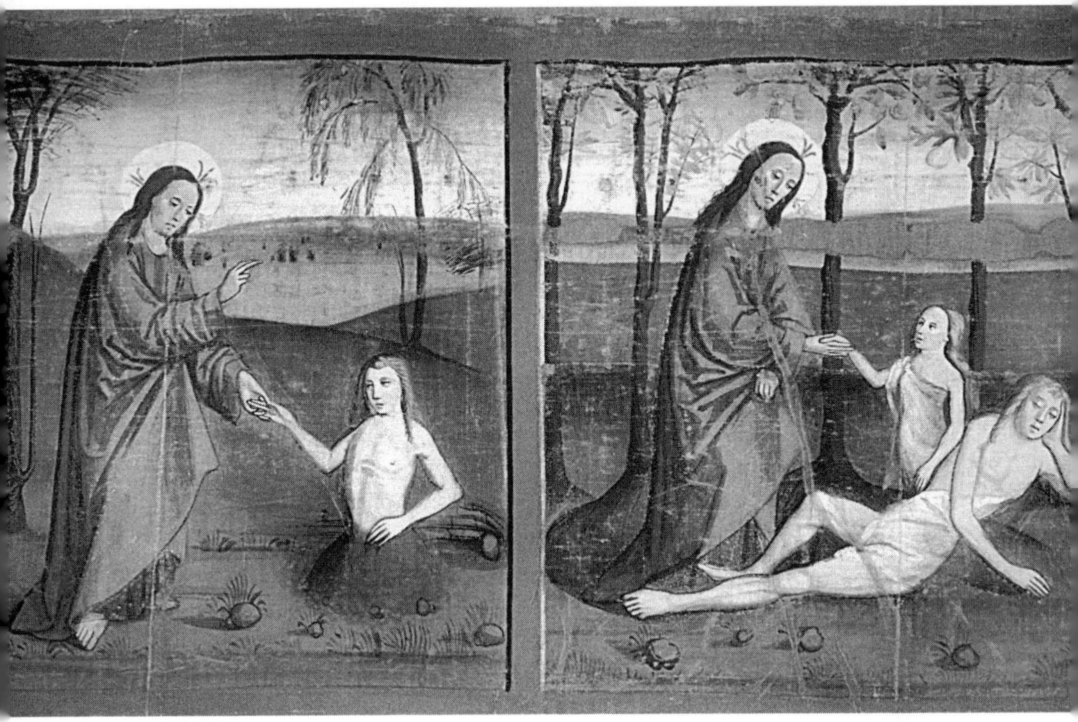

Figure 20. Detail from Figure 19: *Lenten Cloth* (1504) from the parish church in Haimburg bei Völkermarkt, Austria, distemper on linen, 420 × 380 cm. (Photo: Professor Heinz Ellersdorfer. Courtesy of the Katholische Kirche in Kärnten — Diözese Gurk.)

image of a man hanging on a cross takes form in my heart, just as the reflection of my face naturally appears in the water when I look into it."[69] The Deposition rite cultivated the mystery of what was hidden in the sepulcher neither more nor less than LeWitt cultivated the mystery of the cube. Because the crucifix was too familiar to arouse the curiosity of those who were denied a view of it and because, in any case, it would reappear only a short time later, removing it from view functioned more as a disavowal of the image than as a stimulus of the viewer's desire to see it.

In response to all those interpretions of LeWitt's work that take its rationalism at face value and would make a philosopher of the artist, Rosalind Krauss insists that LeWitt deploys reason to unreasonable effect: "'reason' running amok, doing a kind of lunatic dance over an abyss of purposelessness, displaying either by manic hilarity or an almost autistic flatness a reason overwhelmed by emotional chaos. Schizoid reason."[70] In *Buried Cube*, a perfectly reasonable demystification and devaluation of the (art) object opens onto a mystery both hilarious and flat: what are we left with when the mystifications of religion and capital have been consigned to the grave?

On the other hand, the Deposition rite's investment in an alternately seen and unseen but ceaselessly imagined crucifix flattens the mystery and pathos we expect from sacred ritual: what is mysterious, after all, about the predictable rhythms of the cuckoo clock? The affective flatness of the Deposition rite was neither an accident nor a failing: it was precisely this that permitted the rite to do its most important work of *ritualizing* hostility toward the image. In the late medieval church, the mechanical regularity with which familiar images were made to disappear behind shutters and veils and into sepulchers gave ritual form to a sustained ambivalence toward them—freeing those viewers whose ambivalence it was from having to express it.

CHAPTER TWO

Crucifixes with Movable Arms

The Deposition rite was never acknowledged in the liturgy of Rome. It was shaped on a local level and reflected desires not explicitly accounted for in the official documents. The unorthodoxy modern historians tend to associate with late medieval images is a superstitious belief in their sentience and mobility. The Deposition rite encouraged no such thing. On the contrary, I will suggest, it made an annual spectacle of nothing so much as the image's lack of life. Toward the end of the thirteenth century, a special crucifix with movable arms was invented specifically to facilitate the staging of this spectacle (figure 21). The sculpture's movable arms allowed the same image seen hanging on the cross to be lifted off the cross and to be fitted into a narrow coffer. This had the predictable effect of making the reenactment of the deposition more realistic. But the mobility of this crucifix also did something more surprising, in fact, just the opposite of what one might expect: it called attention to the fact that—as moveable as it may be—this image is powerless to move itself.

The Crucifix

In the early Christian period, the cross was a triumphant symbol of Christ's victory over death and the devil. Before the fifth century, the crucifix—a cross with an image of the body of Christ fixed upon it—only appeared in narrative depictions of the crucifixion scene. When isolated crucifixes began to be made in the fifth century, they represented the living Christ. Only in the ninth century, following the Byzantine image controversy and perhaps in response to the

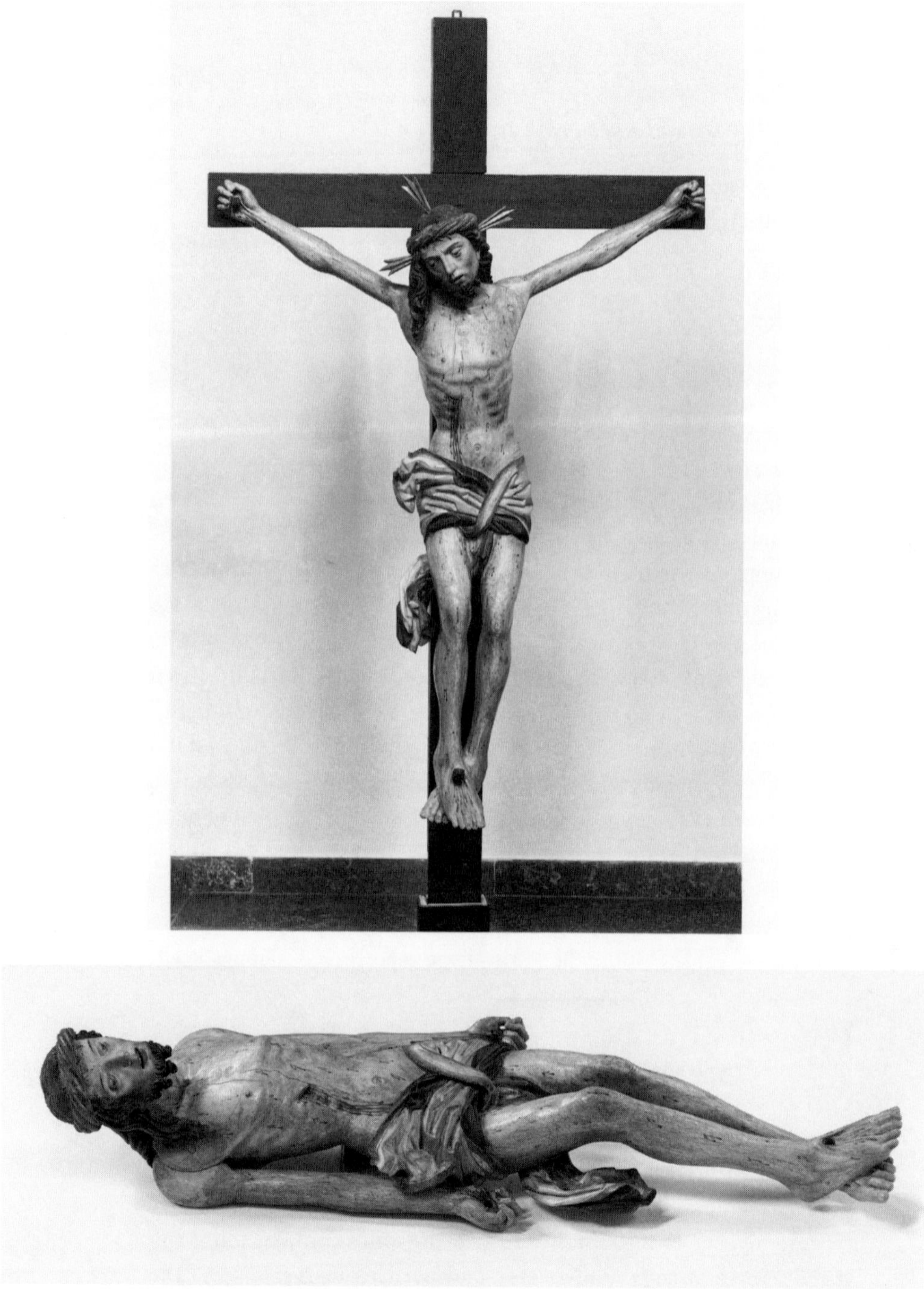

Figure 21. Swabian, *Crucifix with Movable Arms* (ca. 1520) from the Sacristy of St. John the Baptist, Memmingen, Germany, polychromed wood, height 115 cm. (Photo: Haus der Bayerischen Geschichte.)

heresy of monophysitism (the belief that Christ has only one nature: the divine) did Byzantine artists begin consistently representing Christ on the cross with his eyes closed to indicate that he is dead.[1] Crucifixes with the dead Christ appeared at this time in the West as well, although the living crucified Christ persisted there alongside the newer iconography.[2] The ninth-century Irish philosopher Johannes Scotus Eriugena apostrophizes the peculiar death that made it difficult for some to picture Christ lifeless even as he hung on the cross: "O death, death of life, if it is to be called death and not life / I would not dare to call that which supplies life death."[3]

Crucifixes were being made on a monumental scale at least by the late tenth century, which is about when the Deposition rite was first recorded, as far as we know. These crucifixes sometimes carried the living and sometimes the dead Christ, the difference between them being little more than that between open and closed eyes. Only in the thirteenth century did artists begin to graphically represent the suffering and death of Christ on the cross, completing the gradual historical transition from the theomorphic to the anthropomorphic crucifix.[4]

Reading accounts of the Deposition rite, it is often difficult to say what kind of object or image was buried. The *Monastic Agreement* refers to a *sancta crux*, an ambiguous term that can designate either an aniconic cross or a crucifix with an image of Christ's body on it.[5] The term *crucifixus*, which also appears in the documents, would seem to refer to the latter.[6] Even less ambiguous are the terms *imago crucifixi*, *imaginem*, and *imago Domini*.[7] And entirely unambiguous are those cases where the image is described: in Durham Cathedral, for example, one hears of "a goodly large Crucifix, all of gold, of the picture of our Sauiour Christ nailed uppon the crosse."[8] Although the aniconic cross probably never entirely ceased to be used in the Deposition rite, it is likely that figurative crucifixes came to predominate over time and that the representation of the *deadness* of the body became increasingly graphic, as was the case with crucifixion iconography in general.

The invention of the crucifix with movable arms belongs to this trend toward an ever more realistic image of the crucified body. To strengthen its realism, the movable crucifix's simple hinge-mechanisms were sometimes concealed with paint or parchment or both, as are those of a nearly life-size sculpture from Kempten (figure 2, plate 3). Along with the shoulders, the elbows of the Kempten crucifix were once articulated–they have since been filled with plaster–so that when the effigy was placed in the tomb, its hands could be folded over its chest. The use of human hair and beard heightens the realism of a crucifix with movable arms from Bad Wimpfen (figure 22).[9]

Long forgotten, crucifixes with movable arms began to receive attention again in the 1960s.[10] Since then, scholars have naturally associated them with the other movable sculptures used in and around Holy Week.[11] On Palm Sunday, for example, a statue of Christ seated on an ass was processed through the streets as viewers scattered palm leaves before it in celebration of Christ's entry into Jerusalem (figure 23).[12] And on Easter, the resurrection was performed by raising a sculpture of the triumphant Christ from the sepulcher, as I described in Chapter I (figure 24). This same figure was used forty days later to dramatize Christ's ascension to heaven, when a rope was attached to a metal ring in the head of the sculpture by means of which it could be pulled up through an opening in the vaulting of the church (figure 25).[13] Once the sculpture had disappeared through this hole, roses, lilies, Eucharistic Hosts, and sometimes–much to the chagrin of the less theatrically minded–a burning effigy of the devil rained down from the same hole onto the congregation. Kirchmair did not approve:

> The blocke that on the aultar still, till then was seene to stande,
> Is drawne vp hie aboue the roofe, by ropes and force of hande....
> Then out of hande the dreadfull shape of Sathan downe they throw,
> Oft times with fire burning bright, and dasht a sunder tho,
> The boyes with greedie eyes do watch, and on him straight they fall,
> And beate him sore with rods, and breake him into peeces small.[14]

Entirely at odds with the hiding of images during Lent, sculptures like the Palm Sunday ass and the Resurrection figure made

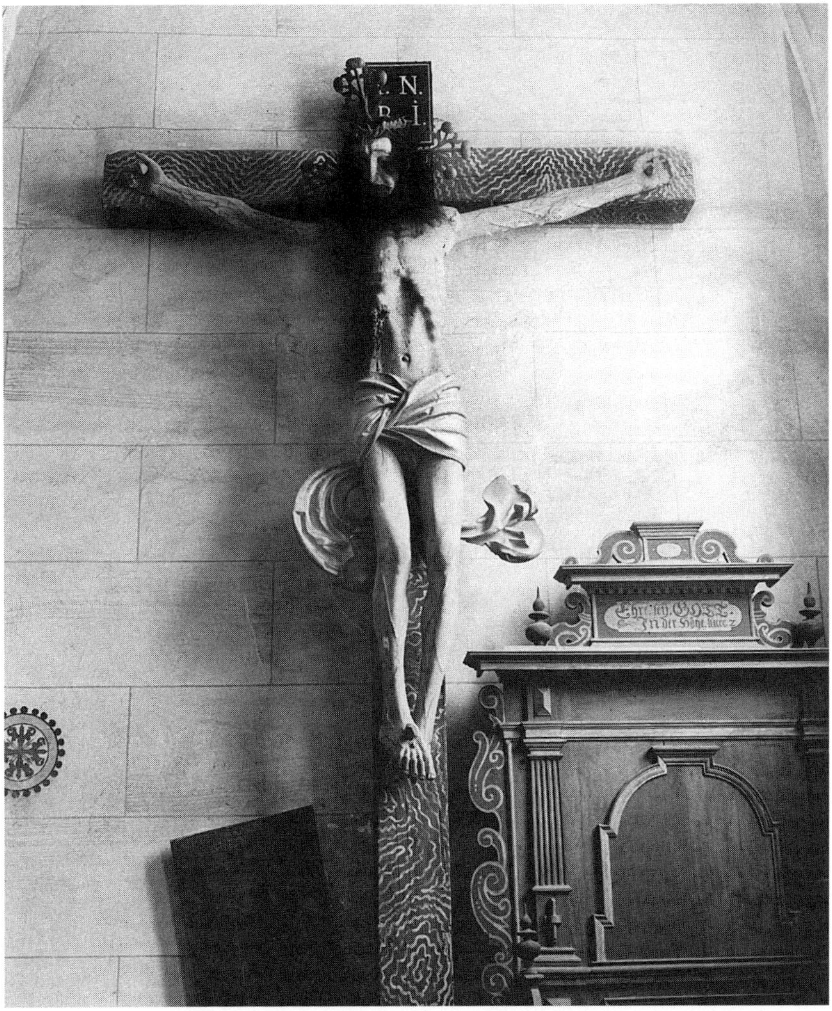

Figure 22. Oswald Bockstorfer aus Memmingen, *Crucifix with Movable Arms* (1481) in the Evangelical Church in Bad Wimpfen am Berg, Germany, polychromed wood with human hair. (Photo: Bildarchiv Foto Marburg.)

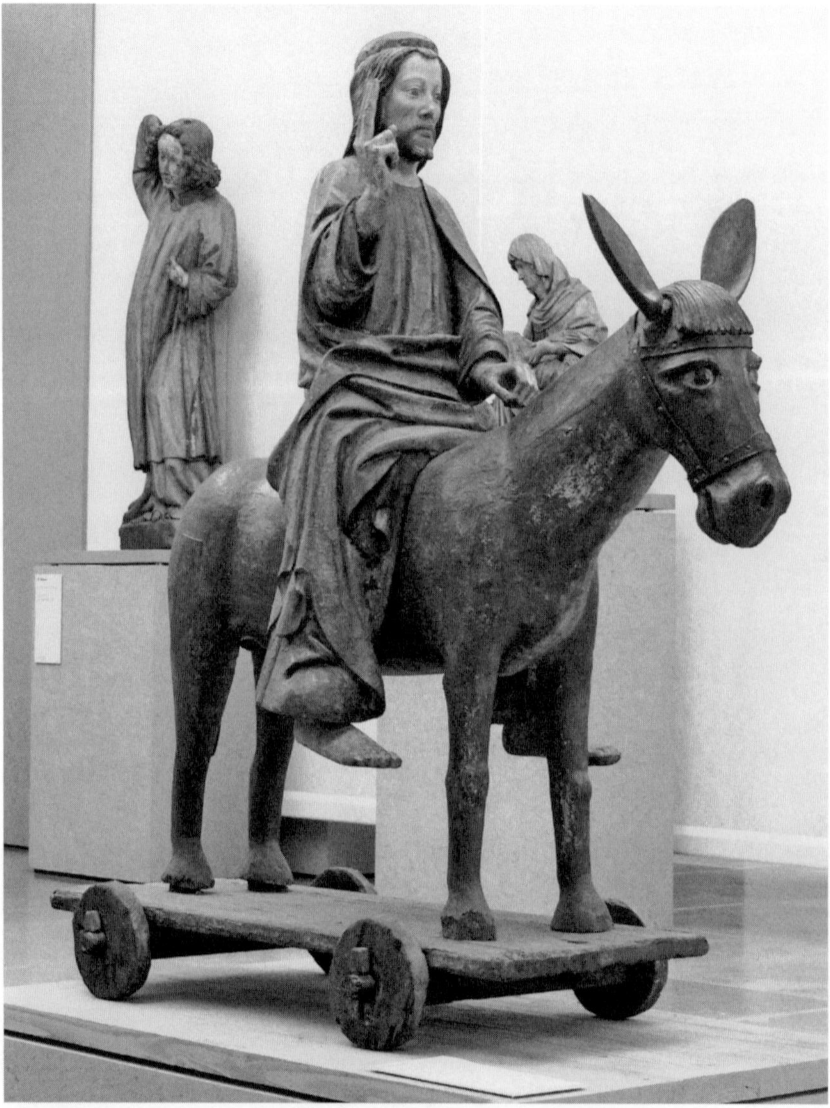

Figure 23. Swabian, *Palm Sunday Ass from Veringendorf* (late 14th c.), polychromed wood, almost life size. Württembergisches Landesmuseum, Stuttgart, Germany. (Photo: Andreas Praefcke.)

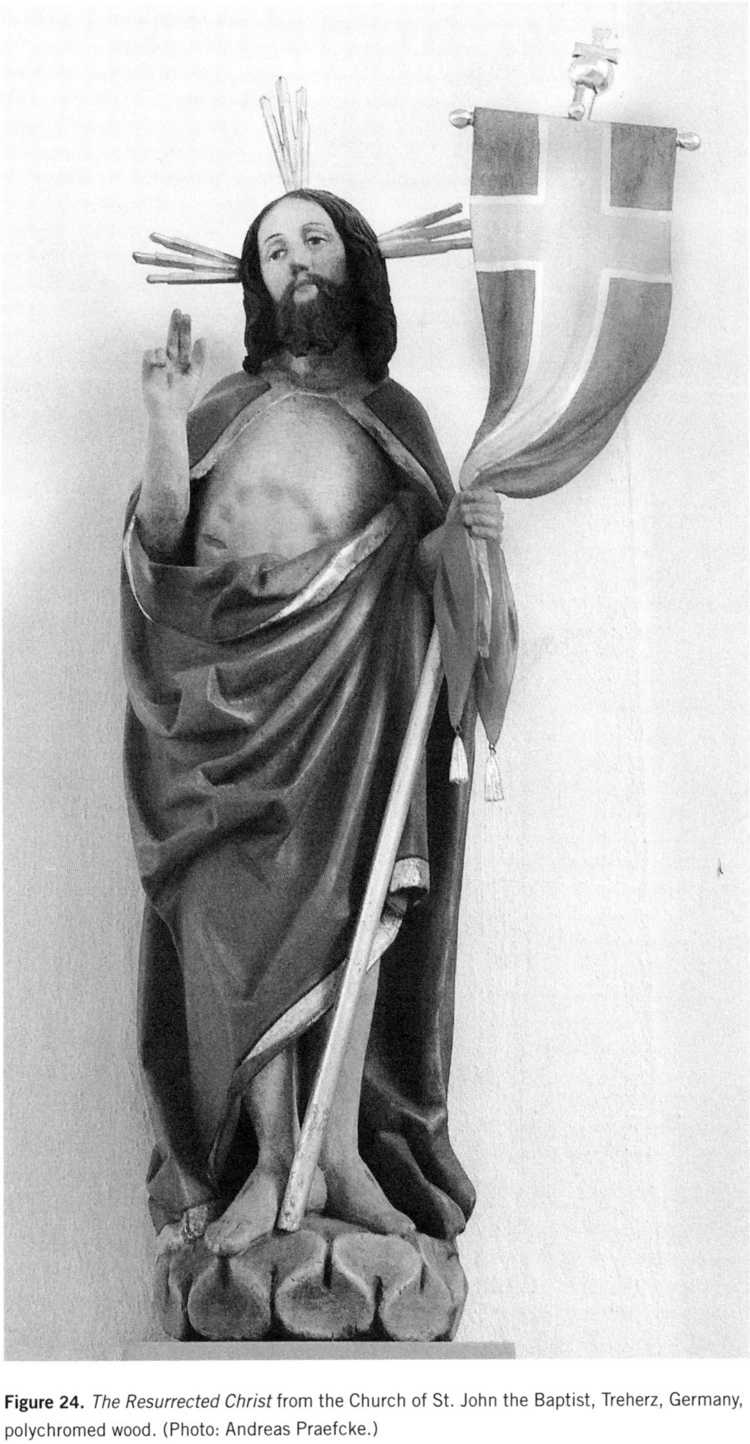

Figure 24. *The Resurrected Christ* from the Church of St. John the Baptist, Treherz, Germany, polychromed wood. (Photo: Andreas Praefcke.)

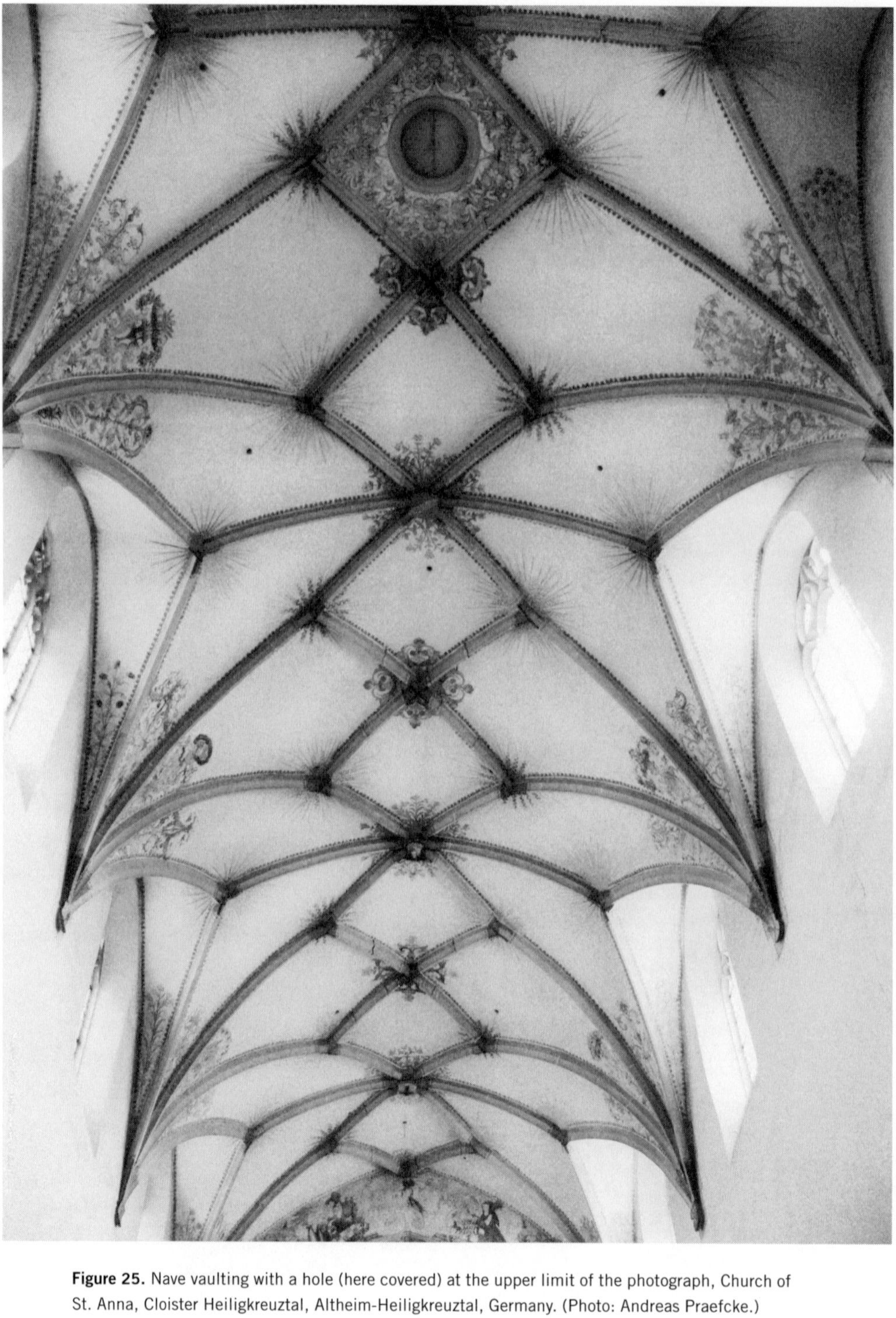

Figure 25. Nave vaulting with a hole (here covered) at the upper limit of the photograph, Church of St. Anna, Cloister Heiligkreuztal, Altheim-Heiligkreuztal, Germany. (Photo: Andreas Praefcke.)

the time around Easter particularly rich not just in images but in images—which "on the aultar *still*, till then were seene to stande" (my emphasis)—put into motion in paraliturgical performances.

The crucifix with movable arms, the Palm Sunday ass, and the Resurrection figure are all mobile in the sense that they can be *made to move*; they cannot move independently. But insofar as the crucifix represents the dead Christ, its movements differ from those of the other two. When the Palm Sunday ass was rolled through the streets of town and when the Resurrection figure was hoisted up through a hole in the vaulting of the church, the fiction was that they were moving of their own accord or, at least, not by means of any human intervention. For this reason, the ass and the Resurrection figure were moved with the help of ropes, wheels, and pulleys, and from a distance great enough to dissociate the mover from the moved: "A wooden Asse they haue," says Kirchmair, "and Image great that on him rides, / But vnderneath the Asses feete, a table broade there slides."[15] By contrast, when the crucifix was taken down from the cross and its arms were laid by its sides, the fiction (and the fact) was that it had no volition whatsoever. Because the fact of the crucifix's stillness coincided with its fiction, it could be handled directly; in fact, it needed to be handled directly since it was its handler who demonstrated its abject passivity.

In his 1697 account of a procession at the Church of the Holy Sepulcher in Jerusalem, Henry Maundrell, chaplain in Aleppo, describes a crucifix with movable arms: "It was an Effigies so contriv'd, that its Limbs were soft and flexible, as if they had been real Flesh: and nothing could be more surprising, than to see the two pretended Mourners bend down the Arms, which were before extended, and dispose them upon the Trunk, in such a manner as is usual in Corpses."[16] Maundrell marvels over just how *yielding* the sculpture's limbs appear to be.

Writing critically about Catholic ritual in 1534, Sebastian Franck describes the same type of Deposition less with awe than indignation: "On Good Friday before Easter one carries a crucifix around in a procession and lays a great dead man-image (*eyen gross gestorben*

Menschen-Bild) in a grave."[17] Franck positions himself as if outside the belief system that gives meaning to the ritual's gestures and words: "As if I were a heathen, I was greatly astonished by the Christian folly."[18] Pretending to simply describe the ritual, he shows how inadequate its clunky maneuvers are to the task of representing the mystery of Christ's sacrifice. Franck relies on the self-evidence of this disparity: he needs only to describe the proceeding, he implies; its inadequacy speaks for itself. For, the better the rite pictures the stillness of its historical character, the more attention it calls to the mere *objectness* of the images that represent him.

In the Deposition rite's insistence on the immobility of the dead Christ, Franck sees and asks his readers to see a humiliating spectacle of what the anonymous author of "An homily against the peril of idolatry" calls the "unmoveable image."[19] John Hooper, Bishop of Gloucester, likewise relies on the irrefutable deadness of the Good Friday effigy to make his iconoclastic point: "What resemblance hath the taking of the cross out of the sepulchre, and going a procession with it, with the resurrection of Christ?" asks Hooper in a pamphlet of 1547. "None at all: the dead post is as dead when they sing *Now he dieth not*, as it was when they buried it with *His place is made in peace*."[20]

Franck and Hooper discover an unconscious mocking of the "unmoveable image" in the Catholic ritual. Although the official explanations of the Deposition rite make no mention of this iconoclastic effect, the iconoclasts' habit of pointing to the image's immobility was too familiar in the late Middle Ages for the mocking implications of the Deposition rite to have gone unnoticed. The Deposition rite let the silence and stillness of the image "speak" for themselves—just as iconoclasts often did: "If you are God, speak"[21]; "if you are God, protect yourself"[22]; "but now may we see, / What Goddes they be, / Euen puppets, mammats and elfes: / Throw them downe thryse, / They can not aryse, / Not ones, to helpe them selues."[23] Unanswered, these taunts demonstrated that images can do nothing in their own defense. According to Franck and Hooper, the Deposition rite demonstrated much the same thing.

Mocking the Image

Several other rituals of the later Middle Ages likewise called attention to the inability of images to "aryse" and help themselves. These included the popular folk rituals of Dead Sunday, the ecclesiastical ritual known as the Humiliation, and the more spontaneous rituals that erupted periodically when images refused to comply with the wishes of the people who relied upon them.

On the fourth Sunday of Lent, which was known as Laetare Sunday or Dead Sunday (*Todtensonntag*), it was common in the Middle Ages and long after to conduct a ritual driving out of "Carnival," "Winter," or "Death," who was personified in the form of an effigy.[24] The similarities between the Deposition rite and the Driving Out of Death would have been readily apparent to late medieval churchgoers since the two rituals occurred each year within weeks of one another. Some versions of the Driving Out ritual even ended with a resurrection.[25] In Chrudim, where the effigy of Death was made of a *cross*—which was decorated with a head, mask, and shirt—the resemblance between the two rituals would have been particularly striking.[26]

The details of the Driving Out varied, but it generally involved the subjection of the effigy to a host of degradations, including taunting, drenching with water, stoning, befouling, beheading, and tearing to shreds. After which, the effigy was either flung into the neighboring village, burned, drowned, or—most notably for my purposes—buried, sometimes in a dung-heap.[27] Each of these acts had the double and somewhat self-contradictory effect of symbolically killing the image *and* demonstrating that it was always already dead—nothing but a defenseless thing. Usually little more than a sack of straw, the effigy was not simply a personification of Death; it was death embodied in the form of inanimate matter.

When James Frazer described these rituals more than a century ago, he characterized them as purification rites intended to protect against plague and other afflictions—to protect, in short, against death. It was for this reason, in his opinion, that the treatment of the puppet was so brutal: "the effigy of Death is often regarded with fear and treated with marks of hatred and abhorrence. Thus the anxiety of the villagers to transfer the figure from their own to their neighbours' land."[28] In Radeberg, after a group of shouting and singing boys paraded the effigy through town, they threw it in a ditch and fled as fast as they could, believing that the last to flee would die that year.[29]

The Driving Out was sometimes explicitly associated with the banishing of idolatry. The Grimms cite the case of Königshain by Görlitz. Here the entire village made its way each Dead Sunday to a neighboring hill called the Todtenstein, where the image of a heathen god was said to have been worshipped. When they later returned to the village, they sang "we have driven out Death, we bring back Summer." "So it is not everywhere," the Grimms conclude, "that the banished idol represented Winter or Death in the abstract; in some cases it is still the *heathen divinity* giving way to Christianity, whom the people thrust out half in sorrow, and uttering songs of sadness."[30] The frequency with which Driving Out songs describe the gouging out of Death or Winter's eyes—a common form of iconoclasm—also suggests that the effigy was conceived of as an idol whose banishment prepared the way for the true religion: "Yes, yes, yes! Summer is here," goes a song from the Middle Rhine, "he scratches the eyes of Winter out."[31] Luther likewise implicitly links the Dead Sunday effigy with the "papist" idol in his satirical version of the Driving Out song, which begins "Now we drive the Pope out, / Out of Christ's church and God's house" and ends by ushering in Christ.[32]

If the Deposition rite shared certain features with the extra-ecclesiastical Driving Out of Death—including its iconoclastic overtones—it also resembled one of the Church's own rituals of image-mortification. Like the Deposition rite, this ritual involved the lowering of images to the ground. Intended to represent the humiliation of a community beset by war, plague, or other iniquity and to plead for God's mercy, the so-called Humiliation was conducted by lowering the crucifix or images of saints from their elevated positions onto the ground, where they were covered with thorns and left until they delivered whatever it was that was being asked of them.[33] The Humiliation functioned not only as supplication but also, according to Patrick Geary and Lester Little, as a means of punishing and finally coercing recalcitrant images into answering prayers.[34] As with the Driving Out, the Humiliation had the double effect of degrading the image at one and the same time that it demonstrated that it was *already* a degraded thing, powerless to get up and defend itself.[35]

The punishment of uncooperative images also occurred spontaneously. Peasants, we are told, shouted and banged sticks on altars to rouse saints to action.[36] In the early sixteenth century, the Madonna of Foix was brutally thrown to the ground when she failed to miraculously produce the weather that had been demanded of her.[37] The monks of Wilton are said to have fallen into a rage when a casket containing the relics of St. Ywius refused to budge from where they had set it down: "They weep, wail, rip their clothing, tear their hair, wring their hands, and beat the reliquary shrine as Balaam struck his ass."[38] Unlike iconoclasts who championed changes in how images were used in churches, the people who committed these acts of aggression turned only temporarily against images they otherwise venerated. They did not reject sacred images altogether but rather deemed certain images under certain conditions worthy of punishment, humiliation, or even destruction. There was room to treat an image with indifference, to vent frustration at it, to use it to vent frustration at the powers that it represented, and to enjoy making a humiliating spectacle of its inability to defend itself, without entirely giving up a belief in the power of images.[39]

While ritual humiliations of images and spontaneous acts of aggression toward images could occur at any time, the Deposition rite and the Driving Out recurred annually when feelings about images (both positive and negative) would have been running particularly high thanks to the many images used in the paraliturgical rites staged around Easter. Iconoclasts found much to object to in the performances with moving images that marked this time of year. Kirchmair complains: "From Thurseday then till Easter come, the fondest toyes haue place Wherein these cathlikes think themselues, great men of wondrous grace."[40] In a Dutch tract written in 1569 and translated into English under the title *The Bee hiue of the Romische Churche*, the Calvinist Philips van Marnix condemns the dramatizations of Christ's life that occurred in the days before Easter: "In summe, Christ hath not done anie thing in his death and passion but they do plaie and counterfeite the same after him, so trimlie and liuelie that no plaier nor iuggler is able to do it better."[41]

Disdain of this kind gave rise to a notable number of late medieval and Reformation iconoclasms in and around Holy Week.[42] On Holy Saturday of 1414, a Hussite interrupted the service in the Church of St. James in Prague and smeared the crucifix with excrement.[43] A 1415 judgment against a Waldensian sect in Bohemia reports that on Good Friday the heretics told the congregation: "today the whores and monks will play with the puppets and idols."[44] In 1466, a man was condemned to death by fire in Regensburg for having shot three times at the crucifix on Good Friday.[45] In 1520, a group of people ringing cow and sheep bells disturbed a procession celebrating the resurrected crucifix in the city of Pirna.[46] On Maundy Thursday of 1524, followers of the radical Thomas Müntzer attacked the Mallerbach Chapel and destroyed a miraculous image of the Virgin.[47] On Easter of that same year in Ammern bei Mühlhausen, a man ripped the crucifix from the hands of a priest as he lifted it from the sepulcher.[48] On Good Friday of 1528, iconoclasm erupted in churches in Basel, leading to the conversion of the city to the Protestant cause.[49] That same day in Augsburg, as the priest placed the Host in the sepulcher, a man showed the blessed bread his ass and was heard to shout in the direction of the monstrance: "Hey you, Christ, what are doing there in that little madhouse?"[50]

In and around Holy Week, iconoclasts were stirred to deflate the fantasy that images move of their own accord. They often did so by demonstrating the powerlessness of the image to defend itself against the insults and degradations to which they subjected it. But long before iconoclasts hurled their insults, a reaction against the fantasy of the moving image had been built into the (para)liturgy itself—a reaction that certain iconoclasts, including Franck and

Hooper, more or less recognized as such. In response to the hyperbolic imaging of God with moving toys, the Deposition rite made a spectacle of the image's wretched stillness and put it away in a box.

The Deposition rite was not aimed at reform and was certainly not intended to rid the Church of images. Nor was it intended to spur unresponsive images to action. Instead of either permanently banishing images or falling into a rage each time one failed to produce a desired miracle, the participants in the Good Friday rite set aside forty hours each year for a ritualized acknowledgment of the image's sustained failure to miraculously move of its own accord. Although the Deposition rite put the image away only temporarily, the object that emerged from the tomb on Easter was shadowed throughout the year by the memory of this rite—that is, the memory of the ritual moment in which the image of a dead man became a stark reminder of the image's own lack of life.

Vignette: Marcel Duchamp's **Unhappy Readymade** *(1919)*

In April 1919, Marcel Duchamp sent his sister Suzanne and her new husband Jean Crotti a wedding gift in the form of instructions for a readymade (figure 26). Duchamp would later describe the gift to Pierre Cabanne: "It was a geometry book, which he had to hang by strings on the balcony of his apartment in the rue Condamine; the wind had to go through the book, choose its own problems, turn and tear out the pages. Suzanne did a small painting of it, 'Marcel's Unhappy Readymade.' That's all that's left, since the wind tore it up. It amused me to bring the idea of happy and unhappy into the readymades, and then the rain, the wind, the pages flying, it was an amusing idea."[51] In one of the notes for his *Large Glass*, Duchamp had earlier written: "Make a sick picture or a sick Readymade."[52] That in the end he made an unhappy rather than a sick readymade suggests a preference for the slightly more anthropomorphic adjective.

The word *(mal)heureux* also has the advantage of affording Duchamp the positive affect of happiness along with its undoing. This doubleness corresponds to the double gesture of making and unmaking that structures the *Unhappy Readymade* and its particular

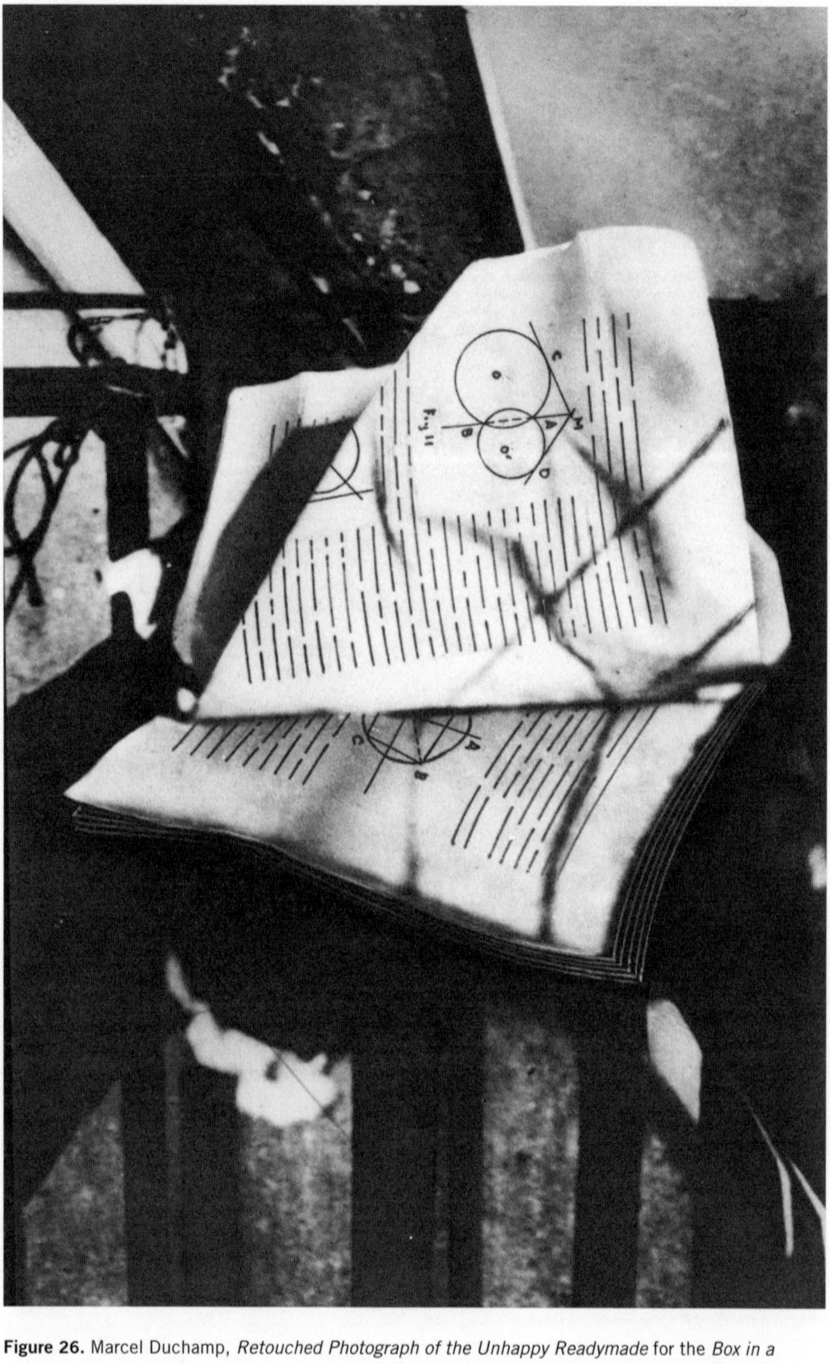

Figure 26. Marcel Duchamp, *Retouched Photograph of the Unhappy Readymade* for the *Box in a Valise* (1935–1941), 16.2×10.5 cm. Philadelphia Museum of Art, The Louise and Walter Arensberg Collection. © 2010 ARS, New York/ADAGP, Paris/Succession Marcel Duchamp. (Photo: PMA Photography Department.)

brand of seriality. In the photograph and painting Suzanne made to document it, the *Unhappy Readymade* has no text. When he retouched the photograph for inclusion in his portable miniature museum, the *Box in a Valise* (1935–1941), Duchamp added text but only the semblance of text, generic text—lines from any geometry book, open to any page. This lack of specificity is fitting since Duchamp had no say in and perhaps no knowledge of the book chosen by his sister and her husband nor in the problems and pages "chosen" by the wind. Moreover, what Suzanne and Jean Crotti and the wind happened to choose in April 1919 made for but one instantiation of the *Unhappy Readymade*, whose iterations are theoretically unlimited.

At the end of a long note that begins "Specifications for 'Readymades,'" Duchamp points to the seriality of the readymade work of art: "By planning for a moment to come (on such a day, such a date, such a minute), '*to inscribe* a readymade.'—The readymade can later be looked for. (with all kinds of delays)"—"*The important thing (then) is just* this matter of timing, this snapshot effect, like a speech delivered on no matter what occasion (but) *at such and such an hour.* It is a kind of rendez-vous.—Naturally inscribe that date, hour, minute (on the readymade), as *information.* also the serial characteristic of the readymade."[53] This reference to seriality is a surprising twist at the end of a full paragraph concerning the readymade's punctuality, that is, its temporal *singularity*. The readymade is caught somewhere between this singularity—the singularity of the moment of its induction into the category of Art—and the seriality of the mass-produced object. Elsewhere Duchamp warns against multiplying the number of readymades: "anything can become very beautiful if the gesture is repeated often enough; this is why the number of my 'ready-mades' is very limited."[54] Despite its "serial characteristic," Duchamp tells us, each readymade represents a singular act and the number of all readymades should be limited.

The *unhappy* readymade must necessarily be something of an exception to these rules, insofar as hanging up the geometry book creates it at the same time that it sets it on course to destruction. The *Unhappy Readymade* is a *double* "rendez-vous," marked with the date and time of its making as well as an indeterminate-as-to-date-and-time-but-otherwise-certain *unmaking*. The unpredictability of wind and rain notwithstanding, the destruction of this object as per Duchamp's instructions is a foregone conclusion. So not only can the *Unhappy Readymade* be endlessly reproduced without becoming a multiple (of existing things); it must be reproduced if it is to continue to exist. Duchamp specifically sanctions reproduction as replacement in the case of the geometry book: "I liked the photograph of the Ready Made sitting there on the balcony," Duchamp told his sister. "When it falls apart you can replace it."[55]

An analogous logic of making-unmaking-remaking structures Man Ray's *Object to be Destroyed* (figure 27). A drawing of the *Object* published in 1932 has the following caption: "Cut out the eye from a photograph of one who has been loved but is seen no more. Attach the eye to the pendulum of a metronome and regulate the weight to suit the tempo desired.... With a hammer well-aimed, try to destroy the whole at a single blow."[56] These instructions might be glossed: create an image of a lost loved one, set it into motion, and then unleash your anger on this substitute for that missing person. As in the case of Duchamp's only slightly less anthropomorphic *Unhappy Readymade*, the making and unmaking of this biomechanical being are inseparable. The execution of the first step (creation) leads inexorably to the final step (destruction).

And again as with Duchamp's *Unhappy Readymade*, destruction would lead back to (re-)creation. According to Man Ray's autobiography, *Object to be Destroyed* met something close to the fate the artist had envisioned for it when a group of art students protesting Dada and Surrealism entered the 1957 exhibition at the Galerie de l'Institut in Paris where the metronome was on display. Although they failed to follow the artist's instructions exactly, they did begin "taking down the works and laying them carefully on the floor... After which they filed out in an orderly manner. But on the way one grabbed the metronome and disappeared with it."[57] The *Object to be Destroyed* was deposed and carried off—for all intents and purposes, destroyed. But it did not meet its end that day, since

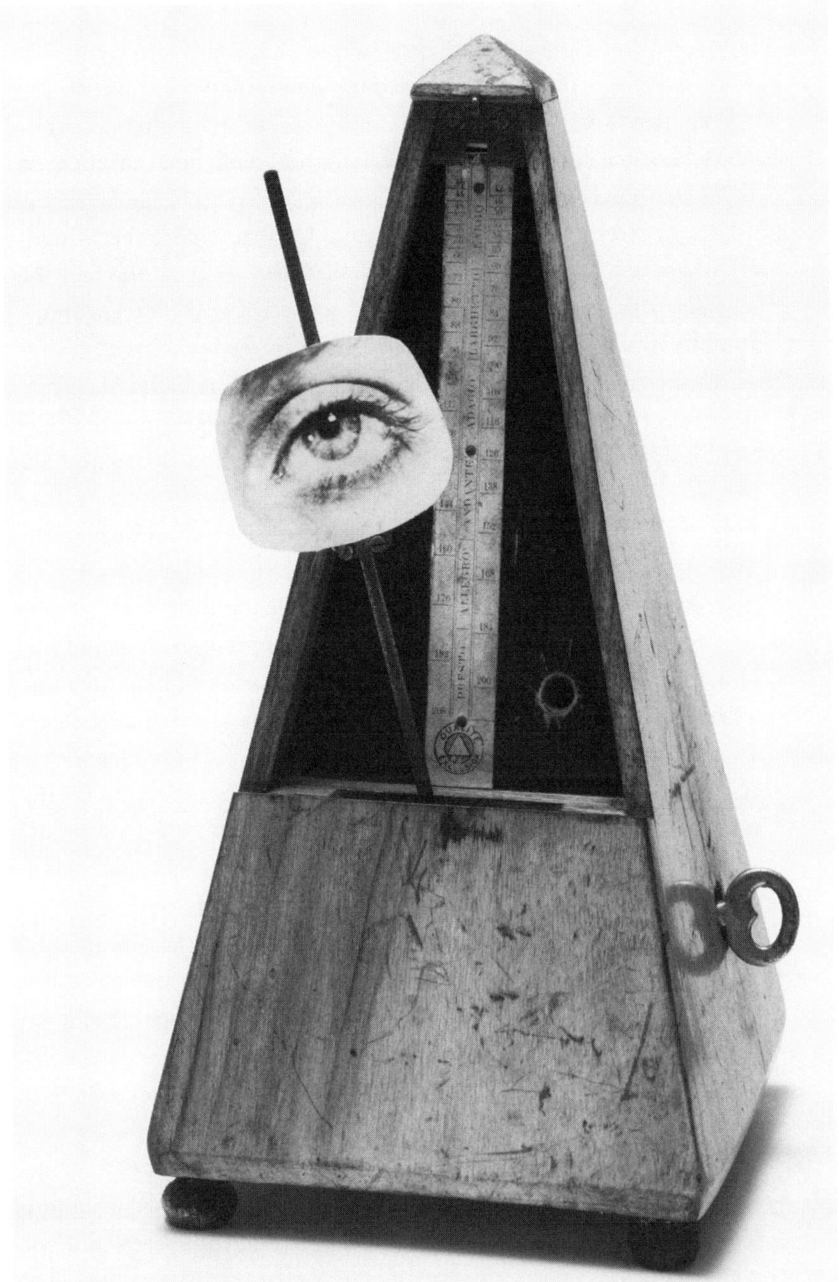

Figure 27. Man Ray, *Object to Be Destroyed* (1964), replica of 1923 original, metronome with cutout photograph of an eye on pendulum, 22.5 × 11 × 11.6 cm. Museum of Modern Art, New York, James Thrall Soby Fund. © 2010 Man Ray Trust/ARS, New York/ADAGP, Paris. (Photo: The Museum of Modern Art/Licensed by SCALA/Art Resource, New York.)

Man Ray used the insurance money grudgingly paid out to him for the lost work to buy a whole new stock of metronomes. These he did not hesitate to use as material for a whole new set of *Objects to be Destroyed*—which he called *Indestructible Objects*. *Indestructible Object* would be renamed several times in turn, before receiving its final and most fitting name, *Perpetual Motif*, to mark the fact that a readymade is too readily replaced to be irretrievably consigned to oblivion.[58]

In the sixteenth century, iconoclastic reformers deposed all but a handful of crucifixes with movable arms. The Deposition rite itself fell into desuetude thanks to the same Reformation that claimed its props.[59] But long before iconoclasts deposed these sculptures, their hinged shoulder joints indicated that they were, at an unspecified time, to be taken down from the cross. Liturgical manuals provided instructions on how and when this should occur, dictating that once a year the crucifix was to be handled in such a way that all could see how inert it was, lowered toward the earth, and put away in a box. These instructions might be glossed: create an image of a lost loved one, set it into the kind of motion that shows just how lifeless it is, and then unleash your hostility on this inanimate substitute for that missing person by banishing it from sight.

While the *Unhappy Readymade* and the *Object to be Destroyed* bear no evidence of the humiliating rituals for which they are destined, knowledge of which is transmitted through their titles and instructions alone, the crucifix with movable arms wears the sign of its annual ordeal on its sleeve in the form of wooden hinges. Equipped with the means of its own deposition—*Abthuung* is the word that Karlstadt uses; "pluck it down to the ground" is how Geoffrey Chamber puts it—the crucifix is ready and waiting to be put away by anyone who wants to do so.[60]

The crucifix with movable arms is made to be deposed—but only temporarily. Like the *Unhappy Readymade* and the *Perpetual Motif*, it is bound to reappear according to well-known formulas. The utterly mechanical, ticking regularity with which these three objects come and go does not in the least, however, diminish the emotional response they elicit. All three anthropomorphic objects are laden with enough feeling to give the viewer a bit of sadistic pleasure. Their anthropomorphism lends poignancy to their mechanically predictable demise, while their replaceability frees the viewer to enjoy their humiliation and "destruction" with impunity. Each offers itself up in all its replaceable glory to the gratification of a viewer whose murderous fantasies it can sustain far more reliably–that is, perpetually–than any living being.

CHAPTER THREE

Dead Images

Iconoclasts developed elaborate and sometimes amusing ways of pointing out the image's inability to do what the living do—witness the taunts discussed in the last chapter—but more often than not they simply called the image dead. This was probably the central trope of medieval and Reformation iconoclasm. Everyone would have been familiar with it, not least of all from its occurrences in the bible, for example, in the Book of Wisdom: "miserable, with their hopes set on dead things, are those who give the name 'gods' to the works of human hands" (Wisdom 13.10). Although no one who performed or watched the Deposition rite is likely to have described it as a comment on the limits of the sacred image, few, I think, would have been able to watch the image buried on Good Friday without hearing an echo of the iconoclastic barb: "dead image."[1]

In the fourteenth and fifteenth centuries, Lollards and Hussites regularly employed the phrase: "suche pilgrimage mai we wel do without seching of dede ymages and of schrynes"[2]; "now men knelyn, and preien, and offren faste to dede ymagis, that han neither hungir neither coold"[3]; "[they ascribe to] these dead images the miracles that God doth alone"[4]; "[Christ] hates everyone who seeks the joys of the world and becomes an enemy of Christ's cross; such a man breaks the image of the living Son of God, but he honors dead images."[5] Lollards often put the phrase to use in condemning the extravagances of the Church, complaining that resources are "veynnely wastid on thes dede ymagis," while the poor, the living images of God, are neglected.[6]

In the sixteenth century, the trope would become a favorite of Protestant iconoclasts, including Karlstadt, who excoriates iconophiles: "For they run to the idols like crows and ravens after a carcass and fly to a lifeless cadaver."[7] Van Marnix complains of "dumb dead blocks of stone" and "lifeless blocks of wood and stone."[8] A 1529 ordinance from the city of Soest argues: "We should turn away from the dead images and rather toward the living saints, the poor, in order to clothe and feed them."[9] An anonymous pamphlet published in the Netherlands in the 1520s mocks the safeguarding of costly images: "the Papists lock them up so that they are not stolen ... like a dead man that one buries."[10] An Anabaptist pleads: "Listen if you will / Whether to the letter or the image / ... Are they not both dead?"[11] Calvin laments: "In all these things the Papists go beyond the Israelites. For they kindle lamps and tapers at the dead images of the dead."[12] In the belief that the blind lead the blind when images are allowed to teach, Bishop Hooper complains: "Oh! blasphemous and devilish doctrine ... to be instructed and taught of a mute, dumb, blind, and dead idol!"[13]

To make the same point, sixteenth-century iconoclasts also buried images. On 2 April 1534, Lutherans in Ulm destroyed a crucifix and threw it into the cemetery of the Dominicans.[14] The day after an iconoclastic riot in April 1525, the images removed from the Cloister of St. Catherine in Stralsund were buried in the garden to guarantee "that no more idolatry or abuse could be committed with them."[15] In February 1529, the great Easter Crucifix in Basel was dragged out of the church with the help of a horse and then ritually "hung" and buried in the horse's stall.[16] In the early 1550s, the miraculous Madonna of Eggerode was buried by the Protestant minister.[17] On Christmas night of 1524, the crucifix and all the other images in the church of Aadorf were broken into pieces and buried in a nearby marsh.[18]

Foes of images were not the only people to associate them with death. Many of their staunchest defenders justified them by recalling God's descent into a body that was born and died and that, for this reason alone, could be pictured. The incarnation was central to the defense of sacred images. John of Damascus's eighth-century formulation of this defense was foundational for later debates: "If we attempted to make an image of the invisible God, this would be sinful indeed.... But we are not mistaken if we make an image of God incarnate, who was seen on earth in the flesh, associated with men, and in His unspeakable goodness assumed the nature, feeling, form and color of our flesh."[19]

In his 1522 *That One Should Not Remove Images of Saints*, Hieronymus Emser explicitly aligns himself with the Damascene: "According to the words of the Holy Father John of Damascus, no one can really imagine or picture God in his divine essence. Nevertheless God appeared to us on earth not, as he did to Abraham, merely in the form of a man, but as an actual man in substance and nature (as he even worked miracles and suffered), who was crucified, died, was buried, and rose again."[20] This argument is a double-edged sword. For, if the God whom death befalls is the only God who can be pictured, then the picturing of God is inextricably bound up with the dying of God. Although not the same as the iconoclast's condemnation of the image as a lifeless block of wood, the incarnational defense of images shares with that condemnation the binding of picturing to death.

Prosopopoeia

According to iconoclasts this intimate relation between pictures and death had grave consequences for viewers. In addition to the hundreds of records of paraliturgical Deposition rites, a few plays portraying the deposition have survived. Although, as Gesine Taubert argues, these were probably performed during the Good Friday liturgy, they have none of the iconoclastic overtones of the Deposition rite.[21] In a play recorded in 1687 but based on an earlier text, actors assume all the roles except that of Christ, who is instead represented by a puppet. Joseph and Nicodemus "climb up and take the Lord down." Joseph speaks: "Come here my heart's cure and comfort. You have now saved the whole world from bitter torment and terrible pain. For this we should all be thankful."[22] Then, Joseph and Nicodemus lay the wooden sculpture on the Virgin's lap. Addressed to a doubly dead interlocutor, the wooden effigy of a corpse, Joseph's words—"come here"—are a form of prosopopoeia: "The fiction of an apostrophe to an absent, deceased, or voiceless entity," as de Man puts it, "which posits the possibility of the latter's reply and confers upon it the power of speech" or the power of movement—as is the case in the Deposition play, where the words addressed to the deceased are "come here."[23]

For de Man, the "latent threat that inhabits prosopopoeia" is that "by making the dead speak, the symmetrical structure of the trope implies . . . that the living are struck dumb, frozen in their own death."[24] Precisely this striking dumb occurs, according to Luther, when images are made to move and speak. The person who reduces God to a toy becomes himself an immobile plaything, frozen in his own death. Perhaps in reference to a Deposition play like the one described above, Luther complains: "they sit God on their laps and play with him as if he were a doll, become so drunk with such thoughts and sweet devil's poison, so proud, hard, and stubborn that they do not want to listen to or follow anyone at all."[25] For Luther, puppets like those used in the Deposition play block the reception of the Word. Where the Word draws the viewer through "listening" into the movement of "following" and thereby away from the fixity of the icon, the image renders this same viewer static—"proud, hard, and stubborn"—like a doll.

The more iconoclastic the reformer, the stronger his belief that idolatry gives rise to a dangerous symmetry. Karlstadt rails: "Images bring death to those who worship or venerate them. Therefore, our temples might be rightly called murderers' caves, because in them our spirit is stricken and slain."[26] Resemblance is the mechanism, according to Karlstadt, that brings death to the viewer: "God ordained that we must become like the things we love. Therefore, in God's sight and in truth, all who love contemptible, useless things, blind idols, deaf stones, or anything abominable become contemptible, useless, deaf, blind, and odious. Then the soul does not remain soul, but becomes an idol with the idol it loves."[27]

The iconoclastic trope of lethal resemblance, which is rooted in the bible—"those who make [idols] are like them" (Psalms 115.8)—was thoroughly exploited by late medieval heretics.[28] A Lollard sermon warns: "for alle suche (as the Hooli Goost seith bi Dauid, the prophete) that tristeth in hem ben maad like to hem; for thei han iyen and seeth noyt, as these ymagis han."[29] The Hussite Nikolaus von Dresden blames "false and dead songs and signs" for a moribund faith: "faith in the Word of Christ... is dead and invisible: they feel neither fear before it nor pleasure in it."[30] The Hussite Matthias von Janow argues that people who invest their hopes in images "do not have a living faith but a dead one."[31] According to the iconoclast, when the viewer venerates the idol, it robs him of the very life he thinks he has discovered in it; mistaking his own life for that of the image, the viewer ends up bereft of life or, as the iconoclast says, dead.

The Reformation would entail a monumental effort to silence prosopopoeic addresses to images and the uncanny echoes they return so that the living Word, delivered through the mouths of human beings, could be heard. The living Word which is said to partake of the Spirit and transcend the inert letter of the law—"the letter kills, but the Spirit gives life" (II Corinthians 3.6)—does not need to be spoken for, answers when it is questioned, and does not feed parasitically on the life of its interlocutor. But well before the Reformation, people were finding ways to hush and still images when they became too gregarious or animated. As a temporary, annual banishment of the lifeless image to the silence and stillness of the grave, the Deposition rite—unlike the Deposition play—blocked the prosopopoeia that Luther denounces and protected the viewer from discovering his or her *own* life reflected back to him or her in the eyes of the wooden doll.

Images of Stone

Well before the Reformation, painters too were finding ways to distinguish between living viewers and dead images. In the 1420s, the Master of Flémalle and Jan van Eyck began decorating the exteriors of altarpieces with monochrome, trompe l'oeil paintings of statues. These simulated stone sculptures would become a common feature of fifteenth and sixteenth-century altarpieces in the Netherlands. When closed, Van Eyck's diminutive *Dresden Triptych* displays the Virgin and the Angel Annunciate in the form of unpainted stone sculptures, each in a narrow vertical niche surrounded by a heavy red-and-black marble frame (figure 28).[32] In his discussion of early Netherlandish grisaille paintings like this one, Paul Philippot writes of two opposing effects: "If, on the one hand, the grisaille is less real than the painting (the object represented is itself nothing but a statue and not a living figure), which justifies its use on the reverse of the wings, visible when the altarpiece is closed, on the other hand, the real presence of the statue is more verisimilar than that of the colored figures, which increases the power of the trompe-l'oeil."[33] The interplay of these two opposing effects gives rise to a situation in which: the more convincing the illusion, the more persuaded the viewer becomes of the image's lifelessness.

The consequences of Van Eyck's uncoupling of illusion and liveliness are far-reaching. His move strikes two targets. First, the cliché that the height of painterly accomplishment is the image that seems to live—a trope that nonetheless quickly found its way into praise of Van Eyck's own work. In 1456, Bartholomaeus Facius described a painting by Van Eyck in the apartments of King Alfonso V of Aragon, including an image of Jerome that was "like a living being" and a portrait of Battista Lomellini that "lacked only a voice."[34] The Italian humanist Cyriacus of Ancona resorts to the same cliché in praising a painting of the deposition that he attributes to Rogier van der Weyden: "There you could see those faces come alive and breathe."[35]

The Christian counterpart to the secular trope of the living image is the second target of Van Eyck's stony conceit. Countless medieval legends told of images of saints that miraculously moved to embrace a devotee or strike an opponent. Statues of the Virgin were known to transport themselves when the need arose. Crucifixes bled, and images of the Christ child leaned forward to receive gifts of fruit. When the devout feeling of the beholder was not strong enough to bring an image to life, prestidigitation could be used to supply animation instead. Virgins were outfitted with irrigation

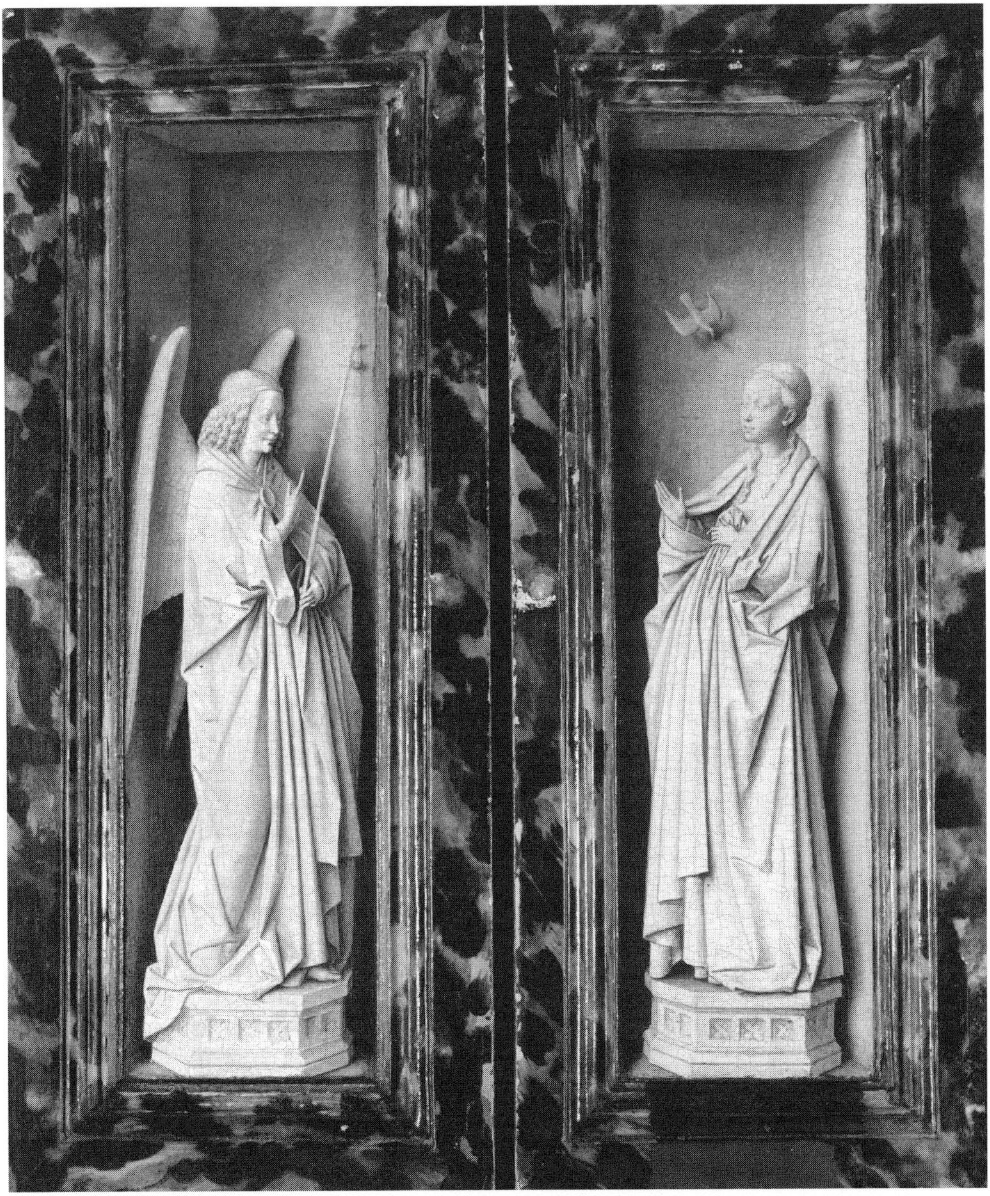

Figure 28. Jan van Eyck, *Annunciation* (ca. 1437), exterior of the *Dresden Triptych*, oil on panel, 33.1 × 27.5 cm. Gemäldegalerie Alte Meister, Staatliche Kunstsammlung, Dresden. (Photo: Bildarchiv Preussischer Kulturbesitz/Art Resource, New York.)

systems that enabled them to weep and mouthpieces through which miraculous voices could be heard.[36]

The understanding of late medieval image-devotion that has taken shape since the second half of the twentieth century makes much of miracles, legends, and fakes like these. Panofsky, Ringbom, Belting, and others understand that devotion to have been predicated on nothing less than the viewer's belief that the image might respond to his or her address *as if it were alive*.[37] Like medieval and Reformation iconoclasts, these art historians argue that the late medieval viewer's relationship to the image was essentially specular. But while medieval and Reformation iconoclasts maintain that the resemblance between image and viewer mortified the latter, art historians say that viewers imparted life to images at no cost to themselves. For Panofsky, the *Andachtsbild* (devotional image) gave to "the individual viewing consciousness the opportunity for a *contemplative absorption* in the viewed content, which is to say, it allowed the subject and the object to merge psychically with one another."[38] For Ringbom, "the intimate quality of the half-length icon made it particularly well suited for the private devotion and profound empathy of the individual. Its character of a 'close-up' gave to meditation the immediacy of a quiet conversation; it had the 'nearness' so dear to the God-seeking devout."[39] Belting likewise compares image-devotion to a conversation, writing of an experience that makes "the partner in the image present as a living participant in [a] dialogue."[40]

At the end of the Middle Ages, "religious images began to 'speak'" and move and live, say the art historians.[41] While tales of miraculous images support this claim, the trompe l'oeil statues on the exterior of Van Eyck's *Dresden Triptych* counter it, countering as well the rhetorical commonplaces, pious legends, and theatrical gimmicks on which this claim is based.[42] Though these grisaille statues have been interpreted as abstemious Lenten images, their abstinence lies less in their refusal of color—for which they generously compensate with chiaroscuro—than in their stunningly illusionistic portrayals of *lifeless* living human forms.[43] They play on the trope of the living image, invoking it with their realism, only to dispel that illusion of life with their stoniness. They invoke the biblical trope of the *lapides vivi*, only to trump it with the iconoclastic trope that Augustine uses in reference to pagan idols: *lapides mortui*.[44] As did Good Friday effigies, these paintings of stone sculptures thereby claim for themselves the taunt "dead image," pre-empting the iconoclasts who would use it against them.

Vignette: Ad Reinhardt's Non-Happening *(1958)*

In the first decades of the twentieth century, the avant-garde repeated the same pronouncements of the death of painting that had accompanied the birth of photography. In 1912, Marcel Duchamp said to Constantin Brancusi and Fernand Léger: "Painting's washed up. Who'll do anything better than that propeller?"[45] At the First International Dada Fair (Berlin 1920), John Heartfield and George Grosz were photographed holding a placard: "Art is dead. Long live Tatlin's new machine art" (figure 29).[46] "One day," they predicted, "photography will suppress and supplant the entire art of painting."[47] Meanwhile, others were predicting that a new kind of painting—the anti-painting of abstraction—would supplant the old. From December 1915 to January 1916, Kazimir Malevich's *Black Square* was exhibited in Petrograd. It hung in the corner of a room in the place of the traditional Russian icon. One critic wrote: "The corpse of the Art of Painting, the art of nature with make-up added, has been placed in its coffin and marked with the Black Square."[48]

Because pronouncements of the death of painting have been calls not only to return to life but also to leave the past behind, they have gone hand-in-hand with condemnations of the museum as the elitist graveyard of an irrelevant patrimony.[49] Marinetti kicked off Futurism in 1909 by consigning the past to the past: "Museums: cemeteries! Identical, really, in the horrible promiscuity of so many bodies scarcely known to one another."[50] In his manifesto *From Easel to Machine* (1923), Nikolai Tarabukin refers to "the fruitlessness of an art divorced from life and the inability of the typical forms of creativity, suitable only for the graveyard of the museum, to survive in contemporary conditions."[51]

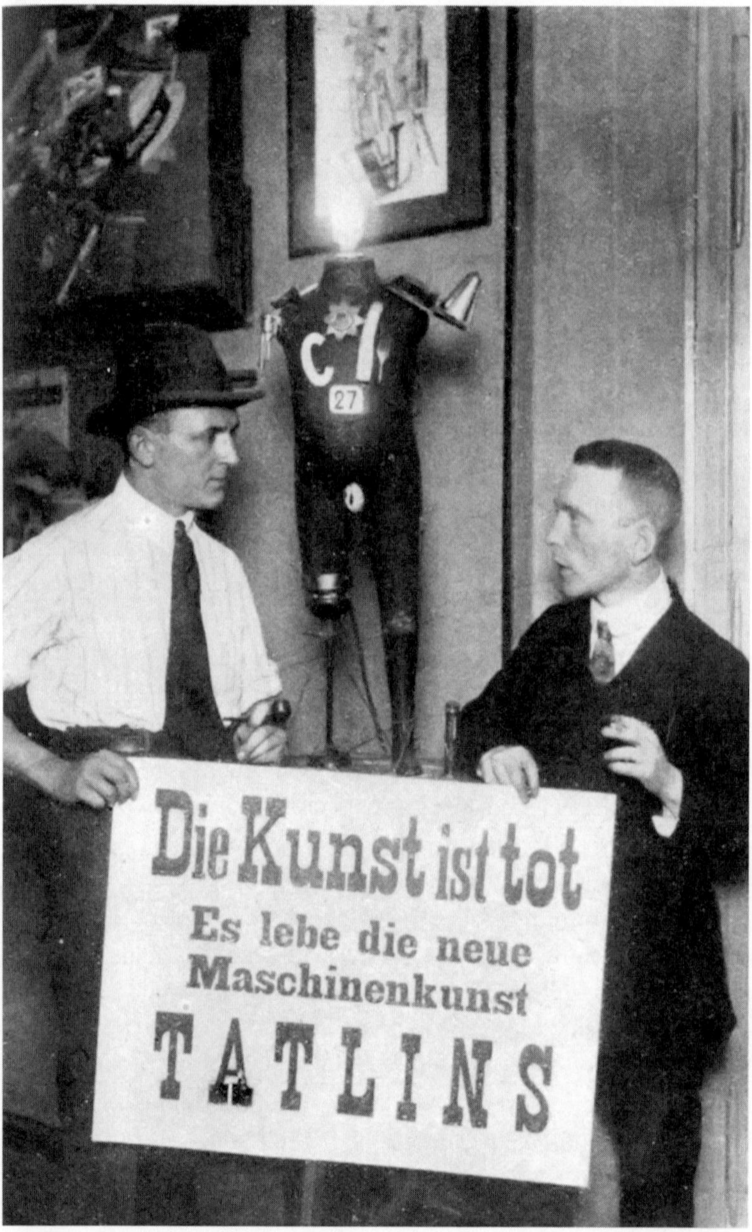

Figure 29. *First International Dada Fair, Room 1, George Grosz and John Heartfield*, photograph from Richard Huelsenbeck, *Dada-Almanac*, Berlin (1920).

The avant-garde declared painting dead and the museum its cemetery in order to release it from the autonomy to which bourgeois aesthetics had confined it and into the flow of social life. The hope was that something open and participatory would replace the autonomous work of art, while the collective would put an end to the singular, expressive artist.[52] For Tarabukin, the 1921 exhibition of Rodchenko's monochrome *Pure Red Color* marked "the death of painting, the death of easel painting as a form."[53] In 1939, Rodchenko confirmed that this was his intention: "I reduced painting to its logical conclusion and exhibited three canvases: red, blue and yellow. I affirmed: It's all over."[54]

In fact, painting was not over. The death of painting has been infamously protracted, in part, because successive waves of abstract art have courted that death while—unlike Rodchenko—holding it at bay as a still impossible dream for the future, whether by pulling back from the pure monochrome or finding ways to vary the monochrome's seemingly invariable theme. "The whole history of abstract painting," Yve-Alain Bois writes, "can be read as a longing for its death"—both an orientation toward it and a feeling of distance from it.[55] At mid-century, according to Barnett Newman, painters including himself and Jackson Pollock were again painting under the shadow of painting's obsolescence: "In 1940, some of us woke up to find ourselves without hope—to find that painting did not really exist. Or to coin a modern phrase, painting was dead a quarter century before it happened to God."[56]

By the late 1950s, Abstract Expressionism had begun to die its own death at the hands of a neo-Dada return to the readymade. In 1958, Allan Kaprow announced that Pollock's near-total destruction of painting should be brought to completion by opening art directly onto life in the form of what he called the Happening.[57] Kaprow's descriptions of this turn toward life sometimes make it sound like a return to nature: "a Happening can be composed by several persons to include, as well, the participation of the weather, animals, and insects."[58] Elsewhere, he describes the Happening as a turn toward the vast, surreal, late capitalist industrial landscape:

"A U.S. Marines' manual on jungle fighting tactics, a tour of a laboratory where polyethylene kidneys are made, a traffic jam on the Long Island Expressway are more useful than Beethoven, Racine, or Michelangelo."[59] Technology here becomes for Kaprow what nature is in Romantic ideology: the standard of truth against which human creativity is to be measured.

To the painter and critic Ad Reinhardt (1913–1967), declarations of the death of painting were the hum of one myth replacing another. For the myth of the immortal work ensconced in the museum, the avant-garde substituted the cult of experience with its "living" present and "real" social conditions.[60] Reinhardt countered pronouncements of the death of painting by declaring that there was nothing there to die in the first place. Shifting the terms of the discussion from the death of painting to *dead paintings*, Reinhardt reverted to something like the early modern trope of the "dead image." Instead of identifying a historically specific turn-of-events—the invention of the camera—he pointed to the corpse-like inertia of each and every work of art, insisting that, "Art is always dead, and a 'living' art is a deception."[61] The museum is a mausoleum: "A museum is a treasure house and tomb, not a counting-house or amusement center."[62] And this is the way it should be: "Any disturbance of a true museum's soundlessness, timelessness, airlessness, and lifelessness is a disrespect."[63] The museum, according to Reinhardt, protects works of art from the coziness of bourgeois ownership. It keeps them out of the *living* room: "There is no reason for art becoming furniture or people living with it. And it ought to be in a public place where it can be seen anytime anybody wants to."[64]

Being true to the lifelessness of painting meant for Reinhardt keeping it apart from everything that is not painting: "I find all romantic attempts to mix up art with anything else extremely offensive intellectually and esthetically. I want to make sharper the lines of demarcation."[65] This drawing of lines was a reaction against Surrealism and Abstract Expressionism and later "all the neo-dadaists, pop and op, happenings and all the assemblage, collage"—all of which, in Reinhardt's view, was too much concerned with blurring the line between art and life.[66] "The one thing to say about art and life is that art is art and life is life, that art is not life and that life is not art. A 'slice-of-life' art is no better or worse than a 'slice-of-art' life. Fine art is not a 'means of making a living' or a 'way of living a life,' and an artist who dedicates his life to his art or his art to his life burdens his art with his life and life with his art."[67] Reinhardt rejected all the conventional accounts of the relation between art and life: "Artists who claim their artwork comes from nature, life, reality, earth or heaven, as 'mirrors of the soul' or 'reflections of conditions' or 'instruments of the universe'...are subjectively and objectively rascals or rustics."[68] If painting does not come from life much less *live*, there is no sense in speaking of its death.

Reinhardt's insistence on the lifelessness of painting is easily mistaken for a modernist feeling of belatedness. After all, he maintained that there was little left for painters to work with in 1960—nothing, in fact, but "monotonous disappearing image."[69] He is also frequently quoted as saying that he was making the last paintings. Less frequently quoted is his account of what he means by last: "If I were to say that I am making the last paintings, I don't mean that painting is dying. You go back to the beginning all the time anyway. There's the idea that art is one thing, that maybe it doesn't have a beginning or an ending, and maybe it isn't as historical as one thinks."[70] Reinhardt's history of art does not recognize firsts and lasts:

> The power of painting is its ability to disappear   reappear.[71]
>
> Creation, destruction, creation, eternal repetition
> Made-unmade-remade   Hope of an absolute end.[72]

Although one may hope or even long for an end, when it comes to painting, there is only repetition.

Reinhardt illustrated the monotony of art in slide shows, for example, the one he presented at the Artists' Club in New York in 1958. In the autobiographical "chronology" for the catalogue of his 1967 exhibition at the Jewish Museum, Reinhardt retroactively named this slide show—which took place one year before Kaprow's *18 Happenings in Six Parts*—a Non-Happening:

> 1957 Forms SPOAF (Society for the Protection of Our Artist Friends) (from themselves), after reading "Nature in Abstraction" statements.
> 1958 Creates first Non-Happening, shows two thousand color slides at Artists' Club.
> 1958 Visits Japan, India, Persia, Egypt.[73]

At the Artists' Club, Reinhardt showed about 2000 slides, drawn from a collection of what would eventually be more than 10,000 slides of art and architecture—pictures taken on his world travels. He grouped the slides pseudomorphologically: crosses, triangles, circles, towers, columns, hands, eyes, torsos, and so forth (figure 30).[74] Reinhardt's taxonomy of world art reflects his interest in André Malraux's *Musée imaginaire*, that photographic space where the arts of all times and places cohabitate. The artist "should have a Malrauxian approach—the André Malraux idea of the imaginary museum in which you just know all the art that's been done," writes Reinhardt. "He certainly should study it and see it in reproductions."[75]

But if Malraux's imaginary museum imperialistically lays hold of the enormous diversity it sets out to democratically embrace, imposing on it the universalizing categories of Style and Man, Reinhardt's museum is meant to do just the opposite: "I traveled around the world in order to get rid of it," Reinhardt explains.[76] Reinhardt does not juxtapose images of objects so as to conjure the "unseen presence, the spirit of art" that urges humans "all on the same quest," as Malraux rhapsodizes.[77] ("The word 'human' is not only disreputable, it's fake," writes Reinhardt. "It is something that hangs around, I suppose, in the romantic."[78]) Nor does Reinhardt kill the work of art with his decontextualizing camera and his timeless imaginary museum, as the avant-garde might have us think. Rather, he uses the camera to "discover" art everywhere *already dead*, that is, always already unmoored from its "living" context. Adopting the decontextualization of Malraux's project without its avarice and pathos, Reinhardt brings the museum's "soundlessness,

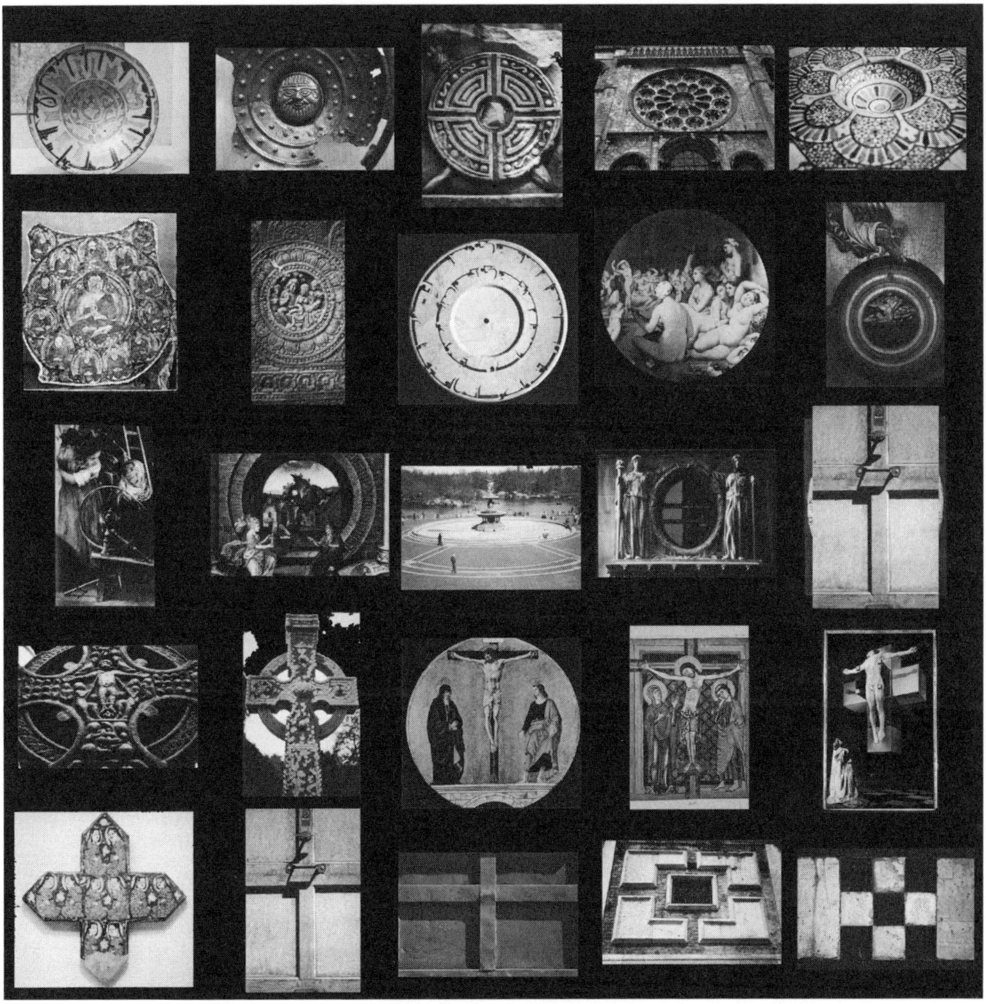

Figure 30. Ad Reinhardt, *Non-Happening* (1958), selection from 2,000 color slides shown at the Artists' Club, New York. Collection Anna Reinhardt, New York. © 2010 Estate of Ad Reinhardt/ARS, New York. © 2010 Salvador Dali, Gala-Salvador Dali Foundation/ARS, New York. (Photo: PaceWildenstein, New York.)

timelessness, airlessness, and lifelessness" into the realm of slide projection.[79]

A well-established feature of the art history lecture, slide projection became in the fifties an artistic (anti-)medium as well. It was one of several such media, including dance, film, painting, live piano, recorded music, poetry, and spoken lecture, assembled in *Theater Piece No. 1*, a collaborative work performed by John Cage and others at Black Mountain College in 1952. In *Theater Piece No. 1*, slide projection was loosely coordinated with these other media by means of what Cage called time brackets.[80] Carroll Williams describes the slides: "35 mm slides, both hand-painted on glass, and sometimes montages—or collages, using colored gelatins and other paints and pigments and materials, sandwiched between glass slides."[81] Cage describes the event: "At one end of a rectangular hall, the long end, was a movie, and at the other end were slides. I was on a ladder delivering a lecture which included silences and there was another ladder which M.C. Richards and Charles Olson went up at different times... Robert Rauschenberg was playing an old-fashioned phonograph... and David Tudor was playing a piano, and Merce Cunningham and other dancers were moving through the audience. Rauschenberg's pictures [the *White Paintings*] were suspended above the audience."[82] The open-ended structure of *Theater Piece No. 1*, its mixing of media, and its embrace of duration would become regular features of Happenings, for which the 1952 event would come to be seen as an important precedent. In this mixed-media context, with live performers moving in and out of projected images, the line between art and life was doubtless hard to draw.

Although Reinhardt's slide shows elided differences between media as diverse as print and architecture, they were anything but attacks on medium-specific formalism. Nor, needless to say, were they calculated to blur the line between art and life—despite his occasional inclusion of a photograph of his daughter. Reinhardt used a projector that required its operator to insert one slide at a time.[83] He moved quickly—about five seconds per slide—but only as quickly as the manual insertion of the slides permitted. And as he advanced

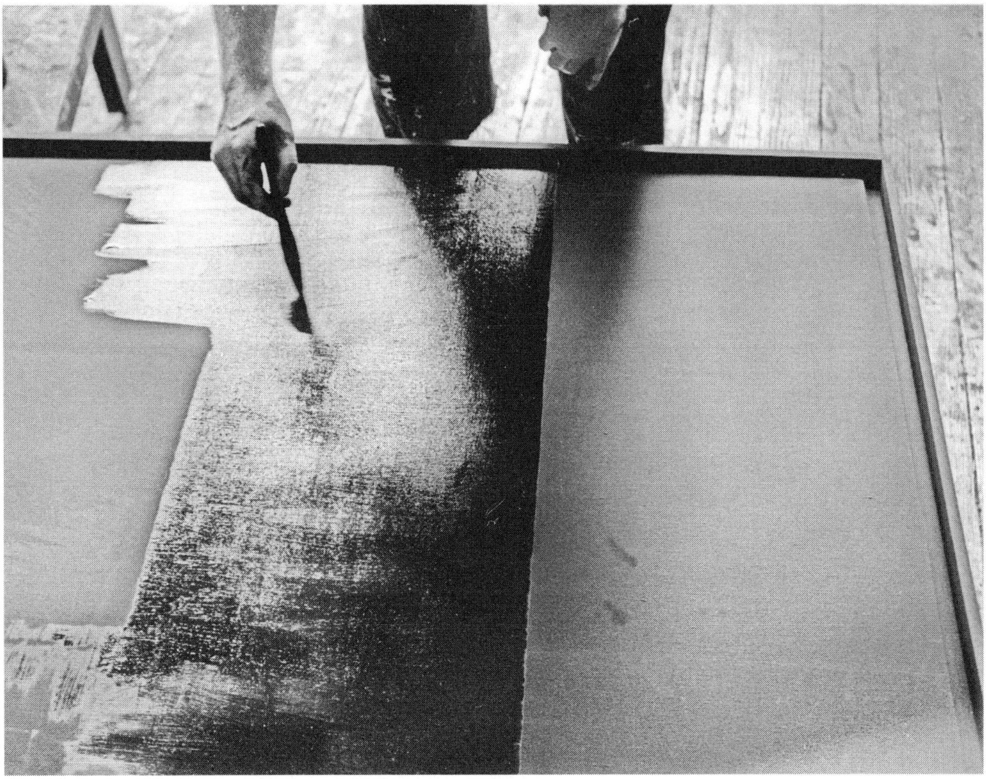

Figure 31. *Ad Reinhardt in His Studio* (1966). (Photo: John Loengard/Time & Life Pictures/Getty Images.)

through his vast collection of perfectly still images, it would have been difficult to forget that this tour through time and space was his own creation: *art not life*. With neither the life-evoking instantaneity of the single photograph nor the seemingly seamless continuity of film, Reinhardt's slide shows showed off the lifelessness of art. If those who declared painting dead treated history (in the guise of technology and especially the camera) as an ineluctable and living force that killed a painting that itself had once lived, Reinhardt used his *manually* operated slide projector to show that neither paintings nor machines are people.

In countering the cliché of the "death of painting," Reinhardt attempted to steer a course clear of both the idolatrous enlivening of images and the iconoclastic replacement of that idolatry with the fetishizing of something else—be it "nature, life, reality, earth or heaven" or, for that matter, technology. Good Friday effigies likewise resisted the fantasies of both the idolater who would enliven them and the iconoclast who would kill them and replace them with the "living" Word. Answering the idolater's demand for liveliness by revealing themselves to be nothing more than wood and paint, they met the iconoclast's attempt to "kill" them with the same wooden retort. In his 1522 defense of images, Emser writes: "Now our images may never be called dumb since they were never able to speak—deprivation presupposes an ability."[84] Like Emser, Reinhardt declared painting dead on arrival. He then set himself about the task of painting what that might mean, leaving little in his wake for iconoclasts who would kill painting's illusion of life and even less for those art historians who would resuscitate it (figure 31).

CHAPTER FOUR

The End of the Deposition Rite

By the late sixteenth century, the Deposition rite had ceased to be performed as widely as it once was. This was true of the paraliturgical rites in general.[1] Protestants abandoned them along with other dramatic aspects of the Catholic liturgy. The Counter-Reformation looked unfavorably upon them as well. The Council of Trent even prohibited the singing of "tropes," those musical and textual additions to the liturgy that were integral to the rites.[2] At the same time, a new sacred theater began to emerge. After initial skepticism, the Jesuits took the lead in developing this theater and in promoting the so-called exposition grave as part of it.[3] With the Eucharistic Host at its center, the Baroque exposition grave that replaced the medieval Easter sepulcher was essentially an oversized tabernacle; Alessandro Galli-Bibiena's simple design is a clear expression of this (figure 32).[4] Although the Host had sometimes been included in the medieval Deposition rite, it became considerably more important in the exposition grave, moving front and center—much to the detriment of attention to the effigy.

A Turn to the Host

The burial of the Host on Good Friday is attested to throughout the history of the Deposition rite.[5] Hosts were occasionally buried alone, as at the Benedictine monastery of St. Blaise in the Black Forest; but they were more often buried along with the crucifix, as in the *Use of Sarum*, the variation of the Roman Rite used in most of England, Ireland, and Wales.[6] By the later Middle Ages, the Host

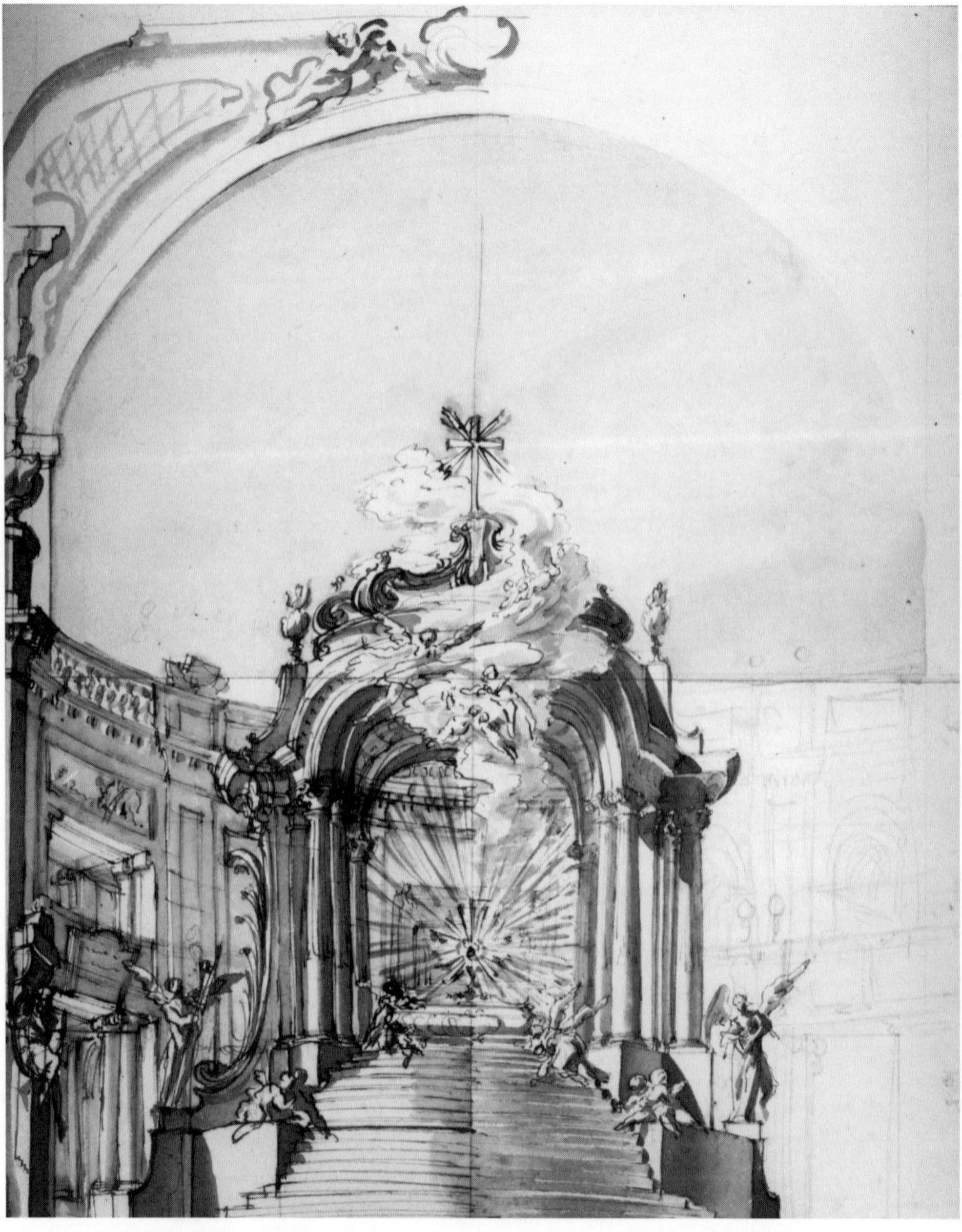

Figure 32. Alessandro Galli-Bibiena, *Design for an Exposition Grave*, pen and wash on paper, 26.2 × 21.8 cm. Staatliche Graphische Sammlung München, Inv. No. 35242 Z. (Photo: Staatliche Graphische Sammlung München.)

was considered to be the historical body of Christ—the body that was born of Mary, that suffered and died, and that was buried and resurrected.[7] Although the historical body with which the Host was associated was usually the body on the cross and though, when it appeared in miraculous visions, that body was sometimes beaten and bloody, still the Host was generally not thought of as a *dead* body. On the contrary, it was held to be "the bred of the blessed couent, the bred of heuene, the bred of angles, the delitable bred, the bred of lif without endynge."[8] The Host was not only thought of as living but also healthy: "Cristes owen bodi in likeness of brede, / Als hale as he toke it of that blessed maiden."[9]

This understanding of the Host made its use on Good Friday problematic. In a Zurich ordinal of 1260, we find an objection to its burial: "It is against all reason, that in certain churches the Eucharist is customarily deposited and closed up in a chest of such a kind that represents a sepulcher. There the Eucharist, which is the true and living body of Christ, actually represents the dead body of Christ, which is indecent, sinful, and absurd."[10] As far as narrative is concerned, the burial of an object that represents the living body may be absurd. But the Host's inclusion in the Good Friday rite made it possible to celebrate the death of Christ without entirely ignoring the everlasting life that his death was believed to have brought about.

Because the Deposition rite delayed the celebration of the final, triumphant outcome of Christ's sacrifice in order to linger over his human death, conducting a funeral for a man who had long since ascended to heaven, it made it possible to forget on Good Friday that Christ's death is not a death in any simple sense but rather the death that *undoes* all death, including the death of Christ.[11] The inclusion of the Host in the Deposition rite served as a reminder of this, helping the beholder to distinguish the historical event of Christ's death from the present moment of its remembrance—a present in which the *imago Dei* was no longer to be found on earth but rather at the right hand of God the Father in heaven, hale, and beyond the reach of the human senses, incapable of being seen, much less adequately represented in the form of lifeless wood.[12]

Perhaps it was this desire to remember the immortal body even in the depths of the darkness of Good Friday that led to a greater emphasis on the Host in the last decades of the fifteenth century. Around this time, Hosts began to be displayed on or near the sepulcher in addition to being buried in it.[13] Some sepulchers were constructed with a built-in tabernacle.[14] When they lacked this feature, a monstrance could be used to display the Host instead. Attention to the Host became still more pronounced in the wake of the Protestant Reformation and the Catholic response to it. It was then that the Host moved to the center of the Good Friday celebrations, and the elaborate, theatrical exposition grave replaced the more modest medieval sepulcher.

The basic design for the exposition grave seems to have derived from sets for the Devotion of the Forty Hours (*L'Orazione delle Quarant'Ore*), which became popular in Italy in the 1520s.[15] Gregory Martin, an Englishman who visited Italy in 1581, describes this forty-hour display of the Holy Sacrament and the spectacle that attended it: "Certayne Companies or Confraternities . . . once a moneth in their Churches, set forth the B. Sacrament with so many lightes, such jewels, and al manner of furniture of tapestrie round about and on the ground, that it semeth a glimpse of paradise: and that for fourtie houres continually, during the which time two and two of the Confraternitie from houre to houre ar upon their knees before it in prayer and meditation, and many out of al the Citie upon devotion visite that place."[16] The Devotion of the Forty Hours was performed at different times of year and was sometimes performed monthly. Exposition graves, by contrast, were erected only in association with Holy Week.

The Jesuits probably began commissioning exposition graves in the 1550s.[17] By 1580, they had incorporated the exposition of the Host into their Holy Sepulcher celebrations in Munich. And by the turn of the century, they had introduced the exposition grave to most areas where they were active.[18] In 1628, Philipp Hainhofer reported visiting nine exposition graves in Innsbruck alone;[19] Vienna had over thirty in the seventeenth century;[20] by 1728, Munich had somewhere on the order of twenty-seven.[21] Exposition graves were built through most of the eighteenth century, before Enlightenment disdain for theatrical church displays brought the period of their widespread use to an end.[22]

Exposition graves took many forms, including banners, stage sets made of painted flats, and full-scale temporary architectural structures adorned with lights and moving figures that transformed altars into visions of lofty spaces extending up as far as heaven. Many exposition graves had moving parts, including one built in Prague in 1570, which was equipped with angels that bowed to the monstrance as they circled in front of it.[23] In an account of his pilgrimage to Rome in 1575, Johann Jakob Rabus marvels over the movement of one of several graves he saw there:

> The whole church of the Order of the Jesuits in the Collegio Romano, named S. Maria della Strada, was covered with beautiful tapestries. High above swayed large angels made out of paper and paints in such a way that one might have thought they were alive. They leaned as if subservient spirits toward the most Holy Sacrament, which stood above in the heights. At the very top was a machine of the celestial spheres filled all around on the inside with little lights. These shone very prettily through several silver stars and also the sun and moon; the larger and smaller stars were different from one another. Also, the planets and the corpus [Christi] moved by means of a hidden weight; all of this moved the pilgrims to a great, inexpressible joy and grace.[24]

Not only does Rabus fail to mention an effigy, he places all his descriptive emphasis on *liveliness and movement*: the movement of the angels, the mechanized celestial orbs, and the "corpus" itself, all of which "moved" the pilgrims in turn. The stillness and sadness of death play no role whatsoever in the spectacle Rabus describes.

Although effigies of the dead Christ had a place in exposition graves, they were less prominently displayed than the Hosts that swayed above them. Nor was the sepulcher any longer the setting only for those ceremonies directly associated with the effigy, including the Deposition and Elevation rites. Instead, it had become the stage for a whole series of dramatic and musical events stretching from Palm Sunday through Ascension Day. On Maundy Thursday, for example, the exposition grave might serve as the setting for a performance of the Last Supper and Christ in the Garden of Gethsemane.[25] In all of this, the effigy probably played only a minor and short-lived role. That said, when the effigy *was* included in the exposition grave, it was laid out on an open bier instead of being placed in a closed structure, as it was in the Deposition rite. In the exposition grave, the effigy was kept on view but only, I would suggest, so as to be more fully and visibly *subordinated to the Host*. Gone, in any case, was the central gesture of the medieval rite: the ritual removal of the abject and immobile image from view.

Largely gone as well was the darkness associated with Good Friday. Although the church itself might be darkened, exposition graves and particularly the Hosts at their center were spectacularly lit. Hundreds of glass vessels filled with colored water were placed in front of candles and oil lamps surrounding the effigy. Lights illuminating the Host were strategically hidden behind canvas flats so that the Host appeared to glow like a celestial body.[26] In comparison with these Baroque ensembles, late medieval sepulchers, even with their candles, cloths, and painted chests, were relatively modest affairs. They certainly made none of the Baroque claims to lead the gaze to celestial heights.

Darkness, mourning, and ritualized hostility toward the motionless image of a dead body gave way in the late sixteenth century to light, celebration, and a vision of the magically animated body of Christ in the form of the *living bread*, leaving hardly a trace on Good Friday of the death that precedes the resurrection. This conversion of the sepulcher into a spectacular exposition of the Sacrament was not without its detractors. In a 1679 treatise on the Host, Jean Baptiste Thiers writes disapprovingly: "Of all the expositions of the uncovered Holy Sacrament in use in our century, there is none that is more universally condemned than that one performed in certain churches on Holy Thursday, Friday, and Saturday."[27] Thiers goes on to list dozens of examples of churches in which the Host is properly hidden during the *Triduum*, preferably under lock and key. He then poses a rhetorical question: "For finally what relation is there between the sadness of these three days and the joy that should be inseparable from the divine Eucharist displayed on our altars? Between darkness and the splendor of our Father?"[28] Despite objections like this one, exposition graves continued to display and celebrate the living Hosts at their center well into the eighteenth century.

Allegories of the Image

The exposition grave's focus on the Host was in keeping with the Counter-Reformation campaign to reaffirm the doctrine of transubstantiation, according to which the Host is literally the body of Christ and not merely the representation that many reformers held it to be.[29] This focus also reflected a change in attitude toward the *image*—here, in the form of the effigy of Christ. The effect of the exposition grave was to repress precisely those more problematic aspects of the sacred image that the medieval Deposition rite had addressed. Whereas the Deposition rite was an iconoclastic allegory of the *lowering of a dead image*, which offered the viewer no recourse but to follow that image in its descent, the exposition grave's allegory was distinctly more Gregorian: encouraging the viewer's happy ascent—in the company of the Host—from the visible to the invisible.[30]

In his allegorical commentary on the Song of Songs, Gregory explains that allegory is "a machine for souls that are far removed from God"—a machine capable of lifting those fallen souls toward their prelapsarian state.[31] This allegory is predicated on a difference between means and ends: "By the grace of a terrestrial language," Gregory explains, "[the soul] is separated from the earth."[32] The *Monastic Agreement* likewise calls attention to the difference between the stuff of allegory and that toward which it ascends: the allegorical words and gestures of the liturgy are an "outward representation of that which is spiritual."[33] And Durand writes: "Allegory is present when what is said literally has another meaning spiritually; for example, when one word or deed brings to mind another."[34] From the obdurate matter of words and deeds (by which he means liturgy), Durand is able to call forth meaning but only because he finds in it something alien to it: "Whatever belongs to the liturgical offices, objects, and furnishings of the Church is full of signs of the divine and the sacred mysteries, and each of them overflows with a celestial sweetness when it is encountered by a diligent observer who can extract *honey from rock and oil from the stoniest ground*" (Deuteronomy 32.13).[35] Celestial sweetness comes to us via stony signifiers, according to Durand, because we would be overwhelmed by anything more direct: "Certainly, he who would attempt to investigate the majesty of heaven would be overwhelmed by its glory."[36]

Gregory sees guilt as the obstacle that prevents us from experiencing spiritual truths directly: "Since the human race was cast out from the joys of paradise, entering into this exile of the present life, it has had a heart blind to spiritual understanding." This fallen soul requires allegories to move it: "by a certain kind of enigma [i.e., allegory] the divine discourse addresses itself to the numbed and cold soul, and, by means of things that the soul knows, it secretly inspires in it a love that the soul does not know."[37] In his *Trauerspiel* book, Walter Benjamin likewise argues that original sin is the motor that drives the allegorical machine: "It was absolutely decisive for the development of [the allegorical] mode of thought that not only transitoriness, but also guilt should seem evidently to have its home in the province of idols and flesh. The allegorically significant is prevented by guilt from finding fulfillment of its meaning in itself.... This view, rooted in the doctrine of the fall of the creature, which brought down nature with it, is responsible for the ferment that distinguishes the profundity of western allegory from the oriental rhetoric of this form of expression. Because it is mute, fallen nature mourns."[38] For Benjamin, allegory only really has force where it is fueled by a Christian guilt that divides the prelapsarian unity of spirit and matter, condemning the latter to a deathly silence.

Johann Anton Gumpp's 1691 design for the exposition grave in the Theatine Church in Munich—here reproduced in an engraving by Michael Hartwanger—pictures this divide (figure 33). A record

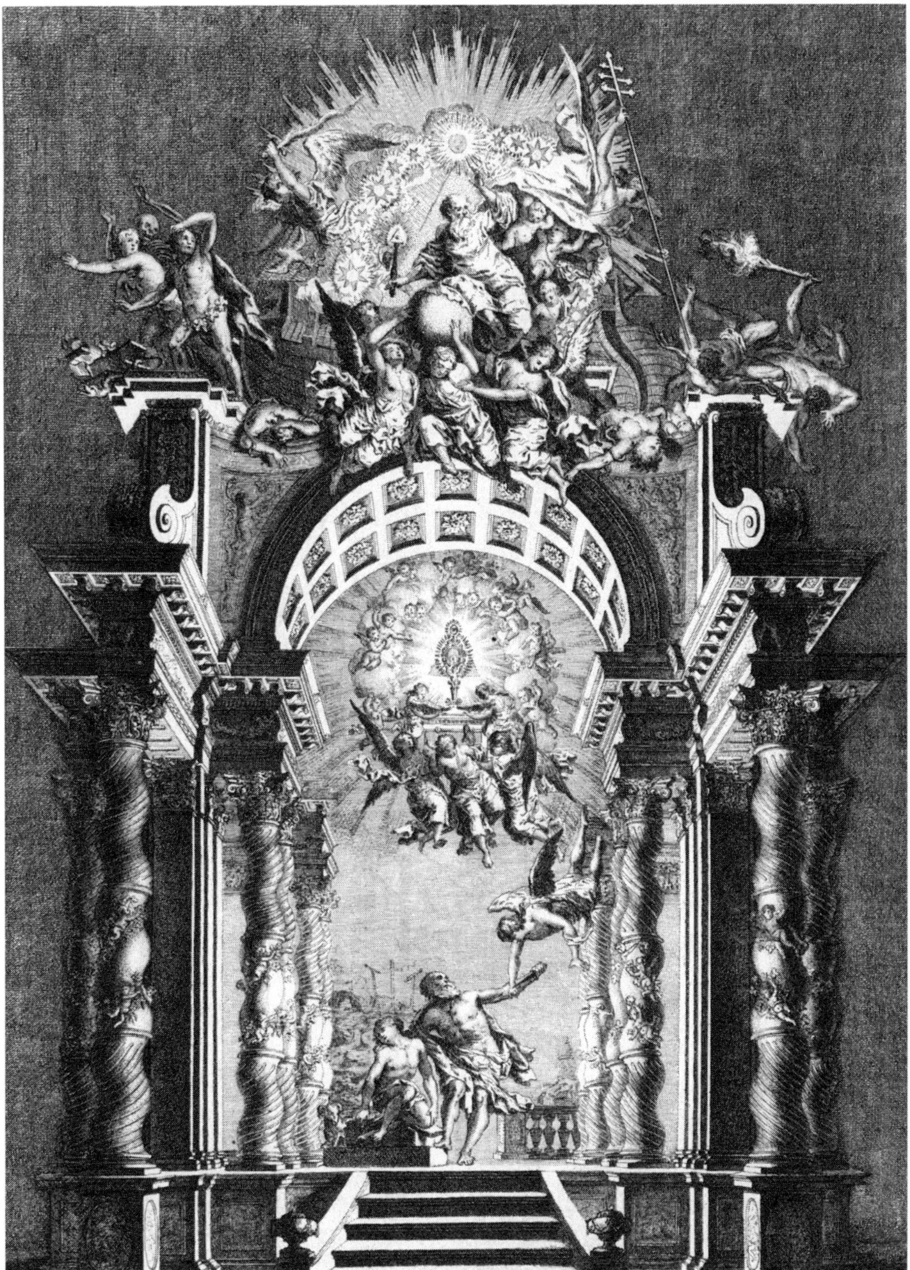

Figure 33. Johann Anton Gumpp, *Holy Sepulcher in the Theatine Church, Munich* (1691), engraving by Michael Hartwanger, 40 x 26 cm. (Photo: Bayerische Staatsbibliothek, Munich.)

of payment for the grave following Gumpp's design informs us that, while the foremost columns of the arch and the platform supporting the sculpture of Abraham's sacrifice of his son were built in three-dimensions, the rest of the architecture was painted on canvas flats placed one in front of another to create the illusion of deep space, including a vista opening onto Golgotha, where three crosses are faintly visible. On Good Friday, the Abraham and Isaac sculpture—an Old Testament prefiguration of Christ's sacrificial death on the cross—was replaced with the effigy of Christ on a bier, which was removed in turn on Easter to signal the resurrection.[39]

While its sculptures were changed according to the days of Holy Week, the central feature of Gumpp's ensemble—the Host in a monstrance surrounded by a corona of light and worshipping angels—remained in place. Perfectly framed by the coffered vault, which springs from an elaborate entablature supported by twisted columns, a real Host in a monstrance would have hung in front of Gumpp's stage-set architecture.[40] Writing about exposition graves in the mid-eighteenth century, Sebastian Sailer confirms that the real body of Christ in the form of the Sacrament is the object of adoration rather than the effigy: "Do we not see in most of the temples of our Christendom the most glorious presentations, in which art and costliness sparkle?... They are illuminated with lamps and candles. The Holy Sacrament, as the true and living body of Christ, is displayed in the most beautiful monstrances for public adoration."[41] Unaffected by the changing of sculptures at the bottom of Gumpp's exposition grave was also the image at the top: God the Father with one arm raised in a gesture of banishment, the other resting on the orb of the world. To his left is the expulsion of Adam and Eve from paradise, to his right, the casting out of the rebel angels—the very events, according to Gregory, that set the allegorical machine (along with everything else) into motion.

Gumpp's exposition grave pictures an apotheosis that connects the real architecture of the church, which it resembles, to the heavenly realm above.[42] The glowing sun that crowns the arch of stars above God's head resembles the light-emanating Host below it.

The heavenly light above the architectural frame, thereby, finds its double beneath the vault, within the illusionistic space that merges with the real space occupied by the viewer. This doubling allows the Host to do its work of reversing the consequences of human and angelic disobedience. The Fall—here represented by humans and angels driven to the edge of an impossibly tall arch from which they are bound to plummet—is reversed by the gentle ascension of the angel-borne monstrance. This reversal includes the sublimation of death, that frightened and frightening skeleton who shadows Adam and Eve. But in what sense is death undone here?

The sacrificed body of Christ *in the form of the Host* is taken up again to a heavenly abode, and the death that afflicts humankind must eventually disappear along with it. The fabulous animation of this allegorical machine, with its writhing figures, flickering lights, and twisting columns, guarantees that the imminent downward motion of the panicked figures—traced in the lance used to cast out Lucifer's rebel angels—will be recuperated by an upward movement along the central axis that connects the sacrificial victim (whether Isaac or Christ) to the Host, God the Father, and the sun. But the gap, the great, white, empty opening onto the sky above Golgotha, interrupts this otherwise unimpeded sublimation of death, marking the ineradicable difference between below and above, rock and honey, signifier and signified, enigma and truth, what we know through the senses and what we can only imagine. This then is the exposition grave's allegory of the image: while the Host—that incorporeal corporeal thing—can pass through the invisible barrier between heaven and earth, the effigy cannot.

Although he brings the Host and effigy closer together than Gumpp does, Johann Andreas Wolff is still careful to distinguish between their relative positions in the allegorical machine (figure 34). In his 1689 design for the exposition grave in the Frauenkirche in Munich, Wolff consigns the allegorical figures of Death, Sin (in the guise of Cupid), and the Devil to the decorative surface of the sarcophagus at the bottom of the scene.[43] Here they appear defeated and bound—bound to one another and hopelessly entangled in drapery

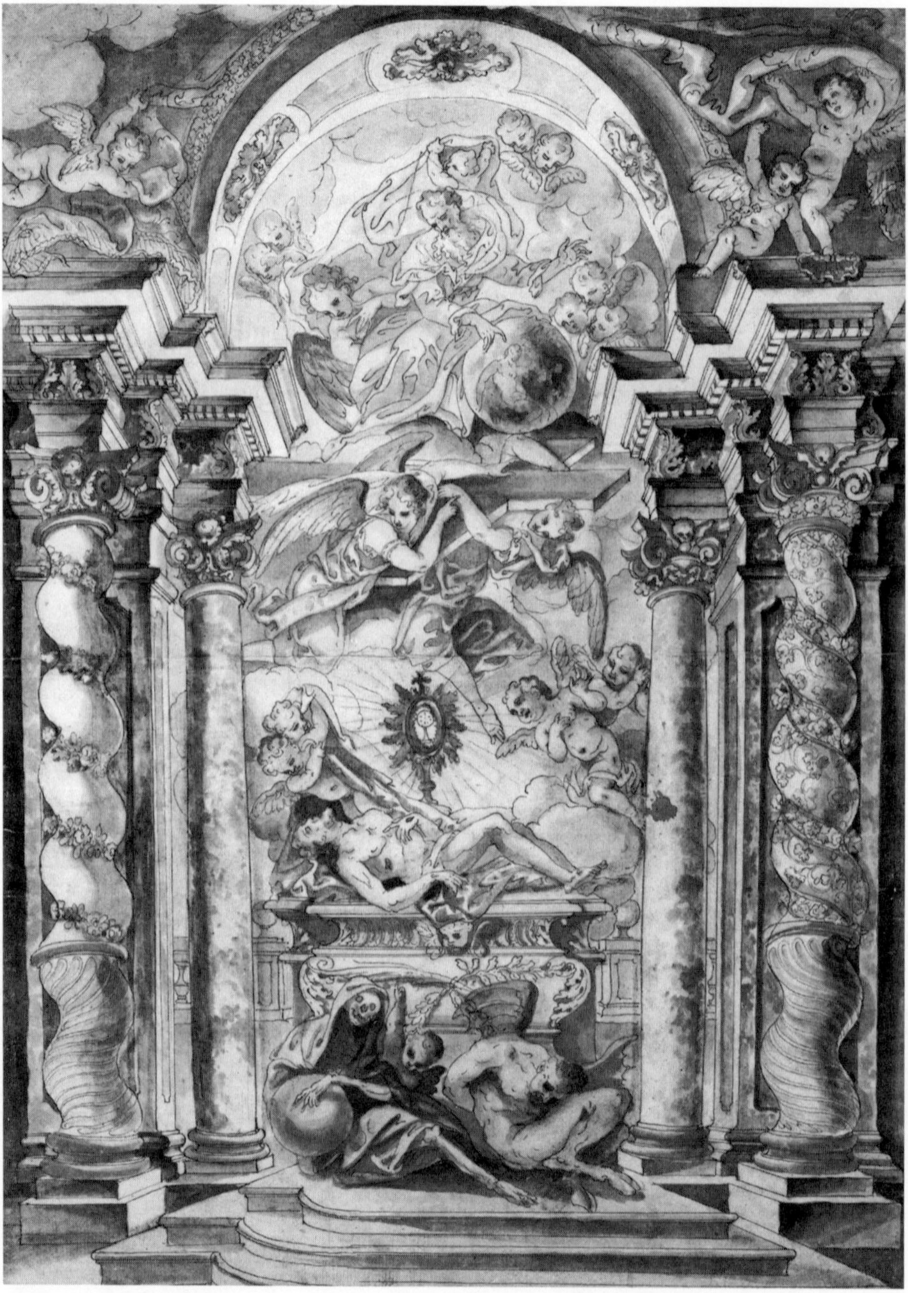

Figure 34. Johann Andreas Wolff, *Design for an Exposition Grave* (1689), ink and watercolor on paper, 58.6 × 42.5 cm. Staatliche Graphische Sammlung München, Inv. No. 14766 Z. (Photo: Staatliche Graphische Sammlung München.)

and swags of greenery, together with which they and the effigy form a decorative whole. To mark the difference between the real presence of Christ in the sacrament and his mere *representation* in the image, Wolff places the effigy in the earthbound space of the proscenium at the bottom of the scene. Too freighted with original sin to ascend, the image is nonetheless the very foundation of the exposition grave. Without it, the machine of allegory could not get the fallen viewer off the ground.

Above the body, the monstrance, and the two angels carrying the cross, God the Father holds a globe and indicates the scene pictured on it: Adam eating the forbidden fruit. This is how the death that now cowers beneath Christ's sacrificial image—an image fit to fuel the machine of allegory but not to be elevated by it—entered the world. The machine of allegory runs on all ordinary matter, according to Benjamin, but most efficiently on the dry bones of the dead because in them matter is purified of spirit. The indwelling meaning that characterizes the symbol in opposition to the allegory is unmistakably absent from the corpse: "If it is in death that the spirit becomes free, in the manner of spirits, it is not until then that the body too comes properly into its own. For this much is self-evident: the allegorization of the physis can only be carried through in all its vigour in respect of the corpse. And the characters of the *Trauerspiel* die, because it is only thus, as corpses, that they can enter into the homeland of allegory."[44]

The corpse is not, for Benjamin, as singular in its allegorical function as this passage might suggest. The idol follows, a close and closely related second: "Allegorical exegesis tended above all in two directions: it was designed to establish, from a Christian point of view, the true, demonic nature of the ancient gods, and it also served the pious mortification of the flesh. It is therefore no accident that the middle ages and the baroque took pleasure in the meaningful juxtaposition of statues of idols and the bones of the dead."[45] Although not a pagan idol, the Good Friday effigy comprises *within itself* the juxtaposition that Benjamin describes: doubly dead, it is an image of a corpse and an image of an idol.

The place to which allegory is capable of elevating the fallen soul lies beyond its own province of idols and flesh, which means that allegory must eventually disavow its own terrestrial language in order to lift the soul above it: "Ultimately in the death-signs of the baroque the direction of allegorical reflection is reversed," Benjamin writes, "on the second part of its wide arc it returns, to redeem."[46] When it returns to redeem, allegory turns away from the idols and corpses that feed it. Only by mortifying, dismembering, and finally giving up its own fallen images and words can allegory fulfill its intention. It is in this sense that allegory means, as Benjamin famously says, "precisely the non-existence of what it presents."[47]

Benjamin describes the crucial moment of allegory as a violent about-face in the depths of melancholic meditation, the moment when all the sensuous objects to which the melancholic has attached himself or herself are given up as so much allegory—as so much self-delusion, for the sake of redemption.[48] This disavowal at the bottom of allegory entails the loss of everything material but, most tellingly, those abject things that seem in their baseness the least likely to deceive: "And this is the essence of melancholy immersion: that its ultimate objects, in which it believes it can most fully secure for itself that which is vile, turn into allegories, and that these allegories fill out and deny the void in which they are represented, just as ultimately, the [allegorical] intention does not faithfully rest in the contemplation of bones, but faithlessly leaps forward to the idea of resurrection."[49]

By diverting attention from the corpse to the Host already on Good Friday, the exposition grave makes precisely this leap from bones to resurrection, subordinating the dead image to a living Host that floats high above the ruins of history. With its proliferation of human figures, its bombastic architectural setting, and its subordination of the effigy to a wafer too small to be seen, the Baroque Good Friday scenography elaborates the stuff of allegory for the sake of turning against it. The exposition grave pictures the Host—whose appearance says nothing of its essence—leaving all this sensuous pomp and circumstance behind. By contrast, the medieval

Deposition rite—which stakes a great deal on the image and relatively little on the transubstantiating power of the Host—postpones the turn from death to everlasting life.

Both before and after the Council of Trent, Good Friday was a day for reckoning with the deadness of a God—that much is clear. But it was also, I have been suggesting, a day for facing the deadness of his *image*. When the *imago Dei* ascends to heaven, the human soul may manage to ride its coattails, but the effigy—the image made by human hands—is left behind as so much unredeemed matter. "In allegory the observer is confronted with the *facies hippocratica* of history as a petrified, primordial landscape," Benjamin says. "Everything about history that, from the very beginning, has been untimely, sorrowful, unsuccessful, is expressed in a face—or rather in a death's head."[50] In the medieval Deposition rite's annual banishment of the effigy to the invisibility of the grave and in the Baroque exposition grave's subordination of the effigy to the Eucharistic Host, the effigy serves as an emblem of this petrified landscape. But where the Baroque exposition grave wasted no time in moving from the disavowal of this effigy to the redemption it affords, the medieval Deposition rite lingered over that disavowal—momentarily entranced by the double melancholy of the idol and the corpse.

Vignette: Sigmund Freud's Game of Fort-Da *(1920)*

With its regular, temporary hiding of an object that seems to stand in for an absent person, the medieval Deposition rite finds an echo in Freud's account of a child's game. There-here, disappearance-return—so goes the game the child plays to cope with his mother's departure: "The child had a wooden reel with a piece of string tied around it.... What he did was to hold the reel by the string and very skillfully throw it over the edge of his curtained cot, so that it disappeared into it, at the same time uttering his expressive 'o-o-o-o.' He then pulled the reel out of the cot again by the string and hailed its reappearance with a joyful '*da*' ('there'). This, then, was the complete game—disappearance and return."[51] Freud recounts the game in *Beyond the Pleasure Principle* (1920), where it serves as an introduction to the related issues of the repetition compulsion, masochism, and, further along, the death drive:

> The child cannot possibly have felt his mother's departure as something agreeable or even indifferent. How then does his repetition of this distressing experience as a game fit in with the pleasure principle? It may perhaps be said in reply that her departure had to be enacted as a necessary preliminary to her joyful return, and that it was in the latter that lay the true purpose of the game. But against this must be counted the observed fact that the first act, that of departure, was staged as a game in itself and far more frequently than the episode in its entirety, with its pleasurable ending.[52]

Freud rejects his own hypothesis that the game subordinates the displeasure of departure to the pleasure of return, reminding his reader that the child repeats the gesture of banishment more frequently. He then suggests two ways in which the game may nonetheless yield a net gain in pleasure: it may afford the pleasure of mastery over a situation that the child has been forced to experience passively or it may allow him to take revenge on the abandoning mother by banishing her.[53] In either case, the game would be dominated by the pleasure principle.

But the specter of repetition—evidence of the death drive—hangs over the game as the tell-tale sign that something is at work which overflows the economy of pleasure. The child's mastery aims at neither the pleasure of banishment nor the pleasure of retrieval but rather the uninterrupted command of the ostensibly lost object so that it can be lost *again*. The game does not yield the satisfaction of resolution, only the melancholic repetition that Benjamin associates with allegory: "The only pleasure the melancholic permits himself, and it is a powerful one, is allegory. It is true that the overbearing ostentation with which the banal object seems to arise from the depths of allegory is soon replaced by its disconsolate everyday countenance; it is true that the profound fascination of the sick man for the isolated and insignificant is succeeded by that disappointed abandonment of the exhausted emblem, the rhythm of which a speculatively inclined observer could find expressively repeated in the behaviour of apes."[54]

Writing some four or five years before Benjamin presented his thesis on the *Trauerspiel*, Freud finds in the child's game the same rhythmic alternation between fascination and disappointment that marks the allegorist's (and the ape's) ambivalent attachment to the objects he invests with meaning. In the rhythmic oscillation between disappearance and reappearance, Freud and Benjamin detect an overproduction of symbolizing activity, which exceeds any strictly economic calculation.

Lacan would later explain the child's repetition of the traumatic scene as his entrance into language and desire: "These are the occultation games that Freud, in a flash of genius, presented to us so that we might see in them that the moment at which desire is made human is also that at which the child is born into language."[55] The game of occultation lays down the linguistic coordinates of the world in which objects will subsequently find their place: "Through the word—which is already a presence made of absence—absence itself comes to be named in an original moment... And from this articulated couple of presence and absence... a language's world of meaning is born, in which the world of things will situate itself."[56]

At the origin of language is a missing person, whose absence compels the child to acquire words. But this absence becomes, in turn, a *function* of those words, the child's symbolizing activity displacing (Lacan calls it killing) the very thing whose absence it names: "the symbol first manifests itself as the killing of the thing, and this death results in the endless perpetuation of the subject's desire."[57] The game initiated in an effort to cope with the mother's departure then becomes an object (of desire) in its own right: "We can now see that the subject here does not simply master his deprivation by assuming it—he raises his desire to the second power. For his action destroys the object that it causes to appear and disappear by *bringing about* its absence and presence in advance. His action thus negativizes the force field of desire in order to become its own object to itself."[58] Sustained over and against the abyss of the mother's absence, the game becomes an end in itself. Casting the object away may, in a certain sense, represent her departure, and bringing the object back may represent her return, but it is the oscillation between the two that figures without picturing what she *is* at any given moment: the uninterrupted loss that is the condition of possibility for the functioning of the symbolic order.

The mother is the enabling cause of the game, but she functions as such only when she leaves and leaves the child alone with his allegorical object, the reel that is at once his most intimate possession and an object of total indifference. This is the paradox of a symbolic order without which there would be no subject but in which the subject is never at home. The world of language is not the child's to create; it is only his to command and only that in a limited sense.[59] For, as soon as the child secures the allegorical object for his use, his control over it destroys its magic.[60] Benjamin describes the price the allegorist pays for keeping the reel tethered to his hand and thereby to his will: "If the object becomes allegorical under the gaze of melancholy, if melancholy causes life to flow out of it and it remains behind dead, but eternally secure, then it is exposed to the allegorist, it is unconditionally in his power. That is to say it is now quite incapable of emanating any meaning or significance of its own; such significance as it has, it acquires from the allegorist."[61]

When it is far away, the reel sustains the child's fascination, but as soon as he greets its "reappearance with a joyful '*da*,'" it will show its "disconsolate everyday countenance," reminding him of its alienating insignificance and its dependence on him for meaning—for which he will need to banish it again. When he banishes the reel, he summons the thing his symbolizing activity kills. Abandoning himself to the repetitions of the death drive, he throws the reel—both signifier of the mother and a lure cast beyond the order of signification—into the curtained bed, attempting once again to escape the petrified landscape of allegory with the very same gesture that he establishes and reestablishes its domain.

In a Good Friday sermon delivered before King Henry VIII in 1535, John Longland employs the word yonder to much the same effect as the child's *fort*:

> Yonder it lyes, yonder is hys bodye, in yonder tombe, in yonder sepulchre. Lett us goo thidre, lett us wepe with these Maryes, lett us turne and wynde thys bodye of Christe, lett us turne it thys wayes and that wayes, to and froo, and pytussely beholde hit. And what shall we fynde. We shall fynde a bloody bodye, a body full of plages and woundes. Not that hit nowe is full of woundes and plages, or nowe deede: but y[e]t thowe oughtest nowe as the tyme of the yere falleth, with the churche to remembere this body.[62]

Through an emphatic four-fold repetition of the word yonder, Longland first locates the body at a distance. Then with three repetitions of lett, he brings himself close enough to the body to "pytussely beholde" it. But even when he has taken the corpse in hand, he keeps it moving, turning it "thys wayes and that wayes, to and froo," as if there were a danger in holding it too steadily under our gaze. And he reminds us, "not that hit nowe is full of woundes and plages, or nowe deede," as if to explain why he will need to cast it away again: like all allegorical objects, this "deede" body "means precisely the non-existence of what it presents."[63]

Although the timing of the annual Deposition and Elevation rites is very different from that of the child's *fort-da* game, analogous is the repetitive hiding and retrieving that does not change—that in fact both depends upon and ensures—the loss of the object to which it refers. The ritual and the game must be compulsively repeated because they are as much about the effigy as they are about what it represents. Casting the object away opens the possibility that it may return as the thing its creation killed; bringing it near forecloses that possibility, which is why it will need to be banished again. This is the back-and-forth movement of the medieval Deposition and Elevation rites—as opposed to the Baroque exposition grave, with its irreversible ascent. Like the child's game, the medieval rites formed an image *in time and space*, a sequence of actions and words that allowed the assertion of the sacred image and its denial, which in fact coexisted throughout the year, to be parceled out into hours and paces, unfolding the insoluble contradictions of the image in the ambivalent form of an allegory without end.[64]

PART TWO

Paintings of the Deposition

CHAPTER FIVE

Rogier van der Weyden's Repeated Forms

The temporal dimension of the liturgy allowed images to be displayed during some parts of the year and hidden during others. This alternation is not possible in the still medium of painting, of course, where the presentation and withdrawal of the image (the complete constellation of the *fort-da*) must occur all at once if they are both to occur.[1] Around the end of the fourteenth century, pictures of Christ's deposition from the cross began to represent these opposing gestures within a single, static frame, condensing the ostension and occultation that the late medieval liturgy spread out in time into one scene.

Pictures of the deposition first appeared in the ninth century, some four hundred years later than the first images of the crucifixion.[2] This is when the story of Christ's life began to be represented in a degree of detail that warranted interest in the somewhat awkward undertaking of the removal of the body from the cross; this is also about the time that the Deposition rite probably began to be performed. At first the body in paintings of the deposition tended to be pictured in the same upright position it takes in the Crucifixion. Over time, the iconography of the Deposition would evolve from a scene with only one or two characters surrounding a body still firmly attached to the cross into a scene in which several figures support and mourn a body on its way to the grave.[3]

In the twelfth century, the Virgin and John the Evangelist, who had formerly been shown standing somewhat apart from the action, were made into more active participants: the mother holds a cloth to receive her son, gazes expectantly toward him, takes hold of his hand, kissing it or pressing it to her cheek, and finally throws both her arms around his body. Additional female mourners, reiterating the Virgin's displays of tenderness, began to be added as well. As the cult of the Virgin grew in the thirteenth and fourteenth centuries, the mother's grief became still more integral to the scene.[4] In addition to giving the Virgin an increasingly important role, trecento painters paid more attention to the difficulty of the task at hand. In Simone Martini's panel, gestures of grief are indistinguishable from straining efforts to lower the body from the cross (figure 35).[5]

Unlike most earlier versions of the scene, Rogier van der Weyden's *Deposition* (ca. 1435) pictures a body completely freed from the cross, which is to say, liberated from the verticality that had governed Christ's posture in earlier paintings (plate 1).[6] The narrative momentum is suspended as Joseph and Nicodemus hold Christ aloft for the viewer's veneration. Al Acres describes the hyphenating effect of this suspension: "Christ has been lowered quite far. Instead of the upper body slumping sideward, the entire figure has descended to a position that was new in the tradition of the subject.... It is, in fact, a perfectly transitional arrangement.... Christ at this moment belongs as much to the cross as to the ground. Where the traditional image of the Descent... associates the event closely with the Crucifixion, the Prado Descent [i.e., Rogier's *Deposition*] looks equally backward and forward between Crucifixion and Entombment."[7] By means of this transitional arrangement, the body in Rogier's painting articulates the visibility of the cross with the invisibility of the tomb, opening up new possibilities for picturing all at once and in a still medium the presentation and iconoclastic withdrawal of the *imago Dei* that occur, in time, over the course of the liturgical year.

Christ as Crossbow

Rogier's *Deposition* was commissioned for the chapel of Louvain's Greater Guild of Crossbowmen, which was dedicated to the Virgin of the Seven Sorrows.[8] This accounts in part for the sorrowing Virgin's prominence in Rogier's altarpiece. Painters had been depicting the Virgin's sorrowful swoon at the foot of the cross since about the

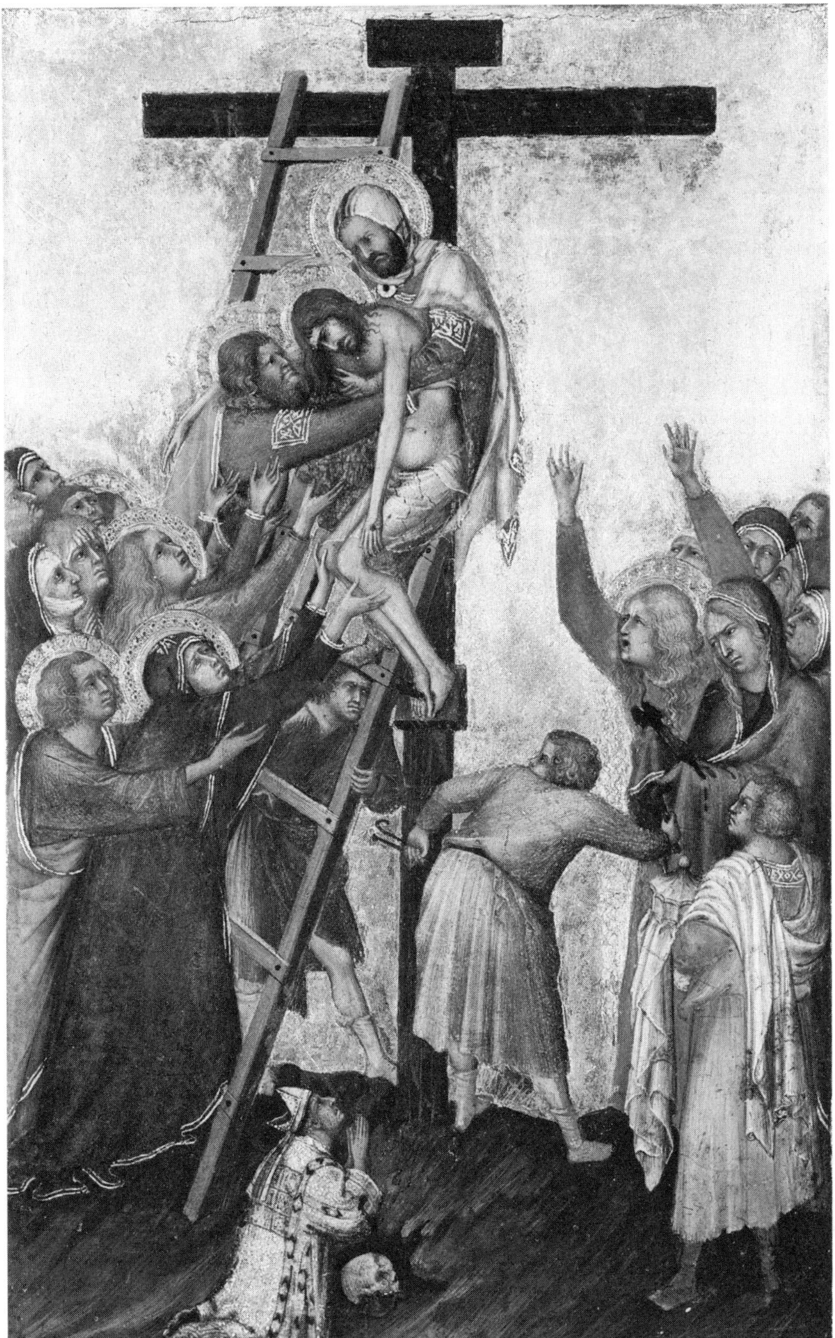

Figure 35. Simone Martini, *Deposition from the Cross* (ca. 1315) from the *Orsini Polyptych*, tempera on panel, 24.5×15.5cm. Koninklijk Museum voor Schone Kunsten, Antwerp. (Photo: Erich Lessing/Art Resource, New York.)

second half of the thirteenth century.[9] But Rogier's rhyme between the bodies of mother and son and the prominence that rhyme gives to the Virgin are unprecedented.[10]

Though often omitted in the numerous fifteenth and sixteenth-century appropriations of Rogier's composition, this rhyme has consistently caught the attention of modern commentators. In 1953, Otto von Simson wrote an influential article on the role of the Virgin's *compassio* in Rogier's painting. Bringing to bear textual accounts of the Virgin's suffering during the crucifixion, von Simson argues that the Virgin's mimetic response to Christ's pain is a model for the viewer's own *imitatio Christi*: moved by the Virgin's compassion, he suggests, the viewer would be encouraged to live a life in accordance with the life of Christ.[11] Though persuasive, von Simson's argument neither exhausts the implications of Rogier's dramatic parallel between the Virgin and Christ nor takes into account the unlikely emptiness that opens between them.

In theological terms, the Virgin's relationship to Christ is complex. Christ appears in the world by taking the Virgin's flesh in the incarnation: "In his presence in flesh taken from the Virgin, on the table of the altar, he visits us by his grace," writes Ranulph de la Houblonnière.[12] Later, when his passion is translated into her compassion, his martyrdom shapes her flesh in turn. In her compassionate suffering at the foot of the cross, the Virgin in Rogier's *Deposition* takes the seal of Christ's body not only upon the heart hidden within her but also upon her visible body, as if according to the Song of Solomon 8.6, where the Bride says: "Set me as a seal upon your heart, / as a seal upon your arm." But the Virgin is more than just a vehicle for Christ's incarnation and a visible sharer in his suffering; she herself is an image of God the Father. For this reason, Alain de Lille calls her "the sister of Christ."[13] Like Christ, she is capable of making God available to human eyes: "she opened her womb to the only king of the world, she who is the image of the invisible god," writes Pierre de Celle.[14]

Of course, medieval theologians distinguished between Christ's likeness to God—a participation in the Holy Trinity—and the

Virgin's more distant resemblance.[15] Without entirely neglecting this distinction, Rogier's *Deposition* stresses the parity of the two. Although Christ holds a position of eminence above the Virgin, her body competes with his for our attention. Moreover, it is only through her presence that his becomes fully legible. If the Virgin gives Christ a body by bearing him, in Rogier's painting, she also gives him a body through a mimicry that anatomizes his form, making visible the shapes and lines that comprise it. The negative space described by Christ's left arm as it is held up by the man on the ladder, the curved edge of Christ's ribcage set against the white shroud, the downward slope of his left hip, over which his loincloth stretches, the hanging weight of his right arm, which falls parallel to the vertical beam of the cross, and the long sinuous line that runs from his throat, between his ribs, and down the length of his legs become conspicuous insofar as they are repeated in the figure of the Virgin. The Virgin takes the measure of Christ's body, helping us see it at the same time that she deprives it of its autonomy.

Made conspicuous by the Virgin's repetition of it, Christ's shape turns out to be highly overdetermined. Two delicate crossbows hanging from the gilded tracery in the upper corners of the frame reveal the identity of Rogier's patrons (figure 36). The shape of these tiny weapons is then reiterated and amplified in the tracery, where the thickest lines mimic the curved front of crossbows with their strings pulled back ready to shoot arrows toward the upper corners of the frame. The shape of the crossbow is reiterated and amplified again in the unusual position of the arms of Mary Magdalene, who stands to the far right of the scene. In fact, the curvature of the Magdalene's entire body, which is contorted by mourning and which is mirrored in the figure of John the Evangelist to the far left, echoes this shape. Finally, Christ himself is a crossbow—the very arrangement of his limbs an allusion to the patrons of the altarpiece.

Rogier makes so much of the crossbow shape in his *Deposition* no doubt because of its fortuitous doubling as a figure for Christ's experience on the cross. In Arnoul Gréban's Passion play of around 1450, the man who nails Christ to the cross says, struggling to

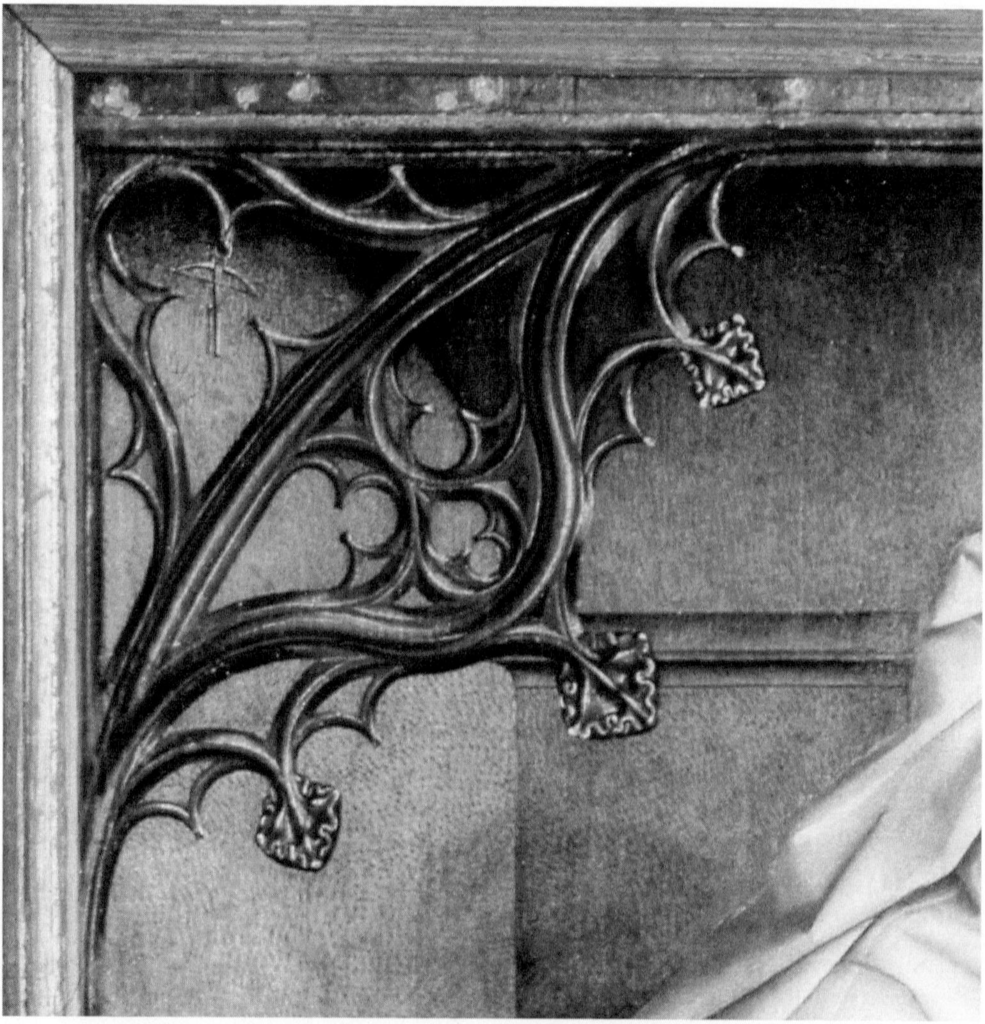

Figure 36. Detail from Plate 1: Rogier van der Weyden, *Deposition from the Cross* (ca. 1435), oil on panel, 220 × 262 cm. Museo Nacional del Prado, Madrid. (Photo: Erich Lessing/Art Resource, New York.)

stretch Christ's hand far enough to reach the hole into which the nail must be driven: "Hard scoundrels! / The hand's getting there, or almost... It's just about there. / Now hammer the nail in. / A bent crossbow never / stretched better than this."[16] In a twelfth-century exegetical work, Gottfried von Admont likewise compares Christ in his passion to a bow stretched nearly to the point of breaking: "A bow consists of a piece of wood or horn and a string, which worthily represents our Lord and Redeemer. The string may be taken to mean his most holy body, which, in the various dire tribulations of his Passion, was wondrously spanned and stretched."[17] Heinrich von Neustadt writes: "They laid him down on the Cross. Then his pure limbs and veins were drawn like the string on a bow."[18] Rogier pictures Christ's removal from the cross as the merciful relaxation of a bow that has released its arrow. The shape of the crossbow, a metonymy for the patron, thereby becomes a metaphor for the release of Christ from the pain of the crucifixion.

The *imitatio* that von Simson identifies as structuring the relationship between mother and son ramifies, therefore, in more ways than he himself explores. It is more than a matter of the Virgin's imitation of Christ and more, even, than a matter of our imitation of the Virgin's imitation in turn. This mimesis echoes through the rest of the composition, in the reiterations of the crossbow's bent form. In theory, this extended imitation might attest to the exemplarity of Christ; here, it has the opposite effect. The dissemination of Christ's form through a series of closely related yet subtly different variations diffuses and ironically undercuts the authority of the model. Because this model needs its copies in order to be recognizable as such, it is neither as autonomous nor as authoritative as one might like to think. Without the dissemination of the crossbow form through all its variations, it might fail to impress us as significant at all.

Our Lady Outside the Walls

Built in 1373, the Crossbowmen's chapel was confiscated from the guild on 23 September 1798, sold at auction along with its contents, and subsequently torn down.[19] Although we know relatively little about this chapel—which is pictured in a book of views of the city of Louvain from about 1615—we do know that Our Lady Outside the Walls (*Onze Lieve Vrouw van ginderbuiten*) was situated beyond the city walls, just outside the Gate of St. Michael in the Hoelstraat (today's Tiensestraat), which is to say on the periphery of the city of Louvain, whose church of St. Peter contained a miraculous statue of the Virgin, which attracted pilgrims and played a major role in the city's annual processions (figure 37).[20]

Even inside the Crossbowmen's chapel, Rogier's altarpiece would not have stood at the center of things, phenomenologically speaking. Though it crowned what the early documents refer to as the chapel's main altar, the altarpiece never would have attracted to itself the undivided attention of the chapel's visitors, which would have been solicited from every direction by other images.[21] At the time Rogier's *Deposition* was installed, Our Lady Outside the Walls was home to a life-size, wooden, polychromed Pietà from the fourteenth century.[22] Toward the end of the fifteenth century, Jan Borreman would be commissioned to make a carved retable representing the martyrdom of St. George for the chapel's transept.[23] It is safe to assume that other altarpieces, crucifixes, freestanding sculptures, stained glass windows, and architectural carvings decorated the chapel as well.

And this only begins to account for the images in the vicinity of Rogier's *Deposition*, many of which would have depicted Christ. The various implements displayed on the altar and used during the Mass were commonly adorned with imagery related to Christ—pictures of the man but also zoomorphic symbols, including the lamb, pelican, phoenix, eagle, and lion.[24] The person officiating at the Mass, repeating Christ's words at the last supper—*Hoc est corpus meum* (This is my body)—was himself an image of Christ. As the twelfth-century theologian Honorius von Autun describes it, "by the extension of his hands he represents the extension of Christ on the Cross."[25] To make this clear, the celebrant sometimes wore a chasuble adorned with an embroidered crucifix (figure 38).[26] Beyond the interior of the chapel, the images of Christ would have continued to multiply: from portal

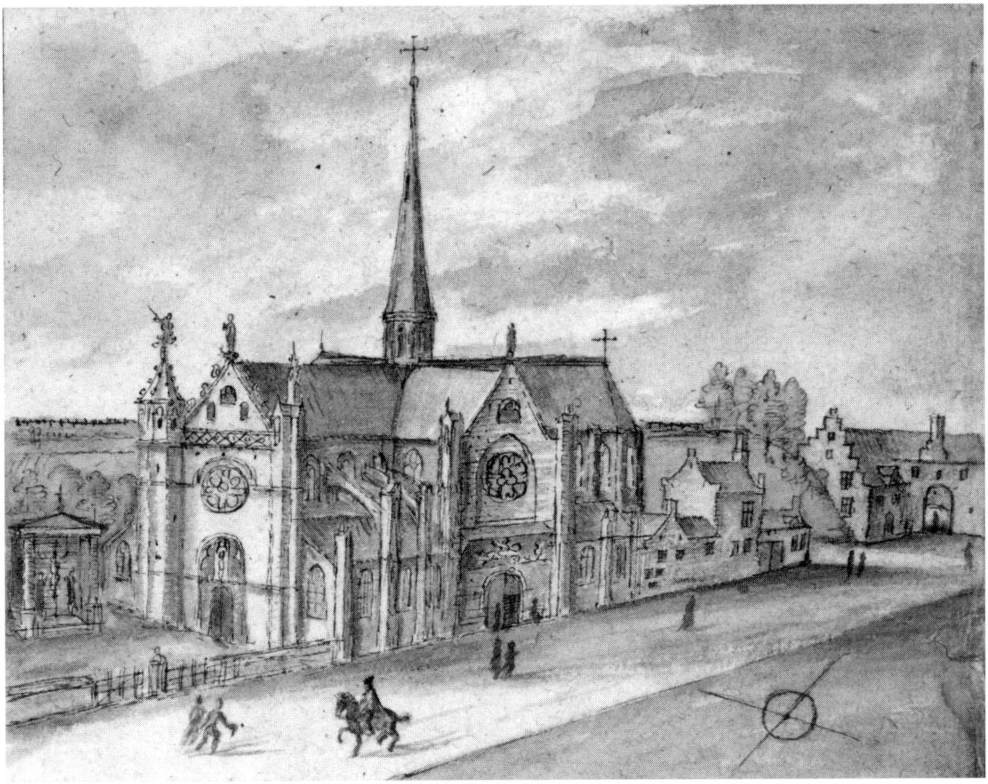

Figure 37. *Our Lady Outside the Walls, Louvain* (ca. 1615), pen and ink with watercolor, 11.1 × 14.4 cm. Koninklijke Bibliotheek van België, Brussels. (Photo: Koninklijke Bibliotheek van België.)

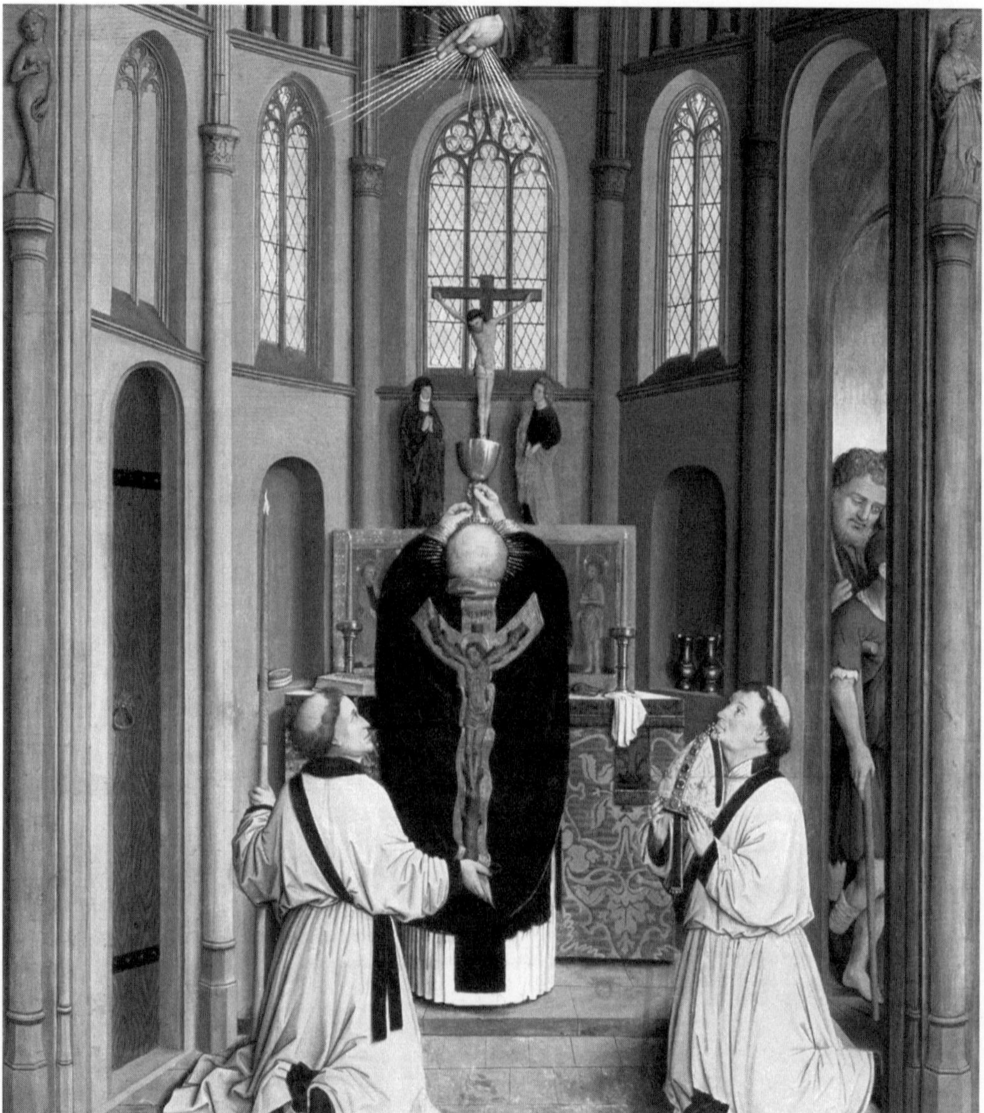

Figure 38. Master of the Augsburg Legend of Ulrich, detail from *Legend of St. Ulrich* (ca. 1450), oil on panel. Church of Sts. Ulrich and Afra, Augsburg. (Photo: Instituts für Realienkunde des Mittelalters und der frühen Neuzeit.)

sculptures, to the cruciform structure of the chapel itself, to the body of the Pope, the *vicarius Christi*, and so on.

In addition to this dizzying collection of objects and humans representing Christ in and around Our Lady Outside the Walls, there was also, of course, that small wheaten wafer elevated each day for all to see during the Mass—a wafer that was itself often stamped with Christ's form.[27] The elevation of the Host was the climactic moment of the Mass—the *manducatio per visum*—for congregants, many of whom whom rarely took communion.[28] What people felt they saw in viewing the Host is difficult to say. At the Fourth Lateran Council of 1215, the Church officially adopted the doctrine of transubstantiation, according to which the Host is the real presence of Christ, in its every part. Although there were numerous images and tales of visions in which the Eucharist miraculously became the infant Christ or the Man of Sorrows, for the average witness to the elevation of the Host, on the average day, Christ's body presumably would have remained veiled behind the appearance of bread.[29]

Those who saw the Host elevated in front of Rogier's *Deposition* would have seen a wafer held before a nearly life-size, painted picture of Christ—a superimposition of two very different representations of the same man.[30] Not only would these viewers have had to reconcile this painted image with the "image" that is the Host but also with the other images in the vicinity of the altar, in the space of the chapel, in the city of Louvain, and beyond.

"The Evil of Superfluity"

One of the major complaints of Protestant reformers was that there were *too many* images.[31] The number of religious images for both public and private use grew in the period leading up to the Reformation. Attempts to restrict their proliferation were already being made in the fifteenth century. Pierre d'Ailly advises that, "images and pictures not be permitted to multiply so," calling that multiplication the "evil of superfluity."[32] One of the articles of the Hussite Synod of St. Wenceslas (1418) stipulates that "images can be kept in the church, but only if they are not in superfluity."[33] In a mid-fifteenth-century response to Wycliffite views on images, Reginald Pecock recommends that they "not be multiplied so wijde that at ech chirche, at ech chapel, at ech stretis eende, or at ech heggis eende in a cuntre be sett such an ymage."[34]

The charge of superfluity became even more common in the sixteenth century. In his 1525 answer to Valentin Compar, Zwingli writes: "Our pious ancestors . . . knew little of paintings and sculptures when they were still in the valleys. But now we have so many of them that if ten ate as much hay as one sheep, we would immediately bring them to market."[35] A pair of German engravings made around 1600 contrasts a "purified" church with its "papist" counterpart. In the former, the congregation is attentive to the preacher; in the latter, every corner is overflowing with images, altars, and sacraments that compete for attention (figure 39).[36]

Many late medieval and Reformation iconoclasts who protested the proliferation of images were also troubled by the proliferation of Hosts. Such a multiplication defied decency, according to Margery Baxter. In her 1428 heresy trial, Baxter attacked the doctrine of Christ's real presence in the Host, suggesting that it led to a fracturing of what is by definition singular: "If every such sacrament were God and Christ's real body, then gods would be infinite in number, because a thousand priests and more confect a thousand such gods every day and then eat them, and once eaten emit them from their back side in filthy and stinking pieces."[37] Most reformers left aside the more scatological implications of the doctrine of the Host, focusing instead on the flaws in its logic. In *The Displaying of the Popish Masse* (1637), Thomas Becon writes: "It is directly against the verity and truth of Christ's natural body to be in more places at once than in one, as he must be in an hundred thousand places at once, if your doctrine be true."[38]

For reformers unhappy with the proliferation of images and Hosts, the corner itself became a rhetorical figure for idolatry. In a sermon of 1533 titled "The Corner Mass (*Winckelmesse*) and the Consecration of Priests," Luther calls for the elimination of private masses held in side chapels: "You clerics who say corner masses

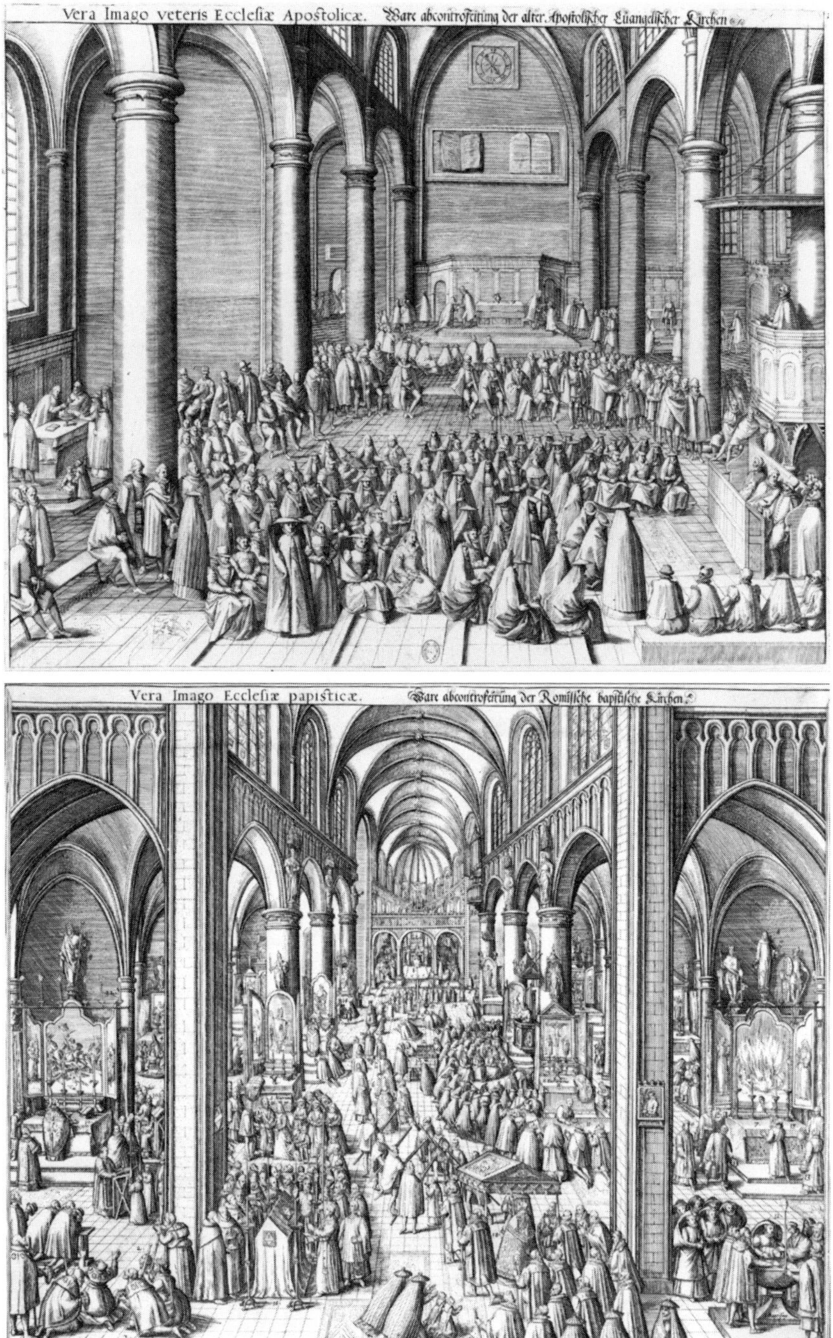

Figure 39. German, *True Image of the Ancient Apostolic Church* (top) and *True Image of the Papist Church* (bottom) (ca. 1600), engraving. Bibliothèque Nationale de France, Paris. (Photo: Bibliothèque Nationale de France.)

(*Winckelmesser*) have never preached one word or confessed Christ in all your corner masses (*Winckel messen*). You partook of the sacrament by yourself. You have whispered it to yourself."[39] In *An Apology of the Church of England* (1564), John Jewel refers to "private Masses in every corner of the temples, now ten, now twenty together in one day."[40] A broadsheet from Nuremburg titled *Complaint of the Poor Persecuted Idols and Church Images* lets the images speak from the corners: "We poor mean church images / and corner idols (*winckel götzen*) big and small."[41] The slurs *Abgott, Beygott, Nebengott, Mitgott, and Seitengott*, all of which mean something like a secondary or side god, likewise reflect an understanding of idolatry as a falling away from the center.[42] In *Toward the Vindication of the Second Commandment*, Edmund Gurnay writes: "While the Lord calleth inwardly, [images] call outwardly: while the Lord calleth to the center, they call to the circumference."[43]

According to Calvin, this proliferation of corner gods comes directly at God's expense. What is given to the idol is taken from Him: "As often as Scripture asserts that there is one God, it is not contending over the bare name, but also prescribing that nothing belonging to his divinity is to be transferred to another."[44] Humans are both seduced by the proximate and lured by the distant: "The greater part of the world thoughtlessly seizes upon whatever is at hand, nay, even flits hither and thither. But godliness, to stand on a firm footing, keeps itself within its proper limits."[45] On the one hand, we mistake whatever happens to be near for the real thing; on the other hand, we flit about in search of something new. This wandering of attention gives rise to idols: "Surely, just as waters boil up from a vast, full spring, so does an immense crowd of gods flow forth from the human mind, while each one, in wandering about with too much license, wrongly invents this or that about God Himself."[46] Despite the freedom he grants the individual to meet God without the elaborate mediation of the Catholic Church, Calvin seeks to limit where and how that meeting takes place. By abolishing the peripheral, strange, and errant gods fabricated by human hands and imaginations, Calvin hopes to centralize authority.

Rogier van der Weyden thematizes precisely the proliferation of peripheral, strange, and errant images that Calvin and other reformers condemn. Instead of simply adding to this proliferation, Rogier's painting *pictures* it. In Rogier's self-reflexive painting there are only "corner gods": the *imago Dei* is split between two rhyming but different bodies—one male, one female, one naked, one clothed, one blue, and one white. In the rhyme between the Virgin and Christ but also in the rhymes between Christ and the crossbow, the crossbow and the Magdalene, the Magdalene and St. John, and so on and so forth, Rogier shows that no single image is adequate to the task of representing God. By ironically recapitulating within his own composition the multiplication of images surrounding it, Rogier reinforces the iconoclastic implications of the deposition scene. The *Deposition* provides an image of *imitatio*, as von Simson describes, but one in which the model to which the viewer is meant to conform himself or herself is being lowered from its central position of authority into a series.

To mark the lack of a first or final image in this series, Rogier opens an abyss between the Virgin and Christ that hollows out the center of the scene. Because of its inverted 'T'-shape format, which was common at the time for sculpted but not for painted altarpieces, there are in fact two ways of determining the center of Rogier's painting.[47] Christ's body predictably occupies the center—his side-wound falling just to the left of and below center—if the center is determined based on dimensions including the raised area at the top of the altarpiece. But if the center of the painting is determined based on dimensions that instead exclude this raised area, the empty space between the Virgin and Christ turns out to occupy the center of the scene. To have two centers is in and of itself remarkable but that—in a painting whose figures are arranged as compactly as they are here—one of these centers should be empty is particularly strange.[48]

The longer one holds this empty center in focus, the more everything in the composition appears to press toward the periphery—despite the figures' state of suspended animation. Christ is being carried off to the right, while the Virgin falls to the left. The bracketing figures of St. John and Mary Magdalene barely manage to hold things in place. That surprisingly deep space between Christ and the fainting Virgin, filled with the impossibly abundant folds of Mary's blue robe, is a portent of what is to come: the hole in the center will expand as the outward push prevails, moving the center toward the periphery and finally completely out of view.

Rounding out the downward pull on Christ's body, this centrifugal movement is part of the iconoclasm that structures Rogier's composition. But even as Rogier's god is being iconoclastically lowered and moved into a modest position in the wings among the other corner gods, a body materializes in the *other* center of the scene. Looked at from the perspective we have been taking, the center of the painting is empty; but if we lift our gaze back to where the center falls when it is determined in the first of the two manners described above, we discover *there* a body.

Vignette: Eva Hesse's Repetition Nineteen III *(1967)*

In an interview with Cindy Nemser first published in 1970, Eva Hesse said of her sculpture *Hang Up* (1966): "It is coming out of something and yet nothing and it is holding. It is framing nothing.... It is like those things I did in Europe" (figure 40).[49] The things Hesse did in Europe in 1965 are machine-bodies of interlocking forms, flesh and industry hooked up in an unlikely exchange that circles around an emptiness.[50] In the drawings she did that year, line separates figure from ground only to relay the one into the other again, articulating the sprouting of shafts that find their way through a series of biomorphic forms back to the flatness of the paper, pumping the energy communicated through them into the reservoir of the ground. *Tomorrow's Apples (5 in White)* (1965) translates these drawn forms into three dimensions (figure 41). Five colored connectors made of metal wire wrapped in painted cord link two low mounds. Where the connectors meet these flesh-colored mounds, an extra loop of cord creates the illusion that they emerge from and penetrate the panel's flesh-like mass, as if they looped around behind it to close

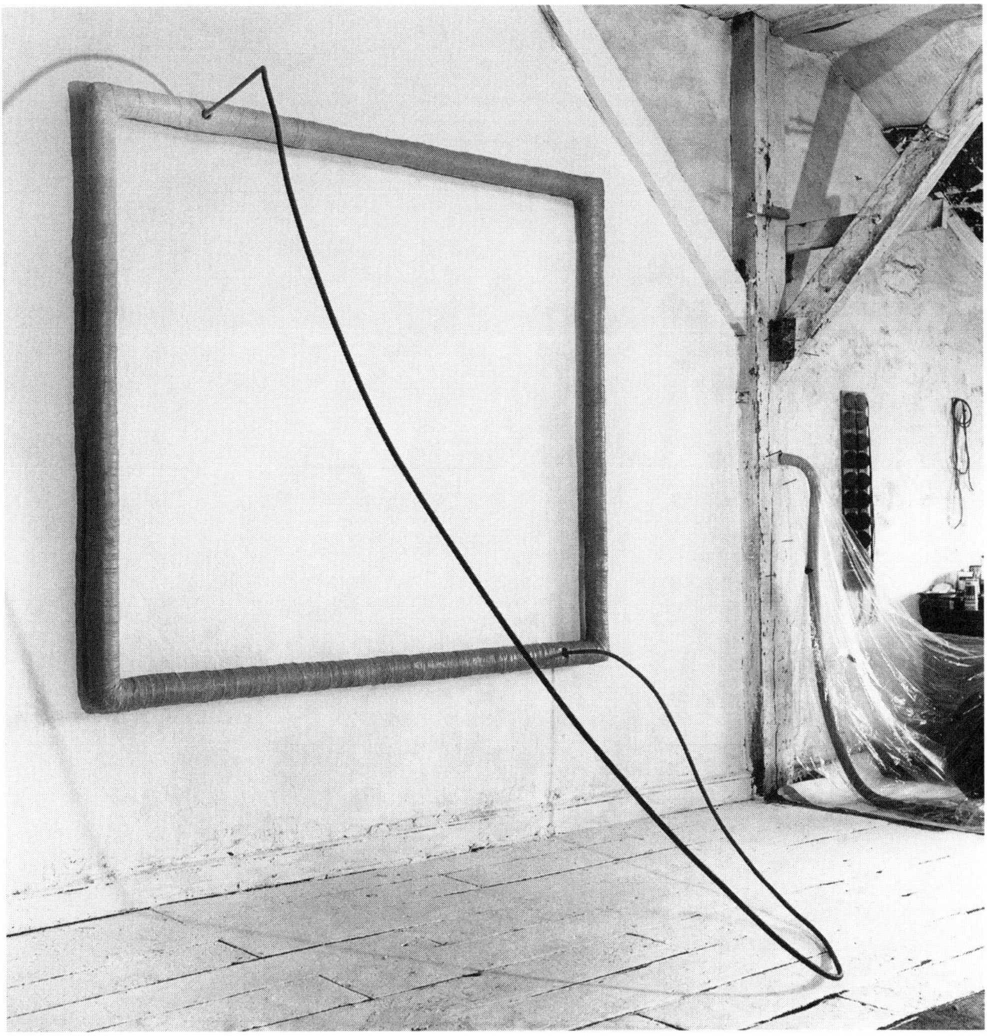

Figure 40. Eva Hesse, *Hang Up* (1966), acrylic, cloth, wood, cord, steel, 182.9 × 213.4 × 198.1 cm. 134 Bowery, New York, 1966. © The Estate of Eva Hesse. Courtesy of Hauser & Wirth Zürich London. (Photo: The Estate of Eva Hesse. Courtesy of Hauser & Wirth Zürich London.)

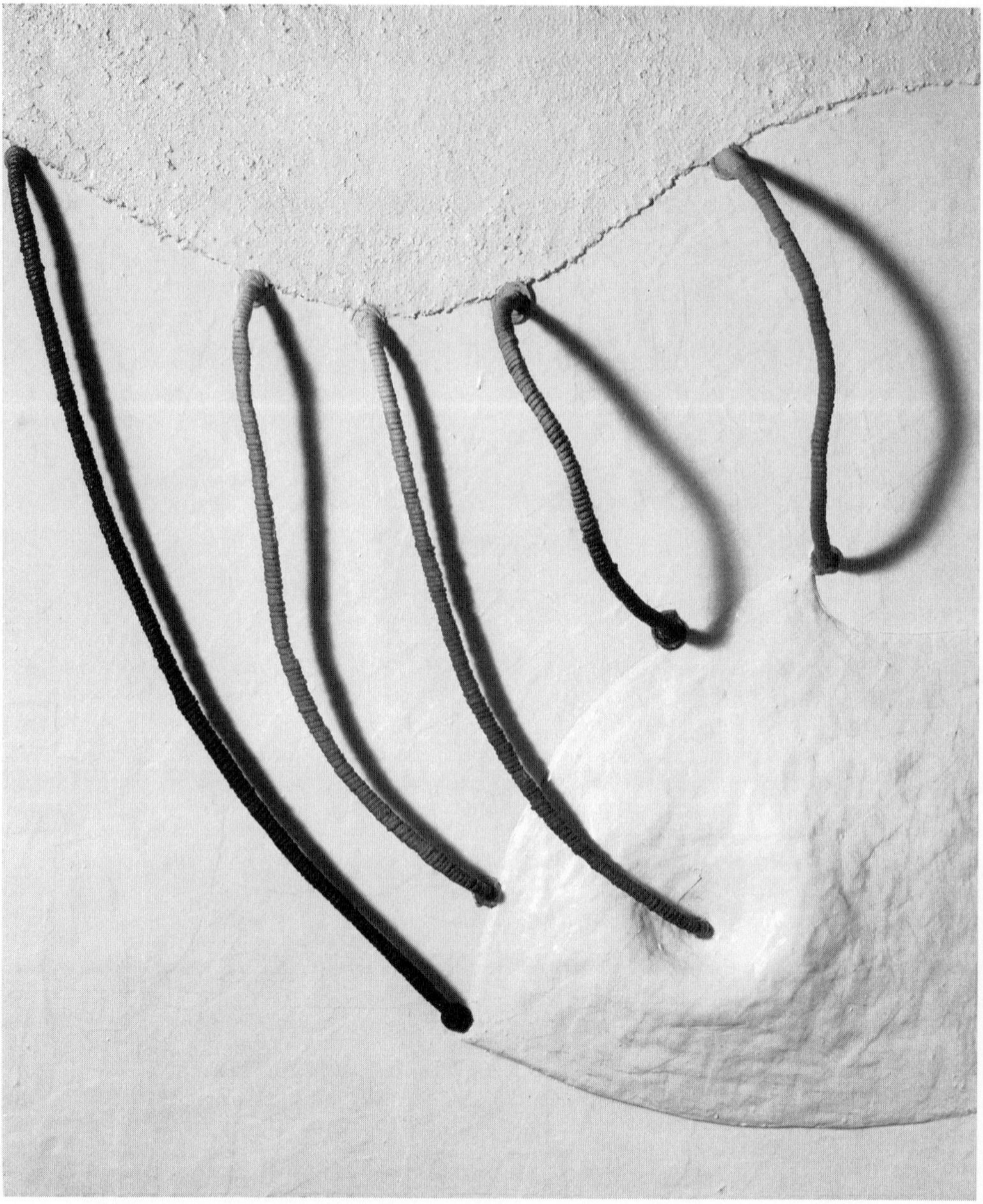

Figure 41. Eva Hesse, *Tomorrow's Apples (5 in White)* (1965), varnish, gouache, enamel, cord, metal, papier-caché, papier-maché, unknown modeling compound, particleboard, wood, 65.4 × 55.6 × 15.9 cm. Tate Modern, London, 1979. © The Estate of Eva Hesse. Courtesy of Hauser & Wirth Zürich London. (Photo: Tate, London / Art Resource, New York.)

off their circuitry. Like *Hang Up*, the drawings and reliefs Hesse did in Europe, including *Tomorrow's Apples*, free line from the task of defining mass. Instead, line itself takes on mass and becomes a kind of circuitry relaying something through its coils.

Although Hesse would leave the pop idiom behind, the framing of an empty center so important in these early works would continue to structure much of what was to come. In 1966, Robert Smithson wrote: "Coils go on and on; some are cracked open, only to reveal an empty center."[51] Mel Bochner characterizes Hesse's work in similar terms in his *Wrap: Portrait of Eva Hesse* (1966), with its concentric circles of closely related words that narrow as they approach the center: "wrap-up. secrete. cloak. bury. obscure. varnish. ensconce. disguise. conceal. / camouflage. confine. limit. entomb. ensack. bag. conceal. hide. / hedge-in. circumcincture. skin. crust. encirclement. cincture. ringed . . ." and so on.

Using a thesaurus, Hesse made a practice of compiling lists of terms like Bochner's—terms related to one another by what we might think of as a kind of drifting meaning: "circumnavigation / circumflexion / circuit / evolution / circumscribe / circuitous, devious / *rotation*, gyration, convolution / vortex . . ."[52] Hesse also used a thesaurus to title her works: "I *do* title them. . . . I use a dictionary and a thesaurus. I usually use a word that sounds right too but that doesn't have a specific meaning in terms of content. It's straight but not another word for it."[53] Just as the terms in her lists are not exactly another word for one another, Hesse's titles are not exactly another word for what they name. With her lists and titles, Hesse creates a verbal equivalent to the relay-effect of the circuitry of *Hang Up* and the work she did in Europe: a synonymia, which leads from one word to another (similar) word to another and another and so on, drifting ever farther from any original word or thing.

In her serial work of the late 1960s, Hesse would transpose this synonymia back into the visual realm, as a means of stringing together the units of her sculptures. In *Repetition Nineteen III*, the bucket shape is not so much repeated as varied (figure 42). Hesse

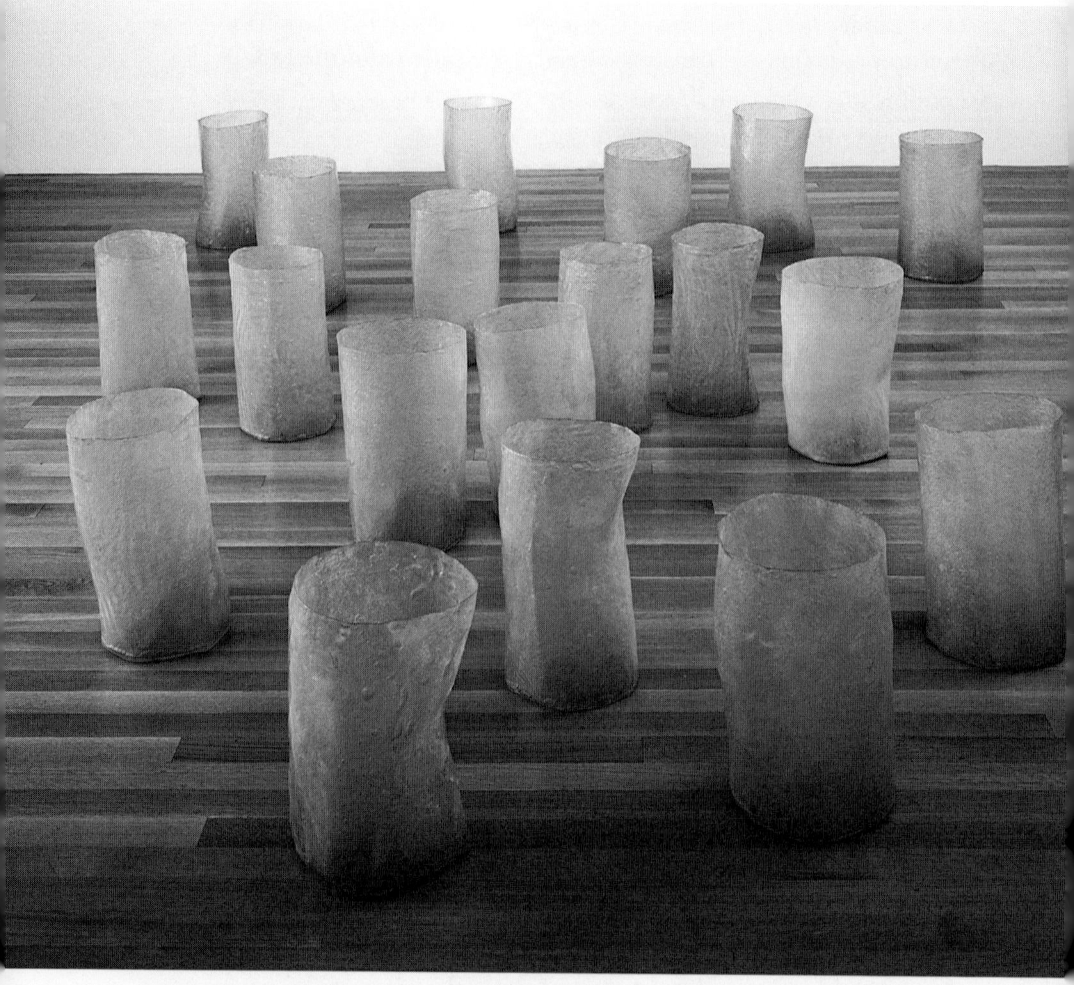

Figure 42. Eva Hesse, *Repetition Nineteen III* (1968), fiberglass, polyester resin, each unit height 48–50 cm, diameter 27.8–32.2 cm. Museum of Modern Art, New York, gift of Anita and Charles Blatt (1004.1969.a–s). © The Estate of Eva Hesse. Courtesy of Hauser & Wirth Zürich London. (Photo: The Museum of Modern Art/Licensed by SCALA/Art Resource, New York.)

wanted each bucket to be a less-than-perfect replica of the others and their arrangement to appear accidental: "irregular structure / random positioning on the floor," she notes on a study for the sculpture.[54] Each bucket mimics the next without being a substitute for it, which helps move the gaze from one to another. And because no bucket holds a privileged position—there is no privileged beginning, middle, or end—the viewer is encouraged to keep cycling through them.

If the overall structure of *Repetition Nineteen III* is reminiscient of the work Hesse did in Europe—in that it generates a movement from part to part—the individual units of the sculpture also harken back to the European work and its culmination in *Hang Up*: like *Hang Up*, the buckets in *Repetition Nineteen III* are "holding" yet "framing nothing." But if one lingers long enough, the emptiness of these buckets begins to acquire substance. A surprising fullness materializes where the milky translucence of the fiberglass transmits the light. The buckets hold the shadows of their own bulging bases—swollen, dark, and irregular—and hovering above that they hold a paler apparition made of nothing but the play of light through their walls. The longer one looks at them, the fuller they become, as if all their circling around an empty center put something there.

Many of Hesse's fiberglass forms have this tendency to generate the appearance of a solid core in what is in fact a hollow shell, their translucent outsides creating the illusion that there is something inside them.[55] In her drawings of *Repetition Nineteen*, Hesse experiments with the mass of the buckets: in some, they look like solid plugs (figure 43); in others, heavy shadows indicate that they are empty. In the final fiberglass version of the sculpture (*Repetition Nineteen III*)—Hesse made other versions with other materials—she maximizes the tension between these opposing possibilities, allowing fullness and emptiness to compete with one another.

In Rogier's *Deposition* the fullness and the emptiness of the center likewise compete. Looked at from one perspective, all the figures in Rogier's altarpiece gather reassuringly around a predictably central, singular, and authoritative model, but when our gaze descends

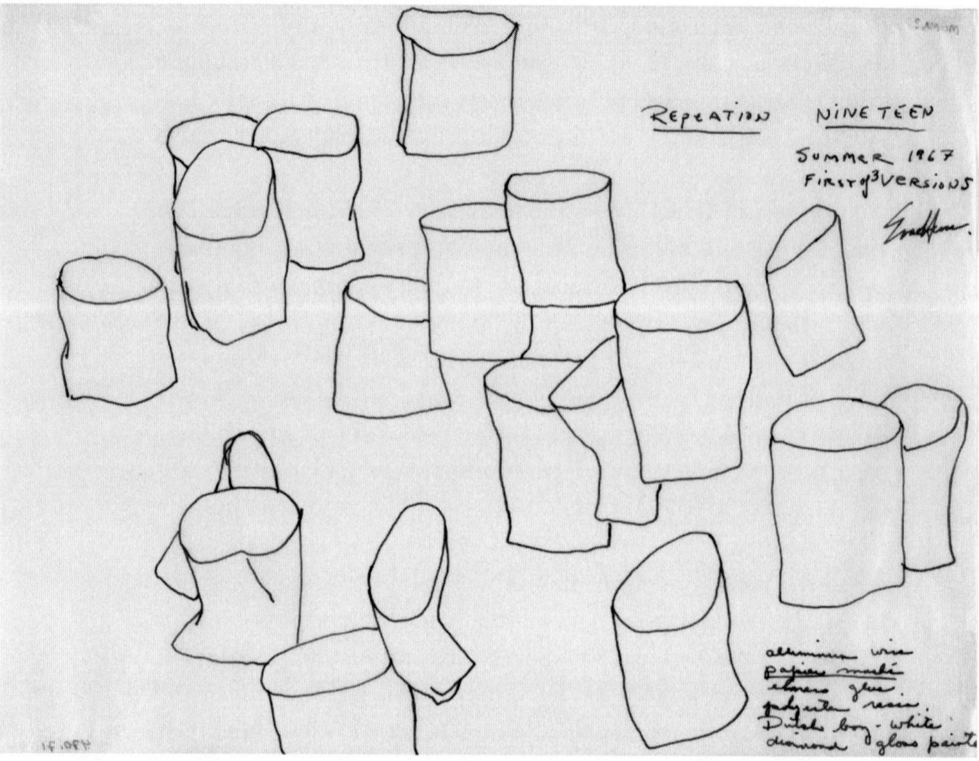

Figure 43. Eva Hesse, *Untitled (Study for Repetition Nineteen)* (1967), pencil and ink on tracing paper, 22.5 × 30.3 cm. Museum of Modern Art, New York, gift of the Eva Hesse Estate (470.1971). © The Estate of Eva Hesse. Courtesy of Hauser & Wirth Zürich London. (Photo: The Museum of Modern Art/Licensed by SCALA/Art Resource, New York.)

to that other center—the one just below Christ's commanding form—we discover there an empty space in the middle: now the bucket appears empty. The tension between these two centers suits the narrative, in which Joseph and Nicodemus show the body even as they move toward depositing it in the grave. This tension also suits the rhetorical structure of the painting, which displays the *imago Dei* for the viewer's veneration even as it lowers it into a series, in which it warrants that veneration neither more nor less than the next image. Only because it has two centers can Rogier's *Deposition* perform this double gesture: giving the body at the same time that it takes it away.

CHAPTER SIX

Broken Bodies in the Antonite Context

Although the empty center of Rogier's *Deposition* usually goes unmentioned in the art-historical literature, a painting of about 1490 by the anonymous Cologne painter known as the Master of the St. Bartholomew Altar suggests that earlier viewers took note of it. The Bartholomew Master adopted the general outlines of Rogier's composition but enlarged the space between the Virgin and Christ so that it hollows out a good quarter of the scene (plate 4). By enlarging it and ringing it with lost limbs, the Bartholomew Master transformed the opening between these two figures into an iconoclastic wound in the body of his painting.

The Bartholomew Master's adaptation of Rogier's composition reflects the hospital context for which the Bartholomew Master's painting was probably made. At the turn of the sixteenth century, Rogier's altarpiece still stood on the high altar of Our Lady Outside the Walls in Louvain. Probably born and trained in the Netherlands before moving to Cologne, the Bartholomew Master may well have seen Rogier's altarpiece firsthand.[1] If not, he would have been familiar with it through an intermediary image.[2] The Bartholomew Master modified Rogier's *Deposition* to fit a context that has been identified based on the four Tau crosses adorned with bells that hang from the gilded tracery on either side of his painting.

The Tau cross had various associations in the Middle Ages but was above all the attribute of St. Anthony and is here evidence that the Antonites were responsible for commissioning the Bartholomew Master's *Deposition*.[3] The bells that hang from the Tau crosses in this

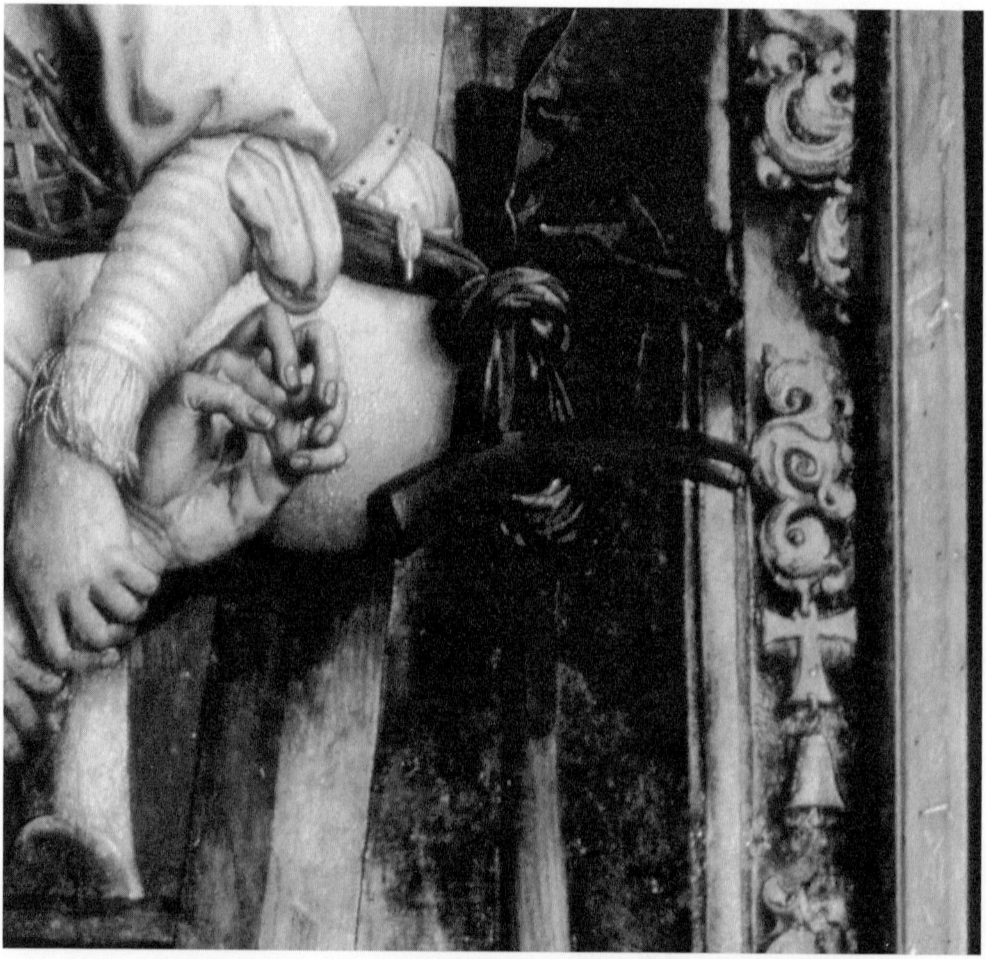

Figure 44. Detail from Plate 4: Master of the St. Bartholomew Altar, *Deposition from the Cross* (ca. 1490), oil on panel, 227 × 210 cm. Musée du Louvre, Paris. (Photo: Erich Lessing/Art Resource, New York.)

painting are also associated with the Antonites, who had the privilege of letting their pigs run free, which they did but not without tying identifying bells around their necks. As if to call attention to this easily overlooked allusion to the patrons of the altarpiece and to play on the logic of Rogier's repeated forms, the hammer elaborately tied to the waist of the helper-figure perched on the ladder in the Bartholomew Master's painting reiterates the shape of the Tau cross beside it (figure 44).[4]

We do not know which of the Antonite houses commissioned the Bartholomew Master's *Deposition*. Before being transferred to the Church of the Val-de-Grâce in Paris in 1763, the painting was in the sacristy of the Jesuits in the Rue Saint-Antoine of the same city, where it may have been already in the sixteenth century. This has led some to speculate that the commission originated in Paris. Others have suggested that the altarpiece originally belonged to the Antonite Hospital in Arnhem.[5] Without sufficient evidence to link the painting to one house in particular, our understanding of the altarpiece's original setting is limited to what can be said about the order in general.

The Antonites traced their history back to the eleventh century, when Anthony's relics were translated from Constantinople to La-Motte-Saint-Didier in the province of the Dauphiné. In 1095, La-Motte-Saint-Didier—renamed Saint-Antoine-en-Viennois—became the motherhouse of the order, which adopted the rule of St. Augustine in 1247.[6] By the end of the fifteenth century, there were more than 370 Antonite hospitals located throughout Europe.[7] From its inception, the order was responsible for the care of people suffering from the disease known as St. Anthony's fire or the holy fire (*ignis sacer*) because of the burning sensations and gangrene it caused in the extremities of the afflicted.[8] Severe intestinal pain, hallucinations, and muscle spasms were among the other symptoms of the disease. Sigebert de Gembloux describes its devastating effects as it swept through Europe in 1089: "It was an epidemic year, particularly in the western part of Lorraine, where many whose insides were afflicted with the holy fire rotted in their ravaged limbs, which were as black as coal. They either died miserably or went on with a miserable life after their rotten hands and feet had been removed."[9]

Periodic outbreaks of the disease in Europe are recorded from the eleventh century down to the twentieth, including major occurrences in 1473, 1494, and 1509.[10] It was only in the seventeenth century that the cause of St. Anthony's fire, now known as ergotism, was identified as a mold that contaminates rye and that was inadvertently consumed when food shortages forced people to eat old grain. The disease remained without cure until the invention of penicillin in the twentieth century.[11]

The Antonites treated the afflicted with St. Vinage, a wine prepared each year on Ascension day by being brought into contact with Anthony's relics.[12] Medicinal herbs considered cold and dry, including verbena, sage, plantain, and poppy, were used to soothe the burning sensations.[13] When these remedies failed, the Antonites resorted to amputation of the gangrenous limbs.[14] In his *Field Book for the Care of Wounds* (1517), a manual for military surgeons with information on the extraction of bullets, arrows, and other things, the surgeon Hans von Gersdorff describes conducting hundreds of amputations at the Antonite hospital in Strasbourg.[15] The book contains a woodcut illustration of amputation with the caption: "There is an art to cutting off an arm or leg to drive out St. Anthony's fire" (figure 45).[16] Because of the practice of amputation, the Antonites' patients were sometimes referred to as the dismembered.[17]

When Pico della Mirandola's nephew Giovanni Francesco visited the cloister of Saint-Antoine-en-Viennois in 1502, he wrote: "We saw scorched limbs as well as bones suspended, as an enduring example, on the doorposts of the holy sanctuaries."[18] The practice of hanging votive *images* of afflicted limbs was common at the time, but what Giovanni saw seems to have been real body parts preserved by the desiccating effects of ergotism. Two Benedictine visitors to the same hospital in the seventeenth century confirm Giovanni's report: "he showed us feet and hands that had been amputated a hundred years ago that are like those that he amputated every day, which is to say black and completely dry."[19] If amputated limbs were put on

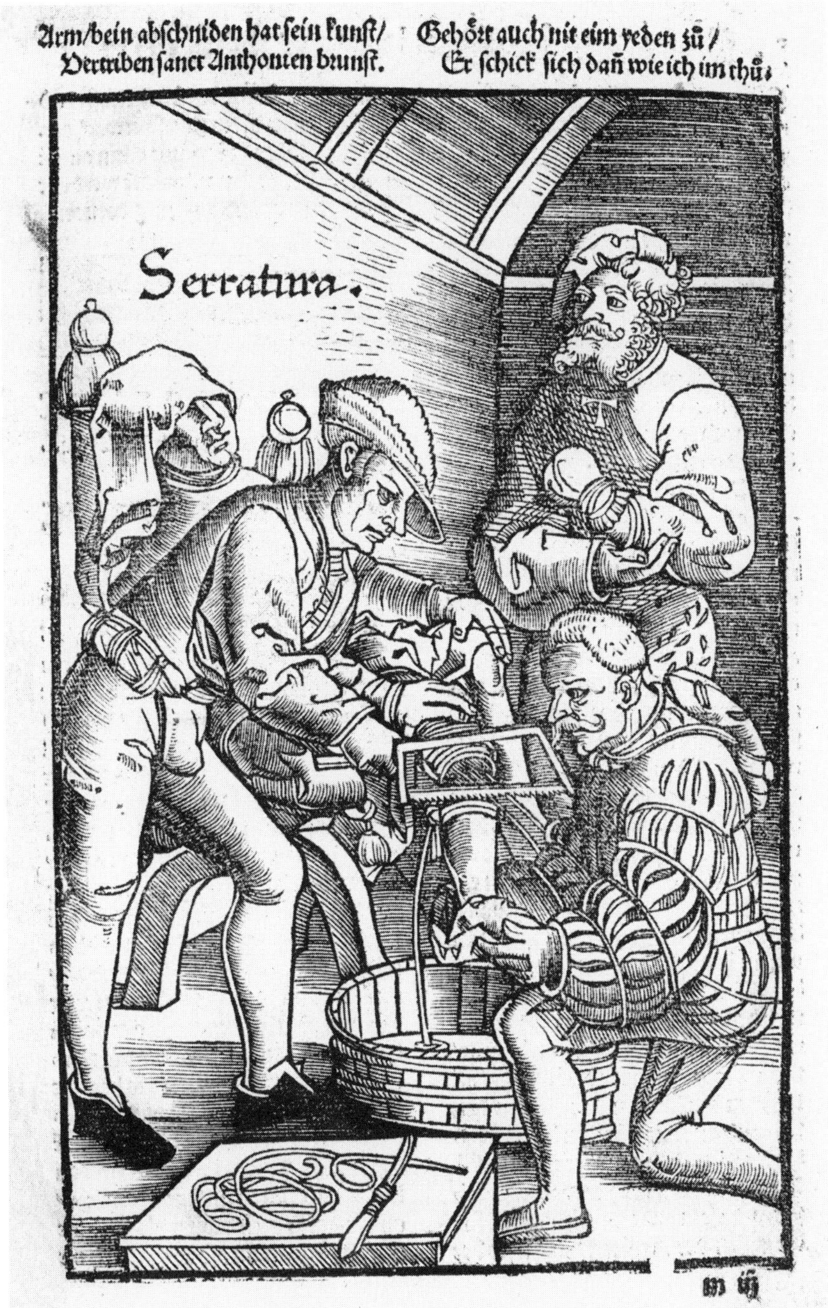

Figure 45. Woodcut illustrating amputation, first illustration in Hans von Gersdorff, *Fieldbook for the Care of Wounds*, Strasbourg (1517). National Library of Medicine, Bethesda, MD. (Photo: Light, Incorporated.)

display, so too were the bodies to which they had formerly belonged. The reforms of the Antonite order enacted in 1478 stipulate: "Let [the men and women] wear their garments or habits in such a way that the amputation of their limbs be apparent, so that, through this, people may be induced to greater devotion and compassion and reverence for Saint Anthony."[20] In this way, the martyrs of St. Anthony, as they were also called, became spectacles of their own sanctified suffering, their mutilated bodies serving as reminders of that saint's wrath as well as his mercy.[21]

At about seven-and-a-half feet by seven feet, the Bartholomew Master's *Deposition* is large enough to have been the central panel of a monumental triptych for an Antonite chapel, where it would have been displayed to the sick residents of the hospital. The 1478 reforms mandate that "each patient be required for every canonical hour to say twelve Our Fathers and as many Ave Marias, and in the church if it is possible."[22] In the Bartholomew Master's *Deposition*, the sick would have found a body much like their own and very much *unlike* the figure of Christ in Rogier's *Deposition*, whose contour can be traced almost without interruption and can be retraced in the figure of the Virgin. In Rogier's painting, the contour of Christ's body is broken only where Nicodemus supports his lower legs.

In the Bartholomew Master's painting, by contrast, Christ's torso is severed from his pelvis by Nicodemus's arm, his thighs from his shins by Joseph's hand, his left arm from his shoulder by Nicodemus's head, his left forearm from his hand by the helper-figure, his right forearm from his hand by the woman in green, and his right arm from his body by the shadow of his own head. Below this fragmented body, another collection of amputated limbs rims the vacuous center: Nicodemus's brown-stockinged left leg perched on the bottom rung of the ladder, Joseph's oddly placed left leg with its flesh-colored sock slipping down from a red-stockinged knee, two empty shoes, a femur and a skull (indicating that this is Golgotha), Christ's loincloth, and the Virgin's strangely limp gown.

Thrown into this mix of body parts and objects are the limbs of a massive ladder. As if they were prostheses, the stiles of this ladder take the place of Nicodemus's darkly clad legs, which nearly disappear into the confusion. Wooden prostheses—like the ones worn by the beggars in a painting by Pieter Bruegel the Elder—must have been a familiar sight in the Antonite context (figure 46). For viewers in that context, the depiction of the bodies in the Bartholomew Master's painting, particularly the body of Christ, would have struck a cord. Instead of presenting a unified image of the *imago Dei*, the Bartholomew Master's *Deposition* showed the sick an image cobbled together from limbs subject to the same dismemberment and prosthetic substitution as were their own.

The Limits of the Senses

The person standing before Rogier's *Deposition* has a more complete view of Christ's body than do any of the participants in the event—much more complete, for instance, than that of the Magdalene, who from her position at far right is only able to see Christ's wounded feet. She is the person perhaps most intently focused on the body and yet least able to see more than fragments of it. But hers is only the most extreme situation: none of the participants have a good view of what is happening. By placing us squarely in front of the body, Rogier affords us the feeling of having transcended the limitations of vision that affect the original witnesses to the event, and the Virgin's repetition of her son's fully visible form strengthens the impression that our view of it is complete.

The Bartholomew Master does away with this repetition of forms. Although the Virgin still participates in her son's unconsciousness, the physical likeness between them is gone. She is limp and shrunken in contrast to his bloated dimensions. Curving away from one another, these two incommensurate bodies form a circle. Along with the rhyme between mother and son has disappeared any sense that our view of Christ is complete. Our lowered vantage point (we are shown the underside of Christ's looming torso) brings us closer to the scene, but that intimacy costs us the privileged prospect we have before Rogier's painting.

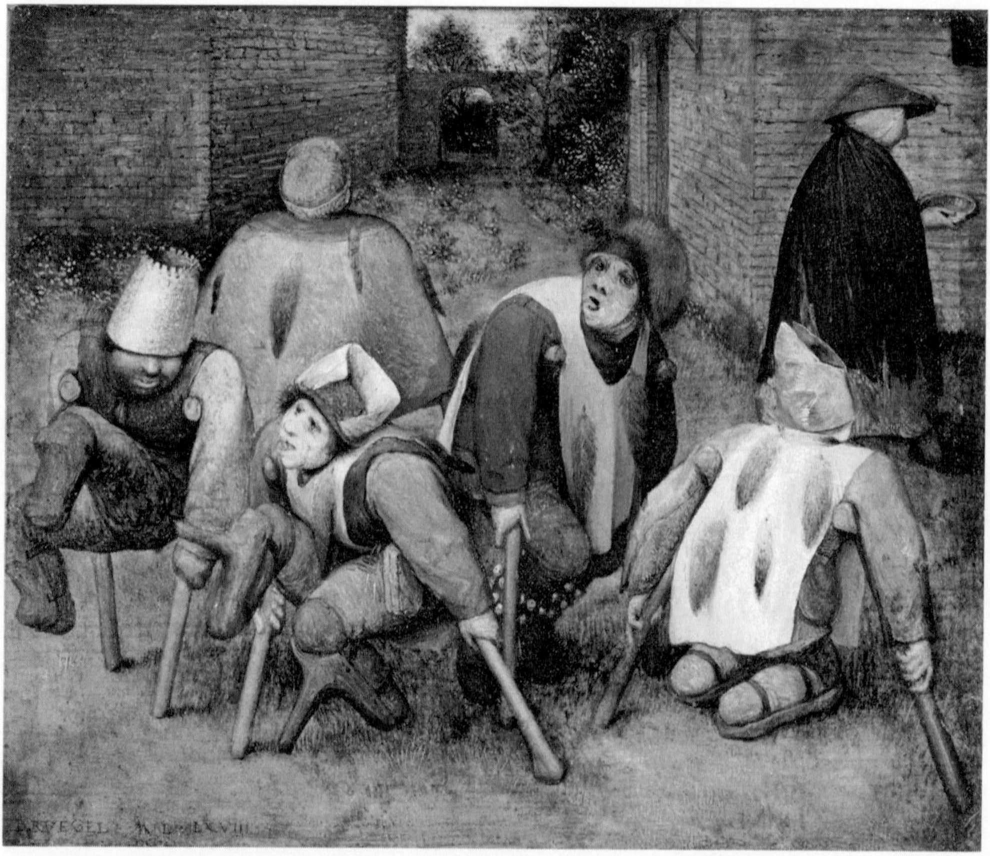

Figure 46. Pieter Bruegel the Elder, *The Beggars* (1568), oil on panel, 185×215 cm. Musée de Louvre, Paris. (Photo: Erich Lessing/Art Resource, New York.)

In the Bartholomew Master's *Deposition*, the difficulty of catching sight of more than fragments of Christ's body—a difficulty we share with the participants in the event—coincides with a problem of touch. Even the men who remove the body from the cross enjoy only limited tactile access to it, and not for lack of trying. In Rogier's painting, these men hold the body almost tentatively, as if touch were not a legitimate form of access to it. At every point of contact there is an intervening bit of cloth. If Rogier's figures treat the touching of the body of Christ as a delicate matter, the Bartholomew Master's cannot get enough of it. We find the painter's customary elongation of fingers and the removal of protective cloth from between hands and Christ's limbs: Mary Salome grabs Christ's right arm and presses it to her cheek; Nicodemus circles Christ's massive torso; the helper-figure above clings to Christ's arm with both hands; Joseph has pulled back his sleeve to take hold of Christ's shins, while the Magdalene has stripped the glove from her right hand specifically, it seems, to lay it bare on Christ's ankle; too far away from the body to touch it, the woman behind the Magdalene eagerly takes hold of the metonymic crown of thorns. But all of this uninhibited touching only demonstrates how little of the body a hand or even two can grasp. The Bartholomew Master emphasizes touch only to drive home the point that it obtains no more than fragments of what it seeks. And, for the viewer of the painting, who cannot touch the body at all, even these fragments lie out of reach.

All the touching in the Bartholomew Master's painting would seem to be motivated by a desire for sensuous proof of Christ's divinity—the kind of proof that the apostle Thomas demanded. In John's account of Thomas's request to see and touch Christ's wounds, the wound becomes the site where sensuous evidence miraculously gives way to an understanding of Christ's intangible divinity.[23] Upon being shown and granted permission to touch Christ's wounds—without, it seems, actually touching them—Thomas' doubts are allayed, and he exclaims, "My Lord and my God" (John 20.28). Christ responds to Thomas' epiphany by praising those who find their way to that divinity without the aid of the senses: "Have you believed because you have seen me? Blessed are those who have not seen and yet have come to believe" (John 20.29).

Augustine takes up this theme when he argues that the apostles could only really know the divinity of Christ after he had ascended to heaven and disappeared from view. Christ's body, he explains, was an impediment to knowledge of his divine nature: "It was necessary that the form of the slave should be taken away from their sight, for by gazing upon it they thought that Christ was only that which they saw.... This is also the meaning of His words: 'Do not touch me, for I have not yet ascended to the Father' (John 20.17). For touch sets as it were a limit to knowledge."[24]

Erasmus follows this iconoclastic line of thought, bringing it to bear on the controversies of his own time. In his colloquy *An Examination Concerning the Faith*, a conversation between an Erasmian and a Lutheran, the former asks, "why did [Christ] will to leave the earth?" The Lutheran replies: "that we might all love him spiritually and no one on earth claim Christ exclusively for himself.... For if men now are so pleased with themselves on account of the colour or shape of a garment, and when some boast of the blood or foreskin of Christ and the milk of the Virgin Mary, what do you think would happen had he remained on earth, clothed, eating, talking? What disagreements would have come about through those things that pertain to the body!"[25] Taking pleasure in the color and shape of garments is perhaps a reference to the veneration of images; boasting of holy blood and milk is certainly a reference to the cult of relics. The Lutheran suggests (and the Erasmian seems to agree) that images and relics generate pride and divisive competition by creating the illusion that Christ can be possessed.

In the Bartholomew Master's *St. Thomas Altarpiece*, Christ guides the apostle's two possessive fingers deep into his wound (figures 47–48).[26] The wound, which falls precisely in the middle of the central panel, invites this touch. Not only the wound but also the buttonholes in Thomas' sleeve and the surrounding folds of cloth encourage the plunging exploration to which Thomas' doubting fingers are given over. Here, at the very center of the composition, Thomas'

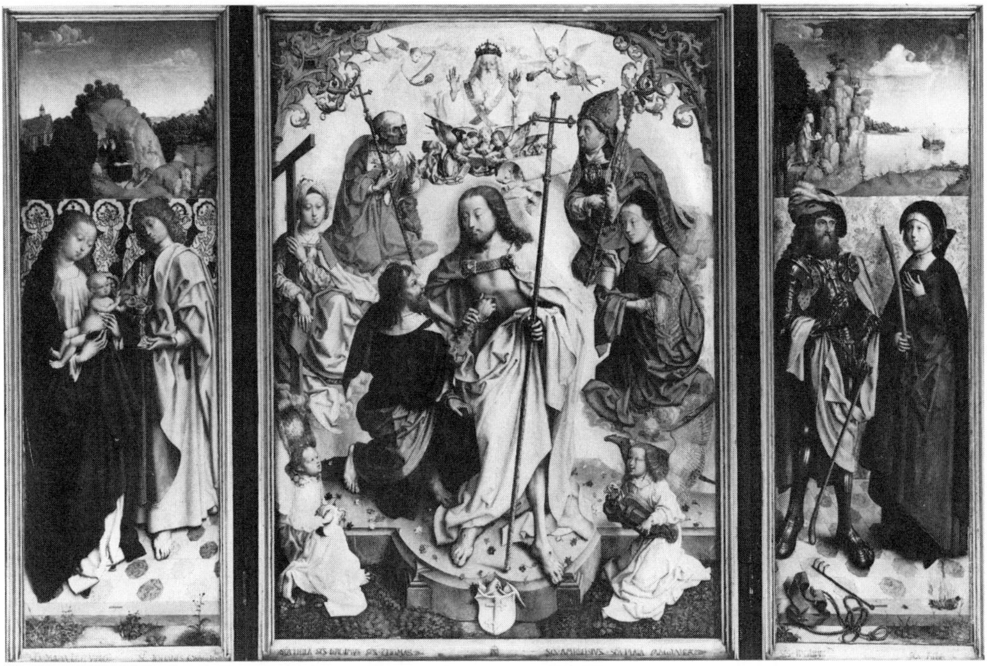

Figure 47. Master of the St. Bartholomew Altar, *St. Thomas Altarpiece* (ca. 1495–1500), interior, oil on panel, 143 × 200 cm. Wallraf-Richartz-Museum, Cologne. (Photo: Rheinisches Bildarchiv.)

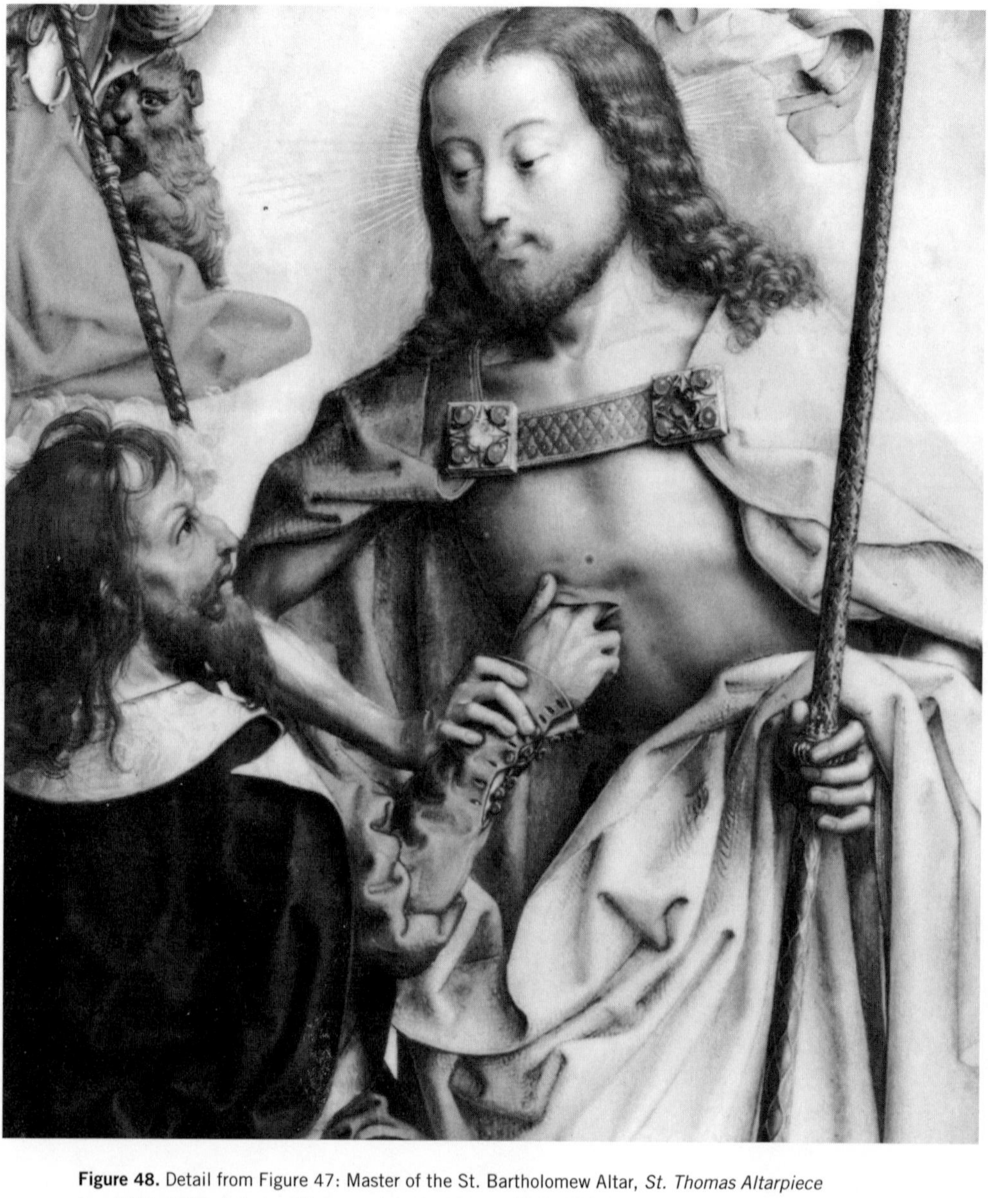

Figure 48. Detail from Figure 47: Master of the St. Bartholomew Altar, *St. Thomas Altarpiece* (ca. 1495–1500), interior, oil on panel, 143 × 200 cm. Wallraf-Richartz-Museum, Cologne. (Photo: Rheinisches Bildarchiv.)

experience of the body becomes an analogy for the viewer's experience of the painting. According to the Gospel account, when Thomas sees the wounds and receives permission to touch them, he discovers something available to neither hand nor eye—which is to say, something that cannot be pictured. But while Thomas may (paradoxically) move beyond the senses in his probing of the wound, the viewer who looks at the Bartholomew Master's painting and imagines touching the wound represented there will have a harder time extricating herself or himself from the sensuous realm. Although the Bartholomew Master pictures a story of *overcoming the senses*, his picturing of that story never stops appealing to them.

Equally ambivalent in its appeal to the senses is a strange type of devotional imagery that began to appear in Books of Hours and woodcuts in the fourteenth century: Christ's side-wound pictured in isolation. The wound in the *Psalter and Hours of Bonne de Luxembourg* (ca. 1345) registers as an aniconic opening in the blue and gold ground of the manuscript page; the picture of a hole in the body here becomes a hole in the image that takes away that body so that the viewer can experience something else—perhaps something as intangible as what Thomas touched. Yet insofar as this wound is as tall as the cross that appears beside it, which is to say roughly as tall as Christ, it itself becomes a body (figure 49).[27] The wound's verticality and bilateral symmetry contribute to this anthropomorphizing effect—healing, so to speak, the iconoclastic wound in the manuscript page.

Just as it does in Bonne de Luxembourg's psalter, the red wound in a late-fifteenth-century German woodcut opens a tear in the fabric of the image. But, again just as it does in the psalter, the anthropomorphic character of this wound sutures that opening (figure 50). Decorated with hands, feet, and a Veronica cloth for its head, the red wound is filled with a cross and heart and flanked by text scrolls. The scroll on the left reads: "This is the length and width of Christ's wound which was pierced in his side on the Cross. Whoever kisses this wound with remorse and sorrow, also with devotion, will have as often as he does this, seven years indulgence

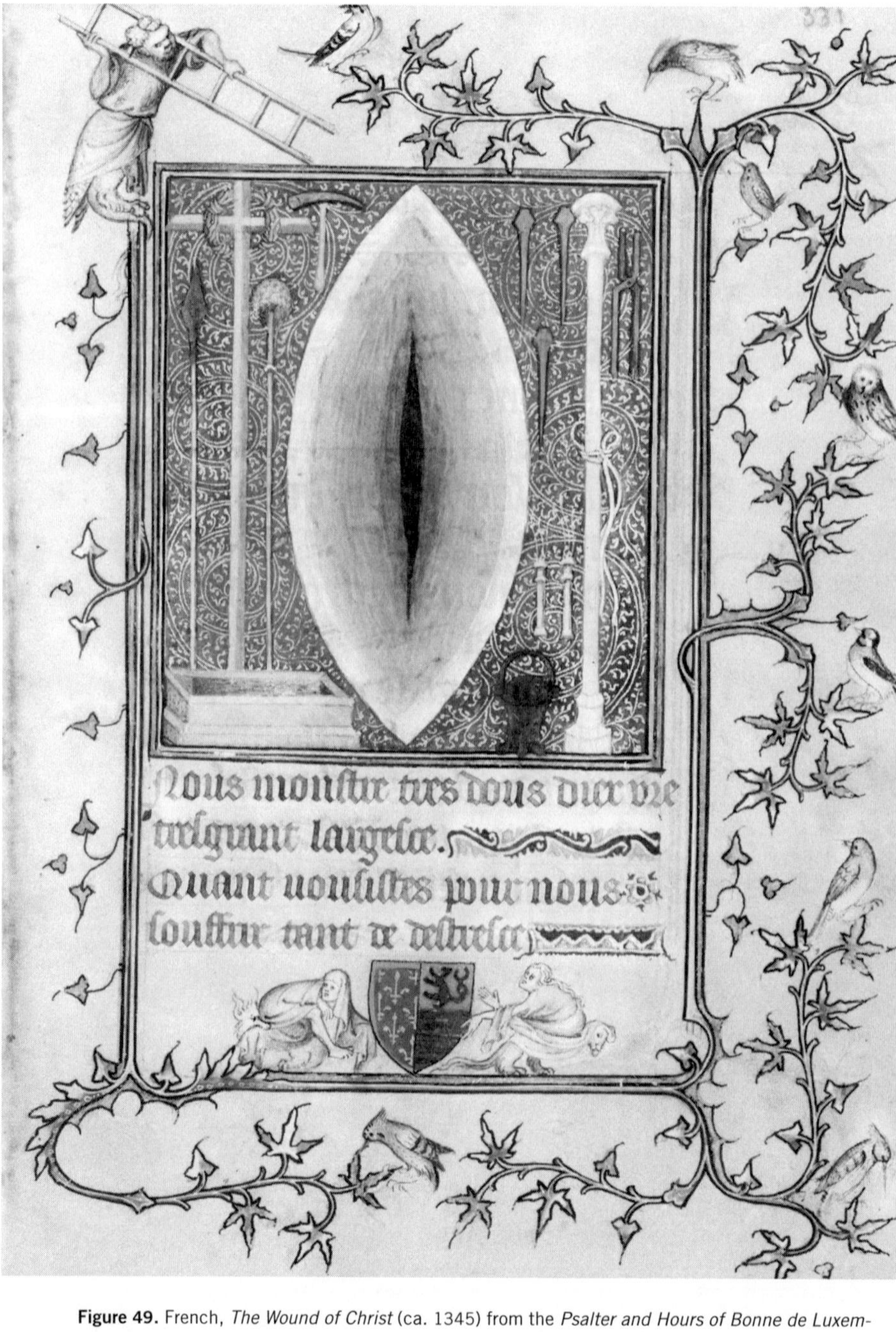

Figure 49. French, *The Wound of Christ* (ca. 1345) from the *Psalter and Hours of Bonne de Luxembourg*, tempera and gold on parchment, 12.6 × 9 cm. Metropolitan Museum of Art, The Cloisters Collection, New York, 1969 (69.86), fol. 331r. (Photo: The Metropolitan Museum of Art.)

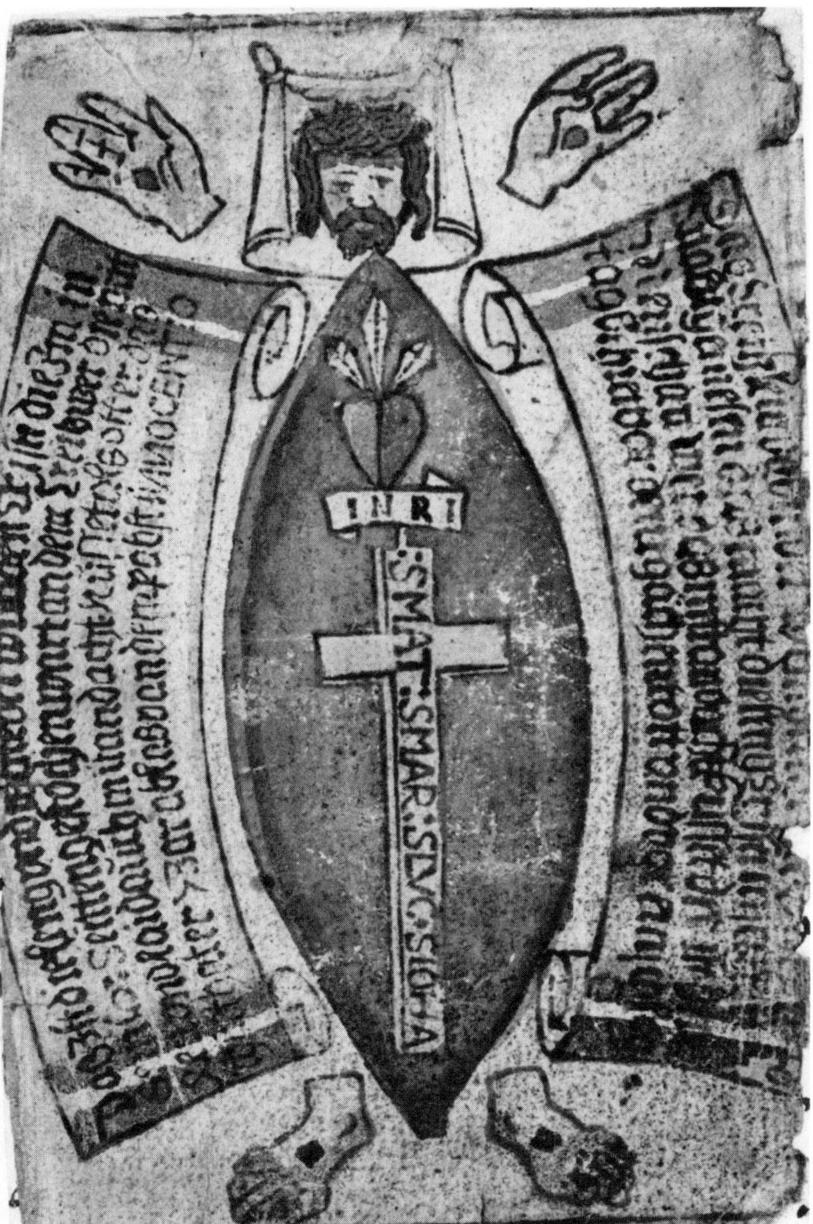

Figure 50. Southeast German, *The Measure of the Side Wound* (ca. 1484–1492), colored woodcut, 12 × 8.1 cm. National Gallery of Art, Washington, D.C., Rosenwald Collection. (Photo: Board of Trustees, Washington, D.C., National Gallery of Art.)

from Pope Innocent." The scroll on the right says: "This little cross standing in Christ's wound measured 40 times makes the length of Christ in his humanity. Whoever kisses it with devotion shall be protected from sudden death or misfortune."[28] Inviting the viewer to understand the wound's length in relation to Christ's own height and to enjoy the wound corporally, that is, with kisses, the scrolls ensure the synecdochic substitution of the anthropomorphic wound for the full body.[29] This hole in the body—which is also a hole in the image—becomes, thereby, a new body and a new image.

In the *St. Thomas Altarpiece*, the Bartholomew Master represents the supersensory something that Thomas discovers in the depths of the side-wound in the sensuous form of musical angels, fragrant flowers, and a vision of the Holy Trinity; in the *Deposition*, by contrast, he pictures that supersensory something—which everyone in the painting seems to be trying yet failing to grasp—as a wound in the image. The *Deposition* is not a picture of Christ's side-wound as such; rather, it is analogous to such pictures in its iconoclastic opening of a hole that asks the viewer to see beyond what can be seen. But it is analogous too in its generation of new bodies and new images: just as we saw the image of the isolated side-wound plug its own hole with its own anthropomorphic shape, the iconoclastic wound in the Bartholomew Master's *Deposition* will turn out to be a powerful generator of new forms to fill the vacuum that it creates.

Vignette: Hans Bellmer's Dolls (ca. 1935)

In 1933, Hans Bellmer assembled a doll out of a metal and wood armature; several articulated limbs; a head, hands and feet carved from wood; and a plaster torso with a "panorama" showing tiny dioramas of "suppressed girlish thoughts."[30] In 1934, Bellmer published *Die Puppe*, a limited edition book with ten photographs charting his construction and manipulation of the doll. That same year, eighteen photographs appeared in the winter issue of the Surrealist journal *Minotaure* as "Doll—Variations on the Assemblage of an Articulated Minor" (figure 51). Published in series, the photographs document the doll's powers of division and multiplication, the means by which it evades being recognized any better than is necessary to trigger certain misprisions.

Bellmer explains: "The main thing to retain from the monstrous dictionary of analogies / antagonisms, which constitute the dictionary of the image, is that any given detail, such as a leg, is perceptible, accessible to memory, and available, (in short is REAL), only if desire does not fatally take it for a leg. The object identical to itself remains devoid of reality."[31] By continually altering its position relative to other parts of the body, Bellmer prevents the leg from falling into fatal self-identity: "It takes only a step for the leg, solitarily perceived and appropriated by memory, to begin triumphantly living its own life and dividing itself freely.... It is free to cling to a head, to sit down, cephalopod-like, on her divided breasts."[32]

In 1935, Bellmer disassembled this first doll and from its parts and others made a second that was even better equipped to "divide itself freely."[33] At its center was a ball joint, to which two pairs of legs, a pair of arms, an upper torso, two pelvises, an extra torso with four breasts, and a second pelvis could be attached—enough parts to preclude the cohering of a human being in any simple sense. A hoop sometimes appears in Bellmer's photographs of this doll, giving a contour to the missing center around which all these solitarily perceived extremities turn. Although it has no arms to cling with, the doll, arrayed against a plaid cloth in a photograph of 1935, adheres to the curvature of this hoop (figure 52). Her volitionless compliance with this circle makes *its* emptiness seem that much more like her own distended self.

In another photograph, the doll has become two pairs of girl's legs that hinge to meet the arc of a tree branch (figure 53). "It takes only a step for the leg, solitarily perceived... to begin triumphantly living its own life," Bellmer says. But what kind of life is this? What kind of being? That this is a *living* being is suggested by the muscular tension of the thighs. Where tree branches brush the inside of those thighs, this questioning takes an erotic turn: what kind of being is experiencing that sensation? In wondering this, one feels the full strangeness of the absence of the central nervous system, the groin,

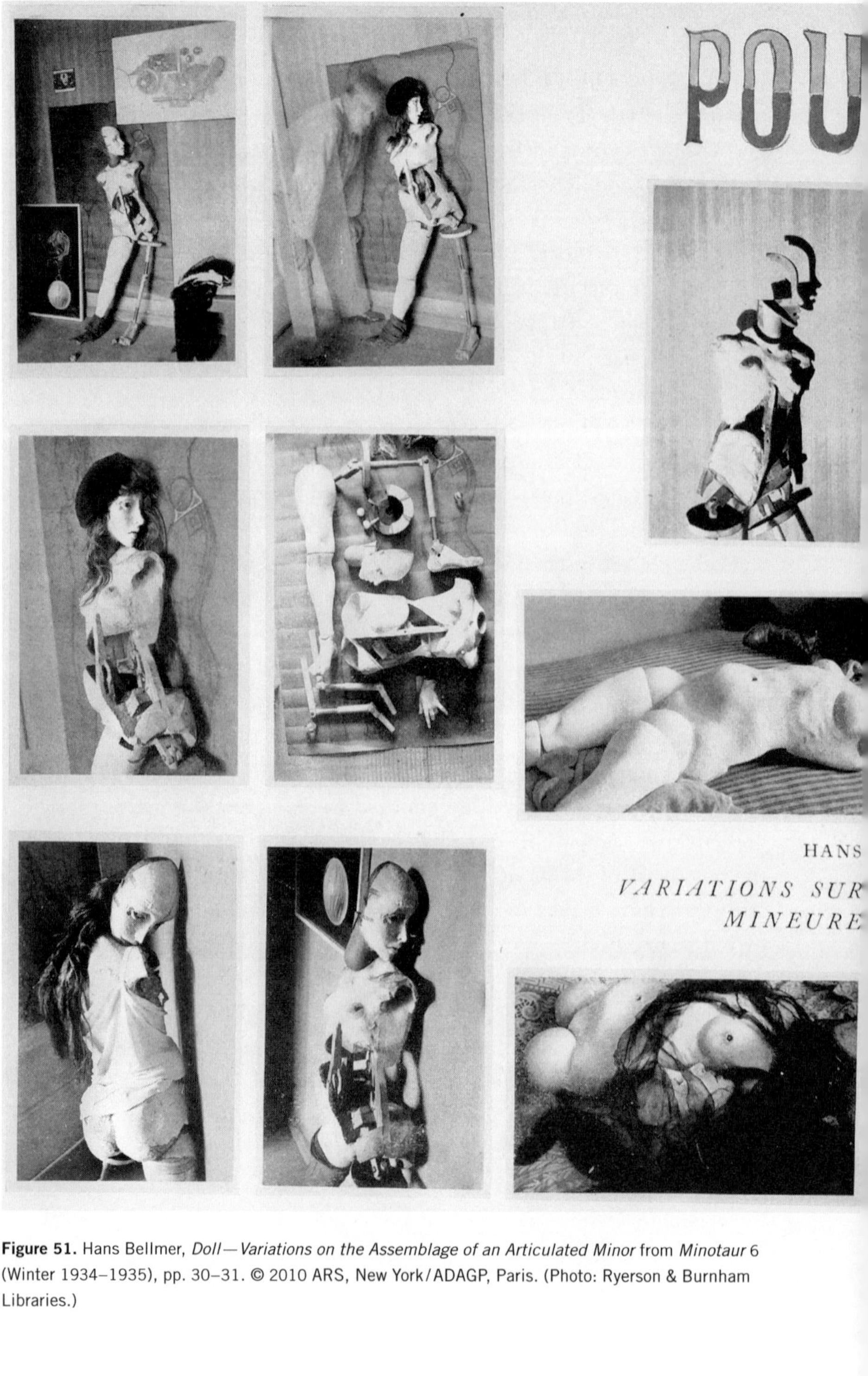

Figure 51. Hans Bellmer, *Doll—Variations on the Assemblage of an Articulated Minor* from *Minotaur* 6 (Winter 1934–1935), pp. 30–31. © 2010 ARS, New York/ADAGP, Paris. (Photo: Ryerson & Burnham Libraries.)

PÉE

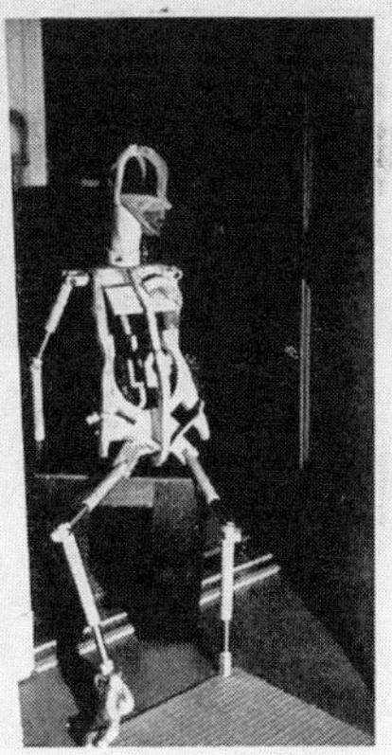

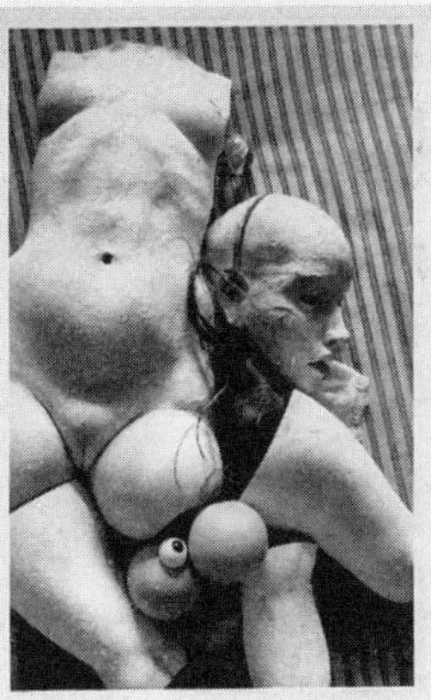

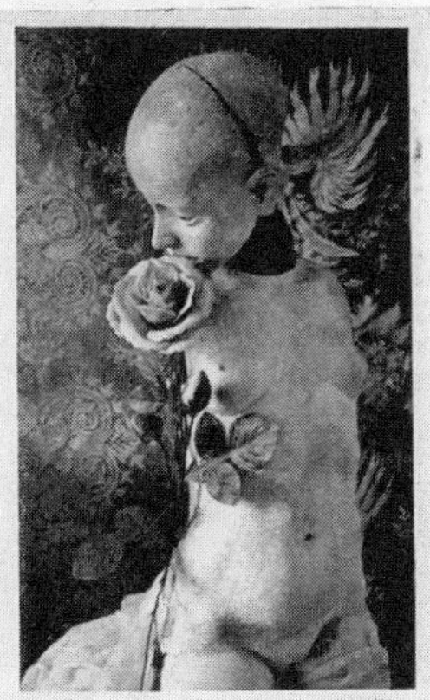

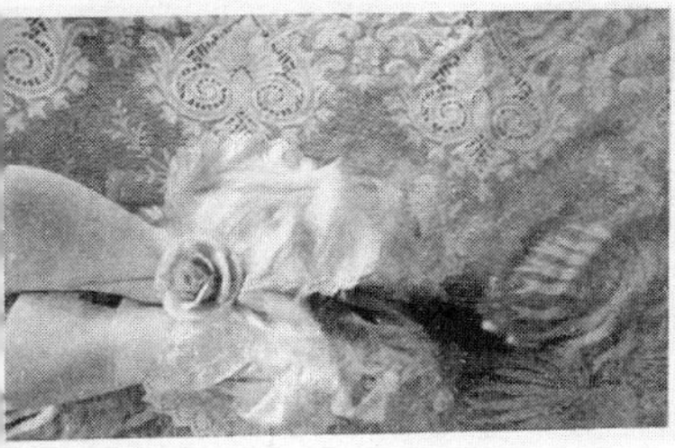

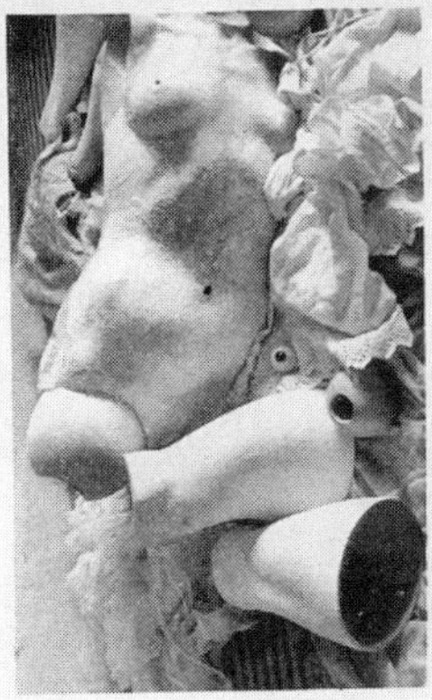

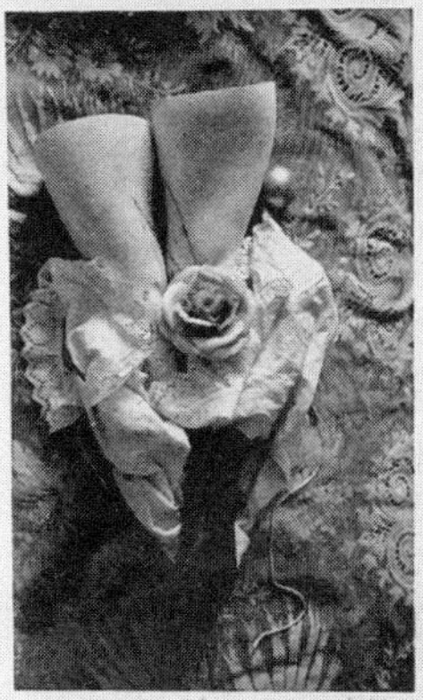

BELLMER

LE MONTAGE D'UNE
ARTICULÉE

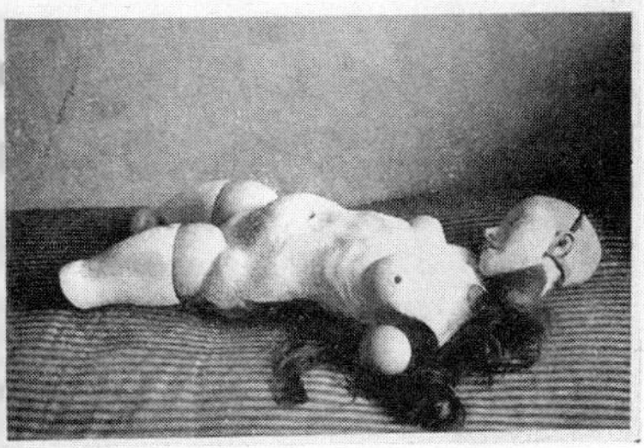

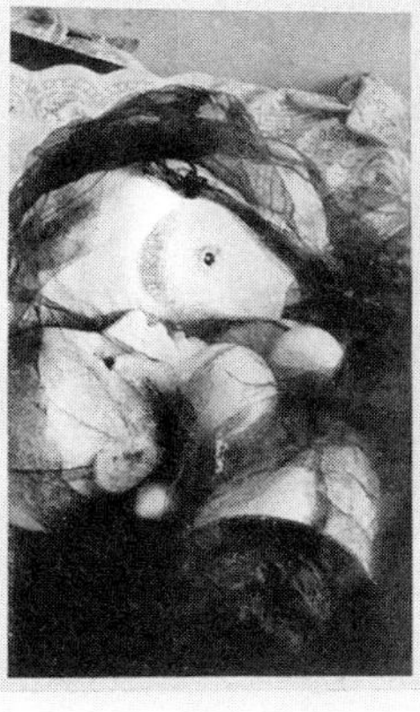

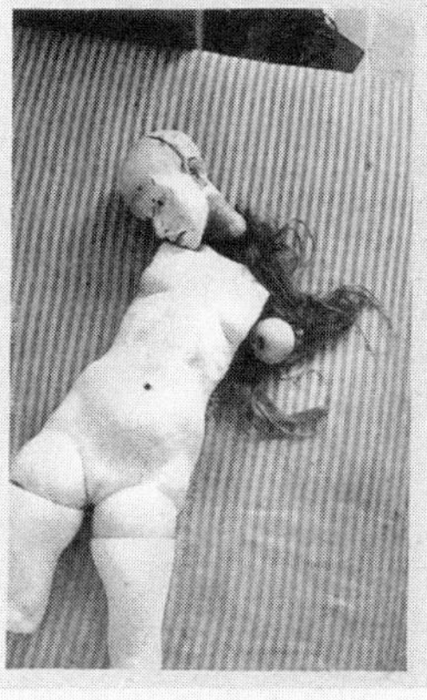

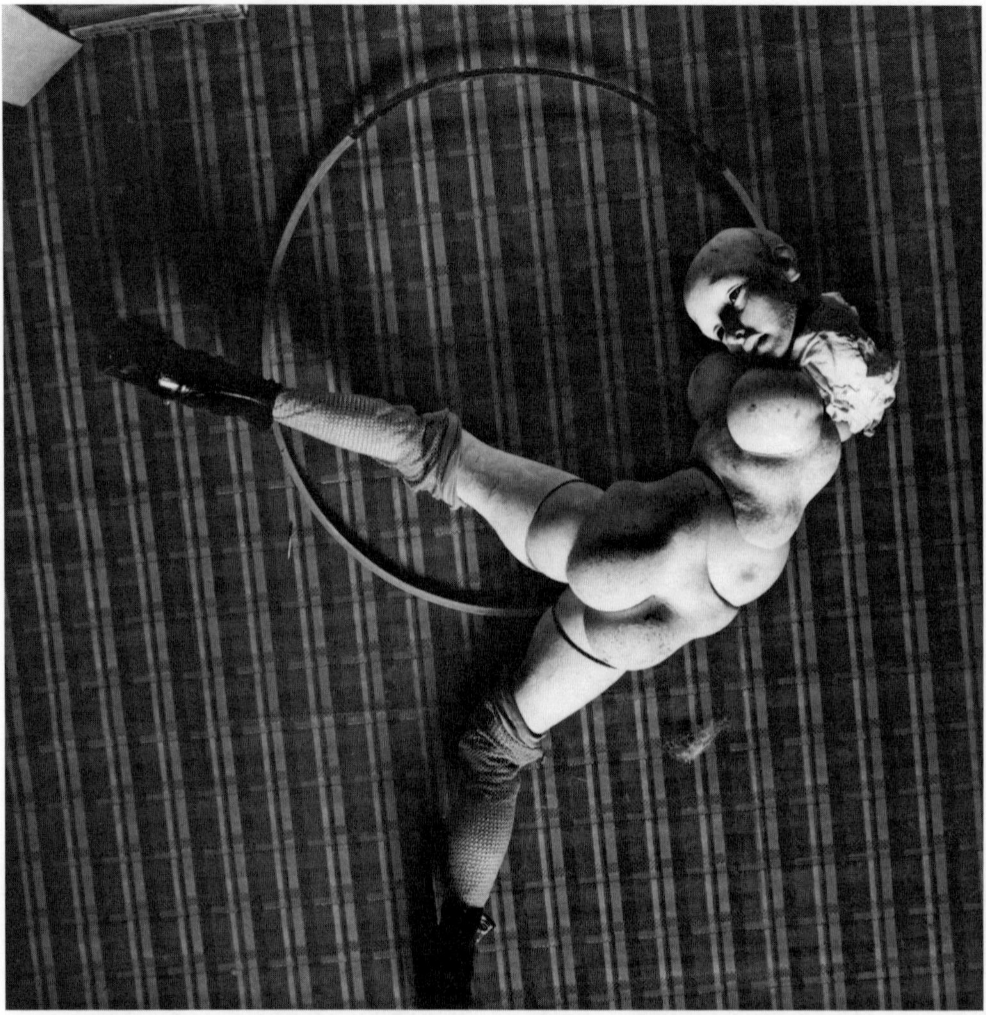

Figure 52. Hans Bellmer, *The Doll* (1935), gelatin silver print, 25.4 × 25.7 cm. International Center of Photography, New York, gift of Mr. Herbert Lust, 1987. © 2010 ARS, New York/ADAGP, Paris. (Photo: International Center of Photography.)

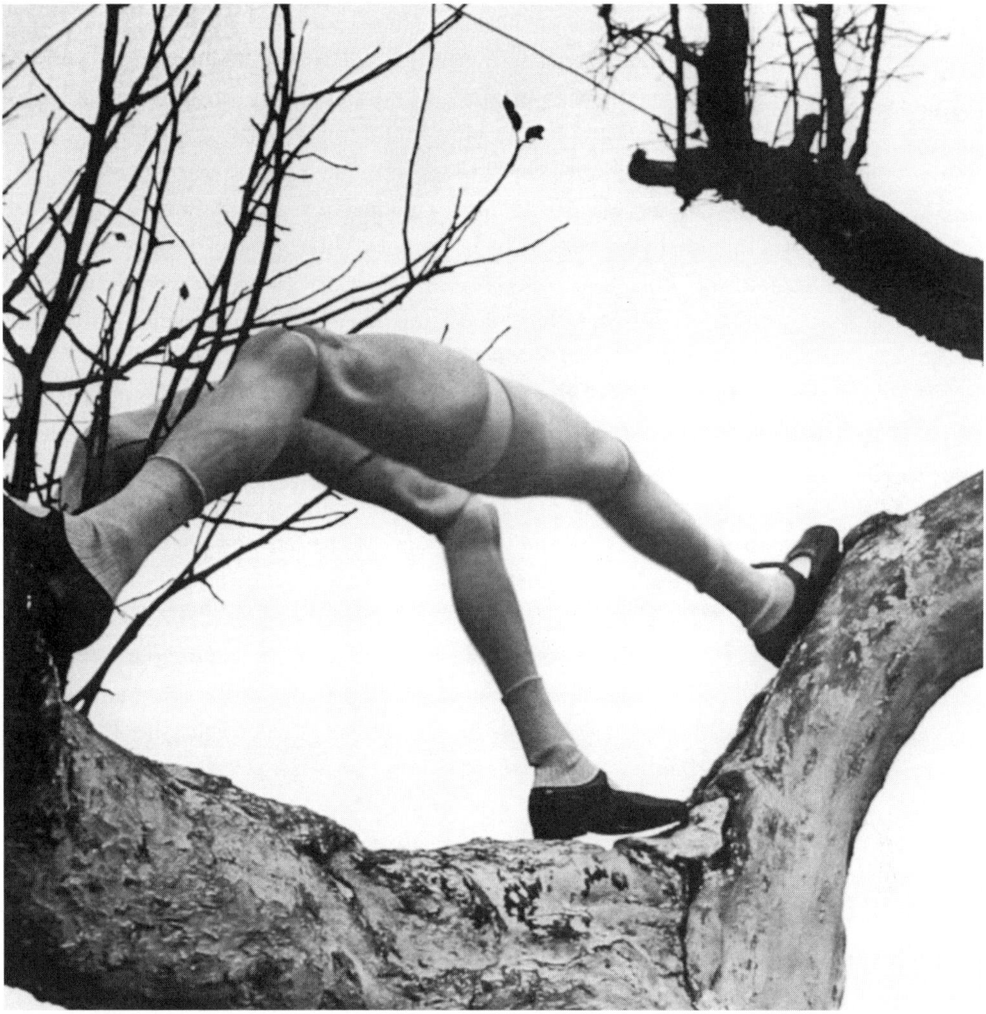

Figure 53. Hans Bellmer, *The Doll* (1935), black and white photograph, 16.2×16.2 cm. Collection of R. Aldoux, Paris. © 2010 ARS, New York/ADAGP, Paris. (Photo: Jacqueline Hyde. Courtesy of Mme Rodica Aldoux.)

and guts. The brushing of the inner thighs makes the uncanny elision of the genitals particularly strange: one feels that something is missing. With its opening onto a bright patch of sky circumscribed by limbs, this photograph is a rather literal image of the female body as castrated. This might, then, seem to make a protective fetish of Bellmer's doll, but Hal Foster has shown just how well Bellmer's doll eludes the fetishist's gaze: "The notion of a 'dictionary of analogues-antagonisms' does not imply a fixing of desire (as in the Freudian account of fetishism); rather its shifting drives the many recombinations of the dolls."[34] The endless recombinations of the doll's parts allow it to slip free of the gaze that would fix it such that it could provide protection against what one does not want to see.

The Bartholomew Master's *Deposition* is also an image of castration without a reliably protective fetish. A hyperbolically phallic male corpse looms over the empty folds of the Virgin's pink gown, but that corpse is unstable. If the image is iconoclastically withdrawn in Rogier's *Deposition* by being indefinitely repeated, it is negated in the Bartholomew Master's *Deposition* by means of fragmentation. Even before it has reached the grave, the body in the Bartholomew Master's painting—crisscrossed by the limbs of the surrounding figures and available to the senses only in pieces—has already begun to come apart, leaving behind a gap in the center of the painting. While from a psychoanalytic point of view, this gap (albeit less vaginal than the isolated side-wound) may pose a threat, from an Augustinian and Erasmian perspective, it represents an opportunity: it opens a passage through which one might move beyond the body and the image toward an invisible God.[35]

But, whether threat or opportunity or both, the opening in the Bartholomew Master's painting is obstructed by a proliferation of new limbs. The Bartholomew Master strikes a blow against his own image in a manner that would become commonplace during the Reformation—that is, by letting the brokenness of the idol speak for itself. Zwingli employed this mode of iconoclasm in a sermon delivered on 28 January 1528, the second of two days of iconoclastic rioting in Bern: "There are still many weak and quarrelsome people who complain about the removal of the idols, even though it is clearly evident that there is nothing holy about them, and that they break and crack like any other piece of wood or stone. Here lies one without its head! Here another without its arms! If this abuse had done any harm to the saints who are near God, and if they had the power which is ascribed to them, do you think you would have been able to behead and cripple them as you did?"[36] Here without its head, here without its arms, the *imago Dei* in the Bartholomew Master's *Deposition* is already a broken idol—an image of its own impotence.

But that is only half the story. The other half concerns the fecundity of that broken idol, its spawning of new bodies, new images. The aniconic hole in the center of the Bartholomew Master's composition is lined with the sorts of amputated arms and legs that were given as votive offerings to St. Anthony in the hope that they might be restored to their rightful owners at the end of time.[37] In the meantime, each of these disjointed limbs is "triumphantly living its own life and dividing itself freely," as Bellmer says. Christ's right arm grows from the cheek of the woman in green, his torso from Nicodemus's chest, while inanimate objects take the place of living limbs. In the Bartholomew Master's painting, the breaking of the body opens a wound through which the viewer is beckoned to move toward (or threatened with) a knowledge that transcends bodies and images. But this very same breaking suspends that iconoclasm—generating new monstrous, combinatory, and prosthetic images to snag the gaze.

CHAPTER SEVEN

Puppets as Idols and Workshop Aids

The Bartholomew Master painted a second version of the Deposition, which is now in the National Gallery in London (plate 5). At less than one-tenth the size of its Paris counterpart, the London *Deposition* probably served as a private devotional panel.[1] Although nothing is known about its patron, the painting shares certain characteristics with the several altarpieces by the Bartholomew Master bequeathed to Cologne's Carthusian monastery of St. Barbara.[2] The London *Deposition* and the altarpieces donated to the Carthusians picture a shallow space with a flat background and carved tracery decorating the upper limits of the frame. This highly artificial setting derives from the shallow gilded box in which Rogier's *Deposition* is staged. Rogier's setting derives, in turn, from the carved and polychromed altarpieces that were produced in large numbers in the Netherlands and Germany during the fifteenth and sixteenth centuries (figure 54).[3]

A chronicle of the city of Cologne from 1499 reports that "the very strictest and holiest order, which is named the Carthusian order . . . is a great jewel and a rose in the church, which has not yet fallen from its perfection and from its rules, as other orders have."[4] Many of the rules and customs of the order of silent monks were intended to enforce segregation from the world.[5] Others pertained to the material culture of monastic life: silver bowls and spoons were prohibited, as were highly decorated equestrian gear and the sealing of documents with red wax.[6] Still other rules regulated the use of images. A 1424 Carthusian charter complains that "in contrast to

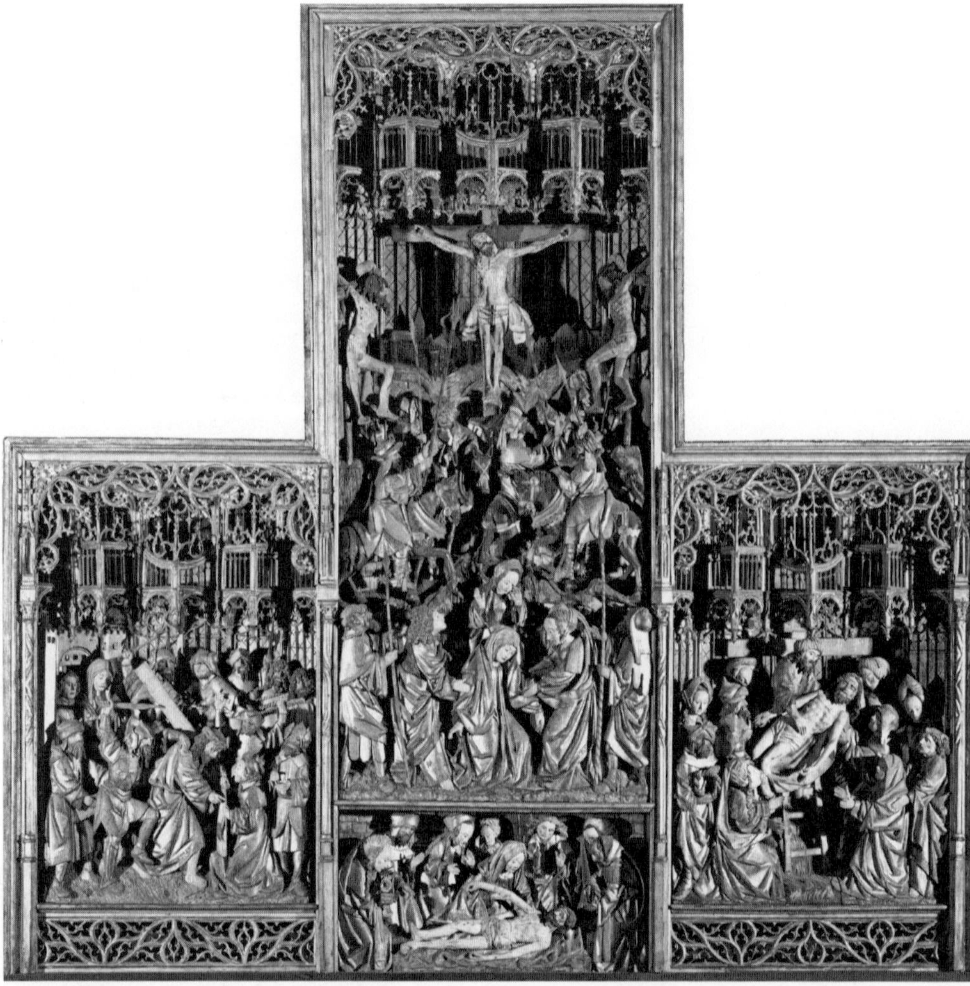

Figure 54. Flemish, *Altarpiece of the Passion* (early 16th c.), gilded and polychromed wood, 227×230×32 cm. Musée des Beaux-Arts, Dijon. (Photo: Erich Lessing/Art Resource, New York.)

the holy simplicity and humility of our Order, paintings wrought on altars with carefully contrived images (*curiosis ymaginibus*) and other different pictures with the shields and weapons of worldly men and female forms are increasing on glass windows and in other places, against the Statutes, in respect of which eminent men are not a little scandalized." The document then stipulates "that all such painted panels and other carefully contrived pictures (*curiose picture*)... be removed."[7]

Evidence suggests that regulations of this kind were in fact carried out, although not very consistently.[8] The 1532 Cologne cloister chronicle reports that the prior hung new images in the lay choir; this was to replace two paintings that were removed and sold some years earlier on account of their being *curiose pictarum* (painted with excessive care).[9] The Bartholomew Master himself appears to have offended the Carthusians' sense of decorum with his *St. Thomas Altarpiece*. An entry in the 1499 cloister chronicle deems the painting "inferior," perhaps because of its unusually graphic representation of the probing of Christ's side-wound.[10]

It is difficult to say why the Carthusians otherwise seem to have prized the Bartholomew Master's work, which has struck most modern commentators as nothing if not "carefully contrived" and full of "female forms." I will suggest that one of the things that made the Bartholomew Master's paintings acceptable in the iconophobic milieu of Cologne's Carthusian monastery is the artificiality of his human figures, which undermines any claims they may seem to make to represent living human beings, much less gods. These figures appear to be assembled out of prefabricated parts, with heads that sit on their bodies rather than being intregral, expressive parts of them. If in the Paris *Deposition*, the Bartholonew Master enlarged the hole in the center of Rogier's composition into an iconoclastic wound, in the London *Deposition*, he transposed the artificiality of Rogier's setting onto the figures who occupy it, transforming Rogier's human beings into puppets—the very emblem of idolatry. In so doing, the Bartholomew Master exploited an iconoclastic strategy latent in Rogier's painting for the purposes of making his work more acceptable to viewers who were ambivalent about images, including the Carthusians.

Gods and Marionettes

Since the nineteenth century, historians have compared the Bartholomew Master's figures to puppets, sometimes attributing their artificiality to the painter's use of wooden models as drawing aids.[11] In general, these comparisons have served to *explain away* the figures' puppet-like appearance as an accidental byproduct of the painter's manner of working. These explanations are based on what is indeed a fair assumption: namely, that the Bartholomew Master had access to wooden models of some kind. For example, he would have been familiar with the puppets used as dramatic props in churches. In fact, the same artists who painted altarpieces were hired to polychrome those sculptures. Nor was it unheard of at the time to keep an articulated mannequin in the studio for use as a drawing aid. But even if we knew that the Bartholomew Master had been personally responsible for polychroming a crucifix with movable arms or that he had a mannequin in his workshop, we would still be left to wonder why some of his human figures resemble articulated dolls. The puppet-like appearance of the Bartholomew Master's figures cannot simply be explained as a reflection of the objects in his purview; while it may in part be that, it is also something more.

This puppet-like appearance is particularly pronounced in the hyperbolic rigor mortis of Christ's body in the London *Deposition*, perhaps for the simple reason that the stiffness of a wooden sculpture can be made to stand in so nicely for the rigidity of a corpse. The affinity between the Bartholomew Master's deposed Christ and the inorganic objects and ornaments that surround him makes it seem as if Christ himself has here become something less supple than flesh. His clenched fists resemble the circular floral motifs in the gilded tracery, his body the wooden ladder which is propped against the cross.[12] This ladder is the same color as Christ's flesh and its circular dowel-joints rhyme with the wounds in his feet, with the hollows in his emaciated chest, and with his navel, which falls right in line with those joints.

The puppetness of the Bartholomew Master's deposed Christ and some of his other figures is surprising given that, around 1500, the puppet had largely negative connotations. It had long been a *vanitas* symbol. The *Garden of Delights*, an illustrated encyclopedia compiled in the late twelfth century by Herrad von Landsberg, Abbess of Hohenbourg, contains a miniature of King Solomon watching children playing a game of dueling marionettes.[13] The scene is decorated with a text scroll: "In monstrous play is depicted the vanity of vanities" (figure 55).[14] Above and below the scene are two more verses that elaborate upon the *vanitas* theme of Ecclesiastes 1.2.[15] Although the iconography of Solomon watching a game of marionettes is unusual, the inscriptions leave no doubt as to what it means.[16] This same association between puppets and vanity is made in Ulrich von Türheim's mid-thirteenth-century version of *Wilhelm der Heilige von Oranse*, where "worldly happiness" is described as "a game of dolls."[17]

By the sixteenth century, if not earlier, the English word "puppet," the German word "Puppe," the Dutch word "pop," and all their variations were being used as pejorative designations for religious images.[18] In fact, by this time the puppet had become virtually synonymous, in the religious context, with idolatry. An early Lutheran church ordinance describes Catholic ceremony as "idle deception and puppet play (*poppen spil*)."[19] In Thomas Becon's *Reliques of Rome* (1563), Nicephorus is remarked as having "destroied al" the Empress Iraene's "poppets, suffryng no images to remayne in the temples."[20] The anonymous author of "An homily against the peril of idolatry" (1562) describes images as "great puppets, wondrously decked and adorned."[21] Heinrich Bullinger complains: "Indeed, in our places of worship, what are representations of the Virgin mother and the other gods and goddesses but huge *puppae*? Are they set up by barbarians? Are we children not only twice but always?"[22] Luther argues that the trappings of the Catholic Church are even worse than puppets and other toys: "Christ will say that . . . the little girls' wreaths and *puppen*, the boys hobby-horses and red shoes please Him

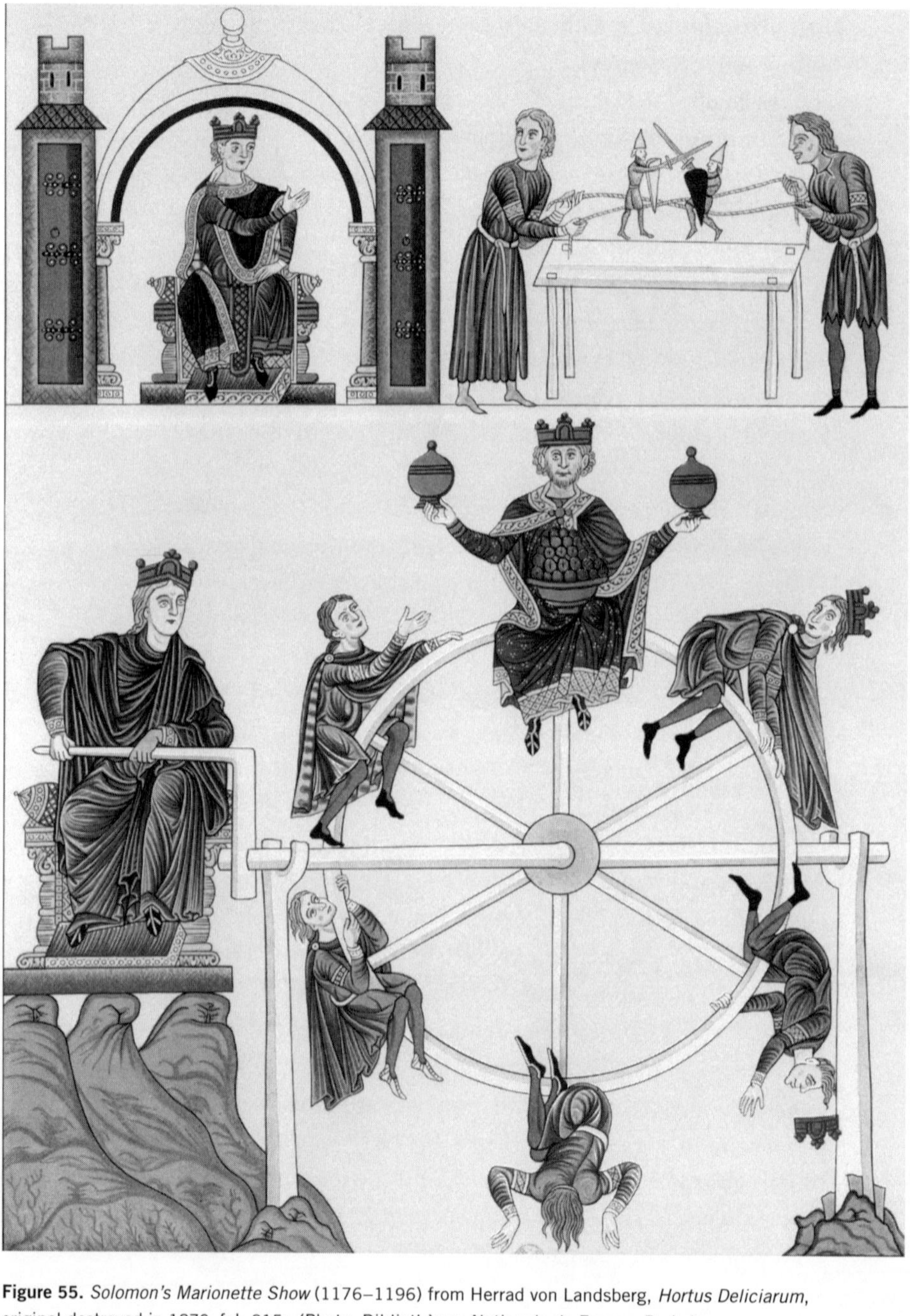

Figure 55. *Solomon's Marionette Show* (1176–1196) from Herrad von Landsberg, *Hortus Deliciarum*, original destroyed in 1870, fol. 215r. (Photo: Bibliothèque Nationale de France, Paris.)

much more than all their hoods, tonsures, surplices, chasubles, and adornments."[23] Other reformers made the same point by simply giving the images they removed from churches to children.[24]

Moving images were especially vulnerable to the accusation that they were nothing but toys for grownups. Reformers made a practice of exposing the workings of mechanized puppets, and the violence they suffered at the hands of iconoclasts suggests that people who were critical of images took particular offense at those that appeared to move. At the end of the sixteenth century, Spanish bishops forbade representing "the actions of Christ, the Blessed Virgin and the saints, either in churches or elsewhere, with clay images moved in some kind of ordered motion."[25] When Dr. Barlow, Bishop of St. David's, preached against idolatry at St. Paul's Cross in London in 1547, he exhibited a puppet that "putt out his legges of sepulchree and blessed with his hand, and turned his heade."[26] After its mechanical apparatus was discovered in 1538, the notorious Boxley rood of Kent was displayed for all to see: "The sayde roode was sett in the market place first at Maydstone, and there shewed openlye to the people the craft of movinge the eyes and lipps, that all the people there might see the illusion that had bene used in the sayde image by the monckes of the saide place of manye yeares tyme out of mynde, whereby they had gotten great riches in deceavinge the people thinckinge that the sayde image had so moved by the power of God, which now playnlye appeared to the contrarye."[27] Not much later, the Boxley rood was destroyed: "and now was heard a tremendous clamour of all sorts of people;—he is snatched, torn, broken in pieces bit by bit, split up into a thousand fragments, and at last thrown into the fire; and there was an end of him!"[28]

While all this was transpiring in churches and public squares, the puppet was establishing a place for itself in the artist's workshop. One of the earliest written accounts attesting to the use of a mannequin as a drawing aid appears in Filarete's *Treatise on Architecture* (1461–1464): "Have a little wooden figure, with jointed arms, legs, and neck. Then make a dress of linen in whatever fashion you choose, as if it were alive. Put it on him in the action that you wish and fix it up."[29] The 1498 will of the painter Bernardin Simondi, who lived in Aix-en-Provance but worked with the Netherlandish painter Josse Lieferinxe, mentions just such a doll.[30] There are at least nine surviving sixteenth-century German mannequins, including one in Berlin who is articulated down to her fingers and toes (figure 56).[31] Mannequins like this one are probably too finely carved to have been workshop aids, but they give some idea of how the painter's model would have been constructed. From as early as the late-sixteenth century, some of the extant mannequins have been attributed to Albrecht Dürer. Although Dürer probably did not make these particular puppets, several of his drawings suggest that he employed something of the kind in his studies of the human body (figures 57–58).[32]

In addition to functioning as a tool for studying drapery and the body, mannequins were probably used to work out problems of foreshortening like the one posed by the helper-figure perched at the top of the ladder in the Bartholomew Master's London *Deposition*. The helper-figure's small size, awkward position, peg-like limbs, rudely foreshortened face, and likeness to the tracery around him make him even less human than the puppet-like Christ whose stiff arm he grasps. A purely mechanical being, the puppet can hold the most difficult poses indefinitely, and because of its diminutive size, it can be inspected from every angle, including from directly above or below. But the puppet exacts a certain price for allowing the painter to circumvent the problems associated with the human body. That price is the subject of Paul de Man's essay "Aesthetic Formalization in Kleist's *Über das Marionettentheater*." The puppet's "increased formalization" of the human body yields an "increased aesthetic pleasure," according to de Man: "That this happens at the expense of stable and determinable meaning is a fair enough price to pay for the mastery over form."[33] This price may be fair, de Man suggests, but it is nonetheless more than one can really afford.

The argument of Herr C., the protagonist of Heinrich von Kleist's 1810 story, is that dance reaches its highest degree of aesthetic perfection in the puppet, whose movements are purified of

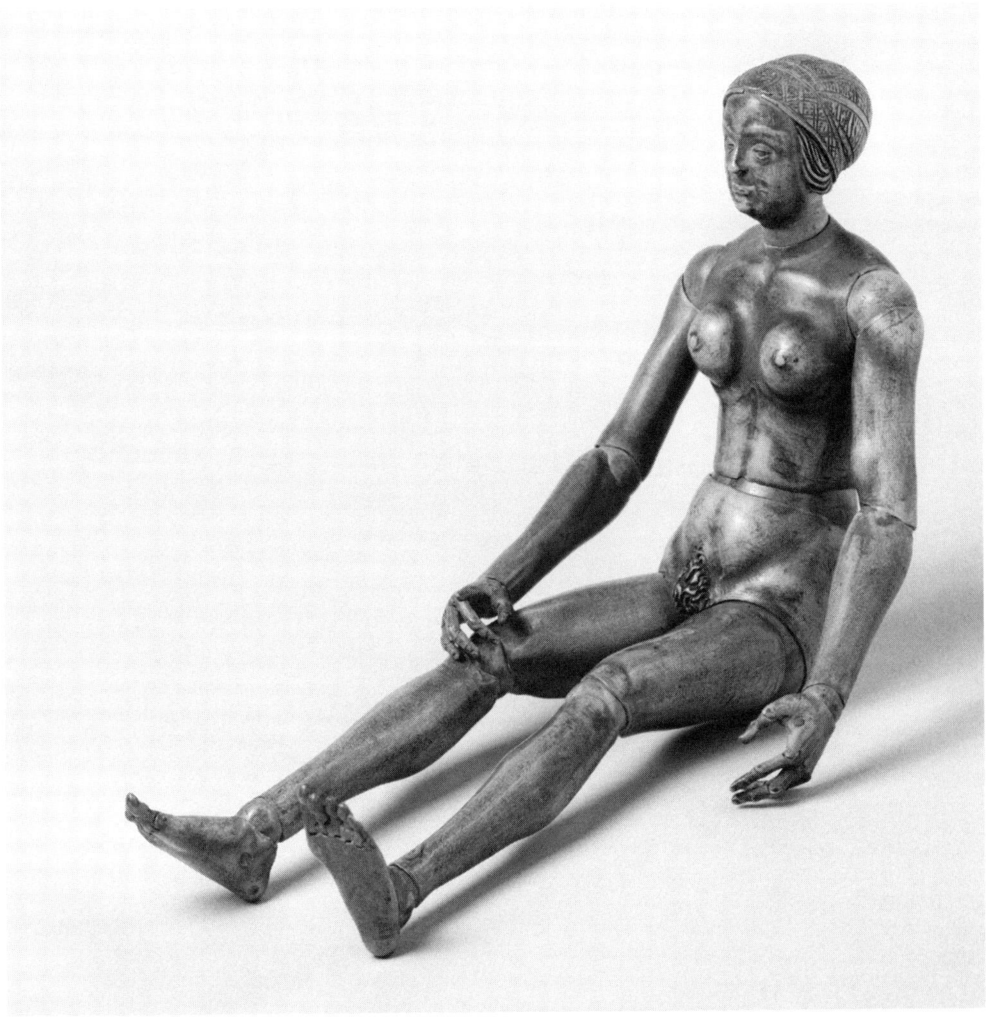

Figure 56. Southern German, *Female Mannequin* (ca. 1520–1530), wood, height 22 cm. Skulpturensammlung und Museum für Byzantinische Kunst, Staatliche Museen zu Berlin. (Photo: Joerg P. Anders/Bildarchiv Preussischer Kulturbesitz/Art Resource, New York.)

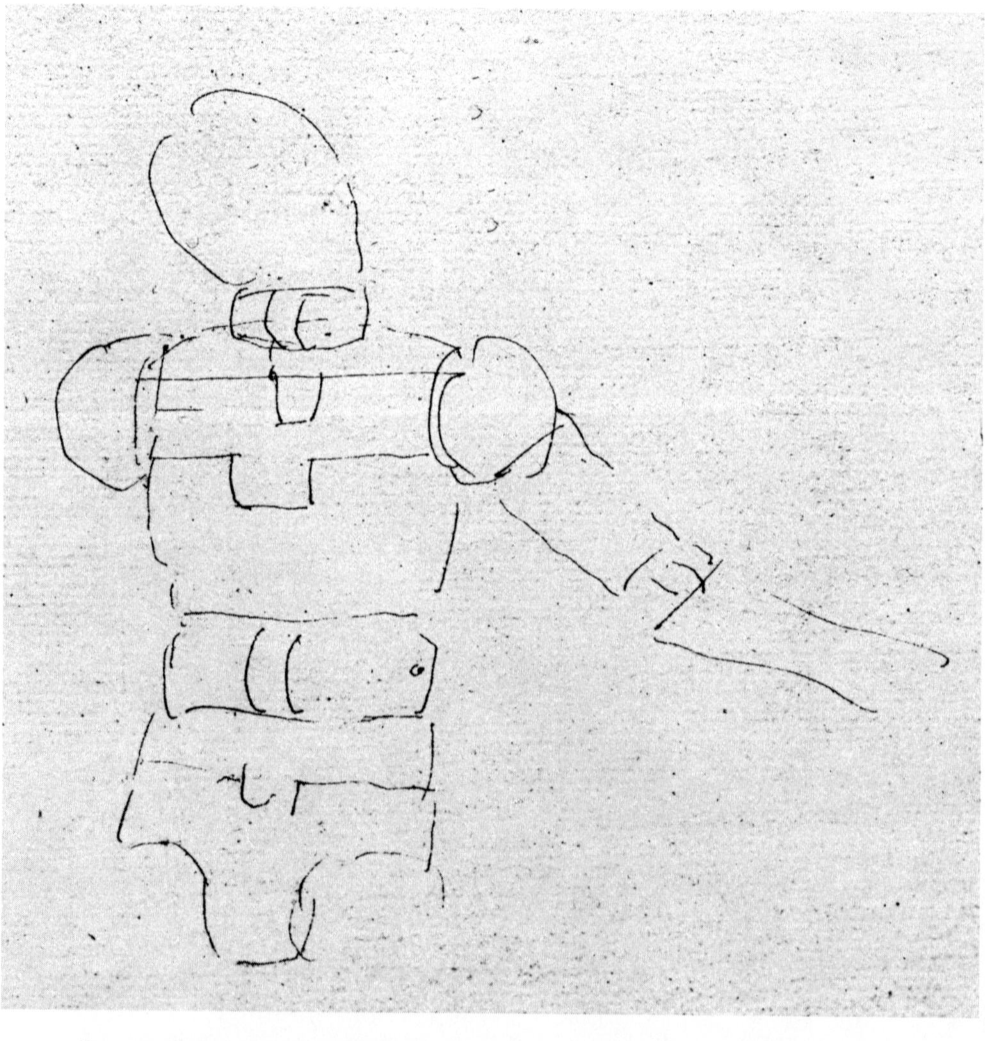

Figure 57. Albrecht Dürer, *Drawing of a Mannequin* (before 1519) from the *Dresden Sketchbook*, 29.3 × 20.8 cm. Sächsische Landesbibliothek—Staats- und Universitätsbibliothek, Dresden. (Photo: SLUB / Deutsche Fotothek / Gundula Körner.)

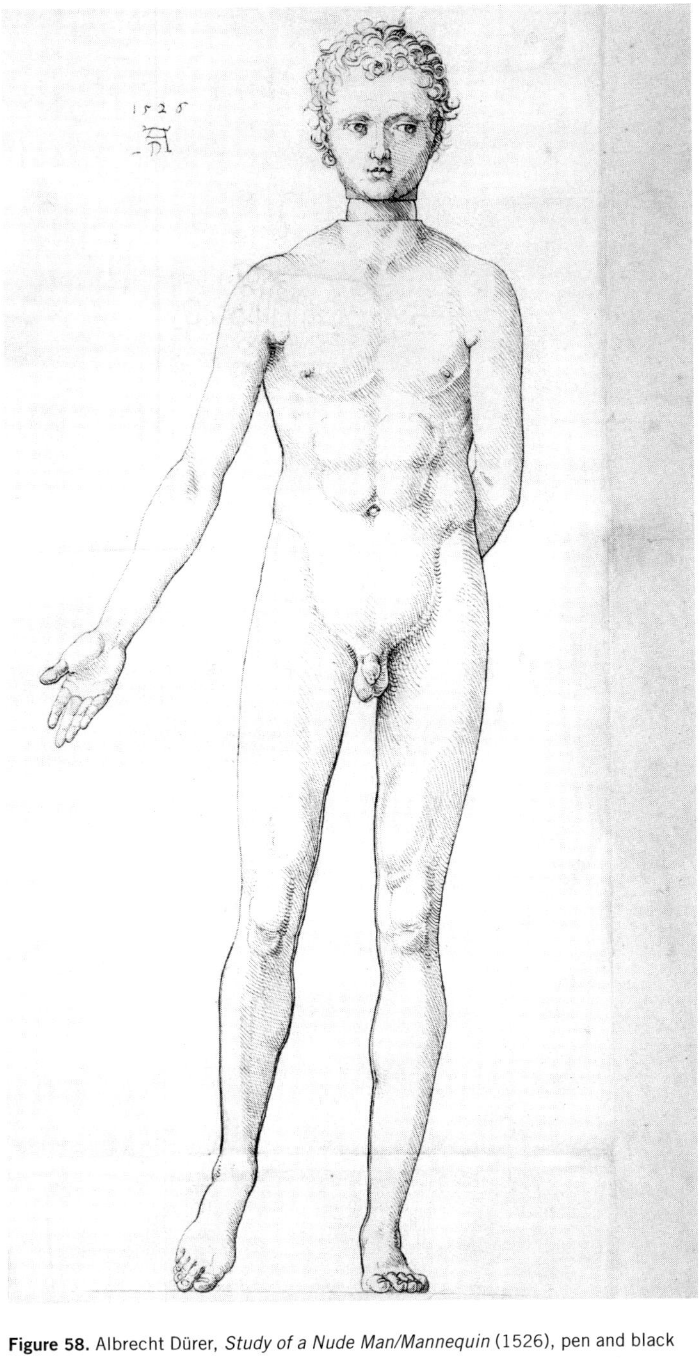

Figure 58. Albrecht Dürer, *Study of a Nude Man/Mannequin* (1526), pen and black ink with light green wash on paper, 45 × 24.8 cm. The British Museum, London. (Photo: The Trustees of the British Museum.)

the affectations of the human dancer.[34] Herr C. explains that "grace will reappear after knowledge (*Erkenntnis*) has gone through infinity. So that we shall find grace at its purest in a body which is entirely devoid of consciousness or which possesses it in an infinite degree; that is, in the marionette or in the god."[35] The difference between impulse and execution that is inescapable for the human dancer collapses in the puppet into a simple unified grace, free of the incongruities of human expression.

But Herr C.'s assertion of the puppet's absolute grace is not, de Man insists, Kleist's final word on the subject. Death and indeterminacy (of meaning) lurk in the innocence regained on the far side of consciousness that the puppet emblematizes.[36] The puppet is graceful, Kleist explains, because its limbs are "what they should be, dead, mere pendula, and they follow the law of pure gravity."[37] In de Man's reading of Kleist's story, this deadness not surprisingly will turn out to characterize the text itself. The puppet is a figure for a linguistic process that is allowed to take its "mechanically predictable" and hence beautiful course: "The memorable tropes that have the most success (*Beifall*) occur as mere random improvisation (*Einfall*) at the moment when the author has completely relinquished any control over his meaning and has relapsed (*Zurückfall*) into the extreme formalization, the mechanical predictability of grammatical declensions (*Fälle*). But *Fälle*, of course, also means in German 'trap,' the trap which is the ultimate textual model of this and of all texts, the trap of an aesthetic education which inevitably confuses dismemberment of language by the power of the letter with the gracefulness of a dance."[38] The puppet in Kleist's story is a figure, finally, for the graceful incoherence of Kleist's own text, where free linguistic play replaces the movements of a language (awkwardly) tethered to sense.

In the Bartholomew Master's London *Deposition*, the Virgin's sympathetic response to Christ's suffering takes the form of a pious collapse, whereas the Magdalene's anguish takes a more exaggerated form.[39] The teetering vacuity of the Magdalene, the dismemberment of the helper-figure, and the stiffness of Christ make it difficult to decide whether the Bartholomew Master's figures are earnest or simply given over to the mechanical predictability of their wooden limbs. Like Kleist's story, the Bartholomew Master's *Deposition* is an "uneasy mixture of affirmation and denial . . . hoax and high seriousness."[40]

In the Bartholomew Master's painting, this denial takes the form of an iconoclastic insistence on the materiality of the image. Not only are the Bartholomew Master's puppets emblems of worldly vanity; they are also lessons in what the image is made of. Following Isaiah 44.14–17, a *rederijker* poem from the first half of the sixteenth century declares: "They are made of wood cut from the forests: How can they be called saints!"[41] Calvin hears the image, echoing Horace, say, "Once I was a little fig tree trunk, a useless bit of wood, when the workman, in doubt whether he should make a stool, preferred that I be a god."[42] Iconoclasts never tired of pointing out that the idol is made of the same material with which one cooks and heats one's home: "With a part of their wood he warms himself, or makes a fire for baking bread; but with another part he makes a god, which he adores."[43] The Bartholomew Master is careful to let the viewer see through his fiction to a model that is nothing but a piece of wood—as good for human survival as for representing Christ.

In the iconophobic milieu of Cologne's Carthusian monastery, the image's mundane matter and manufacture were not meant to be forgotten; images were not meant to be confused with what they represent. By making plain their origins in the workshop and in the play-space of the paraliturgy, the Bartholomew Master's figures made themselves acceptable in the Carthusian context. That the Bartholomew Master painted such figures for the Carthusians and others does not mean that he held a moderate, Gregorian position on images. The issue of representation is much too fraught in his paintings to be explained as that. De Man helps us see that the Bartholomew Master's exposure of the materiality of the image is, instead, another example of that double gesture which we have repeatedly encountered—the *suspended* blow to the image. Here it is the allure of the puppet, what Kleist calls its grace, that counters the Bartholomew Master's iconoclastic transformation of the human figure into a wooden doll. Despite being the surest sign of its deadness, the grace of the puppet repeatedly lures the viewer back to believing in its fiction.

Vignette: Thomas Demand's Clearing *(2004)*

Thomas Demand builds life-size paper replicas of objects and spaces, which he photographs with a large-format camera (figure 59).[44] At first glance, the photographed models seem to represent their subject matter down to the smallest detail. But with a little time, one begins to notice the omissions. The absence of human beings is the most conspicuous. The keys on the typewriter, the writing on the books, and other details, the genre of which it is difficult to put one's finger on, are also missing. Michael Fried describes this lack in terms of human presence: "radically incomplete," Demand's models "have been divested of . . . every mark of use, every trace of human presence and action . . . all traces other than those pertaining to the physical making of the models . . . by the artist."[45] On Fried's account, what is left out here are all indices of human beings other than the human being that is Thomas Demand, whose (past) presence is indexed by the manufacture of the model and particularly poignantly by its small imperfections—pencil marks, creases in the paper, and so on.[46]

The absence of traces of human subjects other than the omnipresent author is all the more striking where Demand constructs what Fried calls "the scene of a crime (loosely speaking)."[47] Many of Demand's banal spaces turn out to be either the now-empty setting of a major historical event or a space incidentally associated with a major historical figure. *Zimmer / Room*, for example, depicts a hotel room where L. Ron Hubbard worked on *Dianetics: The Modern Science of Mental Health* (1950). While Demand's photographs are divested of signs of human subjects—including (in)famous ones—they are thoroughly determined, Fried argues, by their human author. In fact by Fried's estimate, Demand's photographs are nothing less than "images of *sheer authorial intention*."[48]

Although Demand's own (authorial) presence may well be the only significant *human* presence detectable in his photographs, there

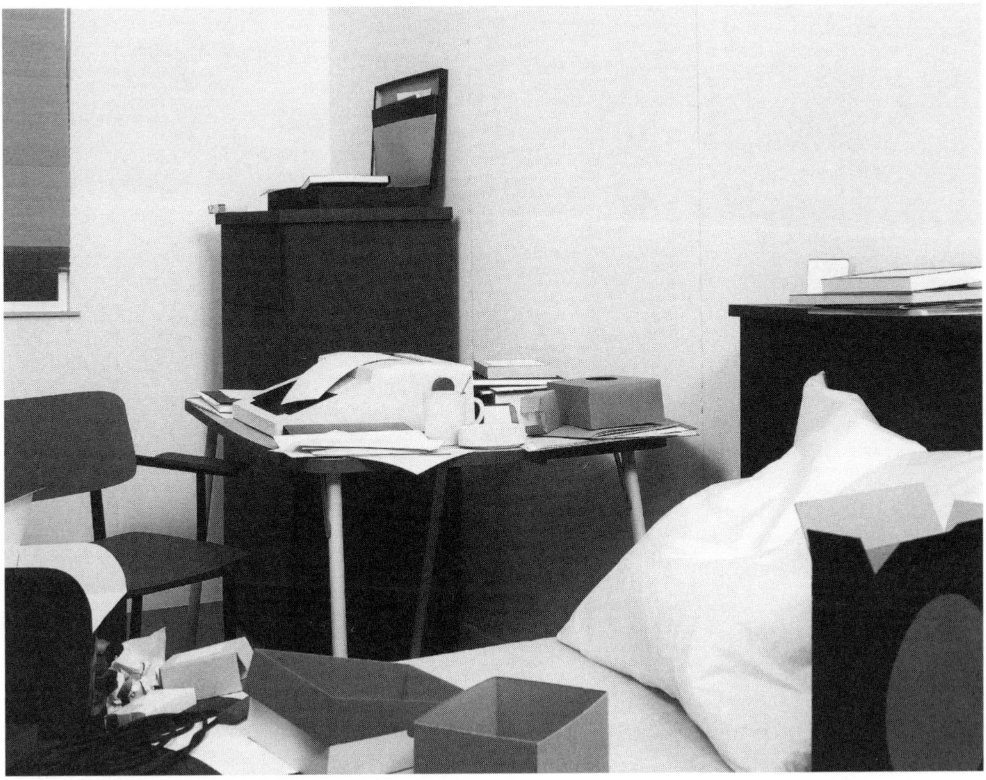

Figure 59. Thomas Demand, *Zimmer/Room* (1996), C-Print/Diasec, 172 × 232 cm. © Thomas Demand/2010 ARS, New York/VG Bild-Kunst, Bonn. (Photo: Matthew Marks Gallery, New York.)

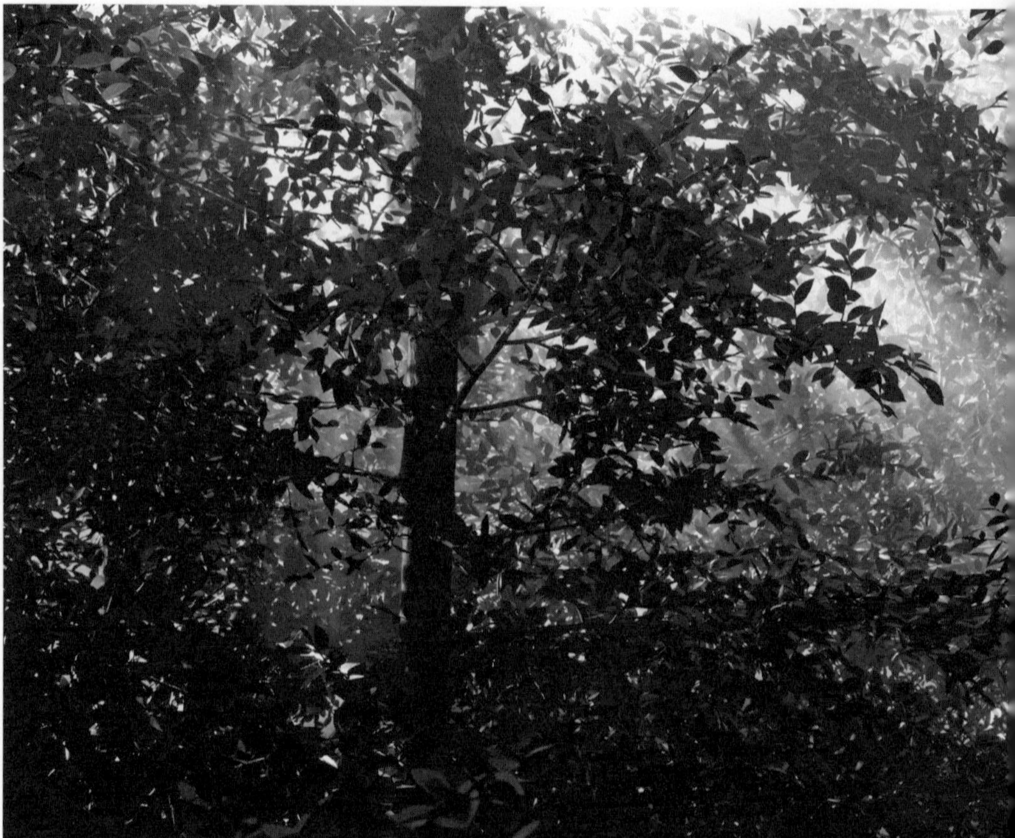

Figure 60. Thomas Demand, *Clearing* (2003), C-Print/Diasec, 192×495 cm. © Thomas Demand/2010 ARS, New York/VG Bild-Kunst, Bonn. (Photo: Matthew Marks Gallery, New York.)

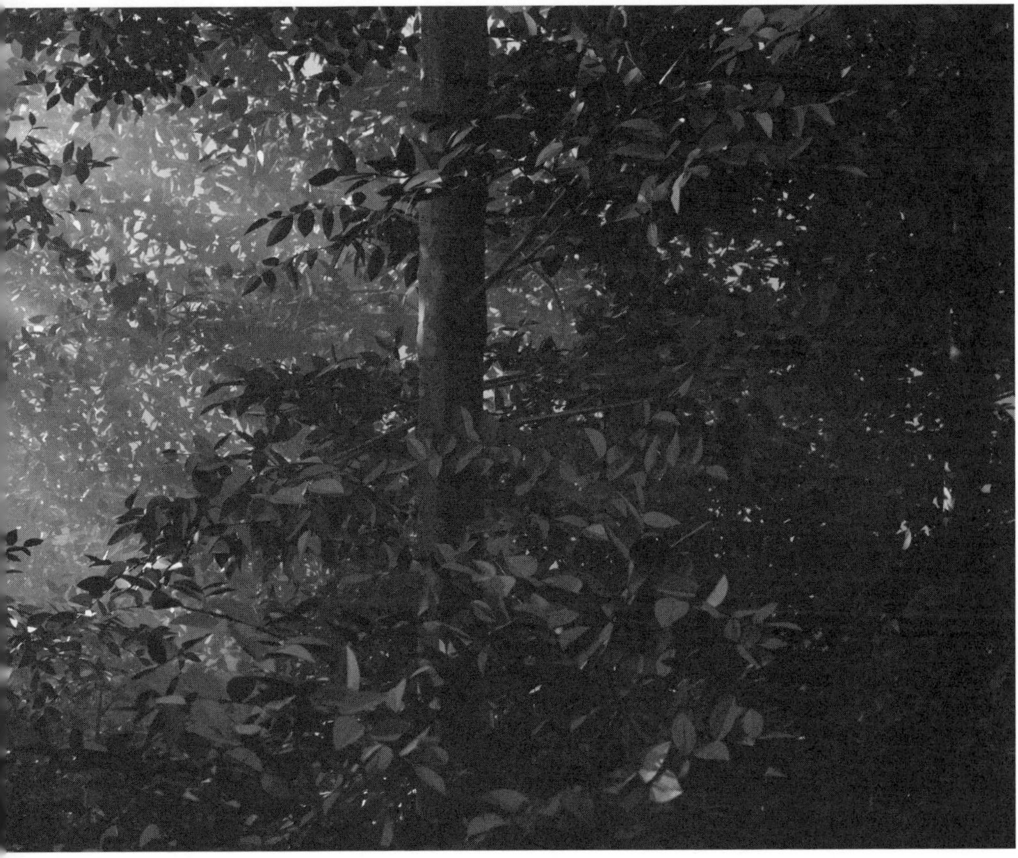

is nonetheless something else that gets in the way of describing these photographs in the way Fried does—namely, paper. To the question: what are Demand's models made of? Duchamp would answer: the ready-made stuff of manufacture. For regardless of where Demand turns for his material, that is all he will find. Even "raw" material is an inheritance, according to Duchamp: "Let's say you use a tube of paint; you didn't make it. You bought it and used it as a ready-made. Even if you mix two vermilions together, it's still a mixing of two ready-mades. So man can never expect to start from scratch; he must start from ready-made things like even his own mother and father."[49] Factory-produced tubes of paint are the mother and father; procreation, Duchamp says elsewhere, is the "Breeding of Colors."[50]

Duchamp's slippages from pigments to bodies, from the inhuman material to the human maker, point to the difficulty of saying where intention ends and the *stuff* of its expression begins. Demand speaks of his paper in more or less Duchampian terms: "When it comes to colour, the first feeling, as with many other factors, is one of a *déjà vu*. The use of paper is of course related to this feeling of the colour's familiarity. The paper I use is the kind you can get in any shop, and the chromatic range always reflects and corresponds to what is currently being produced."[51]

The paper Demand used to make *Clearing*, a six foot by sixteen foot window onto a paper forest, leaves romantically illuminated by rays of sunlight, is no less manufactured than a tube of paint (figure 60). While Demand is able to manipulate his paper to an astonishing degree, his control over that paper only makes more vivid his and our own baffling alienation from it. The material of authorial intention is anything but the author's to intend; someone or *something* else made it. "The way in which I can try to mean is dependent upon linguistic properties that are not only not made by me, because I depend on the language as it exists for the devices which I will be using," writes de Man, "it is as such not made by us as historical beings, it is perhaps not even made by humans at all."[52] In photographing paper worlds, Demand shows not how intentional an image can be but rather how prone we are to misrecognizing ourselves as the authors of our own inheritance. Paper is Demand's language—his puppet, so to speak—the intimate and strange stuff without which he would not know his own intentions but in which his intentions become alien in their mechanical predictability.

Like Demand's photographs, the Bartholomew Master's paintings are second-order fictions: images of images. By letting the wooden puppet that is his model show through, he announces—before any Reformation iconoclasts arrive on the scene—that his image of Christ is nothing but a block of wood. But if the Bartholomew Master makes abundantly clear that the liveliness of his figures does not come *from within them*, he does not quite settle the question as to whether the source of their uncanny animation is divine or human—that is, whether his figures are gods or marionettes.

In allowing for the possibility of both, the Bartholomew Master reveals what they have in common: gods and marionettes are both hard, alien things. Demand's photographs show us that the image made by human hands is never simply that. There is no such thing as an image of *sheer authorial intention*, because no intention can ever divest the wood, paint, or paper of all its madeness. The Bartholomew Master's *Deposition* likewise reminds us that, although the puppet is not a god, it is nevertheless *strange*. It is nothing but a block of wood, and yet an encounter with it can take one outside oneself.

CHAPTER EIGHT

The Shroud as Body Double

The Haarlem-born painter Jan Mostaert adopted many aspects of Rogier's composition but left out the rhyme between the Virgin and Christ—just as the Bartholomew Master had (plate 6).[1] An expanse of creased white cloth extends across the foreground of Mostaert's painting, filling the space that the Virgin occupies in Rogier's composition. Instead of the Virgin's body shaped by compassion, Mostaert offers this shroud as body double of the body of Christ. In casting a blank shroud across the bottom of his painting, I will suggest, Mostaert pictures the invisibility toward which Christ is being lowered.

The Turin Shroud

In his treatise on sacred images, John of Damascus includes the shroud among those things that are holy but secondary to God and therefore to be venerated rather than adored. These include: "the robe, the seamless tunic, the winding-sheet, the swaddling-clothes, the holy tomb which is the fountain of our resurrection."[2] During the Middle Ages, all these things were indeed venerated and turned into relics to be displayed, gifted, and indulgenced. Among the many shroud relics circulating toward the end of the Middle Ages was the cloth that would come to be known as the Turin Shroud, the earliest evidence of which dates to the late fourteenth century. The immense fame this particular relic eventually achieved was due, of course, to the image of Christ that his own sweat and blood were said to have miraculously imprinted on the cloth.

In the first half of the fifteenth century, Marguerite of Charny came into possession of the Turin Shroud and made a lucrative business of displaying it as she moved about in eastern France. Having become embroiled in several legal battles concerning her relic, she gave it to Duke Louis of Savoy in 1453 in exchange for the rents on one of his estates. Various papal bulls promulgated between 1466 and 1552 legitimated the shroud and increased its status. In 1502, it was deposited at Chambéry, in the court chapel of Philibert II of Savoy and his new bride Margaret of Austria. It was put on display there the following year, and in subsequent years, during the Good Friday Mass (figure 61). Margaret of Austria would become a great devotee of the shroud, donating a silver shrine for it and an altarpiece for its chapel.[3]

Following the death of her brother Philip the Fair in 1506, Margaret was appointed governor general (and later regent) of the Burgundian Netherlands and caretaker of her brother's children, including the future Holy Roman Emperor, Charles V. At that time, she returned to the city of Mechelen in Flanders, which would remain her primary residence until her death some twenty-four years later. When she moved to Flanders, Margaret left the Turin Shroud behind in Savoy, in the chapel containing the remains of her late husband. Probably because she no longer had access to the original, Margaret commissioned Bernard van Orley to make a copy of it in 1521. Now lost, the copy was recorded in an inventory of Margaret's bedroom, where it was kept in a cupboard.[4] The appearance of Margaret's lost copy can be inferred from an extant copy of 1516, which is preserved in the Church of St. Gommarus in Lier (figure 62).[5] Margaret's ongoing devotion to the Turin Shroud must have been well known, since the Spanish theologian Juan Luis Vives dedicated several works concerning the shroud to her in 1529.[6]

The little we know about Jan Mostaert places him in the orbit of Margaret's court at Mechelen. Karel van Mander seems to exaggerate when he says that Mostaert "became painter to Lady Margaret, the sister of Duke Philip.... As he was well-regarded and lived everywhere this lady held her court, he remained for 18 years [in this

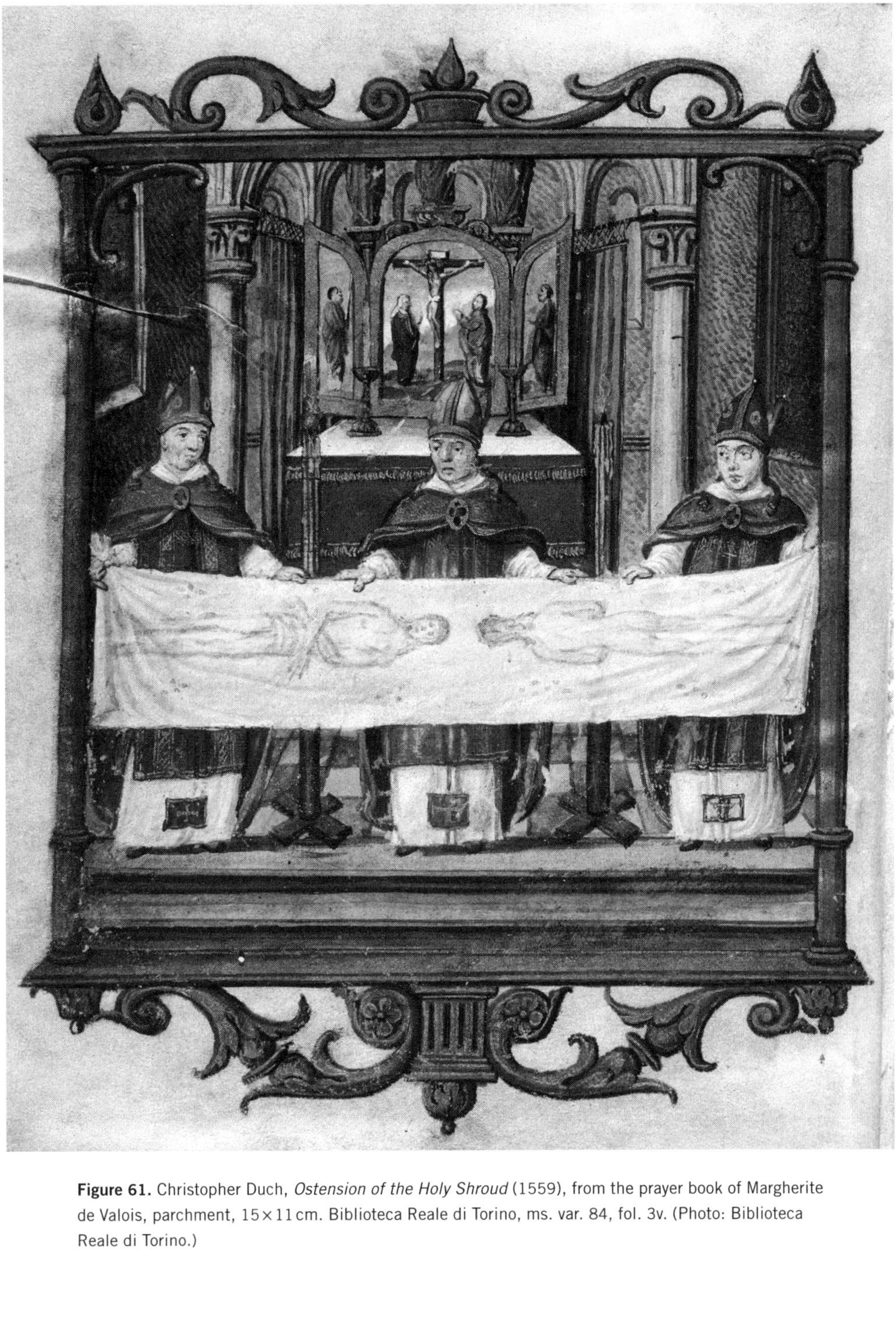

Figure 61. Christopher Duch, *Ostension of the Holy Shroud* (1559), from the prayer book of Margherite de Valois, parchment, 15 × 11 cm. Biblioteca Reale di Torino, ms. var. 84, fol. 3v. (Photo: Biblioteca Reale di Torino.)

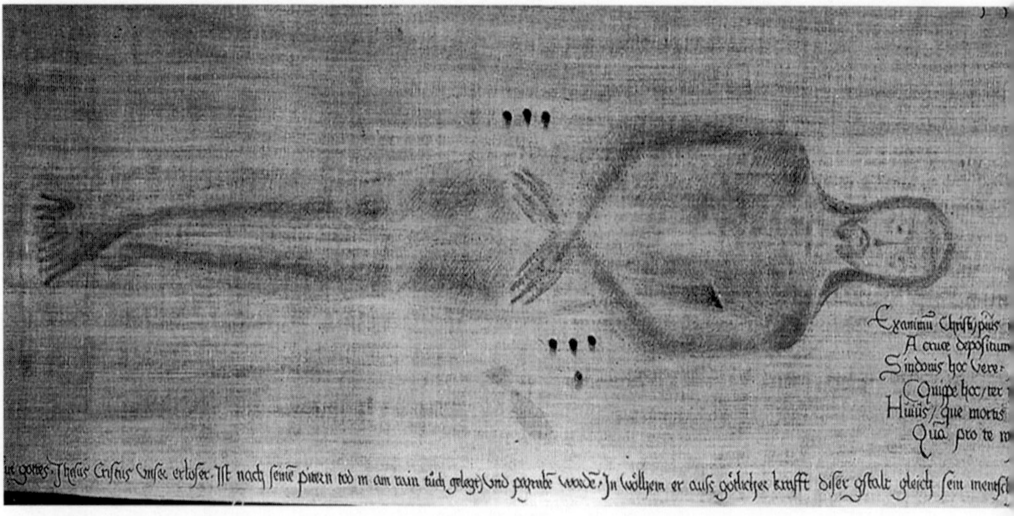

Figure 62. Nuremberg, *Copy of the Turin Shroud* (1516), white taffeta painted with brown and red, 147 × 33 cm. Kerkfabriek Sint-Gummarus, Lier. (Photo: KIK-IRPA.)

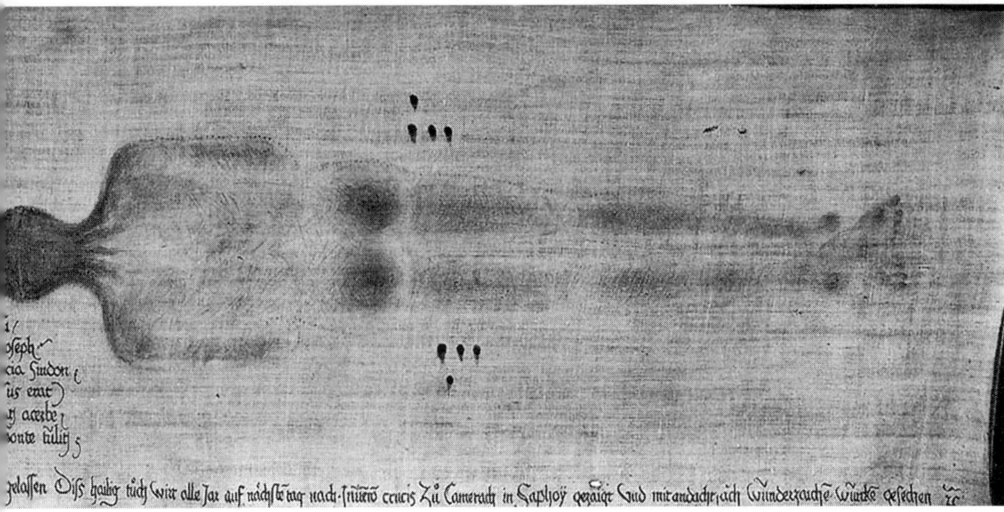
gelassen Diss hailig tüch wirt alle Jar auf nächsten tag nach inventionis crucis Zu Camerach in Saphoy gezaigt Und mit andacht auch Wunderzaiche Würcke gesehen

service], during which time he made various works."[7] The several occurrences of Mostaert's name in Margaret's records suggest that he was not the true court painter he probably wished to be. In fact, he never seems to have enjoyed more than the status of *painctre aux honneur* that Margaret bestowed on him in 1518.[8] But whatever his position at her court may have been, Mostaert would have been familiar with Margaret's famous shroud.

Given the fame of the Turin Shroud, its association with Good Friday, Margaret's attachment to it, and Mostaert's presence at her court, it is not surprising that Mostaert gave such an unusually prominent place to Christ's shroud in his painting of the deposition. Mostaert's *Deposition* is the center panel of a memorial triptych made around 1520 for Albrecht Adriaensz van Adrichem, a wealthy magistrate of Haarlem, to be placed in a side chapel of that city's Church of St. Bavo (figure 63).[9] Just below the horizontal beam of the cross, the coats of arms of the Van Adrichem family and the Van der Laen family (the family of the second of Albrecht's three wives) are suspended from the tracery—not unlike the crossbows in Rogier's *Deposition* and the Tau crosses in the Bartholomew Master's Paris painting.[10] On the exterior of Mostaert's altarpiece, St. Catherine and St. Bavo present Van Adrichem as he kneels directly before the scene of Christ's encounter with Veronica, who has wiped the sweat from Christ's brow with her handkerchief as he makes his way to Calvary (figure 64). This cloth now bears a miraculously imprinted image of the Holy Face that stares out at the viewer. On both the interior and exterior of Mostaert's altarpiece, then, a cloth that represents Christ—the former aniconic, the latter iconic—is a pivotal part of the composition.

Christ as Cloth

Significant cloths appear at the beginning and end of Christ's life. Luke tells us: "she gave birth to her firstborn son and wrapped him in bands of cloth, and laid him in a manger" (Luke 2.7). The mystic Bridget of Sweden expands upon this short Gospel account: "She began to wrap him carefully, first in the linen cloths and then in the woolen, binding his little body, legs, and arms with a ribbon.... And afterward she wrapped and tied on the boy's head those two small linen cloths that she had prepared for this purpose."[11] At the end of Christ's life, "Joseph took the body and wrapped it in a clean linen cloth" (Matthew 27.59). The need for clothing testifies to the vulnerability of Christ's human flesh; the proffering of it signifies the care that the altruistic people, the "sheep," gave him, as opposed to the "goats," "who did not give [him] clothing" (Matthew 25.32–43).[12]

The incarnation, the garbing of Christ in the flesh of the Virgin, is the model for all these subsequent acts of clothing. As Bernard of Clairvaux recounts in a homily on the Virgin, "the angel said 'Hail full of grace, the Lord is with you.' Not only the Lord, your son, is with you, whom you have clothed with your flesh, but also the Lord, the Holy Spirit whom you conceived."[13] Bernard also writes, "He was your Master long before he became your son. He instructed your mind before he clothed himself with your flesh."[14] The shroud in Mostaert's painting merges with the Virgin's robes, as if to suggest that she receives Christ at his death in the same (fleshly) cloth with which she clothed him at the incarnation. In late medieval Pietàs and Lamentations, it is not uncommon for the Virgin's garments and the shroud to merge into a single voluminous piece of fabric (figure 65).[15]

In images of the Virgin of Mercy, the Virgin extends to her devotees the protection she gives to the infant's vulnerable flesh when she wraps him in swaddling cloths and to the dead body when she takes it in the shroud (figure 66).[16] Emblem of the Virgin's protection, the sheltering gown also appears in hagiographical literature: "St. Anne Hettin at one time had much pain in her heart. One day she sat with her task in the workhouse and a woman appeared to her wearing a very beautiful mantle on which was written in golden letters: Ave Maria! And she took [Anne] under her mantle and comforted her and secured for her eternal life."[17] A prayer to the Virgin's mantle recorded in 1502 reads: "That is the devoutly sacred mantle of the mercy and protection of the most praiseworthy Virgin and dignified mother of God, Mary, with which she covers and protects all who go with reverence and righteous hope."[18]

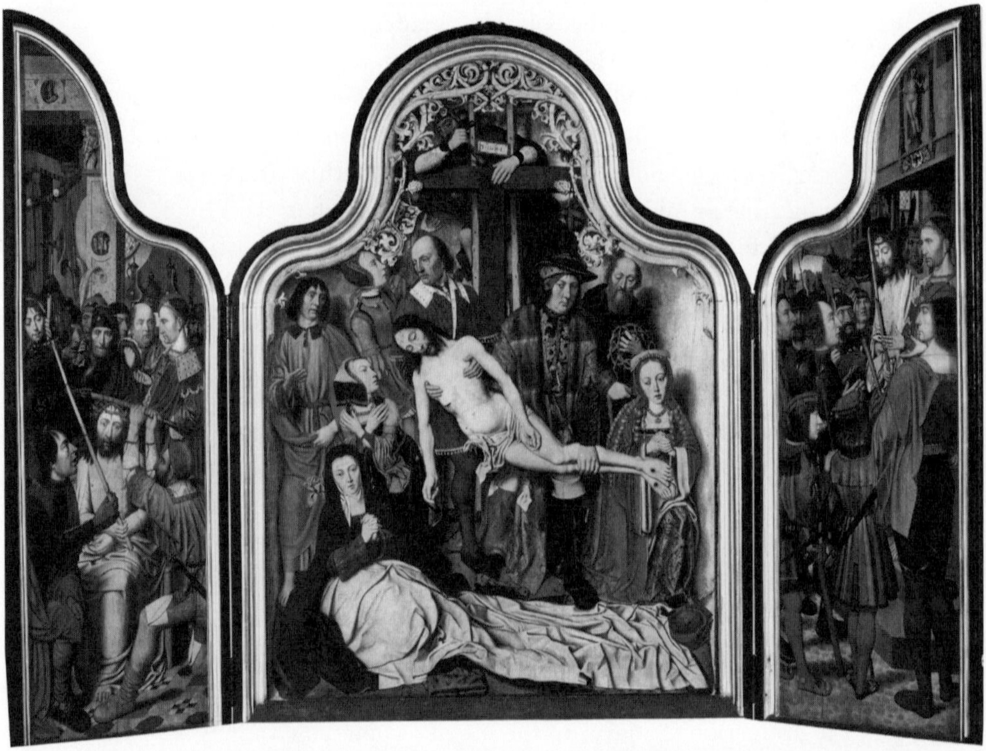

Figure 63. Jan Mostaert, *Triptych of the Deposition from the Cross* (ca. 1520), interior, oil on panel, 140.5 × 97.5–45.5 cm. Musées Royaux des Beaux-Arts de Belgique, Brussels. (Photo: KIK-IRPA.)

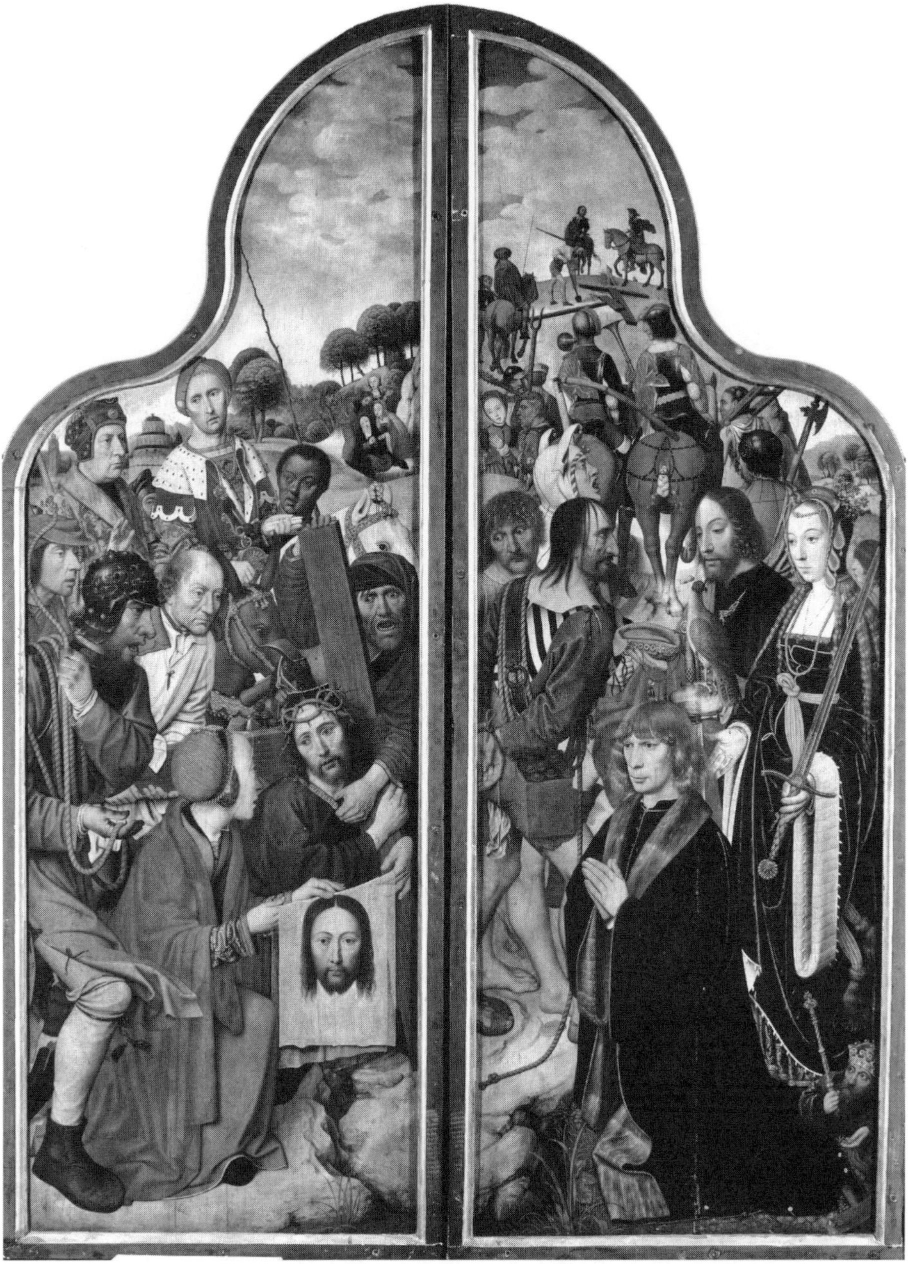

Figure 64. Jan Mostaert, *Triptych of the Deposition from the Cross* (ca. 1520), exterior, oil on panel. Musées Royaux des Beaux-Arts de Belgique, Brussels. (Photo: KIK-IRPA.)

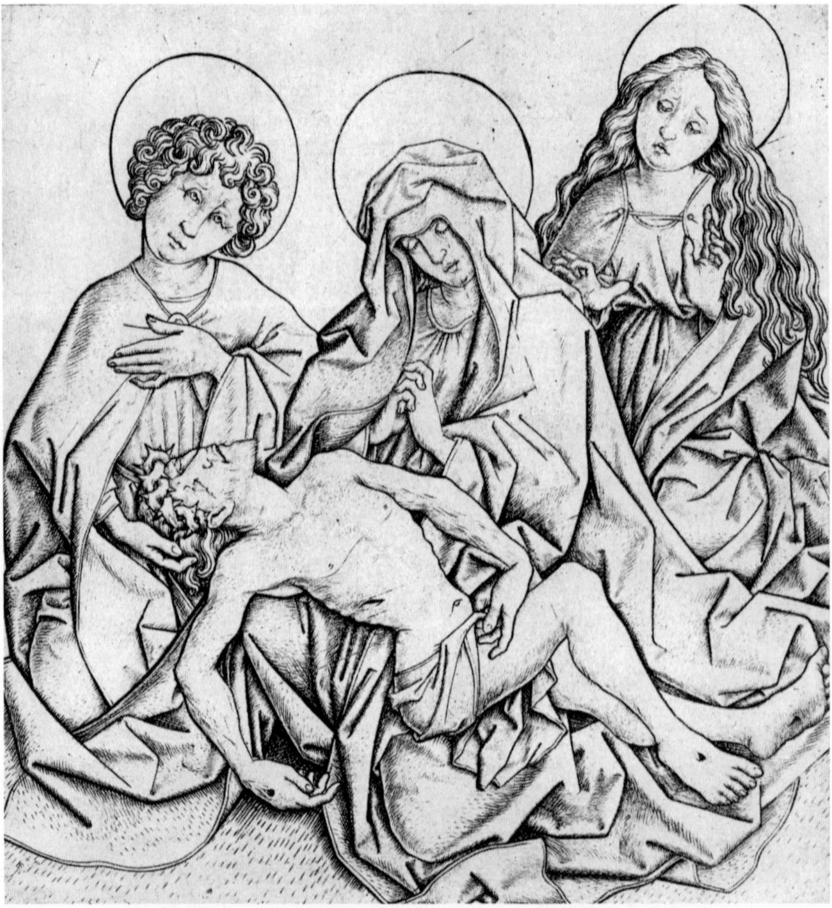

Figure 65. Master ES, *The Lamentation* (ca. 1450–1467), engraving, 11.1 × 10.4 cm. The British Museum, London. (Photo: The Trustees of the British Museum.)

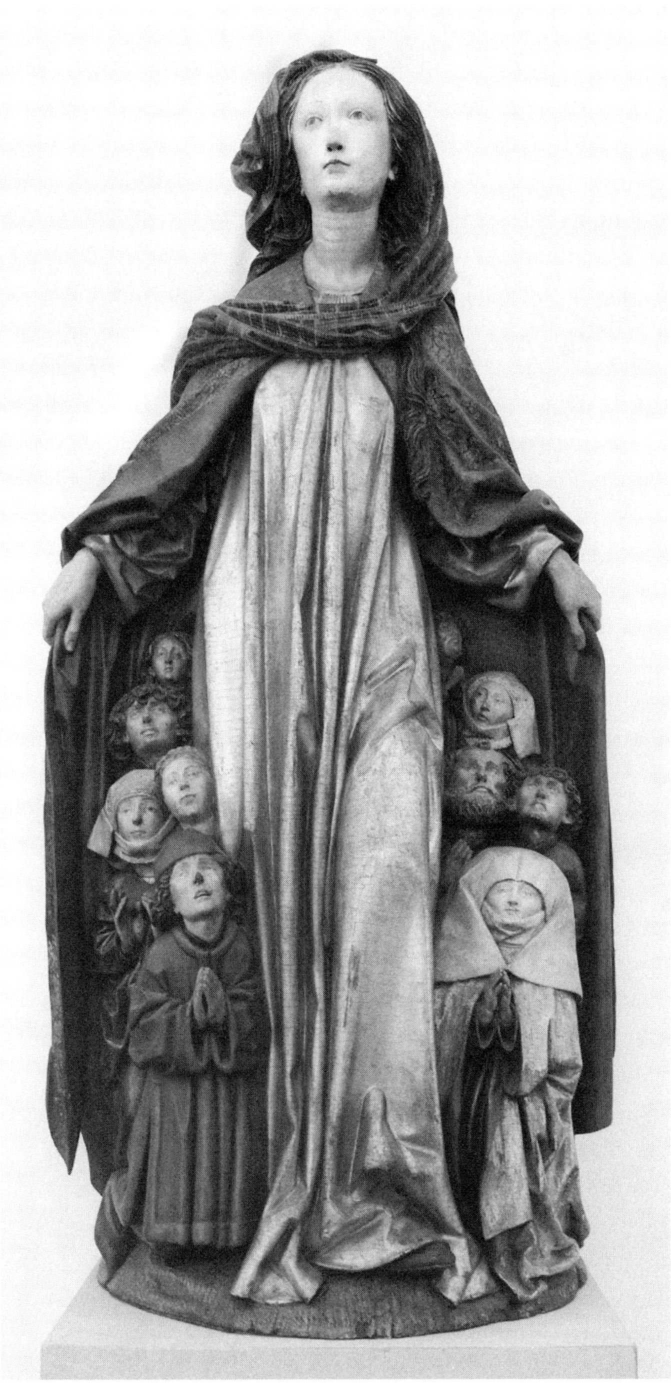

Figure 66. Michel Erhart, *Ravensburg Virgin of Mercy* (ca. 1480–1490), polychromed wood, height 135 cm. Bode Museum, Berlin. (Photo: Andreas Praefcke.)

The cloth with which the Virgin receives Christ in Mostaert's painting is also the cloth with which she receives the viewer. She stares directly at us, as if she were offering *us* the shroud. A generous offer, it nonetheless informs us that access to Christ is to be gained through her alone. While the shroud is a surface onto which we can expect to see the dead body deposited and thereby brought closer to us, it nonetheless holds us at a distance—however small. The shroud represents the Virgin's gift of her body as the medium through which we can know an otherwise invisible God. "May the Word who in the beginning was with God become flesh of my flesh, according to your word," requests the Virgin in Bernard's homily. "I beg that the word be to me not [a word] which once pronounced fades away, but which conceived remains, clothed with flesh and not with air."[19] The Virgin asks for something less fleeting than words, but the flesh she demands will decompose—and faster even than cloth. As the servant says of Israel's oppressors in the third Servant Song: "All of them will wear out like a garment; the moth will eat them up" (Isaiah 50.9).

Before his resurrection, Christ's body was not immune to this same fate. The English mystic Julian of Norwich describes the wearing out of Christ's flesh as it hung on the cross: "[The thorns] cut it in many pieces, like a cloth, and it sagged as if it were on the verge of falling off.... This was a great sorrow and dread to me, for it seemed to me I would not, for my life, have seen it fall.... [The body was] hanging up in the air, as men hang a cloth to dry."[20] Emphasizing the perishability of the flesh, Julian describes gravity turning Christ's body against itself, so that its own weight widens its wounds. As perishable as it is—the Virgin in Mostaert's painting seems to tell us with her gaze—this body of sagging cloth is your only access to God.

The understanding of Christ's flesh as access to the kingdom of heaven finds its definitive figure in the temple curtain: "we have confidence to enter the sanctuary by the blood of Jesus, by the new and living way that he opened for us through the curtain (that is, through his flesh)" (Hebrews 10.19–20).[21] At Christ's death, the curtain hiding the Holy of Holies was parted: "Then Jesus cried again with a loud voice and breathed his last. At that moment the curtain of the temple was torn in two, from top to bottom" (Matthew 27.50–51). Although commentators confidently assert that this tearing signifies the end of the era of the law and the beginning of the era of grace and that Christ's flesh is the means by which one passes from the old to the new, this imagery is complex, even contradictory. While John Chrysostom (d. 407) says that Christ's flesh is "a veil concealing the Godhead," Christ is also the incarnation in whose very flesh the Godhead is *made visible*.[22] Christ's flesh hides the Godhead and yet, also and at once, reveals it.

The Cloths in Mostaert's Painting

The shroud in Mostaert's painting reflects the duplicity of the trope of Christ as veil. While, in some areas, it appears to lie flat on the ground within the painting's illusionistic space—for example, where Nicodemus steps on its edge, as if to hold it down—in other areas, it rises to meet the vertical picture plane. In an already shallow illusionistic space, with figures densely packed together, this white cloth in the foreground comes forward as if into the viewer's space. The series of folds in the lower right corner, running parallel to the right edge of the panel, accentuates this effect. Where the shroud covers the Virgin's lap, it also rises to meet the picture plane. This push forward brings the shroud into alignment with Christ's torso, reinforcing its role as a body double that makes Christ visible (*reveals* him) in his absence. But where the shroud comes up to meet the picture plane, it also resembles a curtain falling in front of Mostaert's altarpiece, *hiding* that altarpiece from view—as if behind a Lenten veil.

In its duplicity, the shroud in Mostaert's composition is comparable to the shroud in the *Visitatio sepulchri*, the paraliturgical rite performed on Easter morning. Representing the visit of the three women to Christ's tomb after the resurrection, this was the most elaborately staged of the paraliturgical rites. The women—generally impersonated by male members of the clergy—arrive at the grave, where the angel greets them with the question: *Quem quaeritis?* "Whom do you seek?" They reply that they are looking for Christ but are summarily dismissed by the angel, who tells them: "He is not here: he is risen, just as he foretold. Go, announce that he is risen from the sepulcher."[23] In many versions of the rite, one of the women or the angel then displays to the congregation the empty cloths left behind in the tomb, saying: "behold the linen cloths and the handkerchief, and the body is not found in the sepulcher."[24] The *Monastic Agreement* describes this moment: "rising and lifting up the veil, [the person playing the part of the angel] shall show them the place void of the Cross and with only the linen in which the Cross had been wrapped."[25] With this ostension and its accompanying words, the linen shroud becomes proof of Christ's resurrection.[26]

Much like the cloth held up at the grave and the words with which the angel scolds the women—"he is not here"—the shroud in Mostaert's painting announces that the body is gone or, rather, that it *will soon* be. Joseph and Nicodemus present the iconic body of Christ, while the blankness of the shroud below them unfolds a proleptic vision of this very body's imminent disappearance. Mostaert's shroud is what Georges Didi-Huberman calls a "dissemblant" patch of painting, which has the effect of "negating or clouding" what the painting affirms "in the mimetic order."[27] In contrast to the iconic image above, the shroud is an "indexical, nondescriptive, and dissemblant" representation of the body.[28]

But in order to truly disturb the mimetic order, the shroud must court the very mimesis it negates. It does so by filling the space given to the compassionate Virgin in Rogier's painting, by resting on a robe whose sleeves resemble the horizontal beam of a cross, and by being made of cloth—a substance metaphorically interchangeable with Christ's flesh. And though there is not yet an image of the body imprinted on this cloth, it already bears small proleptic indices of the body to be deposited there. Two dark streaks to the right of the Virgin's knees read as shadows cast by Christ's arms as they hang in front of his body. These shadows—which are of the same indexical nature as the blood and sweat deposited on the Veronica cloth—anticipate the imminent deposition of Christ onto the shroud and his only slightly less imminent resurrection.

If in Rogier's *Deposition*, the compassionate Virgin repeats Christ's shape, in Mostaert's triptych, that shape finds its double in the guise of cloth—both on the interior and the exterior of the altarpiece. On the interior, that double is a blank shroud; on the exterior, it is a miraculous image imprinted on a sudarium. The exterior of Mostaert's triptych pictures the moment after Veronica has mercifully wiped the sweat from Christ's brow and received a miraculous image of his face lastingly imprinted on her veil. Although the image on Veronica's cloth resembles the flesh-and-blood Christ just behind it, there are telling differences between the two. While the body struggling to bear the cross is firmly planted in illusionistic space, the cloth exists in some other realm. Fully frontal and echoing the shape of the altarpiece's frame, the veil appears to hover at the level of the picture plane—much like the shroud displayed in Mostaert's *Deposition*. And insofar as this veil covers part of the very body whose face it has preserved, it too has the duplicitous effect of hiding and revealing.

By bringing them right up to the picture plane, Mostaert puts the veil and the shroud seemingly within the viewer's reach. The altarpiece's original context, a side altar in the Church of St. Bavo, would have supported this invitation to touch the veil and especially the shroud. In this setting, the white cloth depicted at the bottom of the *Deposition* would have been visually contiguous with a *real* white cloth—the corporal covering the altar.[29] This contiguity would have made possible the fantasy of a bodily reception of Christ—even the fantasy of donning that body in the form of a garment. Gerlach Peters of the *Devotio moderna* writes: "He has clothed us with his example."[30] Julian of Norwich says: "He is our clothing, who, for love, wraps us up, holds us close."[31] And in a lyric from a collection of materials for preaching assembled around 1372, the Franciscan John of Grimestone writes: "I wolde ben clad in cristes skyn."[32]

The tactility of the shroud in Mostaert's *Deposition* and its contiguity with a cloth that could in fact be taken in hand gave concrete form to these strange turns of phrase, so that the beholder could imagine experiencing Christ's body corporeally rather than purely visually. In the shroud—that "dissemblant" patch of painting—mimesis gives way *not to the purity of absence* but rather to a flesh that has slipped free of the body that shapes it. Mostaert's iconoclastic lowering of the icon into the aniconic formlessness of cloth does not release the viewer into an imageless beyond. Rather, it demands that the viewer take on—even that he *put on*—the image's deathly raiment.

Vignette: Robert Rauschenberg's* Untitled (Self-Portrait) *(1952)

In 1952 or so, Robert Rauschenberg photographed himself at Black Mountain College lying on two thin, stacked mattresses (figure 67). Above and slightly behind his body, a narrow strip of painting is visible hanging on the wall—a vertical counterpoint to his prone body. This painting, Rauschenberg's body, and the mattresses together comprise only about one-third of the composition. A white area fills the rest of the frame. Hard to bring into focus, this area reads as a horizontal surface seen from above. In this respect, it resembles a photograph Rauschenberg took that same year, either from a window or a roof, of a slightly out-of-focus and strangely undulating street in Tangier (figure 68).

It feels as if we are looking down at the white area in the self-portrait in part because its blankness reveals all the imperfections of the photograph itself, many of which are indices of either the film or the print's horizontal position during the developing and printing processes. The horizontal impression this blankness makes corresponds to what Leo Steinberg would famously name the flatbed picture plane:

> Something happened in painting around 1950—most conspicuously (at least within my experience) in the work of Robert Rauschenberg and Dubuffet. We can still hang their pictures—just as we tack up maps and architectural plans, or nail a horseshoe to a wall for good luck. Yet these pictures no longer simulate vertical fields but opaque flatbed horizontals. They no more depend on a head-to-toe correspondence with human posture than a newspaper does. The flatbed picture plane makes its symbolic allusion to hard surfaces such as tabletops, studio floors, charts, bulletin boards—any receptor surface on which objects

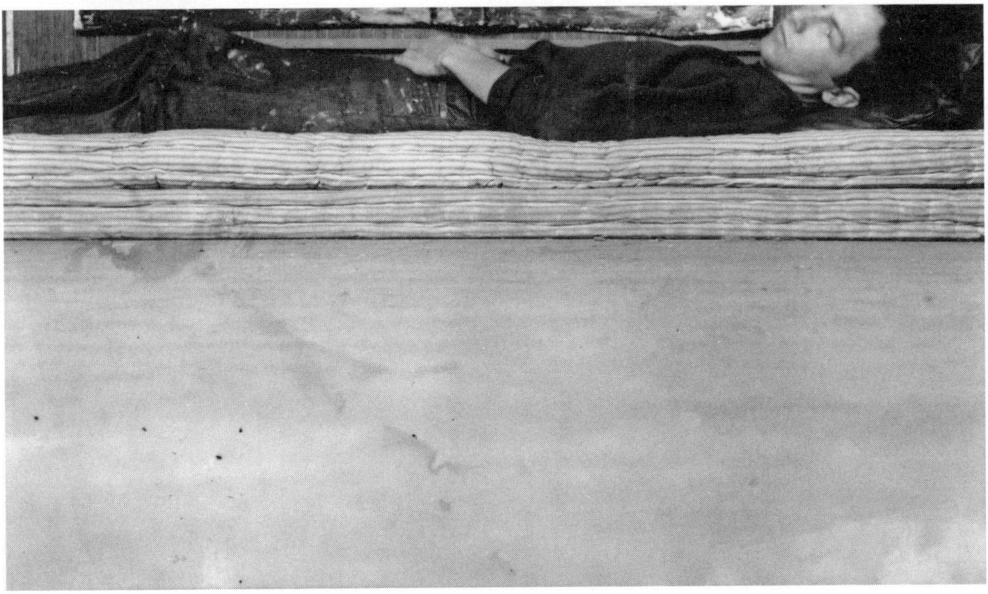

Figure 67. Robert Rauschenberg, *Untitled (Self-Portrait)* (ca. 1952), gelatin silver print, 8.3 × 14 cm. San Francisco Museum of Art, purchased through a gift of Phyllis Wattis. (Photo: San Francisco Museum of Art.)

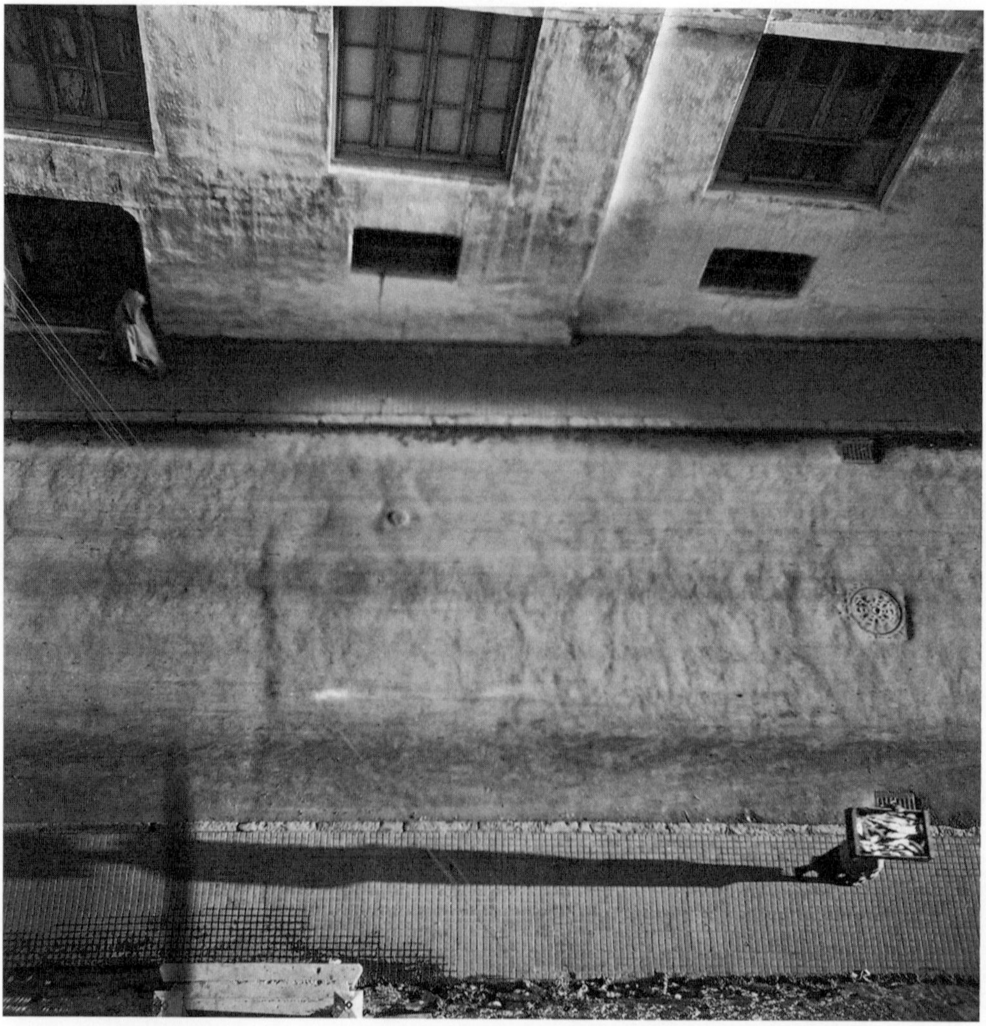

Figure 68. Robert Rauschenberg, *Tangier Street (II)* (1952), gelatin-silver print, 50.8 × 40.6 cm. Collection of the artist. © Estate of Robert Rauschenberg/Licensed by VAGA, New York. (Photo: Robert Rauschenberg, Inc.)

> are scattered, on which data is entered, on which information may be received, printed, impressed—whether coherently or in confusion.[33]

The white area filling two-thirds of the Black Mountain self-portrait is such a "receptor surface," on which particles have been and—its blankness invites us to imagine—will continue to be deposited.

This self-portrait follows directly on the heels of Rauschenberg's 1951 series of white paintings (figure 69). From early on, John Cage recognized the emptiness of the white paintings as an invitation to intervention: "the white paintings were airports for the lights, shadows, and particles"[34]; "the white paintings caught whatever fell on them; why did I not look at them with my magnifying glass? Only because I didn't yet have one? Do you agree with the statement: After all, nature is better than art?"[35] Many of the ideas gathered up in Steinberg's concept of the flatbed picture plane are implicit in Cage's metaphors of landing and falling. Flatness, as Steinberg describes it, and whiteness, as Cage describes it, have a lot in common: the embrace of change, the intermingling of life and art, the uncensored reception of whatever is around, and—perhaps most important—the idea that painting is a matter of letting things fall.

The white paintings—on which gravity deposits whatever is in the atmosphere (to the extent that it is possible to deposit something on a painting *as it hangs on the wall*)—are not authored works of art in any simple sense. Cage remarks of Rauschenberg's work that "the signature is nowhere to be seen" and that it is "an entertainment in which to celebrate unfixity."[36] This unfixity allows the white paintings to receive a fresh coat of paint or even to be entirely refabricated from time to time. In fact, Rauschenberg stipulated that they be periodically retouched; he "didn't want their past to be a mark on them."[37] To continually erase the past of the white paintings is to hold them open to future deposits from the air.

In groping for an account of the attenuated authorship of the white paintings, it seems it was easy to revert to loosely religious metaphors. Rauschenberg mentions God, and a virgin, before naming *Today* as their creator: "They are large white (1 white as 1 GOD) canvases organized and selected with the experience of time and

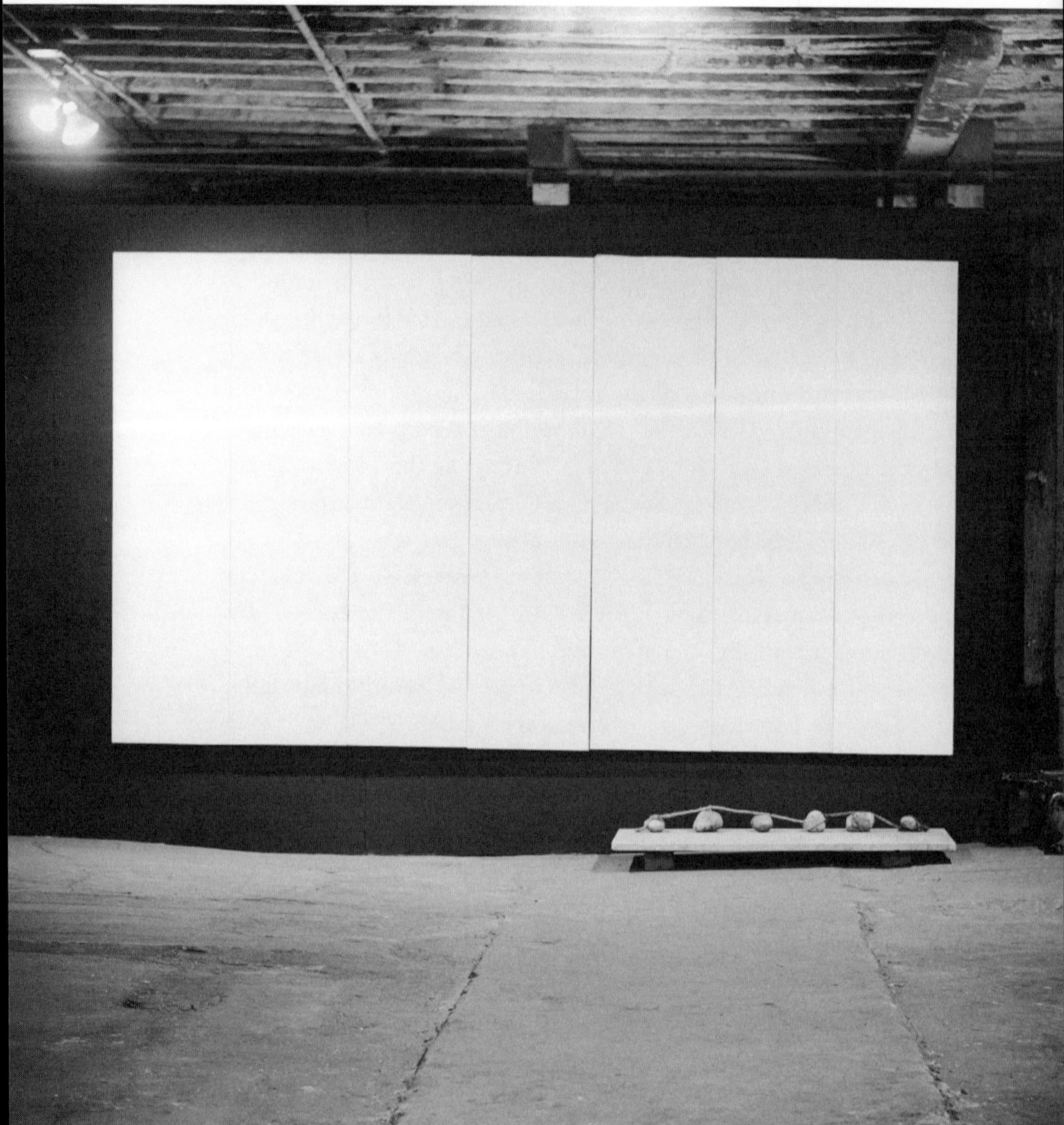

Figure 69. *An Exhibition by Robert Rauschenberg at the Stable Gallery in New York* (1953). © Estate of Robert Rauschenberg/Licensed by VAGA, New York. (Photo: Allan Grant/Time & Life Pictures/ Getty Images.)

presented with the innocence of a virgin. Dealing with the suspense, excitement and body of an organic silence, the restriction and freedom of absence, the plastic fullness of nothing, the point a circle begins and ends. They are a natural response to the current pressures of the faithless and a promoter of intuitional optimism. It is completely irrelevant that I am making them—*Today* is their creator."[38] The painting receptive to deposits of light and dust is open to the interventions of *non-human* as well as human authors; it is an image not made (entirely) by human hands.

Given how emphatic he was that his work be open to everything, above all the ordinary, it might be best to overlook Rauschenberg's reference to God and the "pressures of the faithless" in his explanation of this non-human making. The same could be said of Cage's mention of the gods. For, he also resorted to the divine in describing Rauschenberg's process: "There is in Rauschenberg, between him and what he picks up to use, the quality of encounter. For the first time. If, as happens, there is a series of paintings containing such and such a material, it is as though the encounter was extended into a visit on the part of the stranger (who is divine).... Shortly the stranger leaves, leaving the door open."[39] While to "pick up" something is to encounter the low, to be visited by a divine stranger is generally to be approached from above—though this becomes more complicated when that divine stranger comes, for example, in the guise of a beggar.

Recent scholarship on Rauschenberg rigorously distinguishes between high and low, favoring the former, in accordance with Steinberg's account of the flatbed picture.[40] Although this preference agrees with Rauschenberg's commitment to the ordinary, it risks flattening a process that Cage describes, perhaps more accurately, in *multi-directional* terms. Cage takes into account the fact that the low can become the high, for example, when Rauschenberg picks it up and puts it in the upright painting, and Cage returns again and again to the idea that what enters the painting (be it god or trash) may just as quickly disappear, moving out of the painting *in any direction*: "Shortly the stranger leaves, leaving the door open."[41]

The Black Mountain self-portrait brings together the inviting whiteness of the white paintings and the "symbolic allusion to hard [horizontal] surfaces such as tabletops and studio floors" of the flatbed picture plane. To understand the dynamic this creates, one needs a sense of the multi-directional comings and goings that Cage describes. Cage's sensitivity to mutability is particularly relevant to the medium of photography, whose indexicality registers events of even short duration. In Rauschenberg's photographic self-portrait, the white, flatbed area—a receptor surface lying open to change—stands for this unfixity. Above that, at the very upper limit of the composition, Rauschenberg's body is poised to escape the frame; he would only need to sit up in order to rise out of both the horizontal register and the picture.

Compare the body suspended over the aniconic expanse of white cloth in Mostaert's painting to the body arrayed above the white area in Rauschenberg's self-portrait. In both altarpiece and photograph, the body has been brought low, and below the body is registered a loss of face, a fall from figuration into blankness, as if the lowering of the body had freed up a flat, aniconic space that invites human and non-human intervention alike. In the case of the shroud, that non-human intervention will be a miraculous imprint of Christ's dead body, and in the case of the photograph, the atmosphere's utterly ordinary deposits of light and dust. On the former, one body will be deposited all at once, and on the latter, countless particles over an indefinite period of time—a process that began during the taking of the photograph, continued through its developing and printing, and that will go on indefinitely as the print collects dust.

In Mostaert's painting, the shadows the body casts on the shroud foretell the sweat and blood soon to be registered there; there is no openness in this regard. But in stretching an aniconic white cloth across the bottom of his painting, Mostaert *suspends* the action at the moment of this foretelling: he offers the viewer a shroud whose not-yet-fixed state invites any number of imaginary interventions, including putting on that cloth as if it were a garment. Suspense is once again the operative term here: "the suspense, excitement and body of an organic silence," as Rauschenberg says, "the restriction and freedom of absence, the plastic fullness of nothing."[42] The suspension of the body just above the shroud foretells the depositing of an icon but leaves the cloth forever free of the icon's fixed, authoritative, upright form.

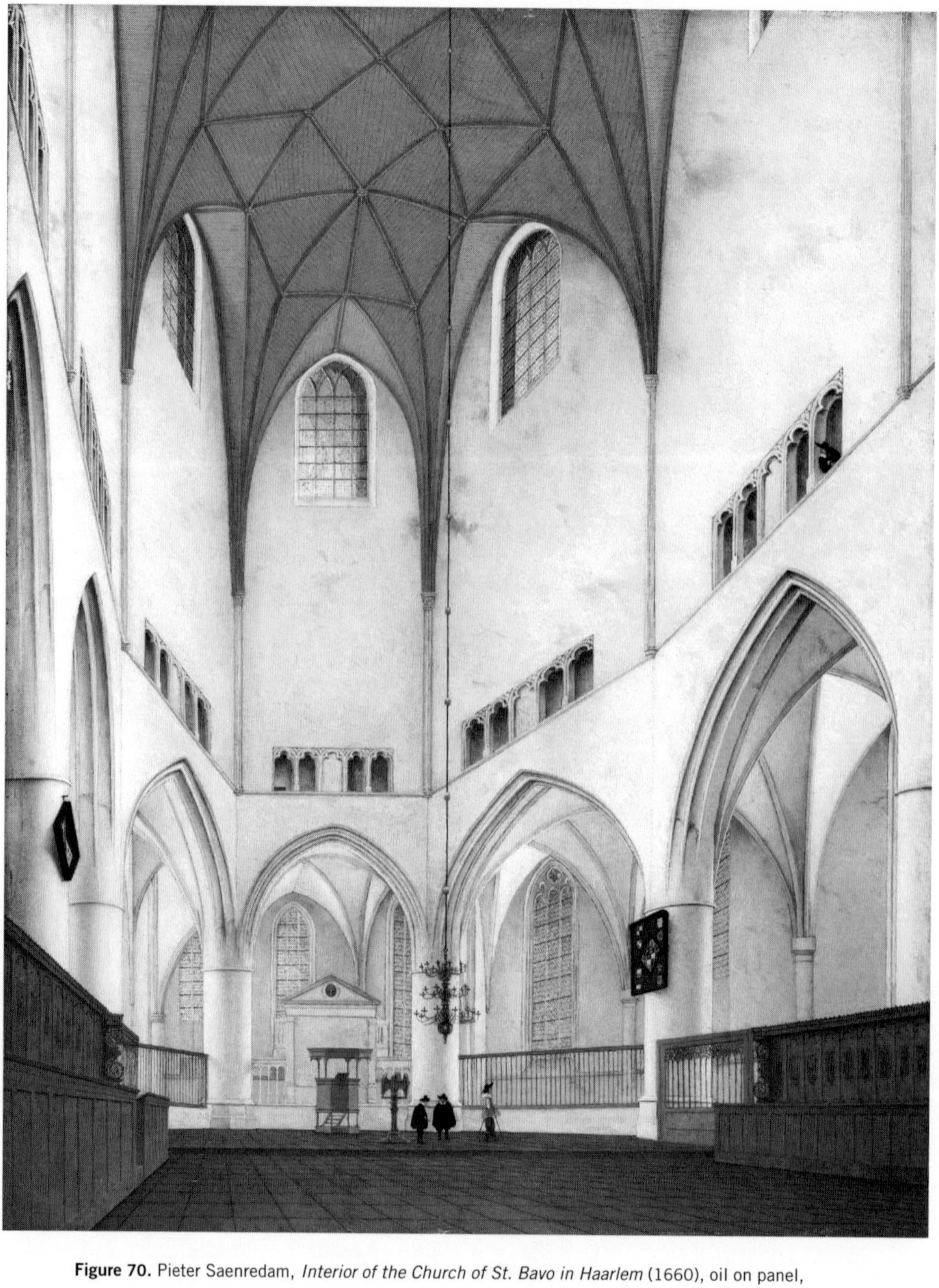

Figure 70. Pieter Saenredam, *Interior of the Church of St. Bavo in Haarlem* (1660), oil on panel, 70.4 × 54.8 cm. Worcester Art Museum, Charlotte E. W. Buffington Fund. (Photo: Worcester Art Museum.)

CONCLUSION

Hans Holbein's *Dead Christ in the Tomb*

Around 1520, Mostaert's *Triptych of the Deposition from the Cross* was installed in the Church of St. Bavo in Haarlem. One hundred and forty years later, Pieter Saenredam painted a picture of the interior of that church, after it had been purged of altarpieces like Mostaert's and whitewashed (figure 70). I hope to have shown in the preceding chapters that the historical divide between Mostaert's triptych and Saenredam's painting is not as absolute as it may at first seem. In the cloths and shutters that covered images during Lent; in the Good Friday Deposition rite that made a spectacle of the deadness of the image and put it away in a box; in crucifixes with movable arms built to disappear; in the rhyme between Rogier's Virgin and Christ; in the wound at the center of the Bartholomew Master's Paris *Deposition*; in the woodenness of that same painter's puppets; and finally, in the aniconic shroud at the bottom of Mostaert's triptych, there are small pre-figurations of the epic deposition of the image that would occur during the Protestant Reformation.

Despite being nowhere visible, the tomb plays an important role in the paintings of the deposition that I have discussed. It is the space beyond the frame toward which the dead body is being conveyed. Unlike the "off-screen" space of the Disappearing Christ—which is nothing less than the supremely sublimatory space of heaven, into which the Gregorian image disappears without a trace—the tomb is where the deposed image persists even after it has been lowered from sight. In the Good Friday Deposition rite, this tomb was not only a visible part of the ceremony but also an object of devotion.

That devotion is reflected in bequests for the maintenance of the Holy Sepulcher and in evidence of the desire to be buried near it.[1] The sepulcher was a place to meditate on the eternal life that Christ's death made possible. To be buried next to it was to pursue the possibility of being resurrected along with Christ.

The attention lavished on the sepulcher and the dead image hidden within it during the annual grave rest is somewhat at odds with late medieval image-devotion as Panofsky, Ringbom, Belting, and others describe it: "The viewer and the person depicted in the image were related to one another mimetically," writes Belting. "The viewer tried to assimilate himself to the depicted person and demanded back from the latter the quality of aliveness which he himself possessed."[2] The image declared dead and removed to the obscurity of the grave was, needless to say, hardly in a position to respond to such a demand. Only insofar as the viewer imagined dying along with the image could an alternate form of reciprocity between the two be achieved. Developing a theme from Paul's letter to the Romans, Thomas Aquinas writes: "those who are baptized ... and who through Christ's death die to their sins, are as it were buried with him by immersion."[3] *The Imitation of Christ* (ca. 1418) takes this "dying with" as one of its leitmotifs: "He is weary of life, and longs for death to release him, that he may be dissolved, and be with Christ."[4] Dying with Christ offers an experience of resemblance within the dark enclosure of the tomb—an experience that holds out the hope of resurrection.

But where this practice of "dying with" involved devotion to an image, an ironic resemblance between the devotee and that image came into play; and here the matter of resurrection was more complicated. Devotion to the sepulcher, adoration of its obscurity and the lifeless image that did not return one's gaze or respond to one's voice from within it, made possible a reciprocity on the far side of death. There, one met a dead image, in whose presence one experienced a commensurate stillness. The crucifix with movable arms, that gratuitously lifeless object, was the ideal image to practice this dying with. But to die with *this* image—as opposed to the *imago Dei* himself—did not bring one any closer to the afterlife since, unlike Christ, the dead image was not destined for heaven.

The Tomb

In his reading of E. T. A. Hoffmann's story "The Sandman," Freud argues that the doll is a narcissistic love object, onto which the protagonist of the story projects his own passivity—the ultimate form of which, one could surmise, would be death.[5] Extrapolating from Freud's reading, one might say that the person who addresses himself or herself to an effigy—as did the person who prayed at the sepulcher during the grave rest—addresses *himself or herself* as a corpse. This experience of oneself as inanimate (and, in the case of the *buried* effigy, unseen) is a proleptic experience of death, which answers to the death drive—the death drive that, according to Freud, fuels the compulsive repetitions of the *fort-da* game.

Lacan will agree that it is the death drive which motivates the repeated banishments of the reel into the bed: "The death instinct essentially expresses the limit of the subject's historical function.... This [limit] is the dead person *(le mort)* that subjectivity takes as its partner.... Thus there is no need to resort to the outdated notion of primary masochism to explain repetitive games in which subjectivity simultaneously masters its dereliction and gives birth to the symbol."[6] The death (or dead person) to which Lacan here refers is not an alien force or being but rather a part of the subject himself; and the reel is, accordingly, "not the mother reduced to a little ball by some magical game... it is a small part of the subject that detaches itself from him while still remaining his, still retained."[7] The compulsive replaying of the mother's unpleasant departure may look like masochism, but in fact it is the testing of a limit—the limit of the subject and the symbolic order alike. The game is structured around the (sepulchral) bed because this curtained space represents what lies beyond that limit, and the child knows that some part of himself exists there.

What would it mean to see beyond that limit? What would it mean, in other words, to see inside the sepulcher? In his 1521 painting *Dead Christ in the Tomb*, Hans Holbein the Younger takes us into the darkness of the grave, the hidden space into which the deposed image (and the child's reel) disappears (plate 7).[8] In taking us there, Holbein professes to show us what cannot be symbolized; this is what the opening of Christ's tomb usually reveals. Pictures of Christ's open tomb generally show it *empty*. This emptiness proves that Christ has been resurrected and signifies, in turn, that his divinity cannot be pictured. But the grave that *Holbein* opens to our view does not point us to a truth that exceeds the image. Instead of finding the longed-for plenitude that has lured us to this hidden place and kept us repeating the iconoclastic sepulchering of the allegorical object—instead, even, of discovering a negative way toward that plenitude—we will discover a body, and an abject one at that.

The original purpose of Holbein's oddly shaped panel remains a subject of debate.[9] The earliest surviving record of it occurs in the 1586 inventory of the Amerbach-Kabinett, a collection established by Bonifacius Amerbach, a Basel lawyer and friend of both Holbein and Erasmus. The record reveals nothing about the panel's function. Christian Müller argues that Holbein made it for the Amerbach family epitaph in the small cloister of the Carthusian monastery of Basel, less than a decade before iconoclasm shook that city, but that it was never installed because it failed to conform to Protestant expectations for religious images.[10]

Whether or not this was the case, there is no doubt that the Reformation had a profound affect on Holbein's life and career. Although it is difficult to say precisely the extent to which Protestant views colored Holbein's attitude toward religious images, the *Dead Christ in the Tomb* offers some insight into the matter. Holbein constructs his painting as if the fourth wall of a stone niche had been removed. The life-size body within completely fills the space. The ribs of the corpse nearly brush the top of the tomb, and the hair and right hand fall over its lower edge, as if the space were not quite large enough to contain the body and opening it had permitted the body to partially escape.

Until fairly recently, commentators saw Holbein's unflinching depiction of Christ's corpse as a radical departure from medieval iconography and piety. Some—notably Fyodor Dostoyevsky—went so far as to say that the painting could only have been the work of a non-believer.[11] Not until Herbert van Einem's article of 1960 was Holbein's panel shown to belong to an iconographic tradition of representing the dead Christ. Van Einem identifies various precedents for Holbein's painting, including the Byzantine *epitaphios*, a large cloth embroidered or otherwise decorated with an image of the dead Christ that was used in the Good Friday liturgy of the Orthodox Church (figure 71).[12]

By identifying precedents for Holbein's composition, van Einem clarifies its relation to a late medieval piety that he summarizes as a call to compassion for the suffering Christ. But if Holbein's painting can now be understood as a pious meditation on Christ's suffering, it is nonetheless strange: it differs from earlier and contemporary images in its isolation of the corpse.[13] Most images of the dead Christ locate the body, by one means or another, within the story of salvation: in the Crucifixion and the Entombment, the narrative clearly frames the body; in the Pietà, the Virgin presents the body and exemplifies a compassionate response to it; in the Man of Sorrows, either angels present the body or Christ presents himself by pointing to his wounds. These various forms of presentation make clear that there is a *reason* for this death. Holbein avails himself of none of these devices for indicating the body's role in the story of salvation. And although the nail-wounds in Christ's hand and foot and the lance-wound in his side are visible, the usual marks of flagellation and crowning with thorns are not.

The perfect coincidence of the edges of Holbein's painting and the limits of the tomb confirms the absolute separateness of this body. Precedent for this sort of isolation is not to be found in images of Christ but rather in representations of ordinary corpses (figure 72). This precedent is surprising since Christ's death is anything but ordinary. This precedent, coupled with Holbein's gruesome depiction of the corpse, was so surprising, in fact, that someone felt

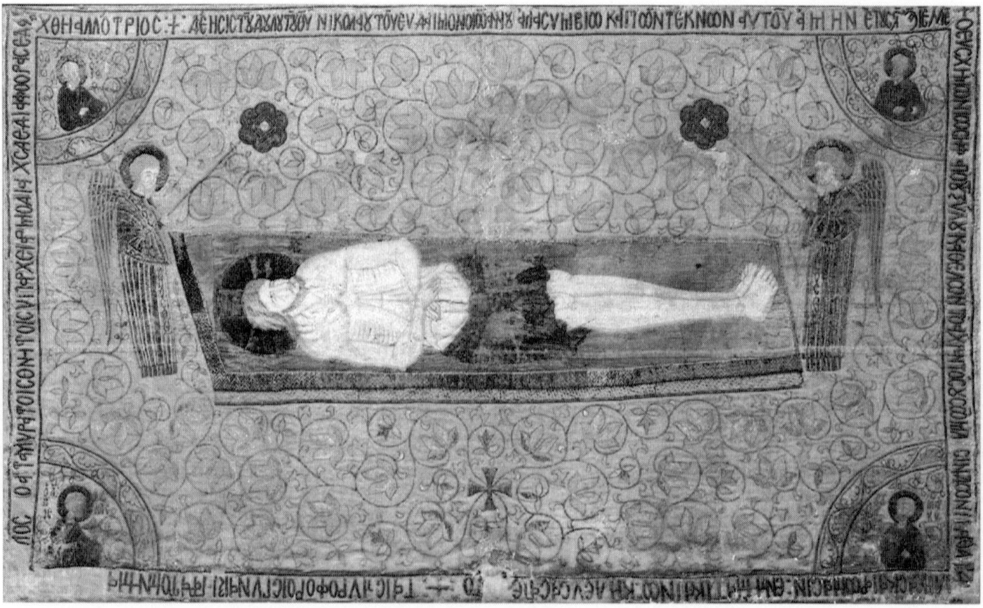

Figure 71. Greek, *Epitaphios* (ca. 1407), embroidered silk, 85.5 × 140.5 cm. Victoria and Albert Museum, London. (Photo: Victoria and Albert Museum.)

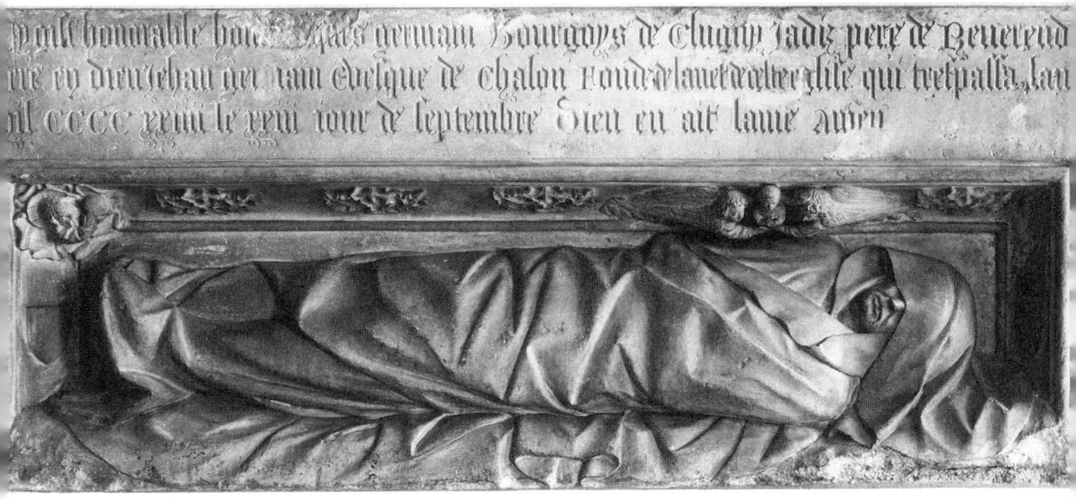

Figure 72. *Tomb Effigy of Jacques Germain* (ca. 1424) from the Carmelite Church, Dijon. Musée des Beaux-Arts, Dijon. (Photo: The Courtauld Institute of Art, London.)

compelled early on to add an identifying label to Holbein's painting. The Amerbach inventory records the panel as: "An image of a dead man by H. Holbein in oil paint on wood." A dead man, the inventory tells us—not Christ.[14] In the margin of the inventory record, the words *cum titulo Jesus Nazarenus Rex Jud* were added at a later date.[15] This annotation reflects the paper titulus with gilded lettering that adorns the upper part of the panel's frame—"Jesus the Nazarene, King of the Jews." Probably added in the later sixteenth century, the titulus (and the corresponding marginal note in the inventory) should eliminate the delay that Holbein builds into our experience of viewing the painting—that delay between our first look at the body and our recognition of it as Christ.[16] But judging from the responses of modern commentators, including Dostoyevsky, the addition of the explanatory title has, in fact, done little to mitigate this effect.

The ongoing capacity of Holbein's painting to baffle viewers is due in part to its rhetoric of surprise—that is, its staging of itself as an uncovering of something not meant to be seen. Horror in the face of the sudden and unexpected revelation of Christ's flesh and a desire to avoid seeing it were expressed in late medieval discussions of the Eucharist that sought to explain the hiddenness of Christ's body and blood behind the "species" of bread and wine. According to these explanations, the deceptive appearance of the bread and wine is necessary because their *truth* would be unbearable to behold. Arguing against Bérenger de Tours' spiritualist understanding of the Host—the belief that it is merely a sign or symbol of Christ—Lanfranc of Bec (d. 1089) writes: "We believe then that the earthly substances, which are on the Lord's Table, are divinely consecrated in the priestly mystery, and are ineffably, incomprehensibly, wonderfully converted by the operation of heavenly power into the essence of the Lord's body, the species of the things themselves being preserved, and certain other qualities, so that men may not shrink through perceiving what is raw and bloody."[17] In 1565, John Rastell would agree that the flesh is veiled "lest some horror & lothsomenes might trouble vs, if it were geaven in visible forme of flesh . . . vnto vs."[18] And the blood is veiled in the form of wine, Thomas Harding writes, "that there might be no abhorring."[19]

Belief that the revelation of what lies beneath the species of bread and wine could offend and even blind was a feature of anti-semitic legends of Host desecration.[20] According to an anonymous account of the murder and expulsion of the Jews of Wroclaw in 1453, the "Jew Jacob son of Solomon" confessed: "In the centre of the synagogue they placed a table and spread a silk cloth upon it, they laid two hosts on the table and, having cursed bishop Peter Novack, they hit them with birches and broke them so that they started to bleed. When this was seen they were terrified and many were blinded."[21] This terror led to the conversion of the offending Jews, the anonymous chronicler tells us. According to the logic of tales like this one, it was a sign of grace *to be spared* the horrifying (though saving) evidence that non-believers, heretics, and Jews required for conversion.

When the veil of appearances was suddenly, miraculously torn to reveal the true nature of the Host as Christ's flesh, the body did not always appear bloody. These miraculous revelations sometimes uncovered an unscathed infant or a man comfortably seated at the right hand of God the Father. But whether or not the body discovered in the Host was in and of itself abhorrent, consumption of it could provoke disgust, so that even those who saw the Eucharistic body as beautiful had reason to avert their eyes when it came to eating it. Durand de Troarn explains the appearance of bread: "It ought to be faithfully believed that this is accomplished by the appointment of God, so that human weakness, which not wont to feed on its own flesh, may find nothing in the appearance to shrink from."[22] Domenico Cavalca reports a horrific vision of the Host as a child cut into bite-size pieces, concluding: "God, knowing that to eat raw flesh horrifies human nature, ordered that this sacrament assume the guise of bread and wine."[23]

With its extraordinary view into the space of a sepulcher that is meant to mercifully hide the body from view, Holbein's painting of the *Dead Christ* is not unlike the sudden revelations of Christ's body in the Host. Like those revelations, the opening of the tomb exposes more than the viewer really wants to see. Instead of following the expected pattern of having the open tomb be decorously empty, Holbein shows us a body that has begun to decompose. The Gospels give conflicting accounts of how long Christ's body lay in the grave. Some passages say it was three days and three nights. Others say that only a day and two nights passed. Thomas Aquinas cites Augustine in arguing for the latter.[24] The question of whether or not the body suffered corruption in the grave was likewise a matter for scholastic debate. Thomas rejects the possibility: "since Christ was not a sinner, he was under no obligation to suffer death, or to return to dust. He died of his own will for our salvation... The corruption or dissolution of his body would have been detrimental to man's salvation, for it would not then have appeared credible that divine power was in him."[25]

Few late medieval images of the dead Christ deal with the vexed question of Christ's corruption as directly as Holbein's. Whereas most Crucifixions, Depositions, Lamentations, Pietàs, and Entombments represent this body in a narrative context which indicates that it is *but newly dead*, the corpse in Holbein's painting could be as many as several days deceased. The green tint of the flesh around the hand and side-wound suggest that this corpse has already begun to decompose. In his *Christian Directory* (1582), Robert Persons warns vain lovers of beauty: "Lett the soule departe but one halfe hower from the bodye, and this loving face is uglye to looke on: lett yt lye but two dayes in the grave, and those whiche were so hote in love withe yt before, will skarse abyde to beholde yt, or come neare yt."[26] Insofar as burial is motivated by not wanting to see a beautiful body transformed into something abhorrent, the opening of the tomb reveals something not only not meant to be seen but also not necessarily capable of being seen—in the sense of being recognized. By isolating the body from the narrative of salvation, stripping it of certain marks of the passion, and picturing it as many as several days dead, Holbein shows us something that has begun to forfeit not only its beauty but also its identity.

Holbein and the Reformation

Holbein worked for both Catholic and Protestant patrons throughout his career. His earliest extant works are drawings in the margins of a copy of Erasmus's *The Praise of Folly* that belonged to Oswald Myconius, a classical philologist, schoolmaster, reformer, and friend of Erasmus.[27] Among these drawings are several that illustrate the folly of image-worship. These include a drawing of two women lighting candles before a statue of the Virgin, which decorates a passage that calls the cult of images superstition (figure 73).[28] Holbein also made woodcut designs for polemical Lutheran publications printed in Basel around 1522.[29] Yet between 1520 and 1526 he produced a number of images for Catholics, including the *Oberried Altarpiece*, the *Solothurn Madonna*, the *Darmstadt Madonna*, and paintings of the passion and the last supper.[30]

Whether or not Holbein sympathized with Protestants, he cannot have welcomed the iconoclasms that prompted him to leave Switzerland for England in 1526.[31] He was back in Basel by August 1528, only to be confronted with another wave of iconoclasm in February 1529.[32] When he and others in Basel were asked to explain their failure to participate in the Reformed Mass, Holbein responded that he needed a fuller explanation of the ceremony. This infraction did not prevent him from receiving commissions from the Reformed city government.[33] But by 1536, Holbein had nonetheless returned to England to serve as court painter to Henry VIII, who was then in the process of carrying out his own dissolution of the monasteries.

Neither a clear confession of faith nor an explicit position on religious images emerges from what we know of Holbein's biography. But his painting of the dead Christ is cautionary in several respects as far as the image is concerned. By making the image coextensive with the tomb, Holbein equates the two, as if to say that the space of the image *is a tomb* and that what it pictures is perforce dead. Nor does the Gregorian belief that images can serve as bibles of the illiterate find much support in Holbein's painting. The deictic finger that falls over the bottom edge of the tomb points to the delicate, linear folds in the shroud as if they could tell us something

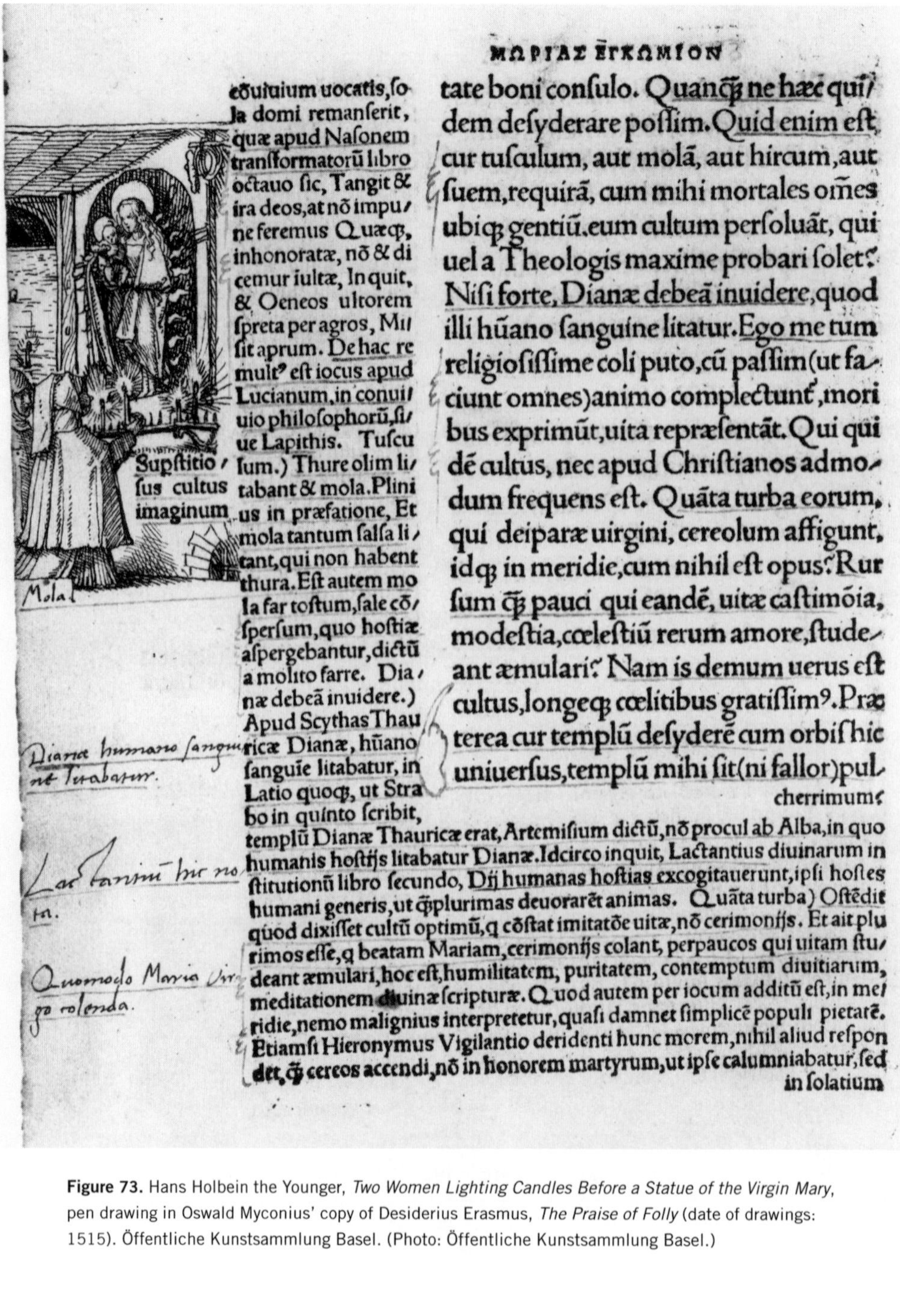

ΜΩΡΙΑΣ ΕΓΚΩΜΙΟΝ

tate boni consulo. Quanquam ne hæc qui/
dem desyderare possim. Quid enim est,
cur tusculum, aut molã, aut hircum, aut
suem, requirã, cum mihi mortales omnes
ubique gentiũ eum cultum persoluãt, qui
uel a Theologis maxime probari solet?
Nisi forte, Dianæ debeã inuidere, quod
illi hũano sanguine litatur. Ego me tum
religiosissime coli puto, cũ passim (ut fa-
ciunt omnes) animo complectunt, mori
bus exprimũt, uita repræsentãt. Qui qui
dẽ cultus, nec apud Christianos admo-
dum frequens est. Quãta turba eorum,
qui deiparæ uirgini, cereolum affigunt,
idque in meridie, cum nihil est opus? Rur
sum quam pauci qui eandẽ, uitæ castimõia,
modestia, cœlestiũ rerum amore, stude-
ant æmulari? Nam is demum uerus est
cultus, longeque cœlitibus gratissim9. Præ
terea cur templũ desyderẽ cum orbis hic
uniuersus, templũ mihi sit (ni fallor) pul-
cherrimum?

cõuiuium uocatis, so-
la domi remanserit,
quæ apud Nasonem
transformatorũ libro
octauo sic, Tangit &
ira deos, at nõ impu/
ne feremus. Quæque,
inhonoratæ, nõ & di
cemur ultæ, Inquit,
& Oeneos ultorem
spreta per agros, Mi/
sit aprum. De hac re
mult9 est iocus apud
Lucianum, in conui/
uio philosophorũ, si/
ue Lapithis. Tuscu
lum.) Thure olim li/
tabant & mola. Plini
us in præfatione, Et
mola tantum salsa li/
tant, qui non habent
thura. Est autem mo
la far tostum, sale cõ/
spersum, quo hostiæ
aspergebantur, dictũ
a molito farre. Dia/
næ debeã inuidere.)
Apud Scythas Thau
ricæ Dianæ, hũano
sanguĩe litabatur, in
Latio quoque, ut Stra
bo in quinto scribit,
templũ Dianæ Thauricæ erat, Artemisium dictũ, nõ procul ab Alba, in quo
humanis hostiis litabatur Dianæ. Idcirco inquit, Lactantius diuinarum in
stitutionũ libro secundo, Dii humanas hostias excogitauerunt, ipsi hostes
humani generis, ut quamplurimas deuorarẽt animas. Quãta turba) Ostẽdit
quod dixisset cultũ optimũ, q cõstat imitatõe uitæ, nõ cerimoniis. Et ait plu
rimos esse, q beatam Mariam, cerimoniis colant, perpaucos qui uitam stu/
deant æmulari, hoc est, humilitatem, puritatem, contemptum diuitiarum,
meditationem diuinæ scripturæ. Quod autem per iocum additũ est, in me/
ridie, nemo malignius interpretetur, quasi damnet simplicẽ populi pietatẽ.
Etiamsi Hieronymus Vigilantio deridenti hunc morem, nihil aliud respon
det, quam cereos accendi, nõ in honorem martyrum, ut ipse calumniabatur, sed
in solatium

Supstitio/sus cultus imaginum

Mola

Dianæ humano sanguine litabatur.

Lactantiu hic nota.

Quomodo Maria Virgo colenda.

Figure 73. Hans Holbein the Younger, *Two Women Lighting Candles Before a Statue of the Virgin Mary*, pen drawing in Oswald Myconius' copy of Desiderius Erasmus, *The Praise of Folly* (date of drawings: 1515). Öffentliche Kunstsammlung Basel. (Photo: Öffentliche Kunstsammlung Basel.)

(figure 74). Indeed, these calligraphic marks register the shape and weight of the corpse—the elbow, finger, and heel each creating its own set of wrinkles. But these wrinkles are not a legible record of that body's role in salvation. Calligraphic and arrayed like a line of text yet unintelligible, these folds index nothing more than the shape and placement of an object. The dead finger in the center of Holbein's painting directs us, then, to a series of unintelligible marks, which bear only an ironic formal resemblance to the meaningful script of the titulus above. Holbein's painting counters the Gregorian defense of images in two ways: it is neither a visible means to the invisible—this body will not release the viewer's gaze from the narrow space of the sepulcher so that it can ascend to higher things; nor is this painting a story for those who cannot read.

Vignette: Donald Judd's **Untitled** *(1972)*

By his own account, Donald Judd was interested in space: "One reason I don't like to make paintings but like three-dimensional work so much is because I like space a great deal. I spent a lot of time sitting around waiting for classes to begin at Columbia—there was a gap between art school and the university—and I realized that the space underneath the desk was a lot more interesting than what was happening down in the art school. It always looked very good under there. That's my particular interest in space."[34] Judd conflates the temporal gap between classes, the ideological gap between schools, and the spatial gap between the floor and desk. His talk of temporal, ideological, and spatial openings all in one breath captures the far-reaching quality of his interest in interstices. Of course, the clearest expression of this interest is Judd's organization of the spaces separating the units of his own sculptures: "The space between the units, the boxes, or whatever they are, is very important."[35]

Judd's boxes tend to be arranged so that the spaces between them resemble the spaces within them. "If you make it too far apart," Judd explains, "it becomes just a space between the boxes, so you've got to make some equivalence between the volume of the boxes or the enclosed space and the open space."[36] In a wall stack of blue anodized

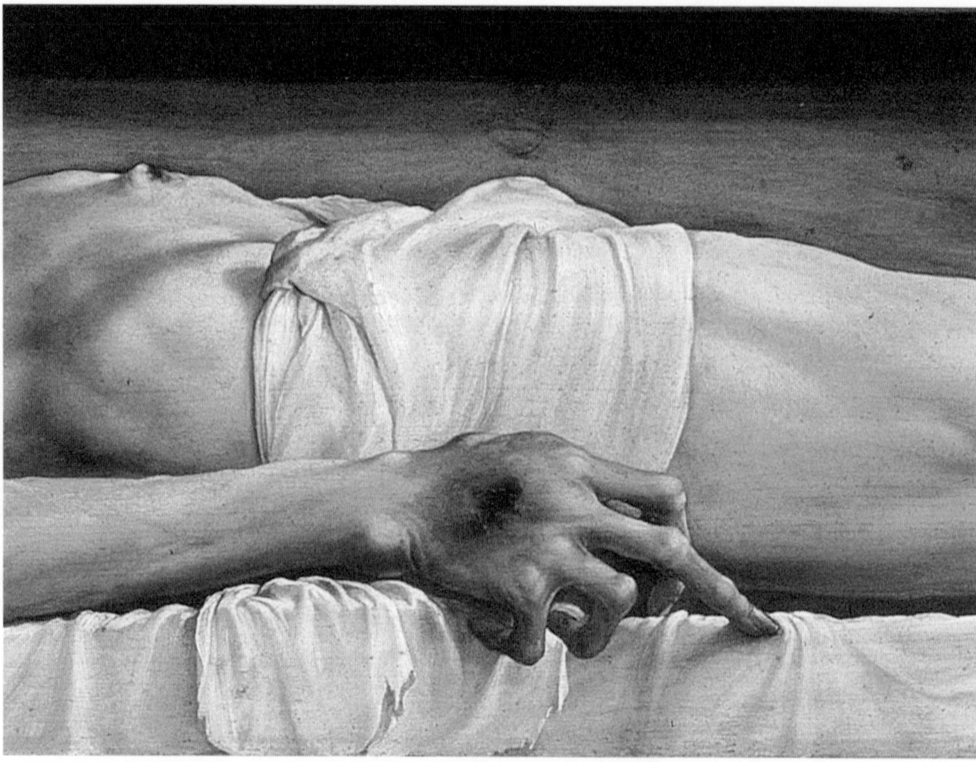

Figure 74. Detail from Plate 7: Hans Holbein the Younger, *Dead Christ in the Tomb* (1521–1522), oil on panel, 30.5 × 200 cm. Kunstmuseum, Basel. (Photo: Erich Lessing/Art Resource, New York.)

aluminum boxes with transparent plexiglass tops and bottoms, the boxes are hung so that the spaces between them have the same dimensions as the boxes themselves (figure 75). By virtue of this equivalence, the interstices take on a kind of mass, making it seem as if the hovering, cantilevered units are no heavier than the gaps that separate them. Judd seems to be referring to both the empty spaces *between* and the empty spaces *within* the units when he says: "I'm also interested in what might be called blank areas, or just plain areas, and what is seen obliquely, like the stack with the plexiglass top and bottom."[37]

According to Judd, exposing the internal space of a box, as he does in his blue stack sculpture, makes for greater clarity: "The use of plexiglass exposes the interior, so the volume is opened up.... It's fairly logical to open it up so the interior can be viewed. It makes it less mysterious, less ambiguous."[38] According to Rosalind Krauss, this opening up does no such thing. Arguing against Judd's own account of his work, Krauss invokes a 1965 essay about Judd by Robert Smithson, where Smithson suggests that the very facts of construction and material that Judd thinks he divests of ambiguity are, in fact, hard to fathom: "What is outside [the boxes] vanishes to meet the inside, while what is inside vanishes to meet the outside. The concept of 'antimatter' overruns, and fills everything, making these very definite works verge on the notion of disappearance."[39]

As an example of what Smithson calls Judd's "uncanny materiality," Krauss cites a large box made of four copper sides, a bottom of aluminum painted with cadmium red enamel, and an open top (plate 8).[40] Inside the box, the copper sides reflect the red of the base so that, although they are simply the reverse of the outside surfaces, they appear very different. In fact, they do not *appear* in quite the same solid way that the exterior surfaces do, dissolved as they are by the pool of reflected color which they seem to hold. Just as Smithson suggests, the opening onto the interior of this box has the somewhat surprising effect of making the facts of its construction less clear. How the box is made and what it is made of become elusive here precisely to the extent that the empty space of the interior takes on a kind of substance, materializing as irrefutably, though nebulously, as a red cloud.

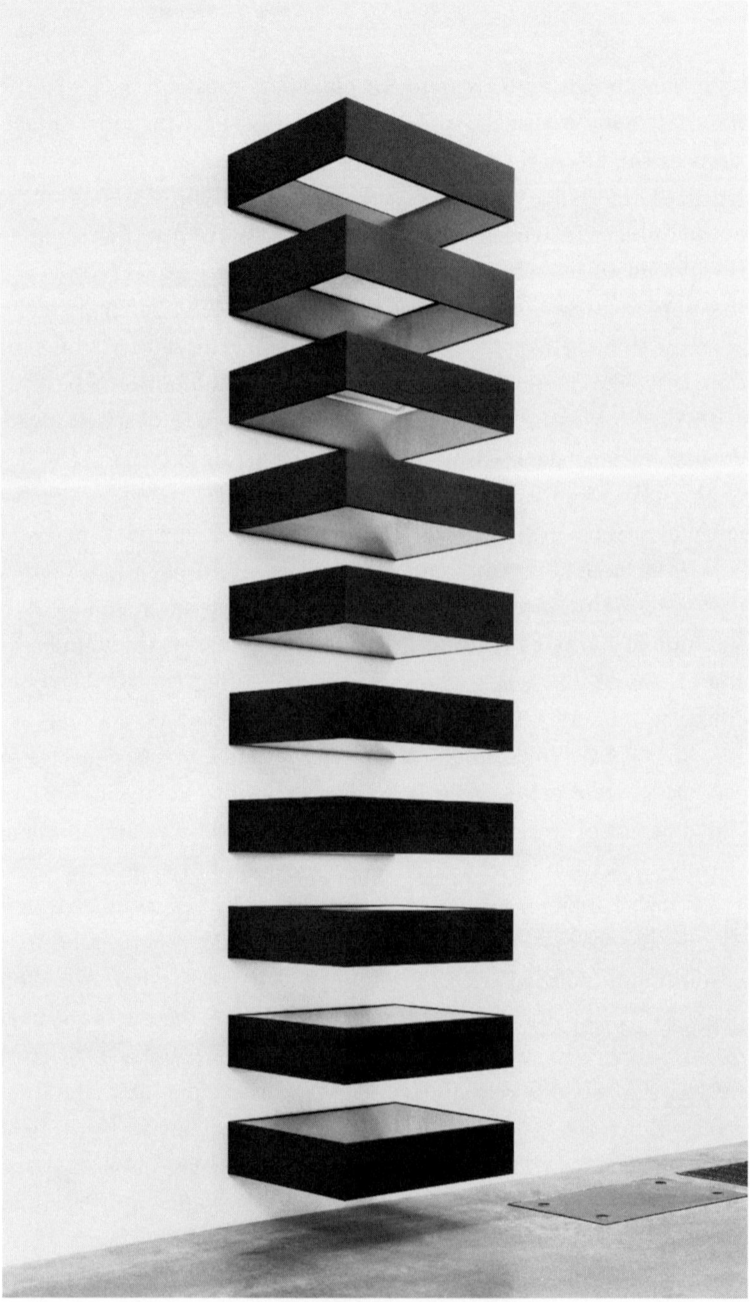

Figure 75. Donald Judd, *Untitled* (1990), anodized aluminum, steel and acrylic, dimensions variable. Tate Modern, London. © Judd Foundation. Licensed by VAGA, New York. (Photo: Tate, London 2009.)

Judd recognizes that even the hardest materials can become elusive: "Sometimes the color is fairly pragmatic and definite, a lot of times it's not. The same with the surface: the metal is often shiny and hard to pin down."[41] But he consistently maintains that this sort of optical indeterminacy does not undermine his commitment to what he sometimes calls objectivity—in opposition to the illusionism of painting.[42] Judd insists that he is only interested in what exists: "Things that exist exist, and everything is on their side. They're here, which is pretty puzzling. Nothing can be said of things that don't exist."[43] Elsewhere, however, Judd says that his work is about making something out of what *does not exist*: "Space doesn't exist; time doesn't exist either. So you have to make them exist. We know space and time, because things occur in them... They are made by positions, events. When you make a work of art, you are making space or further architecture. You are definitely making a space. We have space here in this room, but this is a weak, nondescript, neutral space. If we reorganize the room it could become real space perhaps."[44]

Thinking through this same issue of making spaces that would not otherwise exist, Smithson does something strange in his 1965 essay. In an effort to convey the idea that the internal and interstitial spaces in Judd's sculptures have a kind of palpability and even hardness, he moves from what he calls the dislocation of space, to geological deposits, to the Deposition of Christ: "Space in Judd's art seems to belong to an order of increasing hardness, not unlike geological formations. He has put space down in the form of deposits. Such deposits come from his mind rather than nature. Instead of bringing Christ down from the cross, the way the painters of the Renaissance, Baroque, and Mannerist periods did in their many versions of The Deposition, Judd has brought space down into an abstract world of mineral forms. He is involved in what could be called, 'The Deposition of Infinite Space.'"[45]

Judd publicly distanced himself from Smithson on more than one occasion, and it is hard to imagine him not entirely rejecting this pseudomorphic comparison between his "specific objects" and old-master paintings.[46] But Judd is not so far from Smithson, in fact, when he says, again conflating the temporal, ideological, and spatial: "We are living in a very short time and a very small space in a very big situation. Basically we are living in a little point and everything is infinite in all directions. You have to think about it. I don't think people think about it much."[47] Judd's sculptures do this "thinking" of the relation between the small, interstitial and internal spaces of the work of art and the larger spatial situation in which that work is inscribed. They pull what Smithson calls "infinite space" and what Judd calls "a very big situation" down to earth.

Smithson's discussion of old-master Depositions follows a catalogue of what Judd's art is not: "With Judd there is no confusion between the anthropomorphic and the abstract.... The 'unconscious' has no place in his art.... He translates his concepts into artifices of fact, without any illusionistic representations."[48] In order then to reconcile his reference to the Deposition of Christ with this claim that Judd's work is neither anthropomorphic nor illusionistic, Smithson explains that when Judd puts "space down in the form of deposits," he does not produce a figure: "Time has many anthropomorphic representations, such as Father Time, but space has none. There is no Father Space or Mother Space."[49] Whether or not one accepts Smithson's assertion that space *cannot be anthropomorphized*, it is perhaps still fair to say that Judd, at least, is able to make us aware of space, without putting a face on it.[50] Instead of making images of space, Judd makes facts of space. But precisely because these facts are not organized into a figure, they are "uncanny." Smithson continues: "The important phenomenon is always the basic lack of substance at the core of the 'facts.' The more one tries to grasp the surface structure, the more baffling it becomes. The work seems to have no natural equivalent to anything physical, yet all it brings to mind is physicality."[51]

When Holbein opens the divine sepulcher to view, an equally baffling physicality comes to light—a corpse whose physical presence becomes ever more imposing as its identity fades. This is a body that has been lowered from an anthropomorphic state into what

Smithson calls an abstract world—by which he means a non-figurative form. Holbein's iconoclastic lowering of the image does not free us to move beyond it; his equation of the space of the image with the space of death—his making of the image's frame coextensive with the tomb—is very different, then, from the Gregorian manner of "putting the image in its place." According to Gregory, one acknowledges the limitations of the image so as to transcend it. Had Holbein wanted to move us in that direction, he would have adhered to the convention of picturing Christ's tomb *after the resurrection*. From that empty tomb, from its lack, we might have been able to imagine our way (via opposition) toward the plenitude of presence. Instead, Holbein baffles us with a deposed body, whose fading identity leaves us no choice but to deal directly with its physicality.

POSTSCRIPT

What Became of the Sepulchers

In an *inventarium monumentorum superstitionis* compiled in 1566, we read what became of some fifty-odd Easter sepulchers removed from churches in Lincolnshire: one was "made a shelf to set dishes on"; another was "sold to Hohnne Orson and he haith made a presse thereof to laie clothes therein."[1] Over the course of the Protestant Reformation, the sepulcher became a domestic fixture, a piece of furniture for holding private possessions, including dishes and clothing.[2] With the secularization of the sepulcher, what had held the mystery of an invisible God became a container for personal property.[3] This did not prevent that God from finding his way, via metaphor, back into his cabinet. The seventeenth-century Dutch moralist Dionysius Spranckhuysen holds up the example of the pious woman who, "accepts God . . . and guides him . . . into the cabinet (*het Cabinet*) of her heart, as her most precious treasure."[4] The gradual shift in the function of the sepulcher allowed for coexistence; the effigy of God and the family treasures could, for some time, share the same space. This coexistence confirmed what late medieval dissidents and Reformation radicals had always maintained: the sacred image equals property.

Cabinets filled with more or less precious objects were the quintessential early modern bourgeois furnishing. Over the course of the seventeenth century, massive upright cupboards tended to replace the coffer-shaped chests of the Middle Ages and Renaissance, further (yet never fully) sublimating the cabinet's sepulchral origins.[5] To compensate for a lack of built-in closets and to accommodate a growing quantity of linens, silver, porcelain, and so forth, the uncommonly wealthy homes of seventeenth-century Dutch burghers, for example, had anywhere from eight to twelve large cabinets.[6] The flexibility of the English word cabinet and its cognates in other European languages—all of which designate both a room and a piece of furniture—suggests that the cupboard was understood as a microcosm of the room it stood in.[7]

Pieter de Hooch's painting of two women with a stack of linen pictures the domestic interior as a larger version of the cabinet it houses (figure 76). Here a large, upright, wooden cabinet is nested within a room, within a home, and within a well-ordered, rectilinear urban environment. De Hooch's composition is built upon the opening of each of these enclosures onto the next, with partially open doors and windows permitting views across their thresholds. Half-obscured by the shadow of its open doors, the woman retrieving linen from this cabinet seems to be on the verge of disappearing into its depths, which would be ample enough to accommodate her.

In the nested enclosures of her domestic space and particularly in the anthropometric cabinets that filled it, the early modern subject found a pervasive and elegant metaphor for her own interiority, the careful storing-up of possessions within these cabinets being a rehearsal of the subject's gathering of herself within the privacy of her own head, heart, or soul. The secularization of the Easter sepulcher thus played its small part in helping the modern subject crystallize around a node of the hidden, the mystery of the invisible God becoming the mystery of the interiorized self—more mundane, surely, but no less valuable for having been domesticated.

In a reading of Baudelaire's "Obsession," de Man describes one of the metaphors that has defined this modern, interiorized self: "the subject's presence to itself as a spatial enclosure, room, tomb, or crypt in which the voice echoes as in a cave. The image draws its verisimilitude from its own 'mise-en-abyme' in the shape of the body as the *container* of the voice (or soul, heart, breath, consciousness, spirit, etc.) that it exhales."[8] A (mixed) metaphor of this kind—which confines a *living* lyric voice in a *deathly* architecture—will tend to

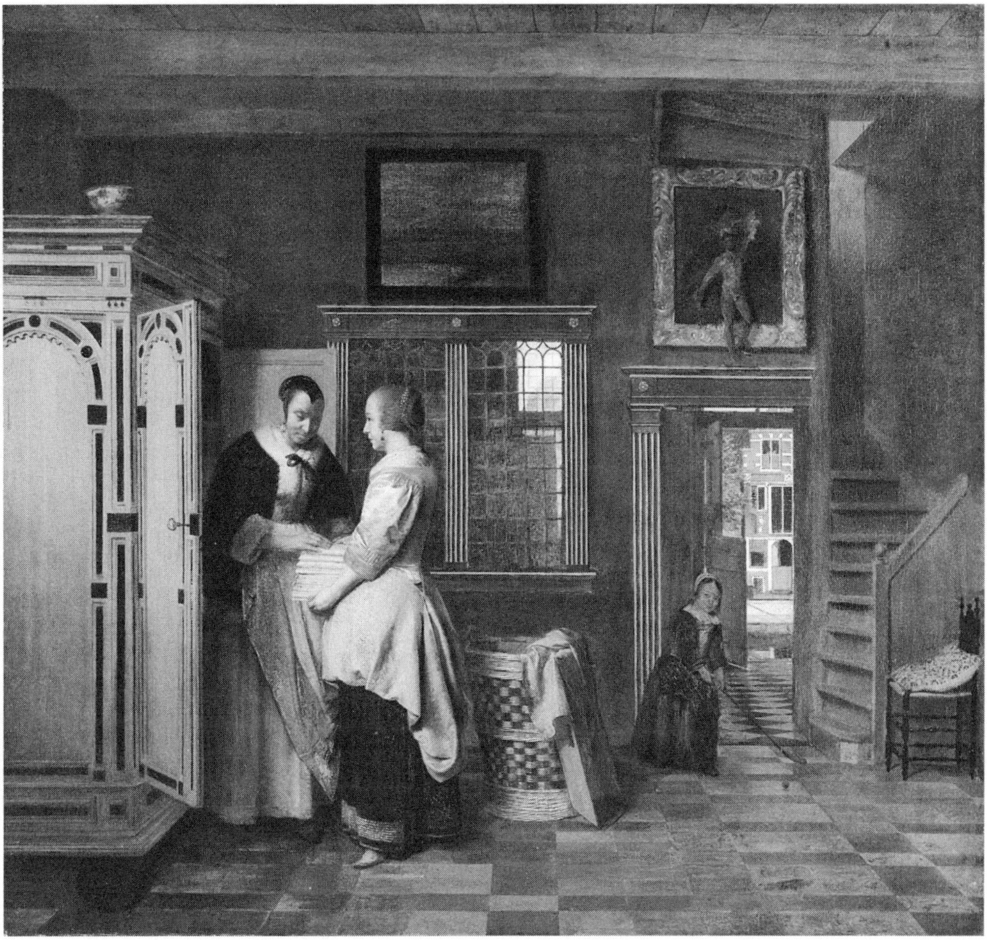

Figure 76. Pieter de Hooch, *The Linen Cabinet* (ca. 1663), oil on canvas, 70 × 75.5 cm. Rijksmuseum, Amsterdam. (Photo: Rijksmuseum.)

come apart, de Man suggests, as it does in Baudelaire's "Spleen II," where the mind is troped as "a hollow container, box, or grave" and where we witness "the transformation of this container, or of the corpse contained in it, into a voice."[9] De Man's reading of "Spleen II" makes clear that this voice, with all its connotations of living self-presence, will be extinguished finally by the sepulchral architecture that houses it.[10]

For Benjamin, from whom de Man's reading of Baudelaire derives, it is the modern subject's identification with the lifeless objects he owns that kills that voice. The subject's identification with his possessions hinges on the domestic interior's isomorphic relation to the decorative box: "The bourgeoisie unabashedly makes impressions of a host of objects. For slippers and pocket watches, thermometers and egg cups, cutlery and umbrellas, it tries to get covers and cases. It prefers velvet and plush covers, which preserve the impression of every touch. For the Makart style, the style of the end of the Second Empire, a dwelling becomes a kind of casing. This style views it as a case for a person and embeds him in it, together with all his appurtenances, tending his traces as nature tends dead fauna embedded in granite."[11] The airless space of the parlor transforms the living subject into one more object in his own collection. And all the rituals of arranging and encasing that domestic life entails—for example, the loving attention to the stack of crisply folded linen in de Hooch's painting—bring one a little closer to death. It is modernity's deathly commodity culture, then, that has kept those late medieval sepulchers, now transformed into cabinets for storing personal possessions, from ever entirely losing their sepulchral aura.

According to Benjamin, while the bourgeoisie was busy enshrouding its dead objects in plush and sentiment, Baudelaire addressed the commodity more heroically.[12] Baudelaire's bearing toward the world of things was made possible by his resuscitation of the obsolete literary form of allegory. Both in its seventeenth and nineteenth-century forms, allegory is grounded in despair over the world: "The allegorical mode of apprehension is always built on a devalued world of appearances. The specific devaluation of the world of things, as manifested in the commodity, is the foundation of Baudelaire's allegorical intention."[13] If the doctrine of original sin once demanded that the pious regard the world as the realm of the fallen, the capitalism of Baudelaire's day required the poet to do the same.[14]

As Benjamin describes it, Baudelaire's allegory differs from its Baroque model in that it has its locus *within the subject*: "In the nineteenth century, allegory withdrew from the world around us to settle in the inner world."[15] This entailed a shift from the flesh-and-blood corpse to its psychic counterpart, the souvenir—the inanimate object lived experience leaves behind: "In [the souvenir] is precipitated the increasing self-estrangement of human beings, whose past is inventoried as dead effects.... The key figure in early allegory is the corpse. In late allegory, it is the 'souvenir.'"[16] Given Baudelaire's obsession with the corpse, Benjamin must mean here that the corpse itself becomes a kind of disembodied memory or souvenir in the nineteenth century. This is what happens in "Spleen II," where Baudelaire takes stock of the mortification of memories within the lyric subject's cluttered head—moving from the cabinet to the graveyard and then back again to the cabinet, this time, in the form of a boudoir:

> Souvenirs?
> More than if I had lived a thousand years!
>
> No chest of drawers crammed with documents,
> love-letters, wedding-invitations, wills,
> a lock of someone's hair rolled up in a deed,
> hides so many secrets as my brain.
> This branching catacombs, this pyramid
> contains more corpses than the potter's field:
> I am a graveyard that the moon abhors,
> where long worms like regrets come out to feed
> most ravenously on my dearest dead.
>
> I am an old boudoir where a rack of gowns,
> perfumed by withered roses, rots to dust;

where only faint pastels and pale Bouchers
inhale the scent of long-unstoppered flasks.[17]

Baudelaire recalls the subject to his origins in the sepulcher. He is both the domestic cabinet and the sepulchral monument, where memories rot like flesh. The brain is a piece of furniture—*un gros meuble à tiroirs*—bloated with "souvenirs" of the now-dead voices of love and law, a graveyard of reified words written in letters and ledgers. The interiorized subject can discover no *living* evidence of himself there, listen as he might for a voice in his own head—the voice "or soul, heart, breath, consciousness, spirit, etc." that, according to the tropes, should echo within him.[18] The lyric voice of "Spleen II" does not transmit the experience of a living subject. Rather, it issues from the same sorts of dead textual and pictorial inscriptions that it will issue in: love-letters, wills, deeds, and *faded paintings*. Along with the sepulcher, then, the dead image buried on Good Friday seems to have been bequeathed to modernity: the poet's cabinet—the secularized sepulcher of his brain—still contains dead images ("faint pastels and pale Bouchers") not unlike those first put there in the Middle Ages.

Anthropomorphism and Art History

In late medieval Depositions, the upright and anthropomorphic God becomes the taken-down God—a (sometimes faceless) image that makes no pretense to life. In light of this, art historians might think twice before attempting to enliven these works of art, the project advocated by Panofsky in his 1940 essay "The History of Art as a Humanistic Discipline"—a project which still holds sway today: "the humanities . . . are not faced by the task of arresting what otherwise would slip away, but of enlivening what otherwise would remain dead."[19]

I wonder what precisely the humanistic discipline of art history purposes to enliven. Did its objects *ever* live? Perhaps this is an unfair question; Panofsky uses a figure of speech after all. But anthropomorphism is the figure to end all figures. "It is a figural affirmation that claims to overcome the deadly negative power invested in the figure," as de Man says.[20] By enlivening its objects, the discipline tries to forget that its objects never in fact belonged to their original contexts, that they have always exceeded those contexts precisely because they are *lifeless things*, which neither live nor die along with the people who make them. Much art history today nevertheless continues to try to breathe life into works of art from the past by imaginatively returning them to the original contexts in which they are said to have lived.

Writing not so long after Panofsky, Adorno was less sanguine about the possibility of resurrecting works of art. More dialectical than either Wimsatt and Beardsley's 1946 essay on the intentional fallacy or Barthes' 1967 essay on the death of the author, Adorno's 1953 meditation on the museum object, "Valéry Proust Museum," stages a confrontation between Valéry's condemnation of the museum as a place in which the deracinated work of art expires—"there, [Válery] says, we put the art of the past to death"—and Proust's celebration of the museum as a place where the work is freed from the life of its maker.[21] In the end, Adorno argues, "neither Proust nor Valéry is right.... Each takes the part of one moment in the truth which lies in the unfolding of contradiction. The fetishism of the object [in Valéry] and the subject's infatuation with itself [in Proust] find their correctives in each other."[22]

Within the framework of this dialectic, Adorno celebrates Proust's refusal to reanimate dead intentions: "For [Proust] works of art are from the outset something more than their specific aesthetic qualities. They are part of the life of the person who observes them; they become an element of his consciousness. He thus perceives a level in them very different from that of the formal laws of the work. It is a level set free only by the historical development of the work, a level which has as its premise the death of the living intention of the work."[23] For Adorno, the death of the living intention of the work of art is unavoidable, nor would we *want* to prevent it: "Works of art can fully embody the *promesse du bonheur* only when they have been uprooted from their native soil and have set out along the path to their own destruction. Proust recognized this. The procedure that today relegates every work of art to the museum . . . is irreversible."[24]

Throughout his essay, beneath, so to speak, his tacking back and forth between Válery and Proust, Adorno shows that the real issue at hand is the very terms of the debate. Symptomatic of the difficulty of these terms is the way they pile up in Adorno's essay: process of dying, mausoleum, fatal situation, frozen creatures, dead visions, entombment, killing, perishing, death, mortality of artifacts, mortal enmity, death of the living intention, process of disintegration, decomposition, death of the work, severance from the living order, estrangement, shriveling up. The debate that Adorno stages depends entirely upon the trope of the death of (the living intention) of the work of art; without this turn of phrase, there would be nothing to argue about. A great deal is at stake, therefore, in Adorno's foregrounding of this trope *as trope*. Through his obsessive re-turnings of it, he exposes the aberrance of the metaphor of the living and dying work of art; and in the process, he shows that humanistic efforts to enliven historical works of art will always come up against the fact that they were not, of course, alive to begin with.

There is perhaps no work of art that invites attempts to enliven it more than the image of the dead God awaiting his resurrection. But such projects only end up reminding us that the *image* will remain forever insusceptible to resurrection. Even were the historian suddenly granted the godlike power of bestowing life on the dead, that power would not extend to dead images: only what has lived (and died) can be, properly speaking, resurrected. The dead image is precisely what gets left behind when the *imago Dei* is brought back to life; unlike the art historian, God is happy to leave it behind.

Although some of us may now hang paintings on walls instead of gods on crosses, things have not changed as much as one might think. Like the dead image of the crucified God, the hung painting has repeatedly lured art historians into trying to resurrect it. But whether crucifix or painting, the dead image returns in the *mechanical form of repetition* rather than by means of the miracle of resurrection. We find this repetition thematized in the Deposition rite and in the suspension of the figure in late medieval Deposition paintings.

Anti-dialetical repetitions and suspensions—which block the Christian dialectic of death and resurrection from ever arriving at its final (imageless) state—also give rise to the pseudomorphic resemblances that have structured this book, including the resemblance between the sepulchering of the divine effigy and the hoarding of the family treasures. The fetishizing of either the cult object or the teacup and the storing-up of either in the enclosure of the sepulchral cupboard is one and the same ritual of relating to those things that are not ours—whether we "own" them now or not, they will outlive us: those dead letters and ledgers that fill our heads just as they fill our homes, and those dead gods and paintings that fill our minds as they do our museums.

By not sharing in our mortality, these things that we sometimes deign to "resurrect" are all the while busy mortifying us. This is not a reason to break them, as the iconoclasts would have us do—as if breaking *them* could free *us* from death. But it is a reason to let these "dead images" have their liaisons with other objects. For, by promiscuously associating with objects from different times and places, they thwart our attempts to bind them to the relatively short lives of their human makers. And by allowing for their promiscuity, we avoid the trap of trying to bring what never lived back to life. I say, let sleeping gods lie and dead paintings hang. The less their deathly stillness resembles my own quickly passing life, the better I like them.

Acknowledgments

Without the brilliant and open-minded mentoring of Joseph Koerner, Jeffrey Hamburger, and Henri Zerner, I would not have felt free to make my own mistakes as I began to write this book. Without the willingness of Jonathan Crary and the rest of the editorial board at Zone Books to take on the project, I would not have had a chance to try to make it, in its final form, what I wanted it to be.

Jessica Buskirk, Wayne Franits, Megan Holmes, Lynn Hunt, Alison Kettering, Kaspar Körner, Justin Kroesen, Ewa Lajer-Burchardt, Thomas Lentes, Susan Merriam, Eric Palazzo, Elizabeth Ross, Ron Spronk, Alison Syme, Hugo van der Velden, and Rebecca Zorach have each guided me at a crucial moment, either by extending an invitation, reading a draft, passing along a bit of wisdom, or lending an ear.

During my time as a Mellon Fellow at Columbia University, conversations with David Freedberg, Hanneke Grootenboer, Robert Harrist, Christopher Heuer, Keith Moxey, and Alicia Walker sparked new ideas. Thomas Crow and Gail Feigenbaum made a magical stay at the Getty Research Institute possible. Michael Ann Holly and Mark Ledbury were kind enough to include me in a memorable Clark/Getty Workshop that same year. For supporting my research while I was teaching at Temple University, I am indebted to Tracy Cooper and Marcia Hall. At the University of California, Irvine, I have benefitted from the thoughts and kindnesses of many people, most of all Elizabeth Allen, Jim Herbert, Lyle Massey, Julia Lupton, Jane Newman, and Cécile Whiting.

I am very fortunate to have had Meighan Gale, Julie Fry, and Bud Bynack turn my manuscript into a book. In addition to the institutional support mentioned above, a Chester Dale Fellowship from the Center for Advanced Study in the Visual Arts gave me time to write. Parts of Chapter Five appear in "The Errant Image: Rogier van der Weyden's *Deposition from the Cross* and its Copies," *Art History* 29 (2006) and "A Point 'Ceaselessly Pushed Back': The Origin of Early Netherlandish Painting," *Art Bulletin* 88 (2006). An earlier version of Chapter Four was written for *The Sensuous Church*, ed. Marcia Hall and Tracy Cooper, which is now forthcoming from Cambridge University Press.

As for my family and friends Danica Ankele, Nadia Herman Colburn, Sarah Demeuse, Andrew Dubois, Evelyn and Marvin Farbman, Sky Feller, Heather Frazar, Julia Livshin, Kiki Pop-Eleches, Gabriel Portnof, Stephanie Schrader, Cristina Vatulescu, and Elizabeth Zirker, I hope that over the years I have conveyed something of the singular way in which I am grateful to each of you for what you help me see.

I thank my mother, Marsha Powell, for teaching me how to make things and my brother, Daniel, for sharing my need to take them apart. Julius for his arrival.

And, for reading so generously and so well, I give my most quotidian loving thanks to Herschel Farbman.

Notes

PREFACE

1. David Summers, "'Form,' Nineteenth-Century Metaphysics, and the Problem of Art Historical Description," *Critical Inquiry* 15, no. 2 (1989), p. 404. Compare Arthur C. Danto, *After the End of Art: Contemporary Art and the Pale of History* (Princeton: Princeton University Press, 1997), pp. 94 and 111. Maleuvre describes well the museum's peculiar marriage of historicism and formalism and gives an overview of the *longue durée* of the museum's disrepute. Didier Maleuvre, *Museum Memories: History, Technology, Art* (Stanford: Stanford University Press, 1999), pp. 7–112.

2. On the new importance of Deposition iconography in the fifteenth century, see Harvey E. Hamburgh, "Aspects of the Descent from the Cross from Lippi to Cigoli" (Doctoral Dissertation, University of Iowa, 1978), vol. 1, p. 115; James Snyder, *Northern Renaissance Art: Painting, Sculpture, the Graphic Arts from 1350 to 1575*, ed. Larry Silver and Henry Luttikhuizen (Upper Saddle River: Prentice Hall, 2005), p. 118. The deposition had already begun to be represented on a monumental scale in thirteenth-century Italian and Spanish sculpture. See Raimond van Marle, "De iconographie der afneming van het kruis tot het eind der 14de eeuw," *Het Gildeboek* 8 (1925), pp. 33, 110–11; Elizabeth C. Parker, *The Descent from the Cross: Its Relation to the Extra-Liturgical "Depositio" Drama* (New York: Garland Pub., 1978), pp. 172–99; Hans Belting, *The Image and Its Public in the Middle Ages: Form and Function of Early Paintings of the Passion*, trans. Mark Bartusis and Raymond Meyer (New Rochelle: Caratzas, 1990), pp. 152–55; Götz Pochat, *Theater und bildende Kunst im Mittelalter und in der Renaissance in Italien* (Graz: Akademische Druck- u. Verlagsanstalt, 1990), pp. 62–63.

3. Cf. "Whoever has seen me has seen the Father" (John 14.9).

4. Recent work in and on anachronistic art histories has inspired my book's experimental form. In studies of Aby Warburg, Carl Einstein, and others, Didi-Huberman has compelled the discipline of art history to see itself anew by revealing how ineluctably anachronistic its projects and objects are. Georges Didi-Huberman, *Devant le temps: Histoire de l'art et anachronisme des images* (Paris: Editions de Minuit, 2000); Georges Didi-Huberman, *L'image survivante: Histoire de l'art et temps des fantômes selon Aby Warburg* (Paris: Editions de Minuit, 2002); Georges Didi-Huberman, "Before the Image, Before Time: The Sovereignty of Anachronism," in Claire J. Farago and Robert Zwijnenberg, eds., *Compelling Visuality: The Work of Art In and Out of History*, (Minneapolis: University of Minnesota Press, 2003), pp. 31–44; Georges Didi-Huberman, *Confronting Images: Questioning the Ends of a Certain History of Art*, trans. John Goodman (University Park: Pennsylvania State University Press, 2005). Viewing Caravaggio, Bernini and others through the lens of contemporary art, Bal has written a "preposterous history" of the Baroque, which takes works of art as "theoretical objects." Mieke Bal, *Quoting Caravaggio: Contemporary Art, Preposterous History* (Chicago: University of Chicago Press, 1999); Mieke Bal, "Ecstatic Aesthetics: Metaphoring Bernini," in Farago and Zwijnenberg, *Compelling Visuality*, pp. 1–30. Profoundly changing our understanding of early modern temporality, Nagel and Wood have recovered a Renaissance understanding of how (art) objects exist in time that is surprisingly different from our own. Alexander Nagel and Christopher S. Wood, "Toward a New Model of Renaissance Anachronism," *The Art Bulletin* 87, no. 3 (2005), pp. 403–15; Christopher S. Wood, *Forgery, Replica, Fiction: Temporalities of German Renaissance Art* (Chicago: University of Chicago Press, 2008); Alexander Nagel and Christopher S. Wood, *Anachronic Renaissance* (New York: Zone Books, 2010). See also Richard Neer, "Godard Counts," *Critical Inquiry* 34, no. 1 (2007), pp. 135–73; and the ideas briefly sketched in James Elkins, "Introduction to an Abandoned Book," in James Elkins and Robert Williams, eds., *Renaissance Theory* (New York: Routledge, 2008), pp. 44–45.

5. On keeping difference and distance in focus while making comparisons, see Hubert Damisch, "Hubert Damisch and Stephen Bann: A Conversation," *Oxford Art Journal* 28, no. 2 (2005), p. 160. See also Damisch's essay for his 1997 exhibition at the Museum Boymans van Beuningen in Rotterdam, *Moves: Playing Chess and Cards with the Museum*, in which he juxtaposes old-master pictures and contemporary works of art, in order to "'precipitate' the distance that normally

keeps these works apart in the space of the museum. To *precipitate* this distance, in the chemical sense of the term, but not to make it disappear." Hubert Damisch and Ernst van Alphen, *Moves: Schaken en kaarten met het museum* (Rotterdam: Museum Boijmans Van Beuningen, 1997), pp. 82–83. *Moves* belongs to a series of exhibitions at the Museum Boymans in which guest curators were asked to choose and arrange objects from the collection. A notable precedent for this kind of exhibition is *Raid the Icebox 1 with Andy Warhol; An Exhibition Selected from the Vaults of the Museum of Art, Rhode Island School of Design* (Providence, 1969). The concept of the "baroque" has also enjoyed a recent vogue as an occasion for exhibitions that juxtapose works from different periods. See, e.g., Lisa G. Corrin, *Going for Baroque: 18 Contemporary Artists Fascinated with the Baroque and Rococo* (Baltimore: The Contemporary and The Walters, 1995); Sabine Folie and Michael Glasmeier, eds., *Eine barocke Party: Augenblicke des Welttheaters in der zeitgenössischen Kunst* (Vienna: Kunsthalle, 2001).

6. Oswald Spengler, *The Decline of the West*, trans. Charles Francis Atkinson (New York: Knopf, 1926), vol. 2, p. 189, see also vol. 1, p. 209.

7. Erwin Panofsky, *Tomb Sculpture: Four Lectures on its Changing Aspects from Ancient Egypt to Bernini*, ed. H. W. Janson (New York: H. N. Abrams, 1964), pp. 26–27. Panofsky sometimes uses the term to name the medieval appropriation of classical forms divested of their classical meaning. Erwin Panofsky, *Studies in Iconology: Humanistic Themes in the Art of the Renaissance* (New York: Harper & Row, 1972), pp. 70–71.

8. This was Judd's irritated response to an interviewer's suggestion that a painting by Barnett Newman could be compared to a Byzantine icon. Gregory Battcock, ed., *Minimal Art: A Critical Anthology* (Berkeley: University of California Press, 1995), p. 163.

9. Bois and Lee use the term in this sense. Yve-Alain Bois, "*La pensée sauvage*," *Art in America* 73, no. 4 (April 1985), p. 183; Yve-Alain Bois, "Force Fields: Phases of the Kinetic," *Artforum* 39, no. 3 (Nov. 2000), p. 146; Pamela M. Lee, "Phase Piece," in Nicholas Baume, ed., *Sol LeWitt: Incomplete Open Cubes* (Hartford and Cambridge: Wadsworth Atheneum Museum of Art; MIT Press, 2001), p. 49. See also Bois' lecture hosted by the Open Practice Committee on 29 November 2007, "Pseudomorphism: What to Make of Look-Alikes?" at http://lucian.uchicago.edu/blogs/opc/video/. Although neither uses the term pseudomorphosis, Buchloh and Danto each argue in different ways that two works of art that look alike (even

monochromes and readymades) can have entirely different meanings. It would be absurd, they suggest, to compare a monochrome painted by Rodchenko to one by Yves Klein. Benjamin H. D. Buchloh, "The Primary Colors for the Second Time: A Paradigm Repetition of the Neo-Avant-Garde," *October* 37 (1986), pp. 48–52; Danto, *After the End*, pp. 153–73.

10. André Breton, *Manifestoes of Surrealism*, trans. Richard Seaver and Helen R. Lane (Ann Arbor: University of Michigan Press, 1969), p. 38, see also p. 302.

11. Bataille—a *dissident* surrealist—gives an account of these "coincidences" in Georges Bataille, *Story of the Eye* (San Francisco: City Lights Books, 1987), pp. 89–96. For Barthes, whose essay I follow closely here, the eroticism of Bataille's text derives from a metonymic operation that crosses the terms of two metaphoric sequences: the eye-egg-testicle sequence and the tears-milk-yolk-sperm-urine sequence. Roland Barthes, *Critical Essays*, trans. Richard Howard (Evanston: Northwestern University Press, 1972), p. 244.

12. On the possibility of understanding form in a non-metaphysical sense, see Summers, "'Form,'" pp. 376–77, 399. On the *impossibility* of such an understanding, see Jacques Derrida, *Margins of Philosophy*, trans. Alan Bass (Chicago: University of Chicago Press, 1982), pp. 155–73. In the final footnote of Derrida's essay, which is an unremitting attack on Husserl's attempt to divest the word "form" of its metaphysical sense, Derrida offers a tiny opening onto the possibility that "form in itself already would be the *trace* (*ikhnos*) of a certain nonpresence, the vestige of the un-formed, which announces-recalls its other" (p. 172 n.16).

13. Georges Bataille, "Human Face," trans. Annette Michelson *October* 36 (1986), p. 19. That this decorous oblivion tends to produce a certain idealism—making meaning intangible and spectral rather than concrete—is nicely illustrated by the metaphor Panofsky uses to distinguish between what he considers to be the *pseudomorphic* revivals of antiquity during the Middle Ages and the true resurrection of antiquity during the Renaissance: "the mediaeval revivals were real but transitory whereas the Italian, or main, Renaissance was, in a sense, academic but permanent. Resurrected souls are somewhat intangible but they have the advantage of being immortal and omnipresent." Erwin Panofsky, "Renaissance and Renascences," *Kenyon Review* 6, no. 2 (1944), pp. 228–29.

14. "Each individual form escapes this common measure and is, to a certain degree, a monster." Georges Bataille, *Visions of Excess: Selected Writings, 1927–1939*, ed. Allan Stoekl (Minneapolis: University of Minnesota Press, 1985), p. 55. See

also Bataille, "Human Face," pp. 17–21.

15. "The notion of the (heterogeneous) *foreign body* permits one to note the elementary *subjective* identity between types of excrement (sperm, menstrual blood, urine, fecal matter) and everything that can be seen as sacred, divine, or marvelous." Bataille, *Visions of Excess*, p. 94. "There is an identity of opposites between glory and dejection, between exalted and imperative (higher) forms and impoverished (lower) forms" (pp. 144–45). On Bataille's splitting of everything in two, including the "heterogeneous," see Yve-Alain Bois and Rosalind E. Krauss, *Formless: A User's Guide* (New York: Zone Books, 1997), pp. 47, 50, 67–73.

16. On "base materialism," see Bataille, *Visions of Excess*, pp. 45–52. On Bataille's "insulting the very opposition of form and content," see Bois and Krauss, *Formless*, p. 16. On Bataille's radical reworking of the idealist philosophical concepts of *form* and *resemblance*, see Georges Didi-Huberman, *La ressemblance informe ou le gai savoir visuel selon Georges Bataille* (Paris: Editions Macula, 1995).

17. "Bataille himself has made any decipherment of his poem futile by giving (at the book's end) the (biographical) sources of his metaphor; he thus leaves no other recourse then to consider, in *Histoire de l'oeil*, a perfectly spherical metaphor." Barthes, *Critical Essays*, p. 242.

18. Critics have pointed in particular to the homogenizing effects of exhibitions that promiscuously mix historically unrelated works of art. Crimp condemns exhibitions that "reaffirm the autonomy of art against the incursion of urgent historical facts." Douglas Crimp, "The Art of Exhibition," *October* 30 (1984), p. 58. And Demos criticizes anachronistic exhibitions for participating in "the institution's generalizing subjection of heterogeneous objects to a homogenizing exhibition space." T. J. Demos, "Duchamp's Boîte-en-Valise: Between Institutional Acculturation and Geopolitical Displacement," *Grey Room* 8 (2002), p. 14. See also Benjamin H. D. Buchloh, "Documenta 7: A Dictionary of Received Ideas," *October* 22 (1982), pp. 104–26; Debora Meijers, "The Museum and the 'Ahistorical' Exhibition: The Latest Gimmick by the Arbiters of Taste, or an Important Cultural Phenomenon?" in Reesa Greenberg, Bruce W. Ferguson, and Sandy Nairne, eds., *Thinking about Exhibitions* (London and New York: Routledge, 1996), pp. 7–20.

19. Louise Lawler and Douglas Crimp, "Prominence Given, Authority Taken," *Grey Room* 4 (2001), p. 78, see also p. 72.

20. F. T. Marinetti, "The Founding and the Manifesto of Futurism (1909)," in Lawrence Rainey, ed., *Modernism: An Anthology* (Malden and Oxford: Blackwell,

2005), p. 3.

21. Buren, for example, writes: "What I later came to realise was that it was the reality of the work, its 'truth,' its relationship to its creator and place of creation, that was irretrievably lost in this transfer. In the studio we generally find finished work, work in progress, abandoned work, sketches—a collection of visible evidence viewed simultaneously that allows an understanding of process; it is this aspect of the work that is extinguished by the museum's desire to 'install.'" Daniel Buren, "Function of the Studio," in A. A. Bronson and Peggy Gale, eds., *Museums by Artists* (Toronto: Art Metropol, 1983), p. 66.

22. Maria Eichhorn, "On the Avertissement: Interview with Daniel Buren (1998)," in John C. Welchman, ed., *Institutional Critique and After* (Zurich: JRP / Ringier, 2006), p. 100. In 1969, the Art Workers Coalition was formed in New York in large part to defend the rights of artists and to protect against the unauthorized instrumentalization of works of art routinely practiced by museums and collectors. See Julia Bryan-Wilson, *Art Workers: Radical Practice in the Vietnam War Era* (Berkeley: University of California Press, 2009).

23. Andre objected to attempts to control the "destiny" of the work of art on precisely these grounds: "The artist may be able to a limited extent to be responsible for the social destiny of the work he or she produces insofar as there may be the possibility of controlling where it's put. Its political destiny is an affair of interpretation and the artist can no more assume final responsibility for that than for any other aspect of its 'meaning.' To try is to lapse into intentionalism." Carl Andre and Jeremy Gilbert-Rolfe, "Commodity and Contradiction, or Contradiction as Commodity," *October* 2 (1976), pp. 101–102. For discussion of this passage and others like it, see Alexander Alberro, *Conceptual Art and the Politics of Publicity* (Cambridge: MIT Press, 2003), p. 169; Andrea Fraser, *Museum Highlights: The Writings of Andrea Fraser* (Cambridge: MIT Press, 2005), p. 61.

24. For a remarkable analysis of the museum's re-contextualizations and colonialism, see Finbarr Barry Flood, "Between Cult and Culture: Bamiyan, Islamic Iconoclasm, and the Museum," *The Art Bulletin* 84, no. 4 (2002), esp. pp. 652–53.

25. "Roger's 'Descent' may be called, without exaggeration, *the* most influential painting of Northern fifteenth-century art, and a study of this influence would fill a sizable monograph." Erwin Panofsky, *Early Netherlandish Painting: Its Origins and Character* (Cambridge: Harvard University Press, 1953), vol. 1, p. 460 n.2. On copies of this painting, see Rudolf Terner, *Die Kreuzabnahme Roger van der Weyden:*

Untersuchungen zu Ikonographie und Nachleben (Münster: Terner, 1973); Micheline Comblen-Sonkes, *The Collegiate Church of Saint Peter, Louvain*, trans. John Cairns (Brussels: Internationaal Studiecentrum voor de Middeleeuwse Schilderkunst in het Schelde- en het Maasbekken, 1996), vol. 1, pp. 139–44; Dirk de Vos, *Rogier van der Weyden: The Complete Works* (New York: Harry N. Abrams, 1999), p. 186. On copies in a half-length format, see Sixten Ringbom, *Icon to Narrative: The Rise of the Dramatic Close-Up in Fifteenth-Century Devotional Painting* (Doornspijk: Davaco, 1984), pp. 117–25; de Vos, *Rogier van der Weyden*, pp. 368–69.

INTRODUCTION

1. Schapiro coined the term Disappearing Christ in Meyer Schapiro, "The Image of the Disappearing Christ: The Ascension in English Art Around the Year 1000," *Gazette des Beaux-Arts* 23, ser. 6 (1943), pp. 133–52. See also Robert Deshman, "Another Look at the Disappearing Christ: Corporeal and Spiritual Vision in Early Medieval Images," *The Art Bulletin* 79, no. 3 (1997), pp. 518–46.

2. On the differences between Byzantine and Western attitudes toward images, see Johannes Kollwitz, "Bild und Bildertheologie im Mittelalter," in *Das Gottesbild im Abendland* (Witten: Eckart, 1959), pp. 109–38; Alain Besançon, *The Forbidden Image: An Intellectual History of Iconoclasm*, trans. Jane Marie Todd (Chicago: Chicago University Press, 2000), p. 4; Jean-Claude Schmitt, "Images and the Historian," in Axel Bolvig and Phillip Lindley, eds., *History and Images: Towards a New Iconology* (Turnhout and Cheltenham: Brepols; European Schoolbooks, 2003), pp. 41–44. On the shift in attitude toward images in the West circa 1000 and the greater resemblance of this new attitude to that of the Eastern Church, see Jean-Claude Schmitt, *Le corps des images: Essais sur la culture visuelle au Moyen Age* (Paris: Gallimard, 2002), pp. 79, 86–88.

3. For differing accounts of what exactly it means for the divine to be present in the Byzantine icon, see Jaroslav Pelikan, *Imago Dei: The Byzantine Apologia for Icons* (Washington, D.C. and Princeton: National Gallery of Art; Princeton University Press, 1990), p. 95; Hans Belting, *Likeness and Presence: A History of the Image Before the Era of Art*, trans. Edmund Jephcott (Chicago: University of Chicago Press, 1994), esp. pp. 144–63; Charles Barber, *Figure and Likeness: On the Limits of Representation in Byzantine Iconoclasm* (Princeton: Princeton University Press, 2002), esp. pp. 107–23; Bissera V. Pentcheva, "The Performative Icon," *The Art Bulletin* 88, no. 4 (2006), pp. 631–36.

4. "The honor given to the image is given to the one portrayed in the image." John of Damascus, *On the Divine Images: Three Apologies Against Those Who Attack the Divine Images*, trans. David Anderson (Crestwood: St. Vladimir's Seminary Press, 1980), p. 36, see also p. 91. John of Damascus is here following St. Basil and will be followed, in turn, by Thomas and Bonaventure.

5. As translated in Herbert L. Kessler, *Spiritual Seeing: Picturing God's Invisibility in Medieval Art* (Philadelphia: University of Pennsylvania Press, 2000), p. 121. Original in Pope Gregory I, *S. Gregorii Magni Registrum epistularum*, ed. Dag Norberg (Turnhout: Brepols, 1982), vol. 2, pp. 1110–11.

6. On the iconography of the Deposition, see Karl Wilhelm Jähnig, *Die Darstellung der Kreuzabnahme, der Beweinung und der Grablegung Christi in der altniederländischen Malerei von Rogier van der Weyden bis zu Quentin Metsys* (Hohenstein-Ernstthal: Frisch, 1914); Erna Rampendahl, *Die Ikonographie der Kreuzabnahme vom 9.–16. Jahrhundert* (Bremen: Jlling & Lüken, 1916); Van Marle, "De iconographie der afneming," pp. 33–112; Parker, *The Descent*; Hamburgh, "Aspects of the Descent"; Yasushi Nagatsuka, *Descente de croix: Son développement iconographique des origines jusqu'à la fin du XIVe siècle* (Tokyo: Presses de l'Université Tokai, 1979); Claudia Bertling, *Die Darstellung der Kreuzabnahme und der Beweinung Christi in der ersten Hälfte des 16. Jahrhunderts: Ein Beitrag zum florentinischen Andachtsbild* (Hildesheim and New York: G. Olms, 1992).

7. On the changes in the iconography that gave rise to this double gesture, see Gertrud Schiller, *Iconography of Christian Art* (London: Lund Humphries, 1971), vol. 2, p. 168; Nagatsuka, *Descente de croix*, 68. Pächt sees the twelfth-century St. Albans Psalter miniature of the Deposition as a turning point in the iconography toward a new tableau-vivant stillness and direct address to the viewer. Otto Pächt, *The Rise of Pictorial Narrative in Twelfth Century England* (Oxford: Clarendon Press, 1962), pp. 30–32.

8. Paul de Man, *The Rhetoric of Romanticism* (New York: Columbia University Press, 1984), pp. 108–109.

9. De Man, *The Rhetoric of Romanticism*, p. 89.

10. Paul de Man, *Allegories of Reading: Figural Language in Rousseau, Nietzsche, Rilke, and Proust* (New Haven: Yale University Press, 1979), p. 17.

11. De Man, *Allegories of Reading*, pp. 26–27.

12. Jeffrey F. Hamburger, "Seeing and Believing: The Suspicion of Sight and the Authentication of Vision in Late Medieval Art and Devotion," in Klaus Krüger

and Alessandro Nova, eds., *Imagination und Wirklichkeit: Zum Verhältnis von mentalen und realen Bildern in der Kunst der frühen Neuzeit* (Mainz am Rhein: P. von Zabern, 2000), p. 48, see also 60. For an excellent critical discussion of the cliché of late medieval "visual piety," see Thomas Lentes, "'As Far as the Eye Can See': Rituals of Gazing in the Late Middle Ages," in Jeffrey F. Hamburger and Anne-Marie Bouché, eds., *The Mind's Eye: Art and Theological Argument in the Middle Ages* (Princeton: Department of Art and Archaeology, Princeton University, 2006), pp. 360–61. Of course, there is work that has avoided the tendency to see the late Middle Ages as unequivocally iconophilic, notably: Michael Camille, *The Gothic Idol: Ideology and Image-Making in Medieval Art* (Cambridge and New York: Cambridge University Press, 1989); Norbert Schnitzler, *Ikonoklasmus—Bildersturm: Theologischer Bilderstreit und ikonoklastisches Handeln während des 15. und 16. Jahrhunderts* (Munich: W. Fink, 1996); Norbert Schnitzler, "Illusion, Täuschung und schöner Schein: Probleme der Bildverehrung im späten Mittelalter," in Klaus Schreiner, ed., *Frommigkeit im Mittelalter: Politisch-soziale Kontexte, visuelle Praxis, körperliche Ausdrucksformen* (Munich: Fink, 2002), pp. 221–39. Scholars of the late medieval heresies have also addressed late medieval iconophobia. In subsequent footnotes, I will give more detailed references to this work. For now, on increased consternation about sacred images in the later Middle Ages, see William R. Jones, "Lollards and Images: The Defense of Religious Art in Later Medieval England," *Journal of the History of Ideas* 34, no. 1 (1973), pp. 27–28; Helmut Feld, *Der Ikonoklasmus des Westens* (Leiden and New York: Brill, 1990), p. 85; Robert W. Scribner, "Das Visuelle in der Volksfrömmigkeit," in Robert W. Scribner, ed., *Bilder und Bildersturm im Spätmittelalter und in der frühen Neuzeit* (Wiesbaden: Harrassowitz, 1990), p. 12. I will not attempt to do justice to the literature that addresses ideals of imageless devotion (and their fraught relation to actual devotional practice) in the monastic context toward the end of the Middle Ages. Suffice it to say that the work of Hamburger and Lentes is essential reading here, e.g.: Jeffrey F. Hamburger, *The Visual and the Visionary: Art and Female Spirituality in Late Medieval Germany* (New York: Zone Books, 1998); Thomas Lentes, "Auf der Suche nach dem Ort des Gedächtnisses: Thesen zur Umwertung der symbolischen Formen in Abendmahlslehre, Bildtheorie und Bildandacht des 14.–16. Jahrhunderts," in Krüger and Nova, *Imagination und Wirklichkeit*, pp. 21–46; Thomas Lentes, "Inneres Auge, äußerer Blick und heilige Schau: Ein Diskussionsbeitrag zur visuellen Praxis in Frömmigkeit und Moraldidaxe des späten Mittelalters," in Schreiner, *Frömmigkeit im Mittelalter*, pp. 179–220.

13. Johan Huizinga, *The Autumn of the Middle Ages*, trans. Rodney J. Payton and Ulrich Mammitzsch (Chicago: University of Chicago Press, 1996), p. 173. Cf. Anton L. Mayer, "Die heilbringende Schau in Sitte und Kult," in Odo Casel, ed., *Heilige Überlieferung: Ausschnitte aus der Geschichte des Mönchtums und des heiligen Kultes* (Münster: Aschendorff, 1938), pp. 234–62. Scribner has helped free analysis of late medieval visual culture from some of the more negative judgments that Huizinga and Mayer brought to it. See, e.g., Robert W. Scribner, "Popular Piety and Modes of Visual Perception in Late-Medieval and Reformation Germany," *Journal of Religious History* 15, no. 4 (1989), pp. 448–69; Robert W. Scribner, "Zur Wahrnehmug des Heiligen in Deutschland am Ende des Mittelalters," in Joachim Kuolt, Harald Kleinschmidt, and Peter Dinzelbacher, eds., *Das Mittelalter: Unsere fremde Vergangenheit* (Stuttgart: Helfant, 1990), pp. 241–67; Robert W. Scribner, "From the Sacred Image to the Sensual Gaze: Sense Perceptions and the Visual in the Objectification of the Female Body in Sixteenth-Century Germany," in *Religion and Culture in Germany (1400–1800)* (Leiden: Brill, 2001), 129–45.

14. The last decade has seen a profound questioning and "queering" of the secularization narrative by scholars of medieval literature and philosophy, including Kathleen Biddick, Andrew Cole, Carolyn Dinshaw, Kathleen Davis, Carla Freccero, Bruce W. Holsinger, and D. Vance Smith. This narrative and the myth of a credulous pre-modernity have remained more stubbornly in place within the fields of art history and visual studies, but things are changing there as well. For demythologizing accounts of pre-modern "belief" in the power of images and "credulity," see respectively Joseph Leo Koerner, *The Reformation of the Image* (Chicago: The University of Chicago Press, 2004), pp. 94–103; Wood, *Forgery, Replica, Fiction*, pp. 1–24. There is also a growing literature that addresses the fact that sacred images did not simply yield their place to aesthetic objects during the Renaissance. On the persistence of the sacred image in the age of Art, see, to take only a few examples, Leo Steinberg, *Leonardo's Incessant Last Supper* (New York: Zone Books, 2001); Michael W. Cole and Rebecca Zorach, eds., *The Idol in the Age of Art: Objects, Devotions and the Early Modern World* (Burlington: Ashgate, 2009); Marcia B. Hall, *The Sacred Image in the Age of Art: Titian, Tintoretto, Barocci, El Greco, Caravaggio* (New Haven and London: Yale University Press, 2011).

15. Belting, *The Image and Its Public*, p. 58. Cf. "l'image de devotion... suscite la vision qui, en retour, lui donne les apparences de la vie, l'illusion du mouvement

et du langage, l'effusion de larmes et de sang divins, autrement dit les signes d'une présence réelle." Schmitt, *Le corps des images*, p. 28, see also p. 31; Belting, *Likeness and Presence*, p. 16. Belting takes up Walter Benjamin's distinction between the auratic cult image and the work of Art in the age of mechanical reproduction. Bredekamp provides important corrections to the Benjaminian view of the medieval cult image in Horst Bredekamp, "Der simulierte Benjamin: Mittelalterliche Bemerkungen zu seiner Aktualität," in Andreas Berndt et al, eds., *Frankfurter Schule und Kunstgeschichte* (Berlin: Dietrich Reimer Verlag, 1992), pp. 117–40. And Wood gives an excellent critical account of Belting's secularization thesis in Christopher S. Wood, "Review of *Bild-Anthropologie: Entwürfe für eine Bildwissenschaft* by Hans Belting," *The Art Bulletin* 86, no. 2 (2004), pp. 370–73; Wood, *Forgery, Replica, Fiction*, pp. 76–77.

16. Kessler, *Spiritual Seeing*, p. 128. See also Herbert L. Kessler, *Seeing Medieval Art* (Peterborough and Orchard Park: Broadview Press, 2004), p. 171.

17. This split is, to some extent, temporal. Kessler concentrates on the moderation of the early and high Middle Ages, while Belting describes an excess that peaked in the late Middle Ages, only to be "corrected" during the Reformation. Kessler writes: "The emphatic distinction between physical and spiritual images had begun to disintegrate around the middle of the twelfth century." Kessler, *Spiritual Seeing*, p. 144. On this historical shift, see also Deshman, "Another Look," pp. 543–45.

18. At points Kessler suggests something close to this internal splitting: "Various aspects of sophisticated works of medieval art—subject matter, form, and material—were devised to engage the viewer in an anagogical process... deploying materials in such a way that physical presence is simultaneously asserted and subverted." Kessler, *Spiritual Seeing*, preface. But Kessler suggests that this anagogical process was meant to resolve itself, finally, in favor of absence: "For most Christian commentators... art's value was precisely its capacity to initiate a process of meditation, starting with physical sight and leading to inner contemplation." Kessler, *Seeing Medieval Art*, p. 167.

19. See, e.g., Philippians 2.6–11 and Colossians 1.15–20. On the *imago Dei*, see Gerhart B. Ladner, *Ad Imaginem Dei: The Image of Man in Medieval Art* (Latrobe: Archabbey Press, 1965); Besançon, *The Forbidden Image*, pp. 84–86. On the *imago Dei recreans*, see Robert Javelet, *Image et ressemblance au 12e siècle, de saint Anselme á Alain de Lille* (Paris: Letouzey et Ané, 1967), vol. 1, pp. 298–315.

20. There is a growing body of work that suggests images were being made in the late Middle Ages with an eye to discouraging idolatry and directing attention beyond the image to an invisible God, whether by purging images of life-like colors, reviving antiquated modes of representation, or inserting frames within frames to hold the viewer at a safe distance. My study of the Deposition borrows much from this line of thinking. Although, where this work tends to find evidence of pictorial reforms more or less in accord with Gregorian ideas about the proper use of images, I will point to something more agonistic. For an excellent critical summary of this work, see Reindert Falkenburg, "Hieronymus Bosch's *Mass of St. Gregory* and 'sacramental vision,'" in Andreas Gormans and Thomas Lentes, eds., *Das Bild der Erscheinung: Die Gregorsmesse in Mittelalter* (Berlin: Reimer, 2007), pp. 179–81. On Tilman Riemenschneider's monochromy, see Michael Baxandall, *The Limewood Sculptors of Renaissance Germany* (New Haven: Yale University Press, 1980), pp. 186, 188–89; Bernhard Decker, "Reform within the Cult Image: The German Winged Altarpiece Before the Reformation," in Peter Humfrey and Martin Kemp, eds., *The Altarpiece in the Renaissance* (Cambridge and New York: Cambridge University Press, 1990), pp. 98–101. On the archaism of German sculpture circa 1500, see Bernhard Decker, *Das Ende des mittelalterlichen Kultbildes und die Plastik Hans Leinbergers* (Bamberg: Lehrstuhl für Kunstgeschichte und Aufbaustudium Denkmalpflege an der Universität Bamberg, 1985), esp. pp. 170–78; Decker, "Reform within the Cult Image," pp. 94–98. On Jan van Eyck's distancing frames, see Lieselotte E. Saurma-Jeltsch, "Bildverfremdung gegen Bildverehrung: Zu einigen Darstellungsstrategien in der nördlichen Tafelmalerei der Spätmittelalters," in Jan-Dirk Müller, ed., *"Auffuhrung" und "Schrift" in Mittelalter und früher Neuzeit* (Stuttgart: Metzler, 1996), pp. 406–28; Hamburger, "Seeing and Believing," p. 47. On a similar type of distancing in Italian art, see Klaus Krüger, "Mimesis als Bildlichkeit des Scheins—Zur Fiktionalität religiöser Bildkunst im Trecento," in Thomas W. Gaehtgens, ed., *Künstlerischer Austausch—Artistic Exchange* (Berlin: Akademie Verlag, 1993), pp. 423–36. On related reforming tendencies in the work of sixteenth-century Catholic artists, see Keith P. F. Moxey, *Pieter Aertsen, Joachim Beuckelaer, and the Rise of Secular Painting in the Context of the Reformation* (New York: Garland Pub., 1977), esp. pp. 229–68; Alexander Nagel, *Michelangelo and the Reform of Art* (Cambridge and New York: Cambridge University Press, 2000).

21. "A deep-rooted distrust of the duplicitous in image-making runs through

the Christian tradition." Camille, *The Gothic Idol*, p. xxvi.

22. Mainstream criticism of images is to be found in the writings of Pierre d'Ailly and John Gerson, late-fourteenth and early-fifteenth-century chancellors of the University of Paris, whose Catholic campaign against image-abuse would find its most famous spokesman in Erasmus of Rotterdam. See, e.g., Pierre d'Ailly, *De reformatione ecclesiae* (1416) in Jean Gerson, *Opera omnia*, ed. Ellies Du Pin (Antwerp: Sumptibus Societatis, 1706), vol. 2, pp. 903–16; Jean Gerson, *Expostulatio ad potestates publicas adversus corruptionem juventutis per lascivas imagines et alia hujusmodi* (1402) in Gerson, *Opera omnia*, vol. 3, pp. 291–92. For a list of Gerson's works that address popular beliefs and superstition, see vol. 10, pp. 73–76. On Pierre d'Ailly's and Gerson's criticism of image abuse, see Carlos M.N. Eire, *War Against the Idols: The Reformation of Worship from Erasmus to Calvin* (Cambridge and New York: Cambridge University Press, 1986), p. 21; Huizinga, *The Autumn*, pp. 175–77; Feld, *Der Ikonoklasmus*, pp. 96–98. For these theologians, whose objections were essentially Gregorian, images were a problem only where they led to abuse. That images symbolized and perpetuated the church's accumulation of wealth worried them less than the possibility that they might give rise to deviant behavior. In his *On Restoring the Unity of the Church* (1533), Erasmus condemns iconoclasm but maintains that "paintings fatuous, smutty, or inflammatory ought not only to be removed from churches but also from the whole commonweal." Desiderius Erasmus, *Erasmus and the Seamless Coat of Jesus: De Sarcienda Ecclesiae Concordia (On Restoring the Unity of the Church) with Selections from the Letters and Ecclesiastes*, trans. Raymond Himelick (Lafayette: Purdue University Studies, 1971), pp. 88–89. On Erasmus's critique of images, see Erwin Panofsky, "Erasmus and the Visual Arts," *Journal of the Warburg and Courtauld Institutes* 32 (1969), pp. 207–14; Eire, *War Against the Idols*, pp. 28–53; Feld, *Der Ikonoklasmus*, pp. 110–15; A.G. Weiler, "Erasmus als kunstcriticus in de geest van de Moderne Devotie," in K. Veelenturf, ed., *Geen povere schoonheid: Laat-middeleeuwse kunst in verband met de Moderne Devotie* (Nijmegen: Valkhof Pers, 2000), pp. 315–41.

23. On apostolic poverty and later medieval religious movements (both orthodox and heterodox), see Gordon Leff, "Heresy and the Decline of the Medieval Church," *Past and Present* 20 (1961), pp. 41–44; Gordon Leff, *Heresy in the Later Middle Ages: The Relation of Heterodoxy to Dissent, c. 1250–c. 1450* (Manchester and New York: Manchester University Press; Barnes & Noble, 1967), pp. 1–13, 51–255, 319–24; Lester K. Little, *Religious Poverty and the Profit Economy in Medieval Europe*

(Ithaca: Cornell University Press, 1978); David Burr, *Olivi and Franciscan Poverty: The Origins of the Usus Pauper Controversy* (Philadelphia: University of Pennsylvania Press, 1989); Herbert Grundmann, *Religious Movements in the Middle Ages: The Historical Links Between Heresy, the Mendicant Orders, and the Women's Religious Movement in the Twelfth and Thirteenth Century, with the Historical Foundations of German Mysticism* (Notre Dame: University of Notre Dame Press, 1995); Malcolm Lambert, *Franciscan Poverty: The Doctrine of Absolute Poverty of Christ and the Apostles in the Franciscan Order, 1210–1323* (St. Bonaventure: Franciscan Institute, St. Bonaventure University, 1998); David Burr, *The Spiritual Franciscans: From Protest to Persecution in the Century after Saint Francis* (University Park: Pennsylvania State University Press, 2001); Malcolm Lambert, *Medieval Heresy: Popular Movements from the Gregorian Reform to the Reformation* (Oxford and Malden: Blackwell, 2002), pp. 209–35; Michael D. Bailey, "Religious Poverty, Mendicancy, and Reform in the Late Middle Ages," *Church History* 72, no. 3 (2003), pp. 457–83; James D. Mixson, *Poverty's Proprietors: Ownership and Mortal Sin at the Origins of the Observant Movement* (Leiden and Boston: Brill, 2009); Beverly Mayne Kienzle, "Religious Poverty and the Search for Perfection," in Miri Rubin and Walter Simons, eds., *The Cambridge History of Christianity: Volume 4, Christianity in Western Europe c. 1100–c. 1500* (Cambridge: Cambridge University Press, 2009), pp. 39–53; Kate Crassons, *The Claims of Poverty: Literature, Culture, and Ideology in Late Medieval England* (Notre Dame: University of Notre Dame Press, 2010).

24. Caecilia Davis-Weyer, ed., *Early Medieval Art, 300–1150: Sources and Documents* (Englewood Cliffs: Prentice-Hall, 1971), p. 48.

25. On the Western Church's reaction to the Byzantine image crisis, see Anthony Ugolnik, "The Libri Carolini: Antecedents of Reformation Iconoclasm," in Clifford Davidson and Ann Eljenholm Nichols, eds., *Iconoclasm vs. Art and Drama* (Kalamazoo: Medieval Institute Publications, Western Michigan University, 1989), pp. 1–32; Helmut Feld, *Der Ikonoklasmus des Westens* (Leiden and New York: Brill, 1990), pp. 14–22; Hans Georg Thümmel, "Die Stellung des Westens zum byzantinischen Bilderstreit des 8. / 9. Jahrhunderts," in Olivier Christin and Dario Gamboni, eds., *Crises de l'image religieuse: De Nicée II à Vatican II* (Paris: Editions de la Maison des sciences de l'homme, 2000), pp. 55–74; Beate Fricke, "Fallen Idols and Risen Saints: Western Attitudes Towards the Worship of Images and the 'Cultura veterum deorum'"; Liz James, "Seeing is Believing But Words Tell No Lies: Captions Versus Images in the Libri Carolini and Byzantine

Iconoclasm," in Anne McClanan and Jeff Johnson, eds., *Negating the Image: Case Studies in Iconoclasm* (Aldershot: Ashgate, 2005), pp. 65–89 and 97–112; Thomas F.X. Noble, *Images, Iconoclasm, and the Carolingians* (Philadelphia: University of Pennsylvania Press, 2009).

26. Jerome's letters on images are collected in Davis-Weyer, *Early Medieval Art*, pp. 37–40, see also pp. 103–105. For examples of ascetic and economic opposition to images throughout the Middle Ages, see Conrad Rudolph, *The "Things of Greater Importance": Bernard of Clairvaux's Apologia and the Medieval Attitude Toward Art* (Philadelphia: University of Pennsylvania Press, 1990), pp. 80–103.

27. Norman Cohn, *The Pursuit of the Millennium: Revolutionary Millenarians and Mystical Anarchists of the Middle Ages* (London: Pimlico, 1993), p. xiii; Michael Frassetto, *Heretic Lives: Medieval Heresy from Bogomil and the Cathars to Wyclif and Hus* (London: Profile, 2007), p. 56.

28. On Cathars and images, see Walter L. Wakefield and Austin P. Evans, eds., *Heresies of the High Middle Ages* (New York: Columbia University Press, 1969), pp. 240 and 313; Anne Brenon, "Cathars and the Representation of the Divine: Christians and the Invisible," in Willem van Asselt et al, eds., *Iconoclasm and Iconoclash: Struggle for Religious Identity* (Leiden and Boston: Brill, 2007), pp. 247–61; Beverly Mayne Kienzle, "The Clash Between Catholics and Cathars over Veneration of the Cross," in Van Asselt et al., *Iconoclasm and Iconoclash*, pp. 263–78.

29. On the Waldensian rejection of church ceremony and images, see Leff, *Heresy in the Later Middle Ages*, pp. 445–85; Wakefield and Evans, *Heresies*, pp. 240 and 349; Feld, *Der Ikonoklasmus*, pp. 92–96; Frassetto, *Heretic Lives*, pp. 56–74. Cameron, by contrast, says that there is inadequate evidence to support the claim that the Waldensians (of the fourteenth and fifteenth centuries) disavowed images. Euan Cameron, *The Reformation of the Heretics: The Waldenses of the Alps, 1480–1580* (Oxford: Clarendon Press, 1984), pp. 100 and 218.

30. On Lollards and images, see Jones, "Lollards and Images," pp. 27–50; Margaret Aston, *Lollards and Reformers: Images and Literacy in Late Medieval Religion* (London: The Hambledon Press, 1984), pp. 135–92; Margaret Aston, *England's Iconoclasts: Laws Against Images* (Oxford: Clarendon Press, 1988), pp. 96–159; Anne Hudson, *The Premature Reformation: Wycliffite Texts and Lollard History* (Oxford and New York: Clarendon Press; Oxford University Press, 1988), pp. 301–309 and index entry for "images"; Kathleen Kamerick, *Popular Piety and Art in the Late Middle Ages: Image Worship and Idolatry in England, 1350–1500* (New York:

Palgrave, 2002); Margaret Aston, "Lollards and the Cross," in Fiona Somerset, Jill C. Havens, and Derrick G. Pitard, eds., *Lollards and Their Influence in Late Medieval England* (Woodbridge and Rochester: Boydell Press, 2003), pp. 99–113; Jeremy Dimmick, James Simpson, and Nicolette Zeeman, eds., *Images, Idolatry, and Iconoclasm in Late Medieval England: Textuality and the Visual Image* (Oxford and New York: The Oxford University Press, 2002); Sarah Stanbury, *The Visual Object of Desire in Late Medieval England* (Philadelphia: University of Pennsylvania Press, 2008). On Hussites and the cult of images, see Howard Kaminsky, *A History of the Hussite Revolution* (Berkeley: University of California Press, 1967), index entry for "images"; Leff, *Heresy in the Later Middle Ages*, pp. 609 and 690; Robert Kalivoda and Alexander Kolesnyk, eds., *Das hussitische Denken im Lichte seiner Quellen* (Berlin: Akademie-Verlag, 1969), pp. 262, 264–65, 268, 270–72, 301–302; Horst Bredekamp, *Kunst als Medium sozialer Konflikte: Bilderkämpfe von der Spätantike bis zur Hussitenrevolution* (Frankfurt am Main: Suhrkamp, 1975), pp. 231–333; Thomas A. Fudge, *The Magnificent Ride: The First Reformation in Hussite Bohemia* (Brookfield: Ashgate, 1998), index entries for "iconoclasm" and "images."

31. On Lollards and church property, see Leff, *Heresy in the Later Middle Ages*, pp. 559–605; Margaret Aston, *Faith and Fire: Popular and Unpopular Religion, 1350–1600* (London and Rio Grande: The Hambledon Press, 1993), pp. 95–131; Anne Hudson, "Poor Preachers, Poor Men: Views of Poverty in Wycliff and his Followers," in František Šmahel, ed., *Häresie und vorzeitige Reformation im Spatmittelalter* (Munich: R. Oldenbourg Verlag, 1998), pp. 41–53. On Hus's accusations of simony, see Leff, *Heresy in the Later Middle Ages*, pp. 608 and 625. On the Hussites and church property, see Leff, *Heresy in the Later Middle Ages*, pp. 605–707. On the egalitarian implications of the Hussites' cult of the chalice, see Fudge, *The Magnificent Ride*, pp. 135–48, 162.

32. As translated in Thomas A. Fudge, "'Neither Mine nor Thine': Communist Experiments in Hussite Bohemia," *Canadian Journal of History* 33 (1998), p. 26. Original in Josef Macek, *Ktož jsú boží bojovníci: čtení o Taboře v husitském revolučním hnutí* (Prague: Melantrich, 1951), pp. 59 and 61.

33. On Taborite iconoclasm, see Bredekamp, *Kunst als Medium*, pp. 265–66; Schnitzler, *Ikonoklasmus*, p. 89; František Šmahel, *Die hussitische Revolution*, ed. Alexander Patschovsky, trans. Thomas Krzenck (Hannover: Hahnsche Buchhandlung, 2002), vol. 2, p. 1106, vol. 3, pp. 1884–85.

34. On the relation between idolatry and money in the Middle Ages, see

Camille, *The Gothic Idol*, pp. 258–71.

35. On the voluntary poverty of Beguines, Beghards, and Free Spirits, see Ernest W. McDonnell, *The Beguines and Beghards in Medieval Culture: With Special Emphasis on the Belgian Scene* (New York: Octagon Books, 1969), pp. 141–53, 477–574; Robert E. Lerner, *The Heresy of the Free Spirit in the Later Middle Ages* (Berkeley: University of California Press, 1972), index entry for "voluntary poverty"; Ute Weinmann, *Mittelalterliche Frauenbewegungen: Ihre Beziehungen zur Orthodoxie und Häresie* (Pfaffenweiler: Centaurus, 1990), pp. 207–13; Walter Simons, *Cities of Ladies: Beguine Communities in the Medieval Low Countries, 1200–1565* (Philadelphia: University of Pennsylvania Press, 2001), index entry for "poverty"; Bailey, *Battling Demons*, pp. 66–74; Frassetto, *Heretic Lives*, pp. 135–50. On voluntary poverty, communal life, and the shunning of external forms of piety in the *devotio moderna,* see Albert Hyma, *The Christian Renaissance: A History of the Devotio Moderna* (New York: The Century Co., 1924), pp. 335–36; Ringbom, *Icon to Narrative*, pp. 20–21; Eire, *War Against the Idols*, pp. 21–22; Martina B. Klug, *Armut und Arbeit in der Devotio moderna: Studien zum Leben der Schwestern in niederrheinischen Gemeinschaften* (Münster and New York: Waxmann, 2005); John H. van Engen, *Sisters and Brothers of the Common Life: The Devotio Moderna and the World of the Later Middle Ages* (Philadelphia: University of Pennsylvania Press, 2008), pp. 162–99.

36. Some Beguines were able to afford lavish images; on the patronage of art in the wealthy Beguinages, see Joanna E. Ziegler, "The *Curtis* Beguinages in the Southern Low Countries and Art Patronage: Interpretation and Historiography," *Bulletin de l'Institut Historique Belge de Rome* 57 (1987), pp. 31–70. On the Beguines and art more generally, see Judith Oliver, *Gothic Manuscript Illumination in the Diocese of Liege (c. 1250–c. 1330)* (Leuven: Uitgeverij Peeters, 1988), esp. pp. 112–19; Walter Simons, "Beguines and Psalters," *Ons Geestelijk Erf* 65 (1991), pp. 23–30; Joanna E. Ziegler, *Sculpture of Compassion: The Pietà and the Beguines in the Southern Low Countries c. 1300–c. 1600* (Brussels and Turnhout: Institut historique belge de Rome; Brepols, 1992); Joanna E. Ziegler, "Reality as Imitation: The Role of Religious Imagery Among the Beguines of the Low Countries," in Ulrike Wiethaus, ed., *Maps of Flesh and Light: The Religious Experience of Medieval Women Mystics* (Syracuse: Syracuse University Press, 1993), pp. 112–26; Penny Galloway, "Neither Miraculous nor Astonishing: The Devotional Practice of Beguine Communities in French Flanders," in Juliette Dor, Lesley Johnson, and Jocelyn Wogan-Browne, eds., *New Trends in Feminine Spirituality: The Holy Women of Liège and their Impact*

(Turnhout: Brepols, 1999), pp. 118–22. Evidence of the production and use of art in the context of the *devotio moderna* remains fairly slim. Veelenturf surveys the literature on this topic in his introduction to an edited volume dedicated to it; see also the essays in this collection. Veelenturf, *Geen povere schoonheid*, pp. 9–30. While many members of the *devotio moderna* lived in extra-monastic communities, the movement also established the Windesheim Congregation of Canons Regular, who lived monastic lives under the rule of the Augustinians. Like the chapels of other monasteries in the period, theirs were decorated with images. See Harry Tummers, "Moderne Devoten en sculptuur: De beeldenschat van het klooster Soeterbeeck," in Veelenturf, *Geen povere schoonheid*, pp. 253–71; Rudolf Th. M. van Dijk, "Toward Imageless Contemplation: Gerard Zerbolt of Zutphen as Guide for *Lectio Divina*," in Hein Blommestijn, Charles Caspers, and Rijcklof Hofman, eds., *Spirituality Renewed: Studies on Significant Representatives of the Modern Devotion* (Leuven: Peeters, 2003), pp. 5–6.

37. Raoul Vaneigem, *The Movement of the Free Spirit: General Considerations and Firsthand Testimony Concerning Some Brief Flowerings of Life in the Middle Ages, the Renaissance, and, Incidentally, our Own Time*, trans. Randall Cherry and Ian Patterson (New York: Zone Books, 1994).

38. Schnitzler argues against drawing such a line. Schnitzler, *Ikonoklasmus*, p. 233. He also questions the idea that medieval viewers understood the image on the model of the real presence of Christ in the Eucharist. Norbert Schnitzler, "'Faules Holz—Toter Stein': Thesen zum Bilderkult des Mittelalters aus ikonoklastischer Perspektive," in *Pictura quasi fictura: Die Rolle des Bildes in der Erforschung von Alltag und Sachkultur des Mittelalters und der frühen Neuzeit* (Vienna: Der Österreichischen Akademie der Wissenschaften, 1996), pp. 175–76.

39. Camille writes: "The rise of the Lollard heresy in late-fourteenth-century England made . . . the vocabulary that divided image from prototype no longer [a matter] for subtle theological speculation but [a matter] of life and death." Camille, *The Gothic Idol*, p. 220. On the late medieval roots of sixteenth-century criticism of images, see p. 346; Schnitzler, *Ikonoklasmus*, p. 67. On the differences between late medieval mystical ideals of imageless devotion and Reformation iconoclasm, see Margaret Aston, "Imageless Devotion: What Kind of an Ideal?" in Rosemary Horrox and Sarah Rees Jones, eds., *Pragmatic Utopias: Ideals and Communities, 1200–1630* (Cambridge and New York: Cambridge University Press, 2001), pp. 188–203.

40. The literature on Byzantine iconoclasm is large. See the classic study

André Grabar, *L'iconoclasme byzantin: Le dossier archéologique* (Paris: Flammarion, 1998). An excellent recent account with bibliography is Barber, *Figure and Likeness*. For bibliography on iconoclasm during the Protestant Reformation, see Linda B. Parshall and Peter W. Parshall, *Art and the Reformation: An Annotated Bibliography* (Boston: G.K. Hall, 1986), pp. 43–66; Cécile Dupeux, Peter Jezler, and Jean Wirth, *Bildersturm: Wahnsinn oder Gottes Wille?* (Munich: Fink, 2000), pp. 430–52. Important work that post-dates these bibliographies includes Michael Gaudio, "The Space of Idolatry: Reformation, Incarnation, and the Ethnographic Image," *RES: Anthropology and Aesthetics* 40 (2002), pp. 72–91; Blickle et al., *Macht und Ohnmacht*; Koerner, *The Reformation of the Image*; Angela Vanhaelen, "Iconoclasm and the Creation of Images in Emanuel de Witte's Old Church in Amsterdam," *The Art Bulletin* 87, no. 2 (2005), pp. 249–64; Mia M. Mochizuki, *The Netherlandish Image after Iconoclasm, 1566-1672: Material Religion in the Dutch Golden Age* (Aldershot and Burlington: Ashgate, 2008); Keith Moxey, "Mimesis and Iconoclasm," *Art History* 32, no. 1 (2009), pp. 52–77.

41. In Zurich, to take but one example, spontaneous individual acts of violent iconoclasm gave way to the orderly removal of images organized by the town council. See Charles Garside, *Zwingli and the Arts* (New Haven: Yale University Press, 1966), pp. 146–60; Sergiusz Michalski, *The Reformation and the Visual Arts: The Protestant Image Question in Western and Eastern Europe* (London: Routledge, 1993), pp. 51–59; Margarete Stirm, *Die Bilderfrage in der Reformation* (Gütersloh: Gütersloher Verlagshaus Mohn, 1977), pp. 130–60; Lee Palmer Wandel, *Voracious Idols and Violent Hands: Iconoclasm in Reformation Zurich, Strasbourg, and Basel* (Cambridge and New York: Cambridge University Press, 1995), pp. 53–101.

42. For discussion of Luther's moderate position on images, which he outlines in "Against the Heavenly Prophets" (1525), see Stirm, *Die Bilderfrage*, pp. 17–68; Carl C. Christensen, *Art and the Reformation in Germany* (Athens: Ohio University Press, 1979), pp. 42–65; Koerner, *The Reformation of the Image*, pp. 153–68. On Zwingli and Calvin's inadvertent fomenting of precisely the popular iconoclasm they condemned, see Eire, *War Against the Idols*, pp. 73–86, 264–70, 276–89.

43. This is not to say that magisterial reformers never advocated the redistribution of the Church's wealth to those in need: "Let us clear out this filth and rubbish!" writes Zwingli, "henceforth, let us devote to other men, the living images of God, all the unimaginable wealth which was once spent on these foolish idols." As translated in Eire, *War Against the Idols*, p. 111, see also p. 164. Original

in Zwingli, *Sämtliche Werke*, vol. 6.1, p. 497. See also Peter Jezler, Elke Jezler, and Christine Göttler, "Warum ein Bilderstreit? Der Kampf gegen die 'Götzen' in Zürich als Beispiel," in Hans-Dietrich Altendorf and Peter Jezler, eds., *Bilderstreit. Kulturwandel in Zwinglis Reformation* (Zurich: Theologischer Verlag, 1984), pp. 92–93. On Zwingli's relationship to the radical Reformation, see W. P. Stephens, *Zwingli: An Introduction to his Thought* (Oxford and New York: Oxford University Press; Clarendon Press, 1992), pp. 23–26, 132–37. On class and iconoclasm, see Michalski, *The Reformation*, pp. 80–82. For a disturbingly uncritical assessment of class and iconoclasm, see Besançon, *The Forbidden Image*, p. 379.

44. George Huntston Williams, *The Radical Reformation* (Kirksville: Sixteenth Century Journal Publishers, 1992), p. 15, see also pp. xxix–xxx, xxxiii. It was Williams who codified the idea of a radical Reformation comprising three major groups: Spiritualists, Anabaptists, and Evangelical Rationalists (p. xxix). A collection of recent essays is dedicated to assessing the validity of the concept of a radical Reformation: Hans-Jürgen Goertz and James M. Stayer, eds., *Radikalität und Dissent im 16. Jahrhundert = Radicalism and Dissent in the Sixteenth Century* (Berlin: Duncker & Humblot, 2002).

45. See Claus Peter Clasen, *Anabaptism, a Social history, 1525–1618: Switzerland, Austria, Moravia, South and Central Germany* (Ithaca: Cornell University Press, 1972), p. 176. Although criticism of the tithes system was widespread among Anabaptists, many were unwilling to disobey secular authorities on the issue. Peter James Klassen, *The Economics of Anabaptism, 1525–1560* (London: Mouton, 1964), p. 116.

46. This is a modified version of the translation in Thomas Müntzer, *The Collected Works of Thomas Müntzer*, ed. and trans. Peter Matheson (Edinburgh: T. & T. Clark, 1988), p. 304. A passage from the anonymously written *To the Assembly of the Common Peasantry* (May 1525) follows similar lines: "This is the intention of St. Paul in Romans chapter 13[.8], on taxes, customs, etc., where he says, 'You do not owe anything to anyone, except that you should love one another, for love is the fulfillment of the law.'" Michael G. Baylor, ed., *The Radical Reformation* (Cambridge and New York: Cambridge University Press, 1991), p. 104. On the Peasants' War and resistance to tithes, see James M. Stayer, *The German Peasants' War and Anabaptist Community of Goods* (Montreal and Buffalo: McGill-Queen's University Press, 1991), index entry for "tithes." On the connections between the Peasants' War and Anabaptism, see Stayer, *The German Peasants' War*, pp. 61–92; Werner O.

Packull, "Die Anfänge des Täufertums in Tirol," in Günter Vogler, ed., *Wegscheiden der Reformation: Alternatives Denken vom 16. bis zum 18. Jahrhundert* (Weimar: H. Böhlaus Nachfolger, 1994), pp. 179–209.

47. Münzer, *The Collected Works*, p. 249, see also pp. 233–34. On Müntzer's iconoclasm, see Christensen, *Art and the Reformation*, p. 69.

48. Münzer, *The Collected Works*, p. 232.

49. "Ir die apgotterey der bildern und altare aus den kirchen bracht; wollt ir nu selig werden, so musten ir auch die apgote in heusern und kasten, sonderlich das schone zynen geschirre von den wenden, cleynot, silberwerk und bargelt aus den kasten auch wegtun." Felician Gess, ed., *Akten und Briefe zur Kirchenpolitik Herzog Georgs von Sachsen* (Cologne and Vienna: Böhlau, 1985), vol. 2, pp. 79–80. Discussed in Abraham Friesen, *Thomas Muentzer, a Destroyer of the Godless: The Making of a Sixteenth-Century Religious Revolutionary* (Berkeley: University of California Press, 1990), p. 231.

50. Baylor, *The Radical Reformation*, p. 255; my italics.

51. Baylor, *The Radical Reformation*, p. 114, see also p. 116. The association of idolatry with tyranny was long standing. See Camille, *The Gothic Idol*, pp. 53–55.

52. Baylor, *The Radical Reformation*, pp. xii and xxi.

53. Martin Luther, *Luther's Works* (Saint Louis: Concordia Pub. House, 1955), vol. 46, pp. 105–106. Cf. "I have never known of a case in which [rebellion] was a just action, and even now I cannot imagine any" (p. 104). "Now that we are under our princes, lords, and emperors, we must outwardly obey their laws instead of the laws of Moses." Luther, *Works*, vol. 40, p. 90, see also pp. 83, 89, 112, vol. 45, pp. 75–129, vol. 46, pp. 3–43, 45–55. In much of this, Luther appeals to Romans 13.1: "Let every person be subject to the governing authorities; for there is no authority except from God, and those that exist have been instituted by God."

54. On Lutheran and Calvinist theories of political resistance, see Eire, *War Against the Idols*, pp. 284–304. On Luther's "two kingdoms" theory, see, e.g., Abraham Friesen, *Reformation and Utopia: The Marxist Interpretation of the Reformation and its Antecedents* (Wiesbaden: F. Steiner, 1974), pp. 15–21; W. D. J. Cargill Thompson, *The Political Thought of Martin Luther*, ed. Philip Broadhead (Brighton and Totowa: Harvester Press; Barnes & Noble Books, 1984); Brent W. Sockness, "Luther's Two Kingdoms Revisited: A Response to Reinhold Niebuhr's Criticism of Luther," *The Journal of Religious Ethics* 20, no. 1 (1992), pp. 93–110; James Martin Estes, *Peace, Order and the Glory of God: Secular Authority and the Church in the*

Thought of Luther and Melanchthon, 1518–1559 (Leiden and Boston: Brill, 2005).

55. In 1534, the Anabaptists stripped Münster's cathedral and churches of altarpieces, sculptures, books, and documents. Max Geisberg, ed., *Die Stadt Münster* (Münster: Aschendorff, 1937), pp. 22–28; Martin Warnke, ed., *Bildersturm: Die Zerstörung des Kunstwerks* (Munich: Carl Hanser, 1973), pp. 80–98; Jeffrey Chipps Smith, *German Sculpture of the Later Renaissance, c. 1520–1580: Art in an Age of Uncertainty* (Princeton: Princeton University Press, 1994), pp. 41–45.

56. On the community of goods practiced in Münster, see Warnke, *Bildersturm*, pp. 75 and 90; Stayer, *The German Peasants' War*, pp. 131–38; Ralf Klötzer, *Die Täuferherrschaft von Münster: Stadtreformation und Welterneuerung* (Münster: Aschendorff, 1992), p. 60. On communitarian experiments during the Reformation more generally, see Hans-Dieter Plümper, *Die Gütergemeinschaft bei den Täufern des 16. Jahrhunderts* (Göppingen: A. Kümmerle, 1972); Klassen, *The Economics of Anabaptism*, pp. 28–82; Clasen, *Anabaptism*, pp. 183–94; Robert W. Scribner, "Practical Utopias: Pre-Modern Communism and the Reformation," *Comparative Studies in Society and History* 36, no. 4 (1994), pp. 743–74. The Hutterites were among the most successful early modern groups to practice a voluntary community of goods with a minimum of hierarchical government. They did not celebrate poverty so much as a detachment from material goods reflected in a person's willingness to give what he or she could to others in need. Klassen, *The Economics of Anabaptism*, pp. 56–65; Stayer, *The German Peasants' War*, pp. 139–59; Werner O. Packull, *Hutterite Beginnings: Communitarian Experiments During the Reformation* (Baltimore: Johns Hopkins University Press, 1995).

57. Williams, *The Radical Reformation*, pp. 553–88. On Anabaptists and violence, see James M. Stayer, *Anabaptists and the Sword* (Lawrence: Coronado Press, 1972); Sigrun Haude, *In the Shadow of "Savage Wolves": Anabaptist Münster and the German Reformation During the 1530s* (Boston: Humanities Press, 2000), p. 2. On anti-semitism and the Reformation, see Heiko Augustinus Oberman, *The Roots of Anti-Semitism in the Age of Renaissance and Reformation*, trans. James I. Porter (Philadelphia: Fortress Press, 1984).

58. "Wir haben ze Zürich gar hälle Tempel; die Wänd sind hüpsch wyss!" Oskar Farner, *Huldrych Zwingli: Seine Verkündigung und ihre ersten Früchte 1520–1525* (Zurich: Zwingli-Verlag, 1954), vol. 3, p. 490.

59. Koerner, *The Reformation of the Image*, pp. 109 and 111.

60. Koerner, *The Reformation of the Image*, p. 114, see also p. 127.

61. Koerner, *The Reformation of the Image*, p. 124, see also p. 208. On resemblance and dissemblance in Christian art, see Georges Didi-Huberman, *Fra Angelico: Dissemblance and Figuration*, trans. Jane Marie Todd (Chicago: University of Chicago Press, 1995), pp. 5, 45–60; Besançon, *The Forbidden Image*, p. 177.

62. Koerner, *The Reformation of the Image*, p. 209, see also p. 12. On the kenosis of the image in the Christian icon, see Jean-Luc Marion, *The Crossing of the Visible*, trans. James K. A. Smith (Stanford: Stanford University Press, 2004), pp. 46–65, 87.

63. Koerner, *The Reformation of the Image*, p. 124.

64. Marin sees in doubleness of this kind the positing of an object of desire: "les discours qui . . . disent simultanément le don et le retrait, l'oblation et la perte du corps de Dieu . . . don et perte par lesquels le corps divin est posé comme objet de désir." Louis Marin, *Opacité de la peinture: Essais sur la représentation au Quattrocento* (Malakoff: Usher, 1989), p. 125.

65. Müntzer condemned the Franciscans for, among other things, believing that "eternal beatitude cannot be called the rule of faith which is already within us; rather eternal beatitude is something present only in our future home." As translated in Steven E. Ozment, "Mysticism, Nominalism and Dissent," in Charles Trinkaus, ed., *The Pursuit of Holiness in Late Medieval and Renaissance Religion* (Leiden: Brill, 1974), pp. 62–63. Original in Thomas Müntzer, *Schriften und Briefe*, ed. Günther Franz (Gütersloh: Gütersloher Verlagshaus G. Mohn, 1968), p. 360.

66. Bredekamp, *Kunst als Medium*, p. 294.

67. On the founding and early history of the Ulmer Verein, see Harold Hammer-Schenk, *Kunstgeschichte gegen den Strich gebürstet? 10 Jahre Ulmer Verein 1968–1978: Geschichte in Dokumenten* (Hannover: Ulmer Verein, 1979). In focusing on the Anabaptists, Warnke followed in the footsteps of earlier Marxist historians of the Reformation, beginning with Engels, who favored the radical reformers associated with the Peasants' War over more politically conservative reformers including Luther. Friesen, *Reformation and Utopia*, pp. 1–27. Engels celebrated Müntzer in an essay of 1850: Friedrich Engels, "The Peasant War in Germany," in *Karl Marx, Frederick Engels: Collected Works* (New York: International Publishers, 1975), vol. 10, pp. 399–482.

68. Warnke, *Bildersturm*, pp. 10–11. See also Martin Warnke, "Ansichten über Bilderstürmer: Zur Wertbestimmung des Bildersturms in der Neuzeit," in Scribner, *Bilder und Bildersturm*, p. 299. Warnke and Bredekamp's work on iconoclasm

provoked an angry debate between defenders and detractors of an overtly politicized art history. For the bibliography of this debate, see Dario Gamboni, *The Destruction of Art: Iconoclasm and Vandalism Since the French Revolution* (London: Reaktion Books, 1997), p. 338 n.10.

69. Recent work on iconoclasm has tended to emphasize its creativity: the breaking of one image is always the making of another. Aligning himself with Warnke and Bredekamp, Gamboni argues against "the binary opposition between creation and destruction." Gamboni, *The Destruction of Art*, pp. 25 and 10. See also Dario Gamboni, "Image to Destroy, Indestructible Image," in Bruno Latour and Peter Weibel, eds., *Iconoclash: Beyond the Image Wars in Art and Science* (Karlsruhe and Cambridge: ZKM; MIT Press, 2002), pp. 88–135. McClanan and Johnson explore this same dialectic in their introduction to a collection of essays: "Our survey of the anthology's contents has emphasized the transformative over the purely destructive energies unleashed in and by iconoclasm." McClanan and Johnson, *Negating the Image*, p. 9.

70. On iconoclasm's uncovering of the limitations of formalist art history, see David Freedberg, *The Power of Images: Studies in the History and Theory of Response* (Chicago: University of Chicago Press, 1989), p. 421; David Freedberg, *Iconoclasts and Their Motives* (Maarssen and Montclair: G. Schwartz; A. Schram, 1985), p. 7.

71. Freedberg, *The Power of Images*, p. 424.

72. Freedberg, *The Power of Images*, p. 427.

73. Freedberg, *The Power of Images*, pp. 425–26.

74. "Why Pollock's intense belief that he could somehow paint pictures which were stripped of their referentiality to nature and to the order and experience of nature? Why the profound attractiveness—at least for a while—of Clement Greenberg's conception of the fruitfulness of painting that does not go in search of the world beyond painting for its subject matter? Because, as I have implied throughout this chapter, of fear." Freedberg, *The Power of Images*, pp. 427–28.

75. "Our century has seen great revolutions, and, once they have abated, law, property, and other institutions long held sacred have had a great deal of trouble finding their footing again. Should we be surprised that it is taking time for the image, which another contemporary revolution dared attack, to reestablish itself?" Besançon, *The Forbidden Image*, p. 382.

76. "'Abstract' art developed within a religious and, more precisely, a mystical movement." Besançon, *The Forbidden Image*, p. 6.

77. For Besançon this indicates the need to return to authoritative traditions. Besançon, *The Forbidden Image*, p. 8.

78. Latour and Weibel, *Iconoclash,* p. 21. Cf. Hans Belting, "Beyond Iconoclasm: Nam June Paik, the Zen Gaze and the Escape from Representation," in Latour and Weibel, *Iconoclash*, pp. 390–91. For an excellent critique of the larger argument to which Belting's rejection of abstraction in this essay belongs, see Wood, "Review of *Bild-Anthropologie*," esp. p. 371.

79. Bruno Latour and Peter Weibel, eds., *Making Things Public: Atmospheres of Democracy* (Cambridge and Karlsruhe: MIT Press; ZKM, 2005), p. 41.

80. Latour and Weibel, *Iconoclash*, p. 32.

81. Latour and Weibel, *Iconoclash*, p. 36.

82. Theodor W. Adorno, *Aesthetic Theory*, ed. Gretel Adorno and Rolf Tiedemann, trans. Robert Hullot-Kentor (Minneapolis: University of Minnesota Press, 1997), p. 19.

83. Roland Barthes, *The Responsibility of Forms: Critical Essays on Music, Art, and Representation* (New York: Hill and Wang, 1985), p. 232. On modernist and postmodernist negation, see, e.g., Douglas Crimp, "The End of Painting," *October* 16 (1981), pp. 69–86; Yve-Alain Bois, *Painting as Model* (Cambridge: MIT Press, 1990), pp. 229–44; Thierry de Duve, *Kant after Duchamp* (Cambridge: MIT Press, 1996), p. 77; T. J. Clark, *Farewell to an Idea: Episodes from a History of Modernism* (New Haven: Yale University Press, 1999), pp. 371–403; Arthur C. Danto et al., "The Mourning After: A Roundtable," *Artforum* 41, no. 7 (2003), pp. 206–11, 267–70.

84. De Duve, *Kant after Duchamp*, p. 148. On historicist myths of beginnings and endings, see Paul de Man, *Blindness and Insight: Essays in the Rhetoric of Contemporary Criticism* (New York: Oxford University Press, 1971), pp. 240–41; Hal Foster, "What's Neo about the Neo-Avant-Garde?" *October* 70 (1994), pp. 12–13.

85. Gustave Flaubert, *Bouvard and Pécuchet: The Last Novel of Gustave Flaubert*, trans. Mark Polizzotti (Normal: Dalkey Archive Press, 2005), p. 286; Cf. "*Photography*: Will dethrone painting" (p. 316); Gaston Tissandier, *Les merveilles de la photographie* (Paris: Hachette, 1874), p. 64; Walter Benjamin, *The Arcades Project*, trans. Howard Eiland and Kevin McLaughlin (Cambridge: Belknap Press, 1999), p. 671.

86. "In reaction to photography, painting begins to stress the elements of color in the picture. By the time Impressionism yields to Cubism, painting has created

for itself a broader domain into which, for the time being, photography cannot follow." Benjamin, *The Arcades Project*, p. 6, see also pp. 671 and 678. Adorno's phrase appears in a letter to Benjamin, in a passage criticizing Benjamin's argument as "undialectical." Theodor W. Adorno et al., *Aesthetics and Politics*, ed. Fredric Jameson (London and New York: Verso, 2007), p. 116.

87. Thierry de Duve, "The Readymade and the Tube of Paint," *Artforum* (May 1986), p. 112; Foster, "What's Neo," p. 9.

88. "The consciousness of the personal and spontaneous in the painting and sculpture stimulates the artist to invent devices of handling, processing, surfacing, which confer to the utmost degree the aspect of the freely made. Hence the great importance of the mark, the stroke, the brush, the drip, the quality of the substance of the paint itself, and the surface of the canvas as a texture and field of operation—all signs of the artist's active presence." Meyer Schapiro, *Modern Art, 19th & 20th Centuries: Selected Papers* (New York: George Braziller, 1978), p. 218. See also Bois, *Painting as Model*, p. 231.

89. The passage continues: "...and by 'mechanizing' their own body at work.... For photography is the principal locus of industrialization's incidence upon painting, and the camera, therefore, also the principal mechanizing device that the painters had to reclaim, which they did by mimicking it and investing it with subjectivity." de Duve, "The Readymade," p. 116. Cf. "The question of the artist-becoming-machine is one that characterized modern painting throughout the nineteenth and twentieth centuries." David Joselit in Danto et al., "The Mourning After," p. 268.

90. Adorno, *Aesthetic Theory*, p. 39.

91. On Seurat and the mechanical, see Schapiro, *Modern Art*, pp. 108–109; de Duve, *Kant after Duchamp*, pp. 175–84; Jonathan Crary, *Suspensions of Perception: Attention, Spectacle, and Modern Culture* (Cambridge: MIT Press, 1999), pp. 150–51.

92. On machinic modernisms, see Hal Foster, *Prosthetic Gods* (Cambridge: MIT Press, 2004), pp. 108–91.

93. "Art is modern art through mimesis of the hardened and alienated; only thereby, and not by the refusal of a mute reality, does art become eloquent." Adorno, *Aesthetic Theory*, p. 21. See also Hal Foster, "Dada Mime," *October* 105 (2003), esp. p. 174.

94. De Duve, *Kant after Duchamp*, p. 171, see also pp. 148–49, 167.

95. Barthes, *Critical Essays*, p. 244. "In order for a part of the past to be touched

by the present instant," writes Benjamin with Surrealism in mind, "there must be no continuity between them." Benjamin, *The Arcades Project*, p. 470.

CHAPTER ONE: RITUALIZED HOSTILITY

1. "Tselve cruys was die meeste affgoederije die in de kercke was." J. Scheerder, *De beeldenstorm* (Bussum: De Haan, 1974), p. 92.

2. Whether or not the liturgy in and of itself and particularly the Mass should be considered dramatic has been too extensively debated for me to do justice to the literature on the topic here. For a partial survey of the matter, see Parker, *The Descent*, pp. 60–80.

3. Neil C. Brooks, Solange Corbin, and Karl Young call these rites extra or para-liturgical, while Kolumban Gschwend, Gesine and Johannes Taubert, and Markus Maisel say that they were *indeed* liturgical. Though the details of the rite vary from place to place, its general outline is consistent. On this consistency, see Solange Corbin, *La deposition liturgique du Christ au Vendredi Saint: Sa place dans l'histoire des rites et du théâtre religieux (analyse de documents portugais)* (Paris: Société d'Éditions "Les Belles Lettres," 1960), pp. 36–37. It is difficult to say how common the rite was. At least two hundred accounts of it have been published. According to Corbin, this number indicates that it was rare. Corbin, *La deposition liturgique*, pp. 14, 22, 200. But others have suggested (either directly or indirectly) that it was performed more widely than the extant evidence alone would suggest. Kolumban Gschwend, *Die Depositio und Elevatio Crucis im Raum der alten Diözese Brixen: Ein Beitrag zur Geschichte der Grablegung am Karfreitag und der Auferstehungsfeier am Ostermorgen* (Sarnen: Ehrli, 1965), pp. 27 and 52; Gesine and Johannes Taubert, "Mittelalterliche Kruzifixe mit schwenkbaren Armen: Ein Beitrag zur Verwendung von Bildwerken in der Liturgie," *Zeitschrift des deutschen Vereins für Kunstwissenschaft* 23 (1969), pp. 102–103. Brooks says simply that the liturgical ceremonies associated with the sepulcher were "quite widespread, but never in universal use." Neil C. Brooks, "The Sepulchre of Christ in Art and Liturgy with Special Reference to the Liturgical Drama," *University of Illinois Studies in Language and Literature* 7, no. 2 (1921), p. 30. And Young asserts that the Deposition and Elevation were "very widely observed, and have persisted from at least the tenth century to the present time." Karl Young, *The Drama of the Medieval Church* (Oxford: Clarendon Press, 1962), vol. 1, p. 112. Nußbaum gives an excellent summary of the geographical and historical extent of the Deposition and Elevation

rites, pointing out that they occurred surprisingly infrequently in the Netherlands and Belgium. Otto Nußbaum, *Die Aufbewahrung der Eucharistie* (Bonn: Hanstein, 1979), pp. 192–95.

4. The paraliturgical rites belonging to the sepulcher, particularly the *Visitatio sepulchri*, also gave rise to more elaborate paraliturgical *dramas*, including the Easter Play. The literature on these dramas is too extensive to do justice to in a footnote. I would, however, like to call attention to one remarkable study: Rainer Warning, *The Ambivalences of Medieval Religious Drama*, trans. Steven Rendall (Stanford: Stanford University Press, 2001).

5. On this participation, see Robert W. Scribner, *Popular Culture and Popular Movements in Reformation Germany* (London and Ronceverte: The Hambledon Press, 1987), pp. 22–31.

6. In a discussion of the most theatrical of the paraliturgical rites, the *Visitatio sepulchri*, Warning writes: "With respect to substantive additions the liturgical Visitatio seems to practice a kind of voluntary self-restraint which sets it sharply apart from the vernacular tradition." Rainer Warning, "On the Alterity of Medieval Religious Drama," *New Literary History* 10, no. 2 (1979), p. 269.

7. On the "latent aggressive function" of medieval religious drama, see Warning, "On the Alterity," p. 284.

8. *The Monastic Agreement of the Monks and Nuns of the English Nation*, trans. Thomas Symons (New York: Oxford University Press, 1953), pp. 44–45. The Deposition rite from the *Monastic Agreement* is discussed in E.K. Chambers, *The Mediaeval Stage* (London: Oxford University Press, 1903), vol. 2, pp. 16–17; Young, *The Drama*, vol. 1, pp. 132–34, 582; Pamela Sheingorn, *The Easter Sepulchre in England* (Kalamazoo: Medieval Institute Publications, Western Michigan University, 1987), p. 21. On the *Monastic Agreement*, see Dunbar H. Ogden, *The Staging of Drama in the Medieval Church* (Newark and London: University of Delaware Press; Associated University Presses, 2002), pp. 19, 23–24; Nils Holger Petersen, "The Representational Liturgy of the *Regularis Concordia*," in Nigel Hiscock, ed., *The White Mantle of Churches: Architecture, Liturgy, and Art Around the Millennium* (Turnhout: Brepols, 2003), pp. 107–17.

9. A 1494 manual from Brixen instructs: "Postea legantur vespere uti brevarius docet: et sub magnificat sepulchrum aspergatur et thurificetur et claudatur." Taubert, "Mittelalterliche Kruzifixe (1969)," p. 106, see also p. 108. The Brixener *Dommesnerbuch* of circa 1553 says: "so sprengt und raucht der Herr Officianto, die

figur jm grab." Gschwend, *Die Depositio*, p. 95, see also pp. 63–64.

10. "Die vier Caplan die leyttern aufsteygen, vnd bildnus ordenlich abnehmen, Vnd das bildnus in die par legen.... wie man zcu den fürstlichen begengnussen vnd iargedechtnussen pflegt zcugebrauchen." Taubert, "Mittelalterliche Kruzifixe (1969)," p. 99, see also p. 101. For other examples, see Gschwend, *Die Depositio*, p. 92 n.151. On the donation of candles, see Gschwend, *Die Depositio*, pp. 33–34.

11. "Ire kappen in clag weyß an die helße tziehen." Taubert, "Mittelalterliche Kruzifixe (1969)," p. 99.

12. On these various sepulcher types, see Alfred Heales, "Easter Sepulchers: Their Object, Nature and History," *Archaeologia, or, Miscellaneous Tracts Relating to Antiquity* 42 (1869), pp. 288–303; J. Charles Cox and Alfred Harvey, *English Church Furniture* (London: Methuen, 1908), pp. 74–78; Francis Bond, *The Chancel of English Churches* (London and New York: Oxford University Press, 1916), pp. 231–41; Brooks, "The Sepulchre," pp. 53–66; Gustaf Dalman, *Das Grab Christi in Deutschland* (Leipzig: Dieterich, 1922), pp. 30–34; Pamela Sheingorn, "The *Sepulchrum Domini*: A Study in Art and Liturgy," *Studies in Iconography* 4 (1978), pp. 37–60; Maria Prokopp, *Das Heilige Grab von Garamszentbenedek im Christlichen Museum zu Esztergom*, trans. Eva Szilágyi (Budapest: Corvina, 1982); Peter Jezler, "Gab es in Konstanz ein ottonisches Osterspiel? Die Mauritius-Rotunde und ihre kultische Funktion als *Sepulchrum Domini*," in Adolf Reinle, Ludwig Schmugge, and Peter Stotz, eds., *Variorum munera florum: Latinität als prägende Kraft mittelalterlicher Kultur, Festschrift für Hans F. Haefele zu seinem sechzigsten Geburtstag* (Sigmaringen: J. Thorbecke, 1985), pp. 91–128; Sheingorn, *The Easter Sepulchre*, pp. 33–45; Justin Kroesen, *The Sepulchrum Domini Through the Ages: Its Form and Function* (Leuven and Sterling: Peeters, 2000), pp. 3–135; Ogden, *The Staging of Drama*, pp. 25–68; Justin Kroesen and Regnerus Steensma, *The Interior of the Medieval Village Church* (Leuven and Dudley: Peeters, 2004), pp. 290–303.

13. Brooks, "The Sepulchre," p. 72, see also pp. 73–75. From the thirteenth century forward, permanent sepulchers were built primarily in Germany and England and only very rarely in France and Italy. Kroesen, *The Sepulchrum Domini*, p. 54. A number of late medieval sculptural types, including monumental entombment scenes, are closely related to the Easter sepulcher. See Annemarie Schwarzweber, *Das heilige Grab in der deutschen Bildnerei des Mittelalters* (Freiburg: Eberhard Albert Universitätsbuchhandlung, 1940); William H. Forsyth, *The Entombment of Christ: French Sculptures of the Fifteenth and Sixteenth Centuries* (Cambridge:

Harvard University Press, 1970); Sheingorn, *The Easter Sepulchre*; Michel Martin, *La statuaire de la mise au tombeau du Christ des XVe et XVIe siècles en Europe occidentale* (Paris: Picard, 1997); Sylvie Aballéa, *Les saints sépulcres Monumentaux du Rhin supérieur et de la Souabe (1340–1400)* (Strasbourg: Presses universitaires de Strasbourg, 2003); Kroesen, *The Sepulchrum Domini*, pp. 83–90, 109–16; Markus Maisel, *Sepulchrum Domini: Studien zur Ikonographie und Funktion großplastischer Grablegungsgruppen am Mittelrhein und im Rheinland* (Mainz: Gesellschaft für Mittelrheinische Kirchengeschichte, 2002); Kroesen and Steensma, *The Interior*, pp. 303–306.

14. *The Monastic Agreement*, p. 45.

15. Bond, *The Chancel*, p. 224.

16. "Ne Christi corpus, per impios, aut haereticos, vel Iudaeos inde auferri, vel alia quaevis contaminatio fieri queat." Young, *The Drama*, vol. 1, p. 173; Peter Wünsche, *Kathedralliturgie zwischen Tradition und Wandel: Zur mittelalterlichen Geschichte der Bamberger Domliturgie im Bereich des Triduum Sacrum* (Münster: Aschendorff, 1998), p. 251.

17. "Zu Stipendien für Scholaren, welche zu Ehren des Leidens and Todes unsers Heilandes bei dem Heilige Grabe von Karfreitag bis zum Osterfeste beständig das Psalterium beten sollten." Josef Andreas Jungmann, "Die Andacht der Vierzig Stunden und das heilige Grab," *Liturgisches Jahrbuch* 2 (1952), p. 190.

18. R. M. Serjeantson and H. Isham Longden, "The Parish Churches and Religious Houses of Northamptonshire: Their Dedications, Altars, Images and Lights," *The Archaeological Journal* 70 (1913), p. 229.

19. "Item nach der metten thue . . . dan du muest doch dieweil jn der Kirchen pleiben unnd auff die Kerzen sehen beim Grab, dan du Kanst die Kirchen vor Neunen, oder Zehen nit zu spörn, die weil das Volckh noch zu Kirchen ist, darnach wan jedermann auß ist, so mögen die Schueler, oder der Junckhmaister Lucaten wol auff hörn vom Psalter zu singen, aber das des morgens umb vier ur widerum kumen zu dem Psalter zu singen, dan das Volckh kumbt auch gewonlich umb die stunt." Walther Lipphardt, *Lateinische Osterfeiern und Osterspiele* (Berlin and New York: De Gruyter, 1975), vol. 6, p. 122. On lay participation in the grave watch, see also Maisel, *Sepulchrum Domini*, pp. 81–82.

20. Jacob Grimm and Wilhelm Grimm, *Deutsches Wörterbuch* (Leipzig: S. Hirzel, 1954), vol. 8, p. 1487. Grimm cites many variations on the expression "es kan niemand dess heyligen grabs vergebens hu'ten" (No one can watch the Holy

Sepulcher for nothing), meaning no one does it simply out of the goodness of his heart. Discussed in Peter Jezler, "Bildwerke im Dienste der dramatischen Ausgestaltung der Osterliturgie—Befürworter und Gegner," in Ernst Ullmann, ed., *Von der Macht der Bilder: Beiträge des C.I.H.A.-Kolloquiums, "Kunst und Reformation"* (Leipzig: E. A. Seemann, 1983), p. 239.

21. "Die schuler bim grab järlichen gar vil verpraucht, haben sich voll getrunken, syen dann gar ongeschickt worden, das es ergerlich gewest, das hab sich von jar zu jar gemeert... pitt derhalben ime ain ordnung zu geben, wie er sich halten sölle." Another complaint was filed in 1564: "das sich die priester bey dem grab singen übel halten mit beweynigen." P. Zinsmaier, "Eine unbekannte Quelle zur Geschichte der mittelalterlichen Liturgie im Konstanzer Münster," *Zeitschrift für die Geschichte des Oberrheins* 104, no. 1 (1956), p. 88 n.76. Discussed in Jezler, "Bildwerke im Dienste," p. 239.

22. "So bestand andererseits auch die Gefahr, daß die willige Hingabe an den Zauber des Zeremoniells verweigert, die illusion zerstört und der Vorgang der Lächerlichkeit preisgegeben wurde." Jezler, "Bildwerke im Dienste," pp. 238–39.

23. Wolfgang Lindow, ed., *Ein kurtzweilig Lesen von Dil Ulenspiegel* (Stuttgart: Reclam, 1966), pp. 39–41.

24. The songs used in the Deposition rite derive from the Easter Saturday liturgy. Corbin lists the responsories and antiphons mentioned in roughly 174 Deposition rites. Corbin, *La deposition liturgique*, pp. 70–84. The most commonly occurring is the *Sepulto domino* responsory, which appears in nearly one hundred accounts. The responsories *Ecce quomodo moritur* and *Recessit pastor* and the antiphons *In pace in idipsum*, *Caro mea*, and *In pace factus est* each appear in approximately fifty accounts. On the frequency of these songs and others, see also Gschwend, *Die Depositio*, p. 64; Lipphardt, *Lateinische Osterfeiern*, vol. 9, pp. 863–98.

25. For the text of the Prüfening Deposition rite, see Young, *The Drama*, vol. 1, pp. 157–58.

26. "Ecce quomodo moritur Justus, et nemo percipit corde; et viri justi tolluntur, et nemo considerat; a facie iniquitatis ablatus est Justus, et erit in pace memoriam ejus." Catholic Church, *Corpus antiphonalium officii*, ed. Renatus-Joannes Hesbert (Rome: Herder, 1963-1979), vol. 4, p. 155.

27. "Recessit pastor noster, fons aquae vivae, ad cujus transitum sol obscuratus est; nam et ille captus est, qui captivum tenebat primum hominem." Catholic

Church, *Corpus antiphonalium officii*, vol. 4, p. 375.

28. "Joseph ab Arimathia petiit corpus Jesu, et sepelivit eum in sepulcro suo." Catholic Church, *Corpus antiphonalium officii*, vol. 3, p. 305.

29. "Sepulto Domino, signatum est monumentum, volventes lapidem ad ostium monumenti, ponentes milites qui custodirent illud." Catholic Church, *Corpus antiphonalium officii*, vol. 4, p. 404.

30. Brixen: "zway turen, so fir das grab gehören, die lain an das grab hinzue auff der obern seitn." Gschwend, *Die Depositio*, p. 93; Taubert, "Mittelalterliche Kruzifixe (1969)," p. 107. Salzburg: "in sepulchro et linteaminibus et sudario cooperiatur, deinde lapis superponatur." Gschwend, *Die Depositio*, p. 68; Taubert, "Mittelalterliche Kruzifixe (1969)," p. 104, see also p. 105. Strasbourg: "sacerdote fila nectente." Brooks, "The Sepulchre," p. 68. On the importance of closing the sepulcher and hiding the object from view, see Maisel, *Sepulchrum Domini*, p. 80 n.318. By contrast, Tripps gives an example of a sepulcher that was constructed so that the body could be seen during the grave rest. Johannes Tripps, *Das handelnde Bildwerk in der Gotik: Forschungen zu den Bedeutungsschichten und der Funktion des Kirchengebäudes und seiner Ausstattung in der Hoch- und Spätgotik* (Berlin: Gebr. Mann, 1998), p. 129.

31. "In pace in idipsum dormiam et requiescam." Catholic Church, *Corpus antiphonalium officii*, vol. 3, p. 276.

32. Augustine, *The Works of Saint Augustine: A Translation for the 21st Century*, ed. John E. Rotelle, trans. Edmund Hill (Brooklyn: New City Press, 1990), part 3, vol. 15, p. 91.

33. On the *Tenebrae* service, see Young, *The Drama*, vol. 1, p. 101; Scribner, *Popular Culture*, pp. 26–27; John Harper, *The Forms and Orders of the Western Liturgy from the Tenth to the Eighteenth Century: A Historical Introduction and Guide for Students and Musicians* (Oxford and New York: Clarendon Press; Oxford University Press, 1991), pp. 141–42; Dupeux, Jezler, and Wirth, *Bildersturm*, pp. 230–31.

34. "Hac die in Ecclesia luminaria non accenduntur, quia in ipso Redemptore crucifixo sidera obscurabantur." Rabanus Maurus, "De clericorum Institutione libri tres" in *Patrologia Latina: The Full-Text Database* (Alexandria: Chadwyck-Healey, 1996), vol. 107, p. 349A. On the abstention from light on Good Friday, with discussion of Maurus, see Gerhard Römer, "Die Liturgie des Karfreitags," *Zeitschrift für katholische Theologie* 77 (1955), pp. 46–49. A fifteenth or sixteenth-century ritual from Soissons dictates that: "Lumen in tota Ecclesia hodie debet

celari. Tenebrae enim factae sunt super universam terram ab hora tertia usque in horam nonam; moriente vero illo qui ait: Ego sum lux mundi, sol obscuratus est et luna non dedit lumen suum" (p. 47 n.3).

35. Thomas Naogeorg (Kirchmair), *The popish kingdome, or reigne of Antichrist, written in Latine verse by Thomas Naogeorgus, and englyshed by Barnabe Googe* (London: Henrie Denham, 1570), fols. 50v–51r. Excerpts from Barnabe Googe's translation are reprinted in Young, *The Drama*, vol. 2, pp. 531–37.

36. *The Monastic Agreement*, p. 49.

37. *Rites of Durham, being a Description or Brief Declaration of all the Ancient Monuments, Rites and Customs belonging or being within the Monastical Church of Durham before the Suppression. Written 1593*, as reprinted in Young, *The Drama*, vol. 1, p. 138.

38. The red on the exterior is apparently not original. See De Vos, *Rogier van der Weyden*, p. 253.

39. On the hierarchical relation between interior and exterior, see Lynn F. Jacobs, "The Triptychs of Hieronymus Bosch," *The Sixteenth Century Journal* 31, no. 4 (2000), esp. pp. 1009–10, 1019–20; Stephan Kemperdick and Jochen Sander, eds., *The Master of Flémalle and Rogier van der Weyden* (Frankfurt am Main, Berlin, and Ostfildern: Städel Museum; Gemäldegalerie, Staatliche Museen zu Berlin; Hatje Cantz, 2008), pp. 117–31. The opening and closing of altarpiece shutters could be used to orchestrate a shifting display of imagery coinciding with the narrative of the life of Christ, the Virgin, or the saints, as these were marked in the liturgical calendar. On the form, history, and use of the winged altarpiece, see Joseph Braun, *Der christliche Altar in seiner geschichtlichen Entwicklung* (Munich: Alte Meister Guenther Koch, 1924), vol. 2, pp. 345–63; Max Hasse, "Der Flügelaltar" (Dissertation, Friedrich-Wilhelms-Universität Berlin, 1941); Harald Keller, "Der Flügelaltar als Reliquienschrein," in Kurt Martin, ed., *Studien zur Geschichte der europäischen Plastik: Festschrift Theodor Müller, zum 19, April 1965* (Munich: Hirmer Verlag, 1965), pp. 125–44; Donald L. Ehresmann, "Some Observations on the Role of Liturgy in the Early Winged Altarpiece," *The Art Bulletin* 64, no. 3 (1982), pp. 359–69; Lynn F. Jacobs, *Early Netherlandish Carved Altarpieces, 1380–1550: Medieval Tastes and Mass Marketing* (New York: Cambridge University Press, 1998), pp. 12–18; Belting, *Likeness and Presence*, pp. 446–53; Annegret Laabs, "Das Retabel als 'Schaufenster' zum göttlichen Heil: Ein Beitrag zur Stellung des Flügelretabels im sakralen Zeremoniell des Kirchenjahres," *Marburger Jahrbuch für*

Kunstwissenschaft 24 (1997), pp. 82–83; Paul Crossley, "The Man from Inner Space: Architecture and Meditation in the Choir of St. Laurence in Nuremberg," in Gale R. Owen-Crocker and Timothy Graham, eds., *Medieval Art: Recent Perspectives, A Memorial Tribute to C. R. Dodwell* (Manchester and New York: Manchester University Press; St. Martin's Press, 1998), pp. 165–82. Kroesen and Steensma point out that no one has yet explained the winged retable's lack of popularity in southern Europe. Kroesen and Steensma, *The Interior*, p. 79. On the hiding and revealing of images in late medieval churches, see Bruno Reudenbach, "Der Altar als Bildort: Das Flügelretabel und die liturgische Inszenierung des Kirchenjahres," in Uwe M. Schneede, ed., *Goldgrund und Himmelslicht: Die Kunst des Mittelalters in Hamburg* (Hamburg: Hamburger Kunsthalle; Dölling und Galitz, 1999), p. 28.

40. Decker argues that altarpiece shutters were developed in response to thirteenth-century monastic reforms that sought to limit image-devotion; he calls them "restrikiv-reformerisch." Decker, *Das Ende*, p. 106, see also pp. 63, 88–92, 113, 171, 293.

41. Jacobs, *Early Netherlandish Carved Altarpieces*, p. 18.

42. For descriptions of the opening of altarpieces as a rare "epiphany," see Decker, *Das Ende*, pp. 79–81, 92; Laabs, "Das Retabel als 'Schaufenster,'" pp. 71–86, esp. p. 81.

43. John Bruce, ed., *Historie of the arrivall of Edward IV in England and the finall recouerye of his kingdomes from Henry VI* (London: J. B. Nichols and Son, 1838), pp. 13–14. Discussed in Philip Nelson, "The Woodwork of English Alabaster Retables," *Transactions of the Historic Society of Lancashire and Cheshire* 72 (1920), pp. 58–59; Francis W. Cheetham, *English Medieval Alabasters: With a Catalogue of the Collection in the Victoria and Albert Museum* (Oxford: Phaidon-Christie's, 1984), pp. 29–30. For an example of instructions for covering images during Lent, see Walter Howard Frere, ed., *The Use of Sarum: The Original Texts* (Cambridge: Cambridge University Press, 1898), vol. 1, pp. 138–41.

44. Lenten cloths were in use as early as the tenth century, and evidence of them becomes abundant in thirteenth-century sources from all over Europe, although the cloths do not seem to have been as common in Italy as elsewhere. Reiner Sörries, "Der Stand der Fastentuchforschung 1998," in Dietmar Damzog, Volker Dudeck, and Gunter Oettel, eds., *525 Jahre Großes Zittauer Fastentuch—und wie weiter?* (Görlitz and Zittau: G. Oettel, 2000), p. 37; Johannes H. Emminghaus, *Die westfälischen Hungertücher aus nachmittelalterlicher Zeit und ihre liturgische*

Herkunft, ed. Rudolf Suntrup and Volker Honemann (Görlitz: G. Oettel, 2004), pp. xiv, 50–65. On variations in the use of Lenten cloths, see Damzog, Dudeck, and Oettel, *525 Jahre großes Zittauer Fastentuch*, p. 19. Emminghaus considers the use of Lenten cloths to have been an attempt to restrict the growing emphasis on visual piety in the later Middle Ages. Emminghaus, *Die westfälischen Hungertücher*, esp. pp. xv, 28–31, 52–55. For more on Lenten cloths, see Bond, *The Chancel*, pp. 101–105; Braun, *Der christliche Altar*, vol. 2, pp. 148–59; Johannes H. Emminghaus, "Fastentuch," in *Reallexikon zur deutschen Kunstgeschichte* (Stuttgart: J. B. Metzler, 1937), pp. 826–48; Molly Teasdale Smith, "The Use of Grisaille as a Lenten Observance," *Marsyas* 8 (1957), pp. 43–54; Paul Engelmeier, *Westfälische Hungertücher vom 14. bis 19. Jahrhundert* (Münster: Aschendorff, 1961); Reiner Sörries, *Die alpenländischen Fastentücher: Vergessene Zeugnisse volkstümlicher Frömmigkeit* (Klagenfurt: Universitätsverlag Carinthia, 1988); Manfred Koller and Margot Schindler, *Fastentuch und Kultfiguren* (Vienna: Österreichischen Museum für Volkskunde, 1996); Friedhelm Mennekes, ed., *Die Zittauer Bibel: Bilder und Texte zum Grossen Fastentuch von 1472* (Stuttgart: Katholisches Bibelwerk, 1998); Dupeux, Jezler, and Wirth, *Bildersturm*, pp. 224–25; Laura Weigert, "*Velum Templi*: Painted Cloths of the Passion and the Making of Lenten Ritual in Reims," *Studies in Iconography* 24 (2003), pp. 199–229.

45. Discussed in Smith, "The Use of Grisaille," p. 49. On non-Lenten veils used around altars, see Emminghaus, *Die westfälischen Hungertücher*, pp. 44–49, 70–71; Kemperdick and Sander, *The Master of Flémalle and Rogier van der Weyden*, pp. 125–26. For depictions of altars with curtains, see Kim Woods, "The Netherlandish Carved Altarpiece, ca. 1500," in Humfrey and Kemp, *The Altarpiece*, pp. 78 and 79, figs. 36, 38, 39, 40, 41.

46. On the Zittau cloth, see Damzog, Dudeck, and Oettel, *525 Jahre großes Zittauer Fastentuch*.

47. On the (il)legibility of the text and images, see Mennekes, *Die Zittauer Bibel*, p. 10; Damzog, Dudeck, and Oettel, *525 Jahre großes Zittauer Fastentuch*, pp. 93 and 105. On the relation between Lenten cloths and Reformation attitudes toward images and words, see Mennekes, *Die Zittauer Bibel*, pp. 12–13. On the compatibility of Lenten cloths and Lutheranism, see Damzog, Dudeck, and Oettel, *525 Jahre großes Zittauer Fastentuch*, pp. 22–24. Many Lutheran churches persisted in hanging their Lenten veils long after the Reformation. The Lenten cloth that Jacob Gürtler gave to the Church of St. John in Zittau in 1472 and a smaller Lenten

veil donated to the same church in 1573 were not retired until deep into the seventeenth century, more than a century after the church had given up the Catholic liturgy. On the surprisingly late donations of the Zittau cloths, see Sörries, *Die alpenländischen Fastentücher*, p. 17; Damzog, Dudeck, and Oettel, *525 Jahre großes Zittauer Fastentuch*, pp. 11–12. As late as 1629, a professed Lutheran by the name of Hans Khevenhüller likewise donated a Lenten cloth to his church in Sternberg. Sörries, *Die alpenländischen Fastentücher*, pp. 17 and 342. These Lutherans continued to hang their Lenten cloths despite the fact that Luther regarded them as part of the "papist" paraphernalia to be expunged: "Lent, Palm Sunday, and Holy Week shall be retained," says Luther, "this, however, does not include the Lenten veil, throwing of palms, veiling of pictures, and whatever else there is of such tomfoolery." Luther, *Works*, vol. 53, p. 90.

48. The sepulcher also has doors on the side that could be opened to reveal that it was empty as well as small openings allowing access to the head and feet of the sculpture. The sepulcher was entirely restored in the nineteenth century, and the painting on the exterior dates from that time, although the iconography reflects the original state. Babette Hartwieg, "Drei gefaßte Holzskulpturen vom Ende des 13. Jahrhunderts im Kloster Wienhausen," *Zeitschrift für Kunsttechnologie und Konservierung* 2, no. 2 (1988), pp. 187–212. This particular effigy was probably not used in the Deposition rite. See Peter Jezler, "Ostergrab und Depositionsbild" (Dissertation, Zürich Universität, 1982), pp. 41–44; Hartwieg, "Drei gefaßte Holzskulpturen," pp. 191–94; Tripps, *Das handelnde Bildwerk*, pp. 129–30. For more on the Wienhausen sepulcher, see Horst Appuhn, *Einführung in die Ikonographie der mittelalterlichen Kunst in Deutschland* (Darmstadt: Wissenschaftliche Buchgesellschaft, 1979), pp. 71–74; Kerstin Hengevoss-Dürkop, *Skulptur und Frauenkloster: Studien zu Bildwerken der Zeit um 1300 aus Frauenklöstern des ehemaligen Fürstentums Lüneburg* (Berlin: Akademie Verlag, 1994), pp. 45–49; Tripps, *Das handelnde Bildwerk*, pp. 128–30; Kroesen, *The Sepulchrum Domini*, pp. 63–68; Dupeux, Jezler, and Wirth, *Bildersturm*, pp. 234–36.

49. Guillaume Durand, *The Rationale Divinorum Officiorum of William Durand of Mende (A New Translation of the Prologue and Book One)*, ed. Timothy M. Thibodeau (New York: Columbia University Press, 2007), p. 42.

50. Durand, *The Rationale*, p. 42. Because the grace that Christ's sacrifice delivered to humanity rent the veil obscuring divine truth during the era of the law, "curtains and veils of this sort are removed on Good Friday," Durand explains

(p. 42).

51. Durand, *The Rationale*, 43. In this passage, Durand also distinguishes between several different kinds of Lenten veil, adding a level of nuance to his discussion that I will leave aside here.

52. The twelfth-century theologian Honorius von Autun links this blindness explicitly to sin: "Vela in ecclesiis suspenduntur, quo populo secreta sanctuarii absconduntur, quia coelestia nobis ob peccata celantur quae ob poenitentiam nobis reserantur." Honorius von Autun, "Speculum ecclesiae" in *Patrologia Latina*, vol. 172, p. 887B. Discussed in Emminghaus, "Fastentuch," p. 831.

53. "Waerom vermomdijse dan, die so schoon staen en blincken, / Inde vastene dan werdense bedect? / Waerom doedij dat? mijn dat vertrect, / Want voorwaer, ghij bevlect // so menighe conscientie." *Een tafelspel van twee personagien te weten de weereltsche gheleerde en de godlicke wijse om te spelen voor een christelicke congregatie*, reprinted in Else Ellerbroek-Fortuin, *Amsterdamse rederijkersspelen in de zestiende eeuw* (Groningen: Wolters, 1937), p. 202. Discussed in Moxey, *Pieter Aertsen*, pp. 160–61.

54. As translated in Garside, *Zwingli and the Arts*, p. 152. Original in Ulrich Zwingli, *Sämtliche Werke*, ed. Emil Egli (Leipzig: Heinsius, 1905), vol. 2, p. 814.

55. Christensen, "Iconoclasm," p. 208; Baxandall, *The Limewood Sculptors*, p. 72; Dupeux, Jezler, and Wirth, *Bildersturm*, pp. 90–92.

56. Maria Sipayllo, ed., *Akta Synodów Różnowierczych w Polsce* (Warsaw: Uniwersytetu Warszawskiego, 1966), vol. 1, p. 113. Discussed in Sergiusz Michalski, "Das Phänomen Bildersturm: Versuch einer Übersicht," in Scribner, *Bilder und Bildersturm*, p. 107; Michalski, *The Reformation*, p. 76.

57. Sol LeWitt, *Sol LeWitt: The Museum of Modern Art, New York*, ed. Alicia Legg (New York: The Museum, 1978), p. 164.

58. Sol LeWitt, *Critical Texts*, ed. Adachiara Zevi (Rome: Libri de AEIUO, 1995), p. 75.

59. Sol LeWitt, *Sol LeWitt: [Exhibition of Drawings and Sculpture] Haags Gemeentemuseum* (The Hague: 1970), p. 43.

60. LeWitt, *The Museum of Modern Art*, p. 164.

61. Robert C. Tucker, ed., *The Marx-Engels Reader* (New York: W. W. Norton, 1978), p. 324.

62. LeWitt, *Sol LeWitt*, p. 76.

63. LeWitt, *Sol LeWitt*, pp. 76–77.

64. LeWitt, *The Museum of Modern Art*, p. 79. The version of *Cubes with Hidden Cubes* made in 1968 was destroyed.

65. LeWitt, *Sol LeWitt*, p. 72.

66. On the Haimburg Lenten cloth, see Sörries, *Die alpenländischen Fastentücher*, pp. 66–72.

67. On the repetition of forms in the Lenten Cloth in Gurk, see Damzog, Dudeck, and Oettel, *525 Jahre großes Zittauer Fastentuch*, p. 109.

68. I doubt LeWitt would have thought much of such a comparison. He objected to pseudomorphosis—without calling it that: "There are many works of artists that superficially resemble the works of other artists.... Single works can always be shown to be similar to other single works. Unless one compares the total work of each artist, one cannot say the work is the same.... Those who understand art only by what it looks like often do not understand very much at all. The physical appearance of a work is often misleading. Art that emphasizes content (such as mine) cannot be seen or understood in a context of form. This is a large and crucial difference. It cannot be said that what looks alike is alike. If one wishes to understand the art of our time one must go beyond appearance." LeWitt, *Sol LeWitt*, pp. 97–99.

69. Luther, *Works*, vol. 40, pp. 99–100.

70. Krauss, "The LeWitt Matrix" in LeWitt, *Sol LeWitt*, p. 453.

CHAPTER TWO: CRUCIFIXES WITH MOVABLE ARMS

1. John R. Martin, "The Dead Christ on the Cross in Byzantine Art," in Kurt Weitzmann, ed., *Late Classical and Mediaeval Studies in Honor of Albert Mathias Friend, Jr.* (Princeton: Princeton University Press, 1955), pp. 189–96; Reiner Haussherr, "Der tote Christus am Kreuz: Zur Ikonographie des Gerokreuzes" (Dissertation, Universität Bonn, 1963), p. 207.

2. When the papal legate Humbert of Silva Candida visited Constantinople in 1054, he decried representations of the dead Christ as blasphemous. Haussherr, "Der tote Christus," pp. 211–12; Belting, *Likeness and Presence*, p. 270. Bloch sees the advent of the *Christus mortuus* in the West as a product of Paschasius Radbertus' *De corpore et sanguine Domini*, which argues that the Eucharist is the historical, human body of Christ. Peter Bloch, *Romanische Bronzekruzifixe* (Berlin: Deutscher Verlag für Kunstwissenschaft, 1992), p. 12.

3. "O mors, mors vitae, si mors, non vita vocanda / (Quod praestat vitam, non

ausim dicere mortem)." Ludwig Traube, ed., *Poetae Latini aevi Carolini* (Berlin: Apud Weidmann, 1881), vol. 3, p. 543. Discussed in Haussherr, "Der tote Christus," p. 215.

4. Paul Thoby, *Le crucifix, des origines au Concile de Trente: Étude inconographique* (Nantes: Bellanger, 1959), pp. 43–44; Bloch, *Romanische Bronzekruzifixe*, pp. 11–13.

5. On the ambiguity and interchangeability of these terms, see Taubert, "Mittelalterliche Kruzifixe (1969)," p. 103; Parker, *The Descent*, pp. 93–96, 142–67; Kroesen, *The Sepulchrum Domini*, pp. 155–57. Some reformers were careful to distinguish between the cross and the crucifix; others found the two equally offensive. Eamon Duffy, "Devotion to the Crucifix and Related Images in England on the Eve of the Reformation," in Scribner, *Bilder und Bildersturm*, p. 32; Wandel, *Voracious Idols*, pp. 78 and 121.

6. For use of the term *crucifixus*, see the Rouen *Book of Ecclesiastical Offices* in Brooks, "The Sepulchre," p. 31; the thirteenth-century gradual of Rouen Cathedral in Young, *The Drama*, vol. 1, pp. 135–36.

7. For *imago crucifixi*, see the Rheinau rite of 1114–1123 in Taubert, "Mittelalterliche Kruzifixe (1969)," p. 104; the Salzburg rite of 1160 in Taubert, "Mittelalterliche Kruzifixe (1969)," pp. 104–107; the Prüfening rite of 1489 in Brooks, "The Sepulchre," p. 39; Taubert, "Mittelalterliche Kruzifixe (1969)," pp. 93 and 96. For *imaginem*, see the rite of the Benedictine Cloister at Barking of ca. 1370 in Taubert, "Mittelalterliche Kruzifixe (1969)," p. 97. For *imago Domini*, see the fifteenth-century *Visitatio Sepulchri* from Passau in Young, *The Drama*, vol. 1, pp. 338, 353, 646; the fifteenth-century *Visitatio Sepulchri* from Salzburg in Young, *The Drama*, vol. 1, pp. 327 and 638.

8. Young, *The Drama*, vol. 1, p. 137.

9. Tripps, *Das handelnde Bildwerk*, pp. 49 and 166.

10. The Tauberts document roughly forty crucifixes with movable arms mainly from Germany, Switzerland, Austria, and Northern Italy, dating from the fourteenth through the sixteenth century, and they discuss textual evidence for the use of such crucifixes in the Deposition rite. They suggest that there are probably more extant crucifixes with movable arms, undocumented in some cases because cloth or another material disguises the joints. Taubert, "Mittelalterliche Kruzifixe (1969)," pp. 79–121; Gesine and Johannes Taubert, "Mittelalterliche Kruzifixe mit schwenkbaren Armen: Ein Beitrag zur Verwendung von Bildwerken in der Liturgie," in Johannes Taubert , ed., *Farbige Skulpturen: Bedeutung, Fassung,*

Restaurierung (Munich: Callwey, 1978), pp. 38–50. The two oldest movable crucifixes, one dated to shortly before 1300 and the other to 1333, are Italian. Margrit Lisner, *Holzkruzifixe in Florenz und in der Toskana von der Zeit um 1300 bis zum frühen Cinquecento* (Munich: Bruckmann, 1970), pp. 11 and 22. Rampold's work confirms the Tauberts' suspicion that there are more crucifixes with movable arms to be discovered. Reinhard Rampold, "Gotische Kruzifixe mit schwenkbaren Armen—Neuentdeckung in Tirol," *Der Schlern* 73 (1999), pp. 425–36.

11. See, e.g., Ulla Haastrup, "Medieval Props in the Liturgical Drama," *Hafnia: Copenhagen Papers in the History of Art* 11 (1987), pp. 133–70; Peter Jezler, "Das 'handelnde Christusbild' und seine Verwendung in der städtischen Zelebration der Herrenfeste im spätmittelalterlichen Deutschland," in Irving Lavin, ed., *World Art: Themes of Unity in Diversity* (University Park: The Pennsylvania State University Press, 1989), pp. 619–22; Tripps, *Das handelnde Bildwerk*; Tanya A. Jung, "The Phenomenal Lives of Movable Christ Sculptures" (Dissertation, University of Maryland, 2006).

12. Josef Anselm von Adelmann, "Christus auf dem Palmesel," *Zeitschrift für Volkskunde* 63 (1967), pp. 182–200; Elizabeth Lipsmeyer, "Devotion and Decorum: Intention and Quality in Medieval German Sculpture," *Gesta* 34 (1995), pp. 20–27; Tripps, *Das handelnde Bildwerk*, pp. 89–113; *Der Palmesel: Geschichte, Kult, Kunst* (Schwäbisch Gmünd: Museum und Galerie Schwäbisch Gmünd, 2000).

13. Marie Grass-Cornet, "Von Palmeseln und tanzenden Engeln," in Nikolaus Grass, ed., *Ostern in Tirol* (Innsbruck: Wagner, 1957), pp. 164–71; Hans-Joachim Krause, "'Imago ascensionis' und 'Himmelloch': Zum 'Bild'-Gebrauch in der spätmittelalterlichen Liturgie," in Friedrich Möbius and Ernst Schubert, eds., *Skulptur des Mittelalters: Funktion und Gestalt* (Weimar: H. Böhlaus Nachfolger, 1987), pp. 281–353; Hans Ruedi Weber, *Die Umsetzung der Himmelfahrt Christi in die zeichenhafte Liturgie* (Bern and New York: Lang, 1987); Tripps, *Das handelnde Bildwerk*, pp. 141–49; Johannes Tripps, "Sakrales Spiel als Motivquelle der Miniaturmalerei: Gedanken zum Oeuvre der Gebrüder Limburg und ihrer Zeitgenossen," in Anna Moraht-Fromm, ed., *Kunst und Liturgie: Choranlagen des Spätmittelatlers—Ihre Architektur, Ausstattung und Nutzung* (Ostfildern: Thorbecke, 2003), pp. 189–206.

14. Naogeorg, *The popish kingdome*, fol. 53r.

15. Naogeorg, *The popish kingdome*, fol. 50r.

16. Henri Maundrell, *A journey from Aleppo to Jerusalem at Easter, A.D. 1697* (Oxford: The Theatre, 1749), p. 74.

17. "Am Karfreitag vor Ostern tregt man aber eyn Creütz herumb in eyner Procession, leget eyen gross gestorben Menschen-Bild inn eyn Grab." Sebastian Franck, *Weltbüch: Spiegel vnd Bildtnisz des gantzen Erdtbodens* (Tübingen: Vlrich Morhart, 1534), fol. 137r. Discussed in Jezler, "Bildwerke im Dienste," p. 239. Cf. "And Christ that euerywhere doth raigne, a laughing stocke to make, An other Image doe they get, like one but newly deade, With legges stretcht out at length and handes, vpon his body spreade." Naogeorg, *The popish kingdome*, fol. 51v.

18. "Ich hab mich als ein heyd der Christen torheit nit gnugsam verwundert." Franck, *Weltbüch*, fol. 134v. Discussed in Dupeux, Jezler, and Wirth, *Bildersturm*, p. 218.

19. "For of surety the glory of God should be more evidently known, if it were declared by reasonable and living creatures rather than by dead and unmoveable images." "An homily against the peril of idolatry and superfluous decking of churches," in John Griffiths, ed., *Certain sermons or homilies appointed to be read in churches in the time of Queen Elizabeth of famous memory (1562)* (London: Society for Promoting Christian Knowledge, 1864), p. 196.

20. John Hooper, *Early Writings of John Hooper* (Cambridge: Cambridge University Press, 1843), pp. 45–46. Hooper also writes, "a man may learn more of a live ape than of a dead image" (p. 322).

21. "Sy tu es Dieu, parle." Solange Deyon and Alain Lottin, *Les "casseurs" de l'été 1566: L'iconoclasme dans le nord* (Paris: Hachette, 1981), p. 173; Michalski, "Das Phänomen Bildersturm," p. 95.

22. "Bistu Got, so wer dich, bistu aber Mensch so blut." As quoted in Robert W. Scribner, "Reformation, Karneval und die 'verkehrte Welt,'" in Richard van Dülmen and Norbert Schindler, eds., *Volkskultur: Zur Wiederentdeckung des vergessenen Alltags (16.–20. Jahrhundert)* (Frankfurt am Main: Fischer Taschenbuch, 1984), p. 121; Robert W. Scribner, "Volkskultur und Volksreligion," in Peter Blickle, Andreas Lindt, and Alfred Schindler, eds., *Zwingli und Europa* (Zurich: Vandenhoeck & Ruprecht, 1985), p. 153; Michalski, "Das Phänomen Bildersturm," p. 95.

23. John Foxe, *The acts and monuments of John Foxe*, ed. Josiah Pratt (London: George Seeley, 1870), vol. 5, p. 409. Discussed in Margaret Aston, "Iconoclasm in England: Rites of Destruction by Fire," in Scribner, *Bilder und Bildersturm*, p. 186.

24. For examples of the Driving Out ritual from the Middle Ages and later, see Adalbert Kuhn, *Sagen, Gebräuche und Märchen aus Westfalen und einigen andern, besonders den angrenzenden Gegenden Norddeutschlands* (Leipzig: F. A. Brockhaus,

1859), vol. 2, p. 131; Paul Sartori, *Sitte und Brauch* (Leipzig: W. Heims, 1914), vol. 3, pp. 123–26; James George Frazer, *The Golden Bough: A Study in Magic and Religion* (London: Macmillan and Co., 1911), vol. 1, pp. 220–65; Karl Theodor Reuschel, *Deutsche Volkskunde im Grundriss* (Leipzig and Berlin: B. G. Teubner, 1920), pp. 52–54; Hanns Bächtold-Stäubli, *Handwörterbuch des deutschen Aberglaubens*, ed. Eduard Hoffmann-Krayer and Gerhard Lüdtke (Berlin and Leipzig: W. de Gruyter & Co., 1927), pp. 1261–63; Paul Sartori, *Westfälische Volkskunde* (Leipzig: Quelle & Meyer, 1929), pp. 151–52; Richard Beitl, *Wörterbuch der deutschen Volkskunde* (Stuttgart: Kröner, 1974), pp. 493–95.

25. Frazer, *The Golden Bough*, vol. 1, p. 233.

26. Frazer, *The Golden Bough*, vol. 1, p. 239.

27. Jacob Grimm, *Teutonic Mythology*, trans. James Steven Stallybrass (Gloucester: Peter Smith, 1976), vol. 2, pp. 772–73, 782–84.

28. Frazer, *The Golden Bough*, vol. 1, p. 239, see also pp. 233–39.

29. Johann Georg Theodor Grässe, *Der Sagenschatz des Königsreichs Sachsen* (Dresden: G. Schönfeld, 1874), vol. 1, pp. 144–46.

30. Grimm, *Teutonic Mythology*, vol. 2, p. 772.

31. "Jajaja! der Sommertag ist da, / er kratzt dem Winter die augen aus." Grimm, *Teutonic Mythology*, vol. 2, p. 765.

32. "Nun treiben wir den Bapst hinaus, / Aus Christus kirch und Gottes haus." Martin Luther, *D. Martin Luthers Werke* (Weimar: H. Böhlau, 1883), vol. 35, p. 569.

33. On the Humiliation, see Patrick J. Geary, "La coercition des saints dans la practique religieuse médiévale," in Pierre Boglioni, ed., *La culture populaire au Moyen Âge* (Montreal: L'Aurore, 1979), pp. 147–61; Patrick J. Geary, "Humiliation of Saints," in Stephen Wilson, ed., *Saints and Their Cults: Studies in Religious Sociology, Folklore, and History* (Cambridge and New York: Cambridge University Press, 1983), pp. 123–40. On the dating of the ritual to the tenth through the thirteenth century and on its geographic concentration in northern Europe, see Geary, "Humiliation of Saints," p. 127; Lester K. Little, *Benedictine Maledictions: Liturgical Cursing in Romanesque France* (Ithaca: Cornell University Press, 1993), pp. 47 and 149.

34. Lester K. Little, "La morphologie des malédictions monastiques," *Annales. Économies, Sociétés, Civilisations* 34, no. 1 (1979), p. 54; Geary, "Humiliation of Saints," pp. 134–37; Little, *Benedictine Maledictions*, pp. 83–85, 133. Marchal calls this phenomenon withdrawal of love (*Liebesentzug*). Guy P. Marchal, "Das

vieldeutige Heiligenbild: Bildersturm im Mittelalter," in Blickle et al., *Macht und Ohnmacht*, p. 316.

35. Given the violence of the Humiliation, it is not surprising that the Church regularly condemned it. Geary, "Humiliation of Saints," pp. 137–38; Little, *Benedictine Maledictions*, pp. 236–37.

36. On popular acts of coercive aggression toward images, see Stephan Beissel, *Die Verehrung der Heiligen und ihrer Reliquien in Deutschland im Mittelalter* (Darmstadt: Wissenschaftliche Buchgesellschaft, 1976), pp. 10–14; Geary, "La coercition des saints," pp. 153–54; Richard C. Trexler, *Public Life in Renaissance Florence* (Ithaca: Cornell University Press, 1991), pp. 118–28; Richard C. Trexler, "Florentine Religious Experience: The Sacred Image," *Studies in the Renaissance* 19 (1972), pp. 24–29; Patrick J. Geary, *Living with the Dead in the Middle Ages* (Ithaca: Cornell University Press, 1994), p. 112; Norbert Schnitzler, "Geschmähte Symbole," in Klaus Schreiner and Gerd Schwerhoff, eds., *Verletzte Ehre: Ehrkonflike in Gesellschaften des Mittelalters und der Frühen Neuzeit* (Cologne: Böhlau, 1995), pp. 290–96; Dupeux, Jezler, and Wirth, *Bildersturm*, p. 112. For an example of a woman punishing an image of the Virgin by stealing her child, see A. G. Little, *Liber exemplorum ad usum praedicantium saeculo XIII compositus a quodam fratre minore Anglico de provincia Hiberniae* (Farnborough: Gregg P., 1966), p. 30; G. G. Coulton, *Life in the Middle Ages* (Cambridge: Cambridge University Press, 1954), vol. 1, p. 152.

37. Théodore de Bèze, *Histoire ecclésiastique des églises réformées au royaume de France*, ed. Ed. Cunitz and G. Baum (Nieuwkoop: B. de Graaf, 1974), vol. 1, p. 957. Discussed in Natalie Zemon Davis, "The Rites of Violence: Religious Riot in Sixteenth-Century France," *Past and Present* 59, no. 1 (1973), p. 77; Olivier Christin, "L'iconoclaste et le blasphémateur au début du XVIe siècle," in Jean Delumeau, ed., *Injures et blasphemes* (Paris: Éditions imago, 1989), p. 39; Schnitzler, *Ikonoklasmus*, p. 129; Marchal, "Das vieldeutige Heiligenbild," p. 319. For other examples of the punishment of statues for bad weather, see Franck, *Weltbüch*, fol. 51v; Ludwig Andreas Veit, *Volksfrommes Brauchtum und Kirche im deutschen Mittelalter: Ein Durchblick* (Freiburg im Breisgau: Herder, 1936), pp. 74–75.

38. "Plorant, eiulant, scindunt uestes, uellunt crines, torquent manus, tundunt feretrum ut Balaam iumentum." A. Wilmart, "La légende de Ste Édith en prose et vers par le moine Goscelin," *Analecta Bolandiana* 56, no. 2 (1938), p. 274. Discussed in Peter Dinzelbacher, "Die 'Realpräsenz' der Heiligen in ihren Reliquiaren und

Gräbern nach mittelalterlichen Quellen," in Peter Dinzelbacher and Dieter R. Bauer, eds., *Heiligenverehrung in Geschichte und Gegenwart* (Ostfildern: Schwabenverlag, 1990), p. 131; Guy P. Marchal, "Bildersturm im Mittelaltar," *Historisches Jahrbuch* 113 (1993), pp. 279–80.

39. See Marchal, "Bildersturm im Mittelaltar," pp. 278–80; Schnitzler, *Ikonoklasmus*, pp. 181–82, 309.

40. Naogeorg, *The popish kingdome*, fol. 50v.

41. George Gilpin, *The bee hiue of the Romishe Churche* (London: Thomas Dawson, 1579), fol. 200v. Reprinted in Young, *The Drama*, vol. 2, p. 537.

42. Michalski points out the frequency of iconoclastic events around Easter and gives examples. Michalski, "Das Phänomen Bildersturm," pp. 91–92.

43. Fudge, *The Magnificent Ride*, p. 178.

44. As translated in Kaminsky, *A History*, p. 166. Original in František Palacký, ed., *Documenta mag. Joannis Hus, vitam, doctrinam, causam in Constantiensi concilio actam et controversias de religione in Bohemia, annis 1403–1418* (Prague: Sumptibus Friderici Tempsky, 1869), p. 637. Discussed in Bredekamp, *Kunst als Medium*, p. 255; Schnitzler, *Ikonoklasmus*, p. 54. For attacks on the Palm Sunday ass, see Dupeux, Jezler, and Wirth, *Bildersturm*, p. 228; Christian von Burg, "'Das bildt vnsers Herren ab dem esel geschlagen': Der Palmesel in den Riten der Zerstörung," in Blickle et al., *Macht und Ohnmacht*, pp. 117–41.

45. Schnitzler, *Ikonoklasmus*, p. 130.

46. Scribner, "Volkskultur und Volksreligion," p. 153.

47. Williams, *The Radical Reformation*, p. 128.

48. Scribner, "Volkskultur und Volksreligion," p. 153. For more examples, see p. 154.

49. Jochen Sander, *Hans Holbein d. J.: Tafelmaler in Basel, 1515–1532* (Munich: Hirmer Verlag, 2005), p. 313; Kaspar von Greyerz, "Basel in Holbein's Day," in *Hans Holbein the Younger: The Basel Years 1515–1532* (Munich and London: Prestel, 2006), pp. 72–74.

50. "Pfue dich, Criste, was thust da in dem narrenhäuslin?" *Die Chroniken der schwäbischen Städte: Augsburg* (Göttingen: Vandenhoeck & Ruprecht, 1966), vol. 23, p. 197. Discussed in Scribner, "Volkskultur und Volksreligion," p. 153.

51. Pierre Cabanne, *Dialogues with Marcel Duchamp*, trans. Ron Padgett (New York: Viking Press, 1971), p. 61. Describing the wedding gift to Schwarz in an interview, Duchamp said, "I knew that the rain would fall and the wind would

blow and the book would be unhappy for being in the open air like that." Arturo Schwarz, *The Complete Works of Marcel Duchamp* (New York: Delano Greenridge Editions, 1997), vol. 2, p. 668.

52. "Faire un tableau malade ou un Readymade malade." Marcel Duchamp, *Notes and Projects for the Large Glass*, ed. Arturo Schwarz (London: Thames & Hudson, 1969), p. 98; Schwarz, *The Complete Works*, vol. 2, p. 668.

53. Duchamp, *Notes and Projects*, p. 90.

54. Octavio Paz, "The Ready-Made," in Joseph Masheck, ed., *Marcel Duchamp in Perspective* (Englewood Cliffs: Prentice-Hall, 1975), p. 86. Cf. "Limit the no. of rdymades yearly (?).... I realized very soon the danger of repeating indiscriminately this form of expression and decided to limit the production of 'readymades' to a small number yearly. I was aware at that time, that for the spectator even more than for the artist, art is a habit forming drug and I wanted to protect my 'readymades' against such contamination. / Another aspect of the 'readymade' is its lack of uniqueness... the replica of a 'readymade' delivering the same message; in fact nearly every one of the 'readymades' existing today is not an original in the conventional sense." Marcel Duchamp, *Salt Seller: The Writings of Marcel Duchamp*, ed. Michel Sanouillet and Elmer Peterson (New York: Oxford University Press, 1973), pp. 33 and 142.

55. Schwarz, *The Complete Works*, vol. 2, p. 669; Marcel Duchamp, *Affectionately, Marcel: The Selected Correspondence of Marcel Duchamp*, ed. Francis M. Naumann and Hector Obalk, trans. Jill Taylor (Ghent and New York: Ludion Press; D.A.P., 2000), pp. 92 and 94.

56. Man Ray, "Object of Destruction," *This Quarter* 5, no. 1 (1932), p. 55. This was a special issue of the journal on Surrealism edited by Breton. On the date of the work's creation, see Man Ray, *Objets de mon affection*, trans. Marie-Hélène Dufour (Paris: Philippe Sers, 1983), pp. 47, 142–43; Janine Mileaf, "Between You and Me: Man Ray's Object to be Destroyed," *Art Journal* 63, no. 1 (2004), pp. 5 and 11.

57. Man Ray, *Self Portrait* (London: A. Deutsch, 1963), p. 391. On Man Ray's various conflicting stories about his own plans to destroy the object, see Mileaf, "Between You and Me," pp. 5–6.

58. On its status as a readymade, see Pamela M. Lee, "How Money Looks: Man Ray's Perpetual Motif and the Economy of Time," *RES: Anthropology and Aesthetics* 36 (1999), pp. 247–48.

59. For examples of iconoclastic condemnations of the Easter sepulcher and its rituals, see Heales, "Easter Sepulchers," p. 304. For examples of the enforcement of the ban on the sepulcher ceremonies, see Pamela Sheingorn, "'No Sepulchre on Good Friday': The Impact of the Reformation on the Easter Rites in England," in Davidson and Nichols, *Iconoclasm vs. Art*, p. 154.

60. Karlstadt's 1522 treatise on images is titled *Von Abthuung der Bilder und daß kein Bettler unter den Christen sein soll.* For the phrase from Chambers, see G.H. Cook, *Letters to Cromwell on the Suppression of the Monasteries* (London: J. Baker, 1965), p. 145. Cf. "puld downe" in Edward Peacock, ed., *English church furniture, ornaments and decorations, at the period of the reformation. As exhibited in a list of the goods destroyed in certain Lincolnshire churches, A.D. 1566* (London: J.C. Hotten, 1866), p. 44; "the roode of the north doore in Paules was taken downe by the Dean." Charles Wriothesley, *A chronicle of England during the reigns of the Tudors, from AD 1485 to 1559* (Westminster: Camden Society, 1875), vol. 1, p. 84, see also p. 88, vol. 2, pp. 145 and 146.

CHAPTER THREE: DEAD IMAGES

1. On the popularity of this phrase among the Lollards, see Aston, *England's Iconoclasts*, pp. 115–16; Stanbury, *The Visual Object of Desire*, pp. 26 and 174.

2. Anne Hudson, ed., *Selections from English Wycliffite Writings* (Cambridge: Cambridge University Press, 1978), p. 23.

3. John Wycliffe, *The Holy Bible: containing the Old and New Testaments, with the apocryphal books, in the earliest English versions*, ed. Josiah Forshall and Frederic Madden (Oxford: Oxford University Press, 1850), vol. 1, p. 34.

4. Aston, *Lollards and Reformers*, p. 152. Cf. "trees growing in a wood are of greater virtue and vigour, and bear a clearer likeness and image of God, than stone or dead wood carved to the likeness and image of God" Aston, *England's Iconoclasts*, p. 115 n.68; "dead images be lewed men's books to learn them how they should worship saints in heaven after whom these dead images are shaped" (p. 116); "dead images that neither thirsteth nor hungereth" (p. 119); "many folks both learned and lewed and covetousness of priests scattereth oft their love upon these dead stocks" (p. 120); "religious men and folk of more perfect life, and more instructed in spiritual wisdom, should let all such dead images pass" (p. 177); "the lively images of Christ should not contend for the dead images" (p. 263); "neither that any true Christian ought to have any ado with filthy and dead images" (p. 322);

"whoso it be, that doth the worship to dead images that is due to God . . . he doth in that, the greatest sin of idol worship." John Foxe, *Foxe's Book of Martyrs: A History of the Lives, Sufferings, and Triumphant Deaths of the Early Christian and the Protestant Martyrs*, ed. William Byron Forbush (Peabody: Hendrickson, 2004), p. 243.

5. As translated in Kaminsky, *A History*, p. 273 n.36. Original in Amedeo Molnár, ed., *Jan Želivský: Dochovaná kázání z roku 1419* (Prague: Nakl. Československé akademie věd, 1953), p. 150.

6. Hudson, *Selections*, p. 83, see also pp. 85 and 87. More pre-Reformation references to "dead images" can be found in: Aston, *Lollards and Reformers*, pp. 90, 152, 155, 159–60, 164; Clifford Davidson, ed., *A tretise of miraclis pleyinge* (Kalamazoo: Medieval Institute Publications, Western Michigan University, 1993), pp. 27 and 98; Michalski, *The Reformation*, pp. 181, 187–88; Schnitzler, *Ikonoklasmus*, p. 42; Aston, "Lollards and the Cross," p. 108.

7. *A Reformation Debate: Karlstadt, Emser and Eck on Sacred Images. Three Treatises in Translation*, trans. Bryan D. Mangrum and Giuseppe Scavizzi (Toronto: Centre for Reformation and Renaissance Studies, 1998), p. 23.

8. As translated in David Freedberg, *Iconoclasm and Painting in the Revolt of the Netherlands, 1566–1609* (New York: Garland, 1988), pp. 63 and 65. The original reads: "Pompe doode blocken ende steenen" and "houte ende steene leeflose blocken." Philips van Marnix van St. Aldegonde, *Philips van Marnix van St. Aldegonde godsdienstige en kerkelijke geschriften*, ed. J. J. van Toorenenbergen (The Hague: M. Nijhoff, 1871), vol. 1, pp. 27 and 34. Cf. "pierres, troncs de bois, ou bois mort." Guillaume Farel, *Du vray usage de la croix de Jesus Christ* (Geneva: Jean Rivery, 1560), p. 199.

9. "Von den toten Bildern weg sollen wir uns lieber den lebendigen Heiligen zuwenden, den Armen, sie kleiden und speisen." Hubertus Carl Friedrich Martin Schwartz, *Geschichte der Reformation in Soest* (Soest: W. Jahn, 1932), p. 76. Discussed in Schnitzler, *Ikonoklasmus*, p. 249.

10. The pamphlet is titled *On the Prophet Baruch*. As translated in Moxey, *Pieter Aertsen*, p. 145. Original in S. Cramer and F. Pijper, eds., *Bibliotheca reformatoria neerlandica: Geschriften uit den tijd der hervorming in de Nederlanden* (The Hague: M. Nijhoff, 1903), vol. 1, p. 262.

11. As translated in Moxey, *Pieter Aertsen*, p. 177 n.2. Original in Angelus Merula, *De verantwoording van Angelus Merula (1553)*, ed. I. M. J. Hoog (Leiden: Van Doesburgh, 1897), p. 57.

12. Jean Calvin, *Tracts and Treatises*, trans. Henry Beveridge (Edinburgh and London: Oliver and Boyd, 1958), vol. 3, p. 46.

13. Hooper, *Early Writings*, p. 39. More sixteenth and seventeenth-century examples can be found in Peter Heylyn, *Ecclesia restaurata, or, the history of the reformation of the Church of England* (London: H. Twyford, 1661), p. 56; Hugh Latimer, *Sermons by Hugh Latimer, sometime bishop of Worcester, martyr, 1555*, ed. George Elwes Corrie (Cambridge: Cambridge University Press, 1844), p. 54; William Tyndale, *An answer to Sir Thomas More's Dialogue: The Supper of the Lord after the true meaning of John VI and I Cor. XI* (Cambridge: Cambridge University Press, 1850), p. 59; "An homily against the peril of idolatry (1562)," pp. 186, 188, 195, 196, 221, 225, 240, 261, 262, 279; James Calfhill, *An Answer to John Martiall's Treatise of the Cross*, ed. Richard Gibbings (New York: Johnson Reprint Corp., 1968), pp. 37 and 39.

14. Jean Wirth, "Aspects modernes et contemporains de l'iconoclasme," in Blickle et al., *Macht und Ohnmacht*, p. 458.

15. "Dat nicht mehr affgöderie edder missbrukes darmit bedreven werden mochte." Alfred Uckeley, "Der Werdegang der kirchlichen Reformbewegung im Anfang der 16. Jahrhunderts in den Stadtgemeinden Pommerns," *Pommersche Jahrbücher* 18 (1917), p. 71. Discussed in Schnitzler, *Ikonoklasmus*, p. 217.

16. Paul Roth, "Eine Elegie zum Bildersturm in Basel," *Basler Zeitschrift für Geschichte und Altertumskunde* 42 (1943), pp. 133–34, 136.

17. Schnitzler, *Ikonoklasmus*, p. 217.

18. Dupeux, Jezler, and Wirth, *Bildersturm*, p. 118.

19. John of Damascus, *On the Divine Images*, pp. 52–53.

20. *A Reformation Debate*, pp. 69–70.

21. Gesine Taubert, "Spätmittelalterliche Kreuzabnahmespiele in Wels, Wien und Tirol," *Jahrbuch des oberösterreichischen Musealvereins* 119 (1974), pp. 53–89.

22. "Sie steigen hinauff, und nemmen den Herrn her- / ab, Joseph spricht: / Komm her meines hertzen heyl und trost, / du hast nun die gantze Welt erlöst, / von der bittern Marter und höllen Peyn, / dess sollen wir alle danckbahr seyn." Taubert, "Mittelalterliche Kruzifixe (1969)," p. 117. In the Wels play, Joseph says to the statue: "Ich pitt dich, her dw wellest mir geben / Ein guet end vnd daß ewig leben." Taubert, "Spätmittelalterliche Kreuzabnahmespiele," p. 89.

23. De Man, *The Rhetoric of Romanticism*, pp. 75–76.

24. De Man, *The Rhetoric of Romanticism*, p. 78.

25. "Sie sitzen Gott im schos und spielen mit im der Tocken, Werden von

solchen gedancken und suessem Teuffels gifft so vol gesoffen, so stoltz, hart und storrig, das sie schlecht niemand hoeren noch folgen wollen." Luther, *Luthers Werke*, vol. 21, p. 244. On Pietàs with removable Christ figures, see Jürgen Michler, "Neue Funde und Beiträge zur Enstehung der Pietà am Bodensee," *Jahrbuch der Staatlichen Kunstsammlungen in Baden-Württemberg* 29 (1992), pp. 29–49; Michaela Burek, Jürgen Michler, and Peter Vogel, "Eine neuentdeckte frühe Bodensee-Pietà in Meersburg," *Zeitschrift für Kunsttechnologie und Konservierung* 6, no. 2 (1992), pp. 315–30; Tripps, *Das handelnde Bildwerk*, pp. 168–69. On a fourteenth-century Lamentation of Mary play from the Friaul in which living actors play the parts of Mary and John and a sculpture takes the part of Christ, see Belting, *The Image and Its Public*, p. 86.

26. *A Reformation Debate*, p. 22.

27. Andreas Rudolff-Bodenstein von Karlstadt, *The Essential Carlstadt: Fifteen Tracts*, ed. and trans. Edward J. Furcha (Waterloo and Scottdale: Herald Press, 1995), p. 238.

28. Cf. Hosea 9.10.

29. Gloria Cigman, ed., *Lollard Sermons* (Oxford: Early English Text Society, 1989), p. 114.

30. My translation is based on the German translation in Petr Chelčický, *Das Netz des Glaubens. Aus dem Alttschechischen ins Deutsche übertragen von Carl Vogl* (Hildesheim and New York: G. Olms, 1970), p. 191. Discussed in Bredekamp, *Kunst als Medium*, p. 286.

31. "Inter hec unum est hoc precipuum et maximum, quod iniquitas capciosa demonum potens est valde in talibus ymaginibus, que sunt Dei vel sanctorum in templo vel domo Dei, dementare homines et ludificare, qui non fide viva habundant, sed mortua." Bredekamp, *Kunst als Medium*, p. 247.

32. On the tripytch, see Rudolf Preimesberger, "Zu Jan van Eycks Diptychon der Sammlung Thyssen-Bornemisza," *Zeitschrift für Kunstgeschicthe* 54, no. 4 (1991), pp. 459–89. For an overview of grisaille painting (of which simulated stone sculpture is a subcategory), see Michaela Krieger, "Zum Problem des Illusionismus im 14. und 15. Jahrhundert—ein Deutungsversuch," *Pantheon* 54 (1996), pp. 4–18; Michaela Krieger, "Die niederländische Grisaillemalerei des 15. Jahrhunderts: Bemerkungen zu neuerer Literatur," *Kunstchronik* 49, no. 12 (1996), pp. 575–88; Jane Shoaf Turner, ed., *The Grove Dictionary of Art. From Renaissance to Impressionism: Styles and Movements in Western Art, 1400–1900* (London: Macmillan Reference,

2000), pp. 672–77.

33. "Si d'une part la grisaille est moins réelle que la peinture (l'objet représenté n'est lui-même qu'une statue et non une figure vivante) ce qui justifie son usage aux revers des volets, visibles lorsque le retable est fermé, de l'autre, la présence réelle de la statue est plus vraisemblable que celle des figures colorées, ce qui accroît le pouvoir de trompe l'oeil." Paul Philippot, "Les grisailles et les 'degrés de réalité' de l'image dans la peinture flamande des XVe et XVIe siècles," *Bulletin des Musées Royaux des Beaux-Arts de Belgique* 15 (1966), p. 230.

34. As translated in Michael Baxandall, "Bartholomaeus Facius on Painting: A Fifteenth-Century Manuscript of the *De Viris Illustribus,*" *Journal of the Warburg and Courtauld Institutes* 27 (1964), p. 102. On the humanist topos of the living image, see Michael Baxandall, *Giotto and the Orators: Humanist Observers of Painting in Italy and the Discovery of Pictorial Composition, 1350–1450* (Oxford: Clarendon Press, 1971), pp. 51–52; Fredrika Herman Jacobs, *The Living Image in Renaissance Art* (Cambridge and New York: Cambridge University Press, 2005).

35. Wolfgang Stechow, *Northern Renaissance Art 1400–1600: Sources and Documents*, ed. H. W. Janson (Englewood Cliffs: Prentice-Hall, 1966), p. 9.

36. On the topos of the living image in medieval art and religion, see Caesarius of Heisterbach, *The Dialogue on Miracles*, trans. Henry von Essen Scott and C. C. Swinton Bland (London: G. Routledge, 1929); Camille, *The Gothic Idol*, pp. 36, 207, 213-14. For examples of fraudulent images, see Frederik Poulsen, "Talking, Weeping and Bleeding Sculptures: A Chapter of the History of Religious Fraud," *Acta Archaeologica* 16 (1945), pp. 192–95; Tripps, *Das handelnde Bildwerk*, p. 167.

37. *Andachtsbild* is a highly contested term. Central to the debate surrounding it is whether it should be defined in terms of form or function. For overviews of the debate, see Belting, *The Image and Its Public*, pp. 41–64; Karl Schade, *Andachtsbild: Die Geschichte eines kunsthistorischen Begriffs* (Weimar: Verlag und Datenbank für Geisteswissenschaften, 1996).

38. "Dem betrachtenden Einzelbewußtsein die Möglichkeit zu einer *kontemplativen Versenkung* in den betrachteten Inhalt zu geben, d. h. das Subjekt mit dem Objekt seelisch gleichsam verschmelzen zu lassen." Erwin Panofsky, "'Imago Pietatis': Ein Beitrag zur Typengeschichte des 'Schmerzensmanns' und der 'Maria Mediatrix,'" in *Festschrift Max J. Friedländer zum 60. Geburtstag* (Leipzig: E. A. Seemann, 1927), p. 264. Panofsky also writes of the viewer's "Selbstidentifikation mit dem Darstellungsinhalt" (p. 266).

39. Ringbom, *Icon to Narrative*, p. 48.

40. Belting, *The Image and Its Public*, p. 3.

41. Belting, *The Image and Its Public*, p. 80.

42. The literature on miraculous images in the early modern period is large. See the important discussions in Trexler, "Florentine Religious Experience"; Freedberg, *The Power of Images*, pp. 283–316. See also the recent collection of essays: Erik Thunø and Gerhard Wolf, eds., *The Miraculous Image: Papers from a Conference Held at the Accademia di Danimarca in Collaboration with the Bibliotheca Hertziana* (Rome: "L'Erma" di Bretschneider, 2004).

43. Smith, "The Use of Grisaille," pp. 50–51.

44. On grisaille and *lapides vivi*, see Marion Grams-Thieme, *Lebendige Steine: Studien zur niederländischen Grisaillemalerei des 15. und frühen 16. Jahrhunderts* (Cologne: Böhlau, 1988), esp. pp. 12, 54–56. Krieger argues against Grams-Thieme's thesis that simulated sculptures were meant to appear alive. Krieger, "Zum Problem des Illusionismus," p. 12. Augustine uses the phrase *lapides mortui* to refer to pagan idols in "Enarratio in psalmum XCVI" in *Patrologia Latina*, vol. 37, p. 1244; "Sermones de scripturis. Sermo XXIV" in *Patrologia Latina*, vol. 38, p. 163. See also Grams-Thieme, *Lebendige Steine*, p. 345 n.121.

45. Duchamp, *Salt Seller*, p. 160.

46. On the photograph, see Irina Antonowa and Jörn Merkert, eds., *Berlin Moskau, 1900–1950 = Moskva Berlin, 1900–1950* (Munich and New York: Prestel, 1995), p. 120; Brigid Doherty, "The Work of Art and the Problem of Politics in Berlin Dada," *October* 105 (2003), pp. 83–84. On Dada and Reformation iconoclasm, see Debbie Lewer, "Hugo Ball, Iconoclasm and the Origins of Dada in Zurich," *Oxford Art Journal* 32, no. 1 (2009), pp. 17–35.

47. Wieland Herzfelde, "Introduction to the First International Dada Fair," *October* 105 (2003), pp. 97 and 100.

48. I. Klyun, *Iskusstvo tsveta (The Art of Color)*, in the catalog of the 10th State Exhibition, "Non-Objective Art and Suprematism," Moscow, 1919, p. 15, as translated in Larissa A. Zhadova, *Malevich: Suprematism and Revolution in Russian Art, 1910–1930* (London: Thames and Hudson, 1982), p. 43. Discussed in Danto, *After the End of Art*, p. 154.

49. See Maleuvre, *Museum Memories*, pp. 19–21.

50. Marinetti, "The Founding," p. 3. (See my preface for a brief discussion of this same passage.)

51. Further along on the same page, Tarabukin writes: "the category of museum objects which have no living or practical purpose . . . finds its final repose in the quiet of the museum graveyard." Francis Frascina and Charles Harrison, eds., *Modern Art and Modernism: A Critical Anthology* (London and New York: Harper & Row, 1982), p. 141. On the museum as cemetery, see also Kazimir Severinovich Malevich, *Écrits*, ed. Andrei B. Nakov, trans. Andrée Robel-Chicurel (Paris: Éditions Champ libre, 1975), pp. 233–36.

52. See, e.g., Bürger, *Theory of the Avant-Garde*, p. 49; Foster, "What's Neo," pp. 8–9.

53. Frascina and Harrison, *Modern Art*, p. 142. For discussion, see Maria Gough, *The Artist as Producer: Russian Constructivism in Revolution* (Berkeley: University of California Press, 2005), pp. 121, 124–25, 127, 138, 216 n.15.

54. As translated in *From Painting to Design: Russian Constructivist Art of the Twenties* (Cologne: Galerie Gmurzynska, 1981), p. 118.

55. Bois, *Painting as Model*, p. 230. For Bois, the deaths that count are those that start at the beginning and work their way ever closer toward an end they never reach. Those that do not count are the facile, manic rushes to the finish line.

56. "Jackson Pollock: An Artists' Symposium, Part I," *ARTnews* 66, no. 2 (April 1967), p. 29.

57. "The Legacy of Jackson Pollock" (1958) in Allan Kaprow, *Essays on the Blurring of Art and Life*, ed. Jeff Kelley (Berkeley: University of California Press, 1993), pp. 1–9. "Pollock's near destruction of this tradition may well be a return to the point where art was more actively involved in ritual, magic, and life than we have known it in our recent past. If so, it is an exceedingly important step and in its superior way offers a solution to the complaints of those who would have us put a bit of life into art" (pp. 6–7). Buchloh comments: "Kaprow's ideas of 1958 are to a certain extent comparable to Benjamin's thoughts of the twenties, when the latter developed the notion of a participatory aesthetic in the context of his discussion of Dadaism. Yet Kaprow speaks with an astonishing naiveté about the historical possibility of a new participatory aesthetic emerging out of Pollock's work." Benjamin H. D. Buchloh, *Neo-Avantgarde and Culture Industry: Essays on European and American Art from 1955 to 1975* (Cambridge: MIT Press, 2000), p. 481.

58. Kaprow, *Essays*, p. 63.

59. Kaprow, *Essays*, p. 62.

60. On the "Dadaist ideology of experience," see Foster, "What's Neo," p. 17.

61. Irving Sandler and Philip Pavia, "The Philadelphia Panel," *It Is* 5 (1960), p. 37.

62. Ad Reinhardt, *Art-as-Art: The Selected Writings of Ad Reinhardt*, ed. Barbara Rose (Berkeley: University of California Press, 1991), p. 54.

63. Reinhardt, *Art-as-Art*, p. 54.

64. Jeanne Siegel, *Artwords* (Ann Arbor: UMI Research Press, 1985), p. 25.

65. Sandler and Pavia, "The Philadelphia Panel," p. 35. This meant no protest art. As a person Reinhardt was a socialist and an activist. As an artist he considered himself to be neither: "I think an artist should participate in any protests against war—as human being. There's no way they can participate as an artist." Siegel, *Artwords*, p. 28. See also "How Effective is Social Protest Art? (Vietnam)" in Siegel, *Artwords*, pp. 101–19.

66. Reinhardt, *Art-as-Art*, p. 27.

67. Reinhardt, *Art-as-Art*, p. 54.

68. Reinhardt, *Art-as-Art*, p. 55.

69. Reinhardt, *Art-as-Art*, p. 114.

70. Siegel, *Artwords*, p. 27. "Paintings are the end of the beginning, beginning of the end." Reinhardt, *Art-as-Art*, p. 76. Reinhardt also makes passing reference to the Second Commandment here and there in his writings. Reinhardt, *Art-as-Art*, pp. 9, 74, 165, 190.

71. Reinhardt, *Art-as-Art*, p. 75.

72. Reinhardt, *Art-as-Art*, p. 193.

73. Reinhardt, *Art-as-Art*, p. 8.

74. "If you're an artist or art historian, you group them stylistically or in periods and so on. And then I got to a point where I was just putting all the slides with navels in them together or slides with feet together. So, in one way or another, I was doing what Magritte did in some paintings, compartmentalize things, skies, feet, navels (audience laughter), trees, and so on." From the unpublished transcript of a lecture at the Institute of Contemporary Arts, London, 28 May 1964. I thank Anna Reinhardt and Susan Sabiston for providing me access to this unpublished transcript and to the one cited below. I also cannot thank Anna Reinhardt enough for discussing with me her father's slide shows.

75. Siegel, *Artwords*, p. 24.

76. From the unpublished transcript of "Art as Art, In the Past," a lecture at the Washington Gallery of Modern Art, 26 January 1966. Transcript courtesy of

Anna Reinhardt.

77. "Yet diverse as they are, all these objects (with the exception of those few whose outstanding genius sets them outside the historic stream) speak for the same endeavor; it is as though an unseen presence, the spirit of art, were urging all on the same quest." André Malraux, *The Voices of Silence*, trans. Stuart Gilbert (Garden City: Doubleday, 1953), p. 46. Criticism of Malraux has been particularly incisive where it contrasts his account of photography's effect on aura with Walter Benjamin's, which is so much more convincingly pessimistic, see Rosalind E. Krauss, "The Ministry of Fate," in Denis Hollier, ed., *A New History of French Literature* (Cambridge: Harvard University Press, 1989), p. 1002; Demos, "Duchamp's Boîte-en-Valise," pp. 14–17; Hal Foster, "Archives of Modern Art," *October* 99 (2002), pp. 91–93.

78. Reinhardt, *Art-as-Art*, p. 29.

79. Reinhardt, *Art-as-Art*, p. 54.

80. Interview with Cage reprinted in William Fetterman, *John Cage's Theatre Pieces: Notations and Performances* (Amsterdam: Harwood Academic Publishers, 1996), p. 103. See also Vincent Katz, ed., *Black Mountain College: Experiment in Art* (Cambridge: MIT Press, 2002), pp. 138–39.

81. Martin B. Duberman, *Black Mountain: An Exploration in Community* (New York: Dutton, 1972), p. 353. Reprinted in Fetterman, *John Cage's Theatre Pieces*, p. 99.

82. Michael Kirby and Richard Schechner, "An Interview with John Cage," *Tulane Drama Review* 10, no. 2 (1965), pp. 52–53. Reprinted in Fetterman, *John Cage's Theatre Pieces*, pp. 98–99.

83. For descriptions of Reinhardt's production and use of slides, see Dale McConathy, "Ad Reinhardt: 'He loved to confuse and confound,'" *ARTnews* (April 1980), pp. 58–59; M. Darsie Alexander, *Slideshow* (Baltimore and University Park: Baltimore Museum of Art; Pennsylvania State University Press, 2005), p. 63.

84. *A Reformation Debate*, p. 73.

CHAPTER FOUR: THE END OF THE DEPOSITION RITE

1. This is not to say that the paralitugical rites disappeared. Even in Lutheran churches, they sometimes persisted well into the sixteenth century: "It is not

generally known to students of the liturgical drama that the Cathedral Church, the Domkirche, of Berlin retained the dramatic *Visitatio sepulchri* and the other sepulcher ceremonies for about sixty years after it had gone over to the Reformation." Neil C. Brooks, "The *Sepulchrum Christi* and its Ceremonies in Late Mediaeval and Modern Times," *The Journal of English and Germanic Philology* 27 (1928), p. 151, see also p. 152. In some Catholic areas, the paraliturgical rites continue to this day. Even at the height of their popularity in the later Middle Ages, they were not acknowledged by Rome, so it is little surprise that they continued in some places long after Rome explicitly condemned the singing of "tropes." For examples of the continued performance of paraliturgical rites beyond the sixteenth century in Catholic contexts, see Nikolaus Grass, "Barock-Heiliggräber: Ein Beitrag zur Kultur- und Kunstgeschichte Tirols," in Grass, *Ostern in Tirol*, pp. 228–29; Josef Andreas Jungmann, "Brauch und Liturgie in der Heiligen Woche," in Grass, *Ostern in Tirol*, p. 319; Gschwend, *Die Depositio*, pp. 128–34.

2. On the banning of "tropes" and the absence of the *Depositio*, *Elevatio*, and *Visitatio sepulchri* from the *Roman Missal* of 1570, see Helmut de Boor, *Die Textgeschichte der lateinischen Osterfeiern* (Tübingen: Max Niemeyer Verlag, 1967), p. 17; Jezler, "Bildwerke im Dienste," p. 240. On the virtual disappearance of the *Visitatio sepulchri*, which involved the *Quem Quaeritis* "trope," in the second half of the sixteenth century, see Brooks, "The Sepulchre," p. 49. On Pius V and Carl Borromeus's banning of the mystery plays or "*sacre rappresentazioni*," see Enzo Bilardello, "L'evoluzione del teatro barocco: pratica e trattati," in *Il Teatro a Roma nel Settecento* (Rome: Istituto della Enciclopedia italiana, 1989), vol. 1, p. 39; Ursula Brossette, *Die Inszenierung des Sakralen: Das theatralische Raum- und Ausstattungsprogramm süddeutscher Barockkirchen in seinem liturgischen und zeremoniellen Kontext* (Weimer: VDG, 2002), p. 51 n.24.

3. On the Jesuits' role in promoting the exposition grave, see Brooks, "The *Sepulchrum Christi*," pp. 155–58; Grass, "Barock-Heiliggräber," pp. 223–26; Jezler, "Bildwerke im Dienste," p. 240; Brossette, *Die Inszenierung*, pp. 44 and 184.

4. On the exposition grave's resemblance to a tabernacle, see Anton Dörrer, "Heiliggräber, Grabandachten, Karwochenspiele: Beispiele aus Tirol," in Grass, *Ostern in Tirol*, pp. 185 and 188.

5. The earliest known account of the burial of the Host occurs in the Life of St. Udalricus, Bishop of Augsburg (d. 973), which was written within about twenty years of the Bishop's death. This is close in date to the *Monastic Agreement* (ca. 970),

which contains the earliest instance of the burial of the cross. Karl Young, "The Dramatic Associations of the Easter Sepulchre," *University of Wisconsin Studies in Language and Literature* 10 (1920), p. 17. On the infrequency of Host burial without a crucifix before the sixteenth century, see Brooks, "The Sepulchre," p. 40; Young, *The Drama*, vol. 1, p. 132; Taubert, "Mittelalterliche Kruzifixe (1969)," pp. 95, 111–12; Nußbaum, *Die Aufbewahrung*, pp. 192–95.

6. For the ceremony at St. Blaise, see Young, *The Drama*, vol. 1, pp. 112–13. For the ceremony dictated by the Use of Sarum, see Frere, *The Use of Sarum*, vol. 2, pp. 165–66. For other examples of the Host and crucifix buried together, see Chambers, *The Mediaeval Stage*, vol. 2, p. 21; Brooks, "The Sepulchre," p. 38.

7. In 831–833, Paschasius Radbertus wrote *Liber de corpore et sanguine domini*, the first monograph devoted to the last supper, in which he identified the sacramental body with the historical body of Christ. This led to the Carolingian Eucharistic debate between Radbertus and Ratramnus of Corbie. In the West, Radbertus' understanding of the Host as Christ's historical body would gradually win out. In 1215, the Church formally adopted the theory of transubstantiation, according to which the bread and wine are transformed into the body and blood of Christ on the altar. Darwell Stone, *A History of the Doctrine of the Holy Eucharist* (London and New York: Longmans, Green, 1909), vol. 1, pp. 216–33; Parker, *The Descent*, pp. 74–75; Bloch, *Romanische Bronzekruzifixe*, p. 12.

8. Dominican Laurent, *The Book of Vices and Virtues: A Fourteenth Century English Translation of the Somme le Roi of Lorens d'Orléans*, ed. W. Nelson Francis (London and New York: Oxford University Press, 1968), p. 109. Discussed in Miri Rubin, *Corpus Christi: The Eucharist in Late Medieval Culture* (Cambridge and New York: Cambridge University Press, 1991), p. 100.

9. John Thoresby, *The lay folks' catechism or The English and Latin versions of Archbishop Thoresby's instruction for the people* (London: K. Paul, Trench, Trübner & Co., 1901), p. 66. Discussed in Rubin, *Corpus Christi*, p. 100.

10. "Nam contra omnem rationem est, quod in quibusdam ecclesiis Eucharistia in huiusmodi archa Sepulchrum representante poni consuevit et claudi. Ibi enim Eucharistia, que est verum et vivum Corpus Christi, ipsum Christi Corpus mortuum representat, quod est indecens penitus et absurdum." Heidi Leuppi, ed., *Der liber ordinarius des Konrad von Mure: Die Gottesdienstordnung am Grossmünster in Zürich* (Freiburg: Universitätsverlag, 1995), p. 254. Discussed in Brooks, "The Sepulchre," p. 40; Young, *The Drama*, vol. 1, p. 132.

11. "It is thus precisely the overloading of the ritual with the 'historical' that exhausts its kerygmatic historicity. For with this overloading, ritualistic repetition no longer takes place in relation to the difference but rather to the identity with the beginning that grounds it." Warning, *The Ambivalences*, p. 36, see also pp. 27–65. Müller makes a similar argument in Jan-Dirk Müller, "Mimesis und Ritual. Zum geistlichen Spiel des Mittelalters," in Andreas Kablitz and Gerhard Neumann, eds., *Mimesis und Simulation* (Freiburg im Breisgau: Rombach Verlag, 1998), p. 553.

12. In the Diocese of Brixen, the grave rest grew ever shorter as the resurrection celebrations came ever sooner. Gschwend, *Die Depositio*, p. 134. Like the inclusion of the Host in the Good Friday ceremonies, this shortening probably reflects a nervousness about lingering over Christ's human death.

13. On the late-sixteenth-century shift from the use of an image to the use of a Host, see Gschwend, *Die Depositio*, pp. 85, 89, 109, 114, 124–26, 134, 158, 168–69 n.37; Nußbaum, *Die Aufbewahrung*, pp. 200–203; Jezler, "Bildwerke im Dienste," pp. 236–49. The *Decreta authentica* lists examples of the Host displayed in a monstrance over the sepulcher from the mid-seventeenth through the nineteenth century. Catholic Church, *Decreta authentica Congregationis Sacrorum Rituum ex actis eiusdem collecta eiusque auctoritate promulgata sub auspiciis ss. domini nostri Leonis Papae XII* (Rome: Ex Typographia Ployglotta, 1898–1901), vol. 4, pp. 429–39. Sometimes the monstrance was covered with a veil on Good Friday, for example, in a 1686 ritual from Salzburg. Catholic Church, *Decreta authentica*, p. 430; Young, "The Dramatic Associations," pp. 35–37. The monstrance was also covered with a veil at the Parish Church of St. Andrä in Lienz. Brossette, *Die Inszenierung*, p. 191.

14. On built-in tabernacles, see Schwarzweber, *Das heilige Grab*, pp. 63 and 71; Kroesen, *The Sepulchrum Domini*, pp. 68–76, 182.

15. On the Devotion of the Forty Hours, which may or may not have developed out of the forty-hour grave rest, see Mark S. Weil, "The Devotion of the Forty Hours and Roman Baroque Illusions," *Journal of the Warburg and Courtauld Institutes* 37 (1974), pp. 218–48. On the relation between the Devotion of the Forty Hours, which was common in Italy but not north of the Alps, and the exposition grave, see Jungmann, "Die Andacht der Vierzig Stunden," pp. 184–98; Andrea Feuchtmayr, *Kulissenheiliggräber im Barock: Entstehungsgeschichte und Typologie* (Munich: Tuduv Verlag, 1989), pp. 27–31; Ewald M. Vetter, *Speculum salutis: Arbeiten zur christlichen Kunst* (Münsterschwarzach: Vier-Türme, 1994), pp. 217–19.

16. Gregory Martin, *Roma sancta (1581)*, ed. George Bruner Parks (Rome: Edizioni di storia e letteratura, 1969), p. 64. Discussed in Weil, "The Devotion of the Forty Hours," p. 222.

17. Rudolf Berliner, *Die Weihnachtskrippe* (Munich: Prestel Verlag, 1955), pp. 32, and 181 n.222; Vetter, *Speculum salutis*, p. 219.

18. Felix Joseph Lipowsky, *Geschichte der Jesuiten in Baiern* (Munich: J. Giel, 1816), vol. 1, p. 200; Berliner, *Die Weihnachtskrippe*, pp. 181–83 n.222.

19. Grass, "Barock-Heiliggräber," p. 226.

20. Brossette, *Die Inszenierung*, p. 184.

21. Ulrike Besch, *Studien zur Ausstattung von St. Kajetan in München: Ein Beitrag zur Funktion ephemerer Systemelemente in der Kunst des Barock* (Munich: Starnberg, 1983), pp. 196–97 n.170.

22. On Enlightenment attitudes toward exposition graves, see Grass, "Barock-Heiliggräber," pp. 253–57; Gschwend, *Die Depositio*, pp. 135–36; Brossette, *Die Inszenierung*, pp. 53 and 598.

23. Berliner, *Die Weihnachtskrippe*, p. 182 n.222.

24. "Die ganz Kirch der Herrn Jesuiter in Collegio Romano, zu S. MARIA AUF DER STRASSEN genannt, war mit schöner Tapezerei überzogen, oben in der Höh schwebten große Engel, von Papier und Farben dermassen zugerichtet, daß einer hätte meinen mögen, sie lebeten, die neigten sich als dienstbare Geister gegen dem hochheiligen Sacrament; das stund oben in der Höh, zu oberst droben war ein machina globi coelestis, inwendig mit kleinen Lichtlin umb und umb besteckt, die schienen durch etliche silberin Sternen gar fein samt Sonn und Mon mit Unterschied der größen und kleinern Sternen, item der Planeten und das Corpus moviert sich durch ein heimlich Gewicht, das alles bewegt die Pilgram zu großer unaussprechlicher Freud und Anmut." Johann Jakob Rabus, *Rom, eine Münchner Pilgerfahrt im Jubeljahr 1575*, ed. Karl Schottenloher (Munich: Münchner Drucke, 1925), p. 113. Discussed in Jezler, "Bildwerke im Dienste," p. 242; Vetter, *Speculum salutis*, p. 219.

25. On the use of the exposition grave for many different performances, see Feuchtmayr, *Kulissenheiliggräber*, pp. 16–18; Brossette, *Die Inszenierung*, pp. 182–83, 190–92, 204.

26. Besch, *Studien zur Ausstattung*, p. 84; Joseph Imorde, "'Allegoricus semper interpres, & historiae fugiens veritatem': Zur Bildervalenz der Eucharistie," in Joseph Imorde, Fritz Neumeyer, and Tristan Weddigen, eds., *Barocke Inszenierung*

(Emsdetten: Edition Imorde, 1999), p. 108; Brossette, *Die Inszenierung*, p. 196. Candles were certainly used during the medieval grave rest. For examples, see Heales, "Easter Sepulchers," pp. 271–77. But it appears that their use was sometimes restricted. The twelfth-century missal of Sarum stipulates: "Candele non accendantur circa altare, nisi ante Corpus Domini." Römer, "Die Liturgie des Karfreitags," p. 49 n.12.

27. "De toutes les expositions du saint Sacrement à découvert qui sont en usage dans notre siécle, il n'y a en a point qui soit plus universellement condamnée que celle qui se fait en certaines Eglises le jeudi, le Vendredi & le Samedi saint." Jean-Baptiste Thiers, *Traité de l'exposition du s. sacrement de l'autel* (Avignon: L. Chambeau, 1777), p. 175.

28. "Car enfin quel rapport y a-t-il entre la tristesse de ces trois jours, & la joie qui doit être inseparable de la divine Eucharistie exposée en evidence sur nos Autels? Entre les tenébres & la splendeur du Pere?" Thiers, *Traité de l'exposition*, p. 191.

29. "Usque ad saeculum decimum quintum SS. Sacramentum in Sepulchro inclusum fidelium adorationi expositum est. Cum autem tempore reformationis haeretici contram realem et essentialem praesentiam Christi in SS. Eucharistia absconditi vehementer praedicarent, eamque exprobrarent et omnio negarent, ac diem Parasceves pro sua confessione festum solemnissimum totius anni elevarent, factum est, ut, ad fideles in confessione verae fidei in Christum in SS. Sacramento vere, realiter et substantialiter praesentem conservandos et confirmandos et ad opponendam luthericae solemnitati die Parasceves aliam catholicam, festivitatem, SS. Sacramentum in Sepulchro non amplius includeretur, sed super Sepulchrum sive in calice sive in ostensorio velato Feria VI in Parasceve adorationi palam exponeretur." Catholic Church, *Decreta authentica*, vol. 4, p. 433. Discussed in Brooks, "The Sepulchre," p. 45.

30. On the differences between the medieval and baroque Good Friday celebrations, see Jezler, "Bildwerke im Dienste," pp. 236–49. On the differences between medieval and baroque allegory, see Walter Benjamin, *The Origin of German Tragic Drama*, trans. John Osborne (London and New York: Verso, 1998), pp. 167–71.

31. "Allegoria enim animae longe a deo positae quasi quandam machinam facit, ut per illam leuetur ad deum." Pope Gregory I, *Commentaire sur le Cantique des cantiques*, trans. Rodrigue Bélanger (Paris: Éditions du Cerf, 1984), p. 68.

32. "Interpositis quippe enigmatibus, dum quiddam in uerbis cognoscit, quod suum est, in sensu uerborum intellegit, quod non est suum, et per terrena uerba serparatur a terra." Gregory I, *Commentaire*, p. 70.

33. *The Monastic Agreement*, p. 36.

34. Durand, *The Rationale*, p. 4.

35. Durand, *The Rationale*, p. 1.

36. Durand, *The Rationale*, p. 1.

37. "Postquam a paradisi gaudiis expulsum est genus humanum, in istam peregrinationem uitae praesentis ueniens caecum cor ab spiritali intellectu habet.... Idcirco per quaedam enigmata sermo diuinus animae torpenti et frigidae loquitur et de rebus, quas nouit, latenter insinuat ei amorem, quem non nouit." Gregory I, *Commentaire*, p. 68.

38. Benjamin, *The Origin*, p. 224.

39. The sculptures were made by Andreas Faistenberger in wood with Venetian glass eyes and cloth drapery. On Gumpp's exposition graves, see Joseph Sebastian Rittershausen, *Die vornehmste Merkwürdigkeiten der Residenz-Stadt München für Liebhaber der bildenden Künste* (Munich: Lentner, 1788), pp. 133–34; Peter Strieder, "Entwürfe zu 'Heiligen Gräbern' in Münchner Kirchen," *Das Münster* 4 (1951), pp. 281–87; Besch, *Studien zur Ausstattung*, pp. 78–80; Peter Wegmann, "'Öfters mehr ein Theater.' Bemerkungen zu barocken Heiligen Gräbern," in Thomas Bolt et al., eds., *Grenzbereiche der Architektur* (Basel and Boston: Birkhäuser, 1985), pp. 251–55.

40. Brossette, *Die Inszenierung*, p. 190 n.86.

41. "Sehen wir nicht in den meisten Tempeln unsers Christenthumes die herrlichsten Vorstellungen, an welchen Kunst und Kostbarkeit glänzen?... Sie werden mit Lampen und Lichtern beleuchtet. Das hochwürdigste Gut, als der wahre und lebendige Leichnam Christi, ist in den schönsten Schaugefässen zur öffentlichen Anbethung darinn ausgesetzet." Sebastian Sailer, *Geistliche Schaubühne des Leidens Jesu Christi, in gesungenen Oratorien aufgeführt* (Weißenhorn: Konrad, 1997), pp. 215–16.

42. On the relation between real and fictive architecture in exposition graves, see Feuchtmayr, *Kulissenheiliggräber*, p. 50; Vetter, *Speculum salutis*, p. 219; Brossette, *Die Inszenierung*, pp. 186–87, 190, 194.

43. According to an inscription on a reproductive print of the grave, the sarcophagus and the figures were built in the round, while the columns, entablature, and vault were painted on canvas flats. Strieder, "Entwürfe," p. 285.

44. Benjamin, *The Origin*, pp. 217–18.

45. Benjamin, *The Origin*, p. 222.

46. Benjamin, *The Origin*, p. 232.

47. Benjamin, *The Origin*, p. 233.

48. "The violence of the dialectical movement within these allegorical depths must become clearer in the study of the form of the *Trauerspiel* than anywhere else." Benjamin, *The Origin*, p. 166.

49. Benjamin, *The Origin*, pp. 232–33.

50. Benjamin, *The Origin*, p. 166.

51. Sigmund Freud, *Beyond the Pleasure Principle*, ed. and trans. James Strachey (New York: W. W. Norton & Company, 1961), p. 14. Decker compares the covering of altarpieces with curtains to the game of *fort-da*. Decker, *Das Ende*, p. 317 n.251.

52. Freud, *Beyond the Pleasure Principle*, p. 15.

53. Freud, *Beyond the Pleasure Principle*, pp. 16–17.

54. Benjamin, *The Origin*, p. 185.

55. Jacques Lacan, *Écrits: The First Complete Edition in English*, trans. Bruce Fink (New York: W. W. Norton & Co., 2006), p. 262.

56. Lacan, *Écrits*, p. 228.

57. Lacan, *Écrits*, p. 262.

58. Lacan, *Écrits*, p. 262.

59. "At the same time, we also see in the game that the value of the object is insignificant (the object the child causes to appear and disappear)... This is the point of insemination for a symbolic order that preexists the infantile subject and in accordance with which he has to structure himself." Lacan, *Écrits*, p. 497.

60. "The mind (*esprit*) that lives as an exile in the creation whose invisible support he is, knows that he is at every instant the master capable of annihilating it." Lacan, *Écrits*, p. 224.

61. Benjamin, *The Origin*, pp. 183–84.

62. John Longland, *A sermond made be fore the kynge hys hyghnes at Rychemunte, uppon good fryday, the yere of our lorde MCCCCCXXXVI* (1535), sig. R4. Although the title dates the sermon to 1536, it was actually delivered in 1535. Discussed in Eamon Duffy, *The Stripping of the Altars: Traditional Religion in England, c. 1400–1580* (New Haven and London: Yale University Press, 1992), p. 36. Cf. "Where shall we fynde hym? where shall we fynde hym? Yonder he lyeth. Where? In yonder

sepulchre. What is he? what is his name, tell vs that we may know hym? His name is Iesus Chryste, Iesus of Nazareth. O Iesus of Nazareth. Yonder in the tombe lyeth thy moost precyous bodye, thy lyuely bodye, not deade, but a lyue. A lyue." John Longland, *A sermonde made before the kynge his maiestye at grenewiche, vpon good frydaye* (London: Thomas Petyt, 1538), n.p. Longland became bishop of Lincoln in 1521 and confessor to Henry VIII a few years later. He was an outspoken proponent of Catholic reform. Margaret Bowker, *The Henrician Reformation: The Diocese of Lincoln Under John Longland 1521–1547* (Cambridge and New York: Cambridge University Press, 1981), pp. 4–16.

63. Benjamin, *The Origin*, p. 233.

64. "The fundamental structure of allegory [is] the tendency of the language toward narrative, the spreading out along the axis of an imaginary time in order to give duration to what is, in fact, simultaneous within the subject." De Man, *Blindness and Insight*, p. 225, see also p. 163.

CHAPTER FIVE: ROGIER VAN DER WEYDEN'S REPEATED FORMS

1. I will not be concerned here with a direct relation between painting and (para)liturgy. The possibility of such a relation has been much debated in a literature that is too large to survey. For a recent review of work on the relation between art and liturgy in general, see Eric Palazzo, "Art and Liturgy in the Middle Ages: Survey of Research (1980–2003) and Some Reflections on Method," *The Journal of English and Germanic Philology* 105, no. 1 (2006), pp. 170–84. On the relation between the pictorial arts and the Deposition rite in particular, see Pächt, *The Rise of Pictorial Narrative*, pp. 30–32; Barbara G. Lane, "'Depositio et Elevatio': The Symbolism of the Seilern Triptych," *The Art Bulletin* 57, no. 1 (1975), pp. 26–29; Parker, *The Descent*, pp. 142–99; Barbara G. Lane, *The Altar and the Altarpiece: Sacramental Themes in Early Netherlandish Painting* (New York: Harper & Row, 1984), pp. 100–103; Belting, *The Image and Its Public*, pp. 65–166.

2. Schiller, *Iconography*, vol. 2, pp. 164–68. The earliest known Deposition appears in the ninth-century Byzantine Codex of Gregory von Nazianz in Paris. Rampendahl, *Die Ikonographie der Kreuzabnahme*, p. 9; Van Marle, "De iconographie der afneming," p. 34. The earliest known Western depiction is in the slightly later Angers Gospel, an Ottonian manuscript of the first half of the ninth century. Parker, *The Descent*, p. 12. In the fourteenth century, the Deposition began to grow

in popularity. Parker, *The Descent*, p. 201.

3. For discussion of the literature on this development as well as exceptions to it, see Parker, *The Descent*, pp. 1–18.

4. Rampendahl, *Die Ikonographie der Kreuzabnahme*, pp. 28–29; Van Marle, "De iconographie der afneming," p. 36.

5. Trecento paintings like Martini's would influence the work of fifteenth-century Burgundian miniaturists in turn. Rampendahl, *Die Ikonographie der Kreuzabnahme*, p. 59.

6. On rare precedents for this freeing from the cross and on Robert Campin and Fra Angelico's use of this device around the time that Rogier painted his *Deposition*, see Hamburgh, "Aspects of the Descent," vol. 1, p. 76; Alfred Acres, "Compositions of Time in the Art of Rogier van der Weyden" (Dissertation, University of Pennsylvania, 1992), pp. 337–41.

7. Acres, "Compositions of Time," pp. 342–43. Cf. Hamburgh, "Aspects of the Descent," vol. 1, p. 79. On the originality of Rogier's conception of the scene, see Nagatsuka, *Descente de croix*, p. 68.

8. On the guild, see Alfons Ising, *Brabantse schuttersgilden vroeger en nu* (Maasbree: Lijster, 1983), pp. 19–23. On Rogier's relationship to the guild, see Mark Trowbridge, "The *Stadschilder* and the *Serment*: Rogier van der Weyden's 'Deposition' and the Crossbowmen of Louvain," *Dutch Crossing: Journal of Low Countries Studies* 23, no. 2 (1999), pp. 5–28.

9. For examples, see Amy Neff, "The Pain of Compassio: Mary's Labor at the Foot of the Cross," *The Art Bulletin* 80, no. 2 (1998), p. 254. On the scarcity of "scenes in which Mary lies completely collapsed on the ground . . . in Netherlandish art in the period 1425–1550," see Reindert Falkenburg, "The Decorum of Grief: Notes on the Representation of Mary at the Cross in Late Medieval Netherlandish Literature and Painting," in M. Terttu Knapas and A. Ringbom, eds., *Icon to Cartoon: A Tribute to Sixten Ringbom* (Helsinki: Society for Art History in Finland, 1995), p. 78. Few Italian Depositions show a swooning Virgin before 1500; this manner of depicting the Virgin only becomes common in the sixteenth century. Harvey E. Hamburgh, "The Problem of *Lo Spasimo* of the Virgin in *Cinquecento* Paintings of the *Descent from the Cross*," *Sixteenth Century Journal* 12, no. 4 (1981), pp. 47–49.

10. Otto von Simson, "*Compassio* and *Co-Redemptio* in Roger van der Weyden's 'Descent from the Cross,'" *The Art Bulletin* 35, no. 1 (1953), p. 11. Neff identifies

something of a precedent for this rhyme in a mid-thirteenth-century Crucifixion in which Mary tilts her head in the same manner as Christ. Neff, "The Pain of Compassio," p. 255.

11. Von Simson, "*Compassio* and *Co-Redemptio*," p. 16.

12. As translated in Rubin, *Corpus Christi*, p. 143. Original in Nicole Bériou, *La prédication de Ranulphe de la Houblonnière: Sermons aux clercs et aux simples gens à Paris au XIIIe siècle* (Paris: Etudes augustiniennes, 1987), vol. 2, p. 107.

13. "Virgini Mariae quae soror dicitur Christi." Alain de Lille, "Elucidatio in Cantica canticorum" in *Patrologia Latina*, vol. 210, p. 107B. Discussed in Javelet, *Image et ressemblance*, vol. 1, p. 365.

14. "Soli Regi saeculorum, quae est imago Dei invisibilis gremium suum expandit." Pierre de Celle, "Sermo 75. De eadem beatissima Virgine" in *Patrologia Latina*, vol. 202, p. 871A. Discussed in Javelet, *Image et ressemblance*, vol. 1, p. 365.

15. Thomas writes: "the name 'Image' does not fit any of the divine persons indifferently, but only the Son; for Augustine says that *only the Son is the Image of the Father.*" Thomas Aquinas, *Summa Theologiae: Latin Text and English Translation, Introductions, Notes, Appendices, and Glossaries* (Cambridge and New York: Blackfriars; McGraw-Hill, 1964), vol. 13, p. 63. On the other hand, Geert Groote (d. 1384) explains that the image of God can take multiple forms: "For even the Most High, condescending to human frailty, employed corporeal forms and figures far removed from God, the angels, and spiritual things for his own external appearances and addresses to men." *Devotio Moderna*, p. 100.

16. Arnoul Gréban, *The Mystery of the Passion. The Third Day*, trans. Paula Giuliano (Asheville: Pegasus Press, 1996), pp. 130–31.

17. As translated in F. P. Pickering, "The Gothic Image of Christ: The Sources of Medieval Representations of the Crucifixion," in *Essays on Medieval German Literature and Iconography* (Cambridge and New York: Cambridge University Press, 1980), pp. 23–24. Original in Gottfried von Admont, "Liber de benedictionibus Jacob patriarchae" in *Patrologia Latina*, vol. 174, pp. 1150A–B. For more examples, see F. P. Pickering, *Literature & Art in the Middle Ages* (Coral Gables: University of Miami Press, 1970), pp. 301–307.

18. As translated in Pickering, "The Gothic Image of Christ," p. 24. Original in Heinrich von Neustadt, *"Apollonius von Tyrland" nach der Gothaer Handschrit, "Gottes Zukunft" und "Visio Philiberti" nach der Heidelberger Handschrift*, ed. S. Singer (Berlin: Weidmann, 1906), p. 373.

19. On the chapel, see Guillaume-Joseph-Charles Piot, *Histoire de Louvain, depuis son origine jusqu'aujourd'hui* (Louvain: Chez l'auteur, 1839), p. 200; Edward van Even, ed., *Geschiedenis van Leuven, geschreven in de jaren 1593 en 1594 door Willem Boonen* (Leuven: Fonteyn, 1880), p. 195; Edward van Even, *Louvain dans le passé et dans le présent* (Louvain: Fonteyn, 1895), pp. 436–38; Raymond van Uytven, ed., *De geschiedenis van het stadsgewest Leuven tot omstreeks 1600* (Leuven: Vrienden Stedelijke Musea, 1980), pp. 304–305.

20. In 1442, the twelfth-century statue was replaced by a new statue, which seems to have been an even more powerful miracle worker than the original. Léon van der Essen, *Notre-Dame de St. Pierre, Louvain, Siège da la Sagesse, 1129–1927* (Louvain: Peeters, 1927), pp. 22–25, 53–69.

21. Kemperdick and Sander point out that there was no high altar in the chapel since chapels do not have high altars. Kemperdick and Sander, *The Master of Flémalle and Rogier van der Weyden*, p. 130. But from as early as the sixteenth century, the original location of Rogier's painting has been identified as the "summum altare" of the Crossbowmen's chapel. See, e.g., Johannes Molanus, *Historiae Lovaniensium libri XIV* (Brussels: M. Hayez, 1861), vol. 1, p. 609. Reprinted in Élisabeth Dhanens, *Rogier van der Weyden: Revisie van de documenten* (Brussels: Paleis der Academiën, 1995), pp. 134–35.

22. Rogier's *Deposition* may have taken the place of this statue. See Edward van Even, *Louvain monumental ou description historique et artistique de tous les édifices civils et religieux de la dite ville* (Louvain: Fonteyn, 1860), p. 237; van Even, *Louvain dans le passé et dans le présent*, pp. 365 and 437.

23. Joseph de Borchgrave d'Altena, *Le retable de saint Georges de Jan Borman* (Brussels: R. Dupriez, 1947), p. 11; *Het laatgotische beeldsnijcentrum Leuven* (Leuven: Stedelijk Museum, 1979), pp. 49–56.

24. Joseph Braun, *Das christliche Altargerät in seinem Sein und in seiner Entwicklung* (Munich: M. Hueber, 1932), pp. 179–85, 340–42, 407–11.

25. As translated in Hardison, *Christian Rite*, p. 40. Original in Honorius von Autun, "Gemma animae" in *Patrologia Latina*, vol. 172, p. 570B.

26. Notice the visual rhyme between the round wafer and the cleric's bald pate. "A priest clothed in sacred vestments occupies the place of Christ, that he may humbly intercede with God for himself and for all men. He wears the sign of the Cross both before and behind him, that he may be ever mindful of His Lord's Passion." Thomas à Kempis, *The Imitation of Christ*, trans. Leo Sherley-Price (London:

Penguin, 1952), p. 195.

27. On the stamping of the Eucharist, see Peter S. J. Browe, *Die eucharistischen Wunder des Mittelalters* (Breslau: Müller & Seiffert, 1938), pp. 96–97, 122–23; Caroline Walker Bynum, *Holy Feast and Holy Fast: The Religious Significance of Food to Medieval Women* (Berkeley: University of California Press, 1987), p. 56.

28. On the infrequency of communion in the later Middle Ages, see Rubin, *Corpus Christi*, pp. 64–82.

29. On Host miracles, see Jules Corblet, *Histoire dogmatique, liturgique, et archéologique du sacrement de l'Eucharistie* (Paris: Société générale de librairie catholique, 1885), vol. 1, pp. 447–515; Caesarius, *The Dialogue on Miracles*, vol. 2, pp. 10–69; Browe, *Die eucharistischen Wunder*, pp. 93–202; V.A. Kolve, *The Play Called Corpus Christi* (Stanford: Stanford University Press, 1966), p. 47; Frederic C. Tubach, *Index Exemplorum: A Handbook of Medieval Religious Tales* (Helsinki: Suomalainen Tiedeakatemia, 1969), pp. 211–12; Peter S. J. Browe, *Die Verehrung der Eucharistie im Mittelalter* (Sinzig: Sankt Meinrad Reprintverlag, C. M. Esser, 1990), index entry for "Wunder"; Nicholas Love, *The Mirror of the Blessed Life of Jesus Christ: A Full Critical Edition*, ed. Michael G. Sargent (Exeter: University of Exeter Press, 2005), pp. 223–40.

30. For liturgical interpretations of the altarpiece, see Carolus Smits, *De iconographie van de Nederlandsche primitieven* (Amsterdam and Brussels, 1933), pp. 102–104; Lloyd W. Benjamin, "Disguised Symbolism Exposed and the History of Early Netherlandish Painting," *Studies in Iconography* 2 (1976), pp. 18–19; Lane, *The Altar and the Altarpiece*, pp. 89–93.

31. William R. Jones, "Art and Christian Piety: Iconoclasm in Medieval Europe," in Joseph Gutmann, ed., *The Image and the Word: Confrontations in Judaism, Christianity and Islam* (Missoula: Scholars Press for the American Academy of Religion; Society for Biblical Literature, 1977), pp. 89–90.

32. As translated in Jones, "Art and Christian Piety," p. 90. Original in Pierre d'Ailly, *De reformatione ecclesiae* (1416) in Gerson, *Opera omnia*, vol. 2, p. 911. Discussed in Huizinga, *The Autumn*, p. 175.

33. As translated in Kaminsky, *A History*, p. 261. Original in Palacký, *Documenta mag. Joannis Hus*, p. 680. Discussed in Bredekamp, *Kunst als Medium*, p. 259; Baxandall, *The Limewood Sculptors*, p. 92; Schnitzler, *Ikonoklasmus*, p. 59.

34. Reginald Pecock, *The repressor of over much blaming of the clergy*, ed. Churchill Babington (London: Longman, Green, Longman, and Roberts, 1860),

pp. 183–84.

35. "Unsere frommen vordren . . . habend von gemelden und bilden wenig gewüßt, als sich noch allenthalb in den teleren erfindt. Nun habend aber wir ietz iro so vil, das, wenn zehen so vil höws ässind als ein schaff, wir sy bald ze merckt tryben wurdind." Zwingli, *Sämtliche Werke*, vol. 4, p. 126. Discussed in Jezler, Jezler, and Göttler, "Warum ein Bilderstreit?" p. 86.

36. Discussed in Werner Hofmann, ed., *Luther und die Folgen für die Kunst* (Munich: Prestel-Verlag, 1983), p. 355.

37. Rubin, *Corpus Christi*, p. 328. For other arguments along these lines, see Miri Rubin, *Gentile Tales: The Narrative Assault on Late Medieval Jews* (New Haven: Yale University Press, 1999), pp. 98 and 102.

38. Thomas Becon, *Prayers and other pieces of Thomas Becon*, ed. John Ayre (Cambridge: Cambridge University Press, 1844), p. 272. Discussed in Catherine Gallagher and Stephen Greenblatt, *Practicing New Historicism* (Chicago: University of Chicago Press, 2000), p. 145.

39. Modified version of the translation in Luther, *Works*, vol. 38, p. 151. *Winckelmesse* seems to have been Luther's own neologistic translation of the Latin term *missa privata*, which is generally translated simply as "private mass." Grimm and Grimm, *Deutsches Wörterbuch*, vol. 30, p. 374.

40. John Jewel, *An Apology of the Church of England* (Ithaca: Cornell University Press, 1963), p. 40. On the proliferation of different kinds of masses, see Erasmus, *Erasmus and the Seamless Coat*, pp. 92 and 94.

41. As translated in Baxandall, *The Limewood Sculptors*, p. 78. The original reads: "Wir armen tempel bilder gemain / Vnd winckel götzen groß und klain."

42. On the concept of *Beygott*, see Michalski, *The Reformation*, p. 190.

43. Edmund Gurnay, *Toward the vindication of the Second Commandment* (Cambridge: Thomas Buck, 1639), pp. 124–25.

44. Jean Calvin, *Institutes of the Christian Religion*, ed. John Thomas McNeill, trans. Ford Lewis Battles (Philadelphia: Westminster Press, 1960), vol. 1, p. 117.

45. Calvin, *Institutes*, vol. 1, p. 117.

46. Calvin, *Institutes*, vol. 1, p. 65.

47. On Rogier's use of this format, see Lynn F. Jacobs, "The Inverted 'T'-Shape in Early Netherlandish Altarpieces: Studies in the Relation between Painting and Sculpture," *Zeitschrift für Kunstgeschichte* 54, no. 1 (1991), pp. 59–62.

48. Developing an observation made by Kurt Forster, Leo Steinberg explains

how the emptiness in the center of Pontormo's *Deposition* is haunted by the Pietà: "The two bodies are separated as by a stretching cord. It is as though the dead Christ had slipped from his mother's knees... that voided middle about which all revolves... is the Virgin's untenanted lap, the widowed center of the design. The prelude to the moment depicted, its implied precondition, emerges for us as a familiar icon, a devotional image in which mourner and mourned overlap and enfold one another." Leo Steinberg, "Pontormo's Capponi Chapel," *The Art Bulletin* 56, no. 3 (1974), p. 387.

49. Cindy Nemser, "A Conversation with Eva Hesse," in Mignon Nixon, ed., *Eva Hesse* (Cambridge: MIT Press, 2002), pp. 7–8.

50. Hesse calls them machines. Lucy R. Lippard, *Eva Hesse* (New York: New York University Press, 1976), p. 38.

51. Robert Smithson, *The Writings of Robert Smithson: Essays and Illustrations*, ed. Nancy Holt (New York: New York University Press, 1979), p. 36. On rotation as a procedure in Hesse's work, see Kathryn A. Tuma, "Eva Hesse's Turn: Rotations Around the Circle Drawings," in Catherine de Zegher, ed., *Eva Hesse Drawing* (New York and New Haven: The Drawing Center; Yale University Press, 2006), pp. 214–71. On emptiness and lack in Hesse's work, see Briony Fer, "Bordering on Blank: Eva Hesse and Minimalism," in Nixon, *Eva Hesse*, pp. 56–85.

52. Lippard, *Eva Hesse*, p. 65. On Hesse's lists, see Rosalind E. Krauss, *The Optical Unconscious* (Cambridge: MIT Press, 1993), pp. 310–13.

53. Nemser, "A Conversation," p. 17.

54. Elisabeth Sussman, *Eva Hesse* (San Francisco and New Haven: San Francisco Museum of Modern Art; Yale University Press, 2002), p. 229. See also Lippard, *Eva Hesse*, pp. 106–109.

55. For example, *Sans II* (1968) and *Accretion* (1968). The latex spheres and demi-spheres of *Sequel* (1967–1968) and *Scheme* (1967–1968) also strike me as ambiguous as far as hollowness is concerned.

CHAPTER SIX: BROKEN BODIES IN THE ANTONITE CONTEXT

1. On the artist's identity and origins, see Stephan Kemperdick and Matthias Weniger, "Der Bartholomäusmeister: Herkunft und Anfänge seines Stils," in Rainer Budde and Roland Krischel, eds., *Genie ohne Namen: Der Meister des Bartholomäus-Altars* (Cologne: Dumont, 2001), pp. 26–43; Roland Krischel, "Der

Meister des Bartholomäus-Altars—Porträt eines Unbekannten," in Budde and Krischel, *Genie ohne Namen*, pp. 13–15.

2. Kemperdick and Weniger argue that the Bartholomew Master's copying of specific colors and textures demonstrates that he saw Rogier's original in Louvain. Kemperdick and Weniger, "Der Bartholomäusmeister," p. 35. On the other hand, a close painted copy may have served as intermediary. Nicole Reynaud, ed., *Les primitifs de l'école de Cologne* (Paris: Editions des Musées nationaux, 1974), p. 31.

3. Timothy B. Husband, "The Winteringham Tau Cross and Ignis Sacer," *Metropolitan Museum Journal* 27 (1992), pp. 19–35.

4. The relationship between the hammer and the Tau cross is pointed out on the website associated with the 2001 exhibition "Genie ohne Name: Der Meister des Bartholomäus-Altars": http://www.museenkoeln.de/ausstellungen/wrm_0108_bartholomaeusaltar/fs.html (accessed 22 July 2010).

5. On the altarpiece's possible origins in Paris, see Reynaud, *Les primitifs*, p. 29; Neil MacGregor, *A Victim of Anonymity: The Master of the Saint Bartholomew Altarpiece* (London: Thames and Hudson, 1994), p. 26. In 1941, vom Rath suggested that two panels depicting the Saints Andrew, Catherine, and Peter, and the Saints John the Evangelist, Apollonia, and Thomas, which are now in Arnhem and which have been attributed to the Bartholomew Master since 1913, are the missing wings of the Paris *Deposition*. Karl vom Rath, *Der Meister des Bartholomäusaltares* (Bonn: Röhrscheid, 1941), pp. 74–77. Nürnberger, however, has used technical analysis to corroborate the earlier objections of Ring and Pieper to this theory, suggesting instead that only the *design* for the wings originated in the Bartholomew Master's workshop. Ulrike Nürnberger, "The Late Medieval Workshop of the Master of the St. Bartholomew Altar: An Investigation of Underdrawings and Paintings" (Dissertation, Indiana University, 1995), pp. 80–84.

6. Adalbert Mischlewski, *Grundzüge der Geschichte des Antoniterordens bis zum Ausgang des 15. Jahrhunderts* (Cologne and Vienna: Böhlau, 1976), pp. 17–47.

7. Adalbert Mischlewski, *Un ordre hospitalier au Moyen Âge: Les chanoines réguliers de Saint-Antoine-en-Viennois*, trans. Hermann Kuhn and Denise Kuhn (Grenoble: Presses Universitaires de Grenoble, 1995), p. 123.

8. Bauer suggests that even very small houses took care of the sick. Veit Harold Bauer, *Das Antonius-Feuer in Kunst und Medizin* (Berlin: Springer, 1973), p. 61.

9. "Annus pestilens, maxime in occidentali parte Lotharingiae, ubi multi, sacro igni interiora consumente computrescentes, exesis membris, instar carbonum

nigrescentibus, aut miserabiliter moriuntur, aut manibus et pedibus putrefactis truncati, miserabiliori vitae reservantur, multi vero nervorum contractione distorti tormentantur." Mischlewski, *Grundzüge der Geschichte*, p. 22 n.27. For other early accounts of the disease, see Henry Chaumartin, *Le mal des ardents et le feu Saint-Antoine* (Vienne: Ternet, 1946), pp. 121–40.

10. Marie Madeleine Antony-Schmitt, *Le culte de saint Sébastien en Alsace: Médecine populaire et saints guérisseurs, essai de sociologie religieuse* (Strasbourg: Librairie Istra, 1977), p. 36.

11. Mischlewski, *Grundzüge der Geschichte*, pp. 349–51.

12. Chaumartin, *Le mal des ardents*, p. 33; Bauer, *Das Antonius-Feuer*, p. 65; Mischlewski, *Grundzüge der Geschichte*, pp. 30–31.

13. Chaumartin, *Le mal des ardents*, p. 94; Andrée Hayum, *The Isenheim Altarpiece: God's Medicine and the Painter's Vision* (Princeton: Princeton University Press, 1989), p. 23.

14. Chaumartin, *Le mal des ardents*, pp. 91–93.

15. Hayum, *The Isenheim Altarpiece*, pp. 31–32.

16. "Arm / bein abschniden hat sein kunst / Vertriben Sanct Anthonien brunst." The illustrations are attributed to Hans Wechtlin. Husband, "The Winteringham Tau Cross," pp. 31–32.

17. "Nous vîmes des démembrés; quelques-uns étaient sans pieds, d'autres sans mains; ceux-ci sans pieds et sans mains." François-Zénon Collombet, *Histoire de la sainte église de Vienne depuis les premiers temps du christianisme jusqu'à la suppression du siège, en 1801* (Lyon: A. Mothon, 1847), vol. 3, p. 347.

18. As translated in Hayum, *The Isenheim Altarpiece*, p. 158 n.42. See also Chaumartin, *Le mal des ardents*, p. 92.

19. "Il nous fit voir des pieds et des mains coupés depuis cent ans qui sont semblables à ceux qu'il coupoit tous les jours, c'est-á-dire noirs et tout secs." Collombet, *Histoire de la sainte église de Vienne*, vol. 3, p. 347.

20. As translated in Hayum, *The Isenheim Altarpiece*, p. 158 n.42. See also Chaumartin, *Le mal des ardents*, p. 100.

21. For an example of the use of the term "martyr" for the victims of Saint Anthony's Fire, see Adalbert Mischlewski, "Der Antoniterorden in Deutschland," *Archiv für mittelrheinische Kirchengeschichte* 10 (1958), p. 43; Bauer, *Das Antonius-Feuer*, p. 65.

22. As translated in Hayum, *The Isenheim Altarpiece*, p. 28. See also Chaumartin,

Le mal des ardents, p. 100.

23. On the wound as a place of passage from the human to the divine, see Deshman, "Another Look," pp. 535–36; Jeffrey F. Hamburger, "Body vs. Book: The Trope of Visibility in Images of Christian-Jewish Polemic," in Ganz and Lentes, *Ästhetik des Unsichtbaren*, p. 120.

24. Augustine, *The Trinity*, trans. Stephen McKenna (Washington: Catholic University of America Press, 1963), pp. 27–28.

25. Desiderius Erasmus, *Colloquies*, trans. Craig R. Thompson (Toronto and Buffalo: University of Toronto Press, 1997), p. 427.

26. On the altarpiece, see Frank Günter Zehnder, *Katalog der Altkölner Malerei* (Cologne: Museen der Stadt Köln, 1990), pp. 422–41; Joachim Gaus, "'Herr, Sie werden im Licht deines Antlitzes wandeln.'—Der Thomas-Altar des Meisters des Bartholomäus-Altares," in Budde and Krischel, *Genie ohne Namen*, pp. 44–51.

27. Suckale describes the *arma Christi*—the collective term for the objects surrounding the wound—as an ascetic form of devotional imagery, insofar as it substitutes *signs* for full-blown images. Robert Suckale, "Arma Christi: Überlegungen zur Zeichenhaftigkeit mittelalterlicher Andachtsbilder," *Städel-Jahrbuch* 6 (1977), p. 194.

28. As translated in Peter W. Parshall and Rainer Schoch, *Origins of European Printmaking: Fifteenth-Century Woodcuts and Their Public* (Washington: National Gallery of Art; Yale University Press, 2005), p. 259.

29. On the substitution of the wound for the body, see David S. Areford, "The Passion Measured: A Late-Medieval Diagram of the Body of Christ," in A. A. MacDonald, H. N. B. Ridderbos, and R. M. Schulsmann, eds., *The Broken Body: Passion Devotion in Late-Medieval Culture* (Groningen: Egbert Forsten, 1998), p. 220.

30. On the construction of the doll, see Therese Lichtenstein, *Behind Closed Doors: The Art of Hans Bellmer* (Berkeley and New York: University of California Press; International Center of Photography, 2001), pp. 21–22. The quotation about the panorama is from Hans Bellmer, "Memories of the Doll Theme," *Sulfur* 26 (1990), p. 33. Many biographies of Bellmer claim that the sixteenth-century articulated mannequins in the Kaiser-Friedrich Museum in Berlin inspired Bellmer's dolls. See, e.g., Peter Webb, *Hans Bellmer* (London and New York: Quartet Books, 1985), p. 47.

31. Hans Bellmer, *Little Anatomy of the Physical Unconscious: Or The Anatomy of the Image*, trans. Jon Graham (Waterbury Center: Dominion, 2004), p. 31.

32. Bellmer, *Little Anatomy*, p. 36.

33. On the construction of the second doll, see Webb, *Hans Bellmer*, pp. 47–48; Lichtenstein, *Behind Closed Doors*, p. 50.

34. Hal Foster, *Compulsive Beauty* (Cambridge: MIT Press, 1993), p. 103.

35. For discussion of the vaginal form of late medieval images of Christ's side-wound, see Flora Lewis, "The Wound in Christ's Side and the Instruments of the Passion: Gendered Experience and Response," in Lesley Smith and Jane H.M. Taylor, eds., *Women and the Book: Assessing the Visual Experience* (London: The British Library, 1996), pp. 212–17; Karma Lochrie, "Mystical Acts, Queer Tendencies," in Karma Lochrie, Peggy McCracken, and James A. Schultz, eds., *Constructing Medieval Sexuality* (Minneapolis and London: University of Minnesota Press, 1997), pp. 189–96; Amy Hollywood, "'That Glorious Slit': Irigaray and the Medieval Devotion to Christ's Side Wound," in Teresa Krier and Elizabeth D. Harvey, eds., *Irigaray and Premodern Culture: Thresholds of History* (London and New York: Routledge, 2004), pp. 105–25.

36. As translated in Eire, *War Against the Idols*, pp. 111–12. Original in Zwingli, *Sämtliche Werke*, vol. 6.1, p. 497.

37. On the resurrection of body parts, see Caroline Walker Bynum, *Fragmentation and Redemption: Essays on Gender and the Human Body in Medieval Religion* (New York: Zone Books, 1991), pp. 239–97.

CHAPTER SEVEN: PUPPETS AS IDOLS AND WORKSHOP AIDS

1. It is generally dated to about 1500, with no agreement having been reached as to whether it was painted before or after the Paris version. Nürnberger, "The Late Medieval Workshop," pp. 343–44. Nürnberger suggests that a copy now in a small church in Cunavarrabias, Spain, which has wings depicting John the Evangelist and Jerome and a curved top, may represent the original state of the London *Deposition*. She also points out that the barb of the London *Deposition* is not intact, which means that the panel has been cut down from its original size (p. 340). But even if it was originally slightly larger and had wings, it would not have been suitable for a major altar.

2. These include the *Crucifixion Altarpiece*, the *St. Thomas Altarpiece*, and the *St. Bartholomew Altarpiece*. Budde and Krischel, *Genie ohne Namen*, pp. 376–77, 416–17, 532–33.

3. On Rogier's allusion to sculpture, see Panofsky, *Early Netherlandish Painting*, vol. 1, p. 258; K.M. Birkmeyer, "The Arch Motif in Netherlandish Painting of the Fifteenth Century: Part One," *The Art Bulletin* 43, no. 1 (1961), p. 15; de Vos, *Rogier van der Weyden*, p. 15.

4. "Den allervernoemsten strengsten und hillichsten orden, der genoempt is der Carthuser orden, der der hilliger kirchen ein grois schatz ind rose is, der welche noch nie gefallen is von sinre volkomenheit ind van sinre regulen, as ander orden gedain haven." *Die Chroniken der niederrheinischen Städte: Cöln* (Leipzig: S. Hirzel, 1876), vol. 2, p. 463. Discussed in Marijan Zadnikar, ed., *Die Kartäuser: Der Orden der schweigenden Mönche* (Cologne: Wienand, 1983), p. 206.

5. In 1525, for example, the monastery of St. Barbara built a small house near its outer wall to allow monks to speak to women in the event that it should become absolutely necessary. See Brigitte Corley, *Painting and Patronage in Cologne, 1300–1500* (Turnhout: Harvey Miller, 2000), p. 292 n.23.

6. Gerhard Jaritz, "Klosteralltag und Welt im Spätmittelalter: Das Beispiel der Kartaeuser," *Analecta Cartusiana* 113, no. 3 (1985), p. 54.

7. "Tabule curiosis ymaginibus depicte in altaribus et alie diuerse picture cum clipeis et armis secularium et formis mulierum contra sanctam Ordinis nostri simplicitatem et humilitatem tam in fenestris vitreis quam et alijs locis contra Statuta multiplicant, de quo notabiles viri non modicum scandalizantur; ordinamus vt tales omnes picture et tabule ac alie curiose picture vt predictitur amoueantur, vbi sine graui scandalo fieri poterit, et noue de cetero fieri non permittantur." James Hogg and Michael Sargent, eds., *The Chartae of the Carthusian General Chapter* (Salzburg: Institut für Anglistik und Amerikanistik, Universität Salzburg, 1982), p. 61. Discussed in Jaritz, "Klosteralltag und Welt," p. 57.

8. For evidence that these regulations were commonly ignored, see Wolfgang Schmid, *Stifter und Auftraggeber im spätmittelalterlichen Köln* (Cologne: Kölnisches Stadtmuseum, 1994), p. 134; Schmid, "Netzwerk-Analysen," p. 62.

9. "In choro laicorum, in locum duarum tabularum nimis curiose pictarum ideoque iussu visitatorum ab annis aliquot 150 aureis venditarum, duas alias e vitalitio f. Ioannis Petit conversi pretio 183 aureorum comparatas parietibus utrimque affixit." Werner Schäfke, ed., *Die Kölner Kartause um 1500: Aufsatzband* (Cologne: Kölnisches Stadtmuseum, 1991), p. 50.

10. "On 8 February of the year 1501 died the famous Peter Rinck.... He was our special benefactor, who...left in his will 200 ordinary gulden, half the content

of his chapel, namely a retable for the altar of the Holy Cross in the screen gallery (he had earlier given a similar retable for the altar of St Thomas, which had a contemporary value of 250 gold coins, but is thought inferior, despite being very valuable)." As translated in Corley, *Painting and Patronage*, p. 237. Original in Schäfke, *Die Kölner Kartause*, p. 46.

11. See, e.g., Johann Jacob Merlos, *Kölnische Künstler in alter und neuer Zeit* (Düsseldorf: L. Schwann, 1895), p. 1180; Ludwig Scheibler and Carl Aldenhoven, eds., *Geschichte der Kölner Malerschule* (Lübeck: Nöhring, 1894), p. 266; vom Rath, *Der Meister des Bartholomäusaltares*, pp. 64–65, 68, 71; Paul Pieper, "Miniaturen des Bartholomäus-Meisters," *Wallraf-Richartz-Jahrbuch* 15 (1953), p. 144; Paul Pieper, "Das Stundenbuch des Bartholomäus-Meisters," *Wallraf-Richartz-Jahrbuch* 21 (1959), p. 124; Rolf Andree, Helmut R. Leppien, and Horst Vey, "Nachlese der Ausstellung 'Kölner Maler der Spätgotik,'" *Wallraf-Richartz-Jahrbuch* 23 (1961), p. 333; Regina Urban, "Der Meister des heiligen Bartholomäus: Untersuchungen zur Kleidung, Gestik und Vorbilderverarbeitung im Oeuvre des Malers" (Dissertation, Technischen Universität Berlin, 1997), p. 11; Krischel, "Der Meister des Bartholomäus-Altars," pp. 15–16.

12. This affinity between hands and tracery is also found in the Bartholomew Master's *Crucifixion Altarpiece*.

13. Herrad of Landesberg, *Hortus deliciarum*, ed. Rosalie B. Green et al. (London: The Warburg Institute, 1979), vol. 1, p. 200, vol. 2, fol. 215r. This is a reconstruction of the lost original. Green calls the Solomon scenes "moderately well recorded" (vol. 1, p. 28). Illustrations of booths with glove-puppet shows appear in Jehan de Grise, *Li Romans d'Alixandre*, 1344 (Bodleian ms. 264, fols. 76r and 54v), reproduced in Allardyce Nicoll, *Masks, Mimes and Miracles: Studies in the Popular Theatre* (London: G.C. Harrap, 1931), p. 168. For late medieval references to puppets at court, see George Speaight, *The History of the English Puppet Theatre* (London: Hale, 1990), pp. 27–32.

14. "In ludo monstrorum designatur vanitas vanitatum." Herrad, *Hortus deliciarum*, vol. 1, p. 200.

15. The verse below: "Versus de vanitate et quod nichil vanus sit homine. / Unde superbit homo cujus conceptio culpa / Nasci poena, labor vita, necesse mori, / Vana salus hominis, vanum decus, omnia vana. / Inter vana nihil vanius est homine / Post hominem vermis post vermem fit cinis, eheu! / Sic in non hominem vertitur omnis homo." The verse above: "De eo quod spernendus sit mundus. /

Spernere mundum, spernere nullum, spernere sese. / Spernere sperni se, quatuor haec bona sunt." Herrad, *Hortus deliciarum*, vol. 2, fol. 213v, nos. 734–35.

16. Gérard Cames, *Allégories et symboles dans l'Hortus deliciarum* (Leiden: Brill, 1971), p. 84.

17. "Der warlde wroude ist tokken spil." Ulrich von dem Türlin, *Wilhelm der Heilige von Oranse. Erster Theil*, ed. W. J. C. G. Casparson (Kassel: Johann Jacob Cramer, 1781), p. 16. Discussed in Charles Magnin, *Histoire des marionnettes en Europe depuis l'antiquité à nos jours* (Paris: Michel Lévy frères, 1852), p. 269; Grimm and Grimm, *Deutsches Wörterbuch*, vol. 2, p. 1210; Cames, *Allégories et symboles*, p. 85.

18. See entries for "puppet" and "poppet" in *Oxford English Dictionary Online* (Oxford and New York: Oxford University Press, 2000); "Puppe" in Keith Spalding, *An Historical Dictionary of German Figurative Usage* (Oxford: Blackwell Reference, 1992), vol. 5, pp. 1919–20; and "pop" in *Het woordenboek der Nederlandsche taal* (Rotterdam: AND Publishers, 2000).

19. "Ydel weifelerent vnde poppen spil edder kinder spil der Papen." Johannes Bugenhagen, *Der ehrbaren Stadt Hamburg christliche Ordnung 1529: De Ordeninge Pomerani*, ed. Hans Wenn (Hamburg: F. Wittig, 1976), pp. 4–6. Discussed in Koerner, *The Reformation of the Image*, p. 49.

20. Thomas Becon, *The reliques of Rome: contayning all such matters of religion, as haue in times past bene brought into the Church by the Pope and his adherentes* (London: Iohn Day, 1563), p. 88.

21. "An homily against the peril of idolatry (1562)," p. 276. Discussed in Margaret Aston, "Gold and Images," in W. J. Sheils and Diana Wood, eds., *The Church and Wealth* (Oxford: Basil Blackwell, 1987), p. 197.

22. As translated in Moxey, *Pieter Aertsen*, pp. 136–37. Original in Heinrich Bullinger, *De origine erroris libri duo* (Tigvri in officina Froschoviana mense martio, 1539), pp. 156–57. For other examples of the iconoclastic trope of the image as a doll or puppet, see Heales, "Easter Sepulchers," p. 280.; Michalski, *The Reformation*, pp. 188–89.

23. Luther, *Works*, vol. 20, p. 272. See also Luther, *Luthers Werke*, vol. 21, p. 500. In another instance, Luther *defends* images as innocent playthings. Luther, *Luthers Werke*, vol. 28, p. 678.

24. For example, in Biberach: "Den heiligen Geist, den man am Pfingstfest abersandte, hund die Kind beim Spielen zerbrochen"; "viel der Ding haben die

Kinder vertragen." Albert Angele, *Altbiberach um die Jahre der Reformation* (Biberach-Birkendorf: Stadtpfarramt St. Josef, 1962), pp. 163 and 164. "Pixes ar defacid and geve awaie . . . this yeare vnto a child to plaie wth all." Peacock, *English church furniture*, p. 55. For other examples, see Scribner, "Volkskultur und Volksreligion," p. 157; Michalski, "Das Phänomen Bildersturm," p. 88.

25. As translated in Speaight, *The History of the English Puppet Theatre*, p. 34. Original in Catholic Church, *Collectio maxima Conciliorum omnium Hispaniae, et Novi Orbis* (Rome: Typis J. J. Komarek Bohemi apud S. Angelum Custodem, 1693), vol. 3, pp. 718–19. Discussed in Magnin, *Histoire des marionnettes*, p. 58.

26. Wriothesley, *A chronicle of England*, vol. 2, p. 1. Discussed in Chambers, *The Mediaeval Stage*, vol. 2, p. 158. On the same page, Chambers also quotes a description of a sixteenth-century resurrection play performed by "certein smalle Puppets, representinge the Parsons of *Christe*, the Watchmen, *Marie*, and others." The quotation is from William Lambarde, *Dictionarium Angliæ topographicum & historicum: An alphabetical description of the chief places in England and Wales* (London: F. Gyles, 1730), p. 459. This resurrection play is also discussed, along with an example from Salisbury, in Sheingorn, "'No Sepulchre on Good Friday,'" p. 153. On medieval automata more broadly, see, e.g., Tripps, *Das handelnde Bildwerk*, pp. 13–16; Camille, *The Gothic Idol*, pp. 244–58; Caroline Walker Bynum, *Metamorphosis and Identity* (New York: Zone Books, 2001), pp. 59–61.

27. Wriothesley, *A chronicle of England*, vol. 1, p. 74.

28. George Cornelius Gorham, *Gleanings of a few scattered ears during the period of the reformation in England* (London: Bell and Daldy, 1857), p. 19. See also Clarence Hopper, ed., *London chronicle during the reigns of Henry the Seventh and Henry the Eighth* (Westminster: Camden Society, 1859), pp. 11–12.

29. Filarete, *Treatise on Architecture: Being the Treatise by Antonio di Piero Averlino, Known as Filarete*, trans. John R. Spencer (New Haven: Yale University Press, 1965), vol. 1, p. 315; vol. 2, fols. 184r–v. For other accounts of Italian artists, including Fra Bartolommeo, using dolls as models, see Francis Ames-Lewis, *The Intellectual Life of the Early Renaissance Artist* (New Haven: Yale University Press, 2000), pp. 46–57.

30. Numa Coste, "Recherches sur l'art provençal: Liste des peintres, sculpteurs, architectes, enlumineurs ayant séjourné en Provence depuis le Moyen-Age jusqu'au XIXème siècle," *Revue historique de Provence* (1901–1902), pp. 298–99. Discussed in Lorne Campbell, *The Fifteenth Century Netherlandish Schools* (London:

National Gallery Publications; Distributed by Yale University Press, 1998), p. 27.

31. The inventory of Margaret of Austria registers a number of such puppets. Ernst Friedrich Bange, *Die Kleinplastik der deutschen Renaissance in Holz und Stein* (Florence and Munich: Pantheon; K. Wolff, 1928), p. 49. On the German mannequins in general, see Arpad Weixlgärtner, "Von der Gliederpuppe," *Göteborgs Konstmuseum Arstryck* (1954), pp. 37–71; Anton Legner et al., eds., *Spätgotik in Salzburg: Skulptur und Kunstgewerbe 1400–1530* (Salzburg: Salzburger Museum Carolino Augusteum, 1976), pp. 162–64. On the female mannequin in Berlin, whose fingers and toes are also articulated, see Hanna Gagel, ed., *Der Mensch um 1500: Werke aus Kirche und Kunstkammern* (Berlin: Staatlichen Museen Preussischer Kulturbesitz, 1977), pp. 166–67. On the male mannequin in the Hamburg Museum für Kunst und Gewerbe, see Michael J. Liebmann, "Studien zur deutschen Kleinplastik: Eine Adam-Statuette im Puschkin-Museum zu Moskau und die Salzburger Bildschnitzerwerkstatt um 1520–1530," *Münchner Jahrbuch der bildenden Kunst* 12, no. 3 (1961), p. 200; Jörg Rasmussen, *Deutsche Kleinplastik der Renaissance und des Barock* (Hamburg: Museum für Kunst und Gewerbe Hamburg, 1975), pp. 85–86; Herbert Beck and Peter C. Bol, eds., *Dürers Verwandlung in der Skulptur zwischen Renaissance und Barock* (Frankfurt am Main: Liebieghaus Museum Alter Plastik, 1981), pp. 187–89. The Grassi Museum für Angewandte Kunst in Leipzig is home to a female figure that is thought to be the counterpart of the figure in Hamburg. Arpad Weixlgärtner, "Dürer und die Gliederpuppe," in *Beiträge zur Kunstgeschichte: Franz Wickhoff gewidmet von einem Kreise von Freunden und Schülern* (Vienna: A. Schroll, 1903), pp. 82–84. The Landesmuseueum Ferdinandeum in Innsbruck has a pair. Bange, *Die Kleinplastik*, p. 49; *Het schildersatelier in de Nederlanden 1500–1800* (Nijmegen: De Waag, 1964), nr. 69.

32. On the attributions to Dürer, see Beck and Bol, *Dürers Verwandlung*, p. 189; Bernhard Decker, "Gelingen oder Mißlingen des Fortschritts," in Beck and Bol, *Dürers Verwandlung*, pp. 471–75. For the drawings, see Weixlgärtner, "Dürer und die Gliederpuppe," pp. 80–82; Gagel, *Der Mensch*, pp. 167–70.

33. De Man, *The Rhetoric of Romanticism*, p. 272.

34. On Kleist's story, seventeenth-century automata, and the Kunstkammer, see Horst Bredekamp, *The Lure of Antiquity and the Cult of the Machine: The Kunstkammer and the Evolution of Nature, Art, and Technology*, trans. Allison Brown (Princeton: Markus Wiener Publishers, 1995), pp. 106–107.

35. As translated in de Man, *The Rhetoric of Romanticism*, p. 267. "Wenn die

Erkenntnis gleichsam durch ein Unendliches gegangen ist, die Grazie wieder ein; so, daß sie, zu gleicher Zeit, in demjenigen menschlichen Körperbau am reinsten erscheint, der entweder gar keins, oder ein unendliches Bewußtsein hat, d. h. in dem Gliedermann, oder in dem Gott." Heinrich von Kleist, "Über das Marionettentheater," in *Sämtliche Werke* (Munich: Winkler, 1967), pp. 11–12.

36. De Man, *The Rhetoric of Romanticism*, pp. 267–68.

37. As translated in de Man, *The Rhetoric of Romanticism*, p. 288. "Was sie sein sollen, tot, reine Pendel, und folgen dem bloßen Gesetz der Schwere." Kleist, "Über das Marionettentheater," p. 8.

38. De Man, *The Rhetoric of Romanticism*, p. 290.

39. In his discussion of Passion plays, Speirs compares Christ to a puppet: "But in these episodes of the Mystery Cycle Christ has something of the mysterious impersonal or non-human quality of the sacrificial victim, something even of the passivity or immobility of a masked figure or of a sacred doll or puppet, image of a god." John Speirs, *Medieval English Poetry: The Non-Chaucerian Tradition* (London: Faber and Faber, 1957), p. 353.

40. De Man, *The Rhetoric of Romanticism*, p. 272.

41. As translated in Moxey, *Pieter Aertsen*, p. 159. Original in C.G.N. De Vooys, "Een onbekende verzameling refereinen uit de eerste helft van de zestiende eeuw," *Nederlands Archief voor Kerkgeschiedenis* 21, no. 1 (1928), pp. 211–12.

42. Calvin, *Institutes*, vol. 1, p. 104. Cf. "a block of wood will be our Father in heaven." Calvin, *Tracts and Treatises*, p. 46.

43. As translated in Michalski, *The Reformation*, p. 188. Original in Adolf Laube, *Flugschriften der frühen Reformationsbewegung (1518–1524)* (Vaduz and Berlin: Topos; Akademie-Verlag, 1983), vol. 275.

44. Roxana Marcoci, *Thomas Demand* (New York: Museum of Modern Art, 2005), p. 9.

45. Michael Fried, "Without a Trace," *Artforum* 43 (March 2005), pp. 200–201.

46. "I don't cut out paper on purpose so that you can see how it was cut. But it is true that at every stage I can choose whether or not to leave these visible flaws." Thomas Demand, *Thomas Demand* (New York: Thames & Hudson, 2000), p. 52.

47. Fried, "Without a Trace," p. 199.

48. Fried, "Without a Trace," p. 202.

49. Katharine Kuh, *The Artist's Voice: Talks with Seventeen Modern Artists* (New York: Da Capo Press, 2000), p. 90. Discussed in de Duve, *Kant after Duchamp*, p.

162. Duchamp also writes: "Since the tubes of paint used by the artist are manufactured and ready made products we must conclude that all the paintings in the world are 'readymades aided' and also works of assemblage." Duchamp, *Salt Seller*, p. 142.

50. Duchamp, *Notes and Projects*, p. 56.

51. Demand, *Thomas Demand*, p. 68.

52. Paul de Man, *The Resistance to Theory* (Minneapolis: University of Minnesota Press, 1986), p. 87.

CHAPTER EIGHT: THE SHROUD AS BODY DOUBLE

1. On Mostaert's *Deposition*, see Jules Helbig, "Les peintures des maîtres inconnus: Un triptyque du XVIe siècle," *Revue de l'art chrétien* 9, 4th ser. (1898), pp. 349–57; Camille Benoit, "Le triptyque d'Oultremont et Jan Mostaert," *Gazette des Beaux-Arts* 21, 3rd ser. (1899), pp. 265–79, 368–80; Winfried Wilhelmy, *Der altniederländische Realismus und seine Funktionen: Studien zur kirchlichen Bildpropaganda des 15. Jahrhunderts* (Münster: Lit, 1993), pp. 106–10. First proposed by Benoit in his article of 1899, the attribution to Mostaert is now widely accepted. For an argument against the attribution, see Georges Hulin de Loo, *Exposition de tableaux flamands des XIVe, XVe et XVIe siècles* (Ghent: S. Siffer, 1902), pp. 70–72.

2. John of Damascus, *On the Divine Images*, p. 86.

3. For this early history of the shroud, I rely on John Beldon Scott, *Architecture for the Shroud: Relic and Ritual in Turin* (Chicago: University of Chicago Press, 2003), pp. 12–16.

4. On Margaret's attachment to the shroud, see Dagmar Eichberger, *Leben mit Kunst, Wirken durch Kunst: Sammelwesen und Hofkunst unter Margarete von Österreich, Regentin der Niederlande* (Turnhout: Brepols, 2002), pp. 230–34; Dagmar Eichberger and Yvonne Bleyerveld, *Women of Distinction: Margaret of York, Margaret of Austria* (Leuven: Davidsfonds; Brepolis, 2005), pp. 49–55.

5. Hertha Leemans, ed., *De Sint-Gummaruskerk te Lier* (Antwerp and Utrecht: De Nederlandsche Boekh., 1972), pp. 293–94.

6. Juan Luis Vives, *Joannis Ludovici Vivis Valentini opera omnia* (London: Gregg Press, 1964), pp. 41–91. Discussed in Eichberger, *Leben mit Kunst*, p. 234.

7. Modified version of the translation in Karel van Mander, *The Lives of the Illustrious Netherlandish and German Painters*, ed. and trans. Hessel Miedema (Doornspijk: Davaco, 1994), p. 174.

8. Jozef Duverger, "Jan Mostaert: Ereschilder van Margareta van Oostenrijk," *Aachener Kunstblätter des Museumvereins* 41 (1971), pp. 113–17; Eichberger, *Leben mit Kunst*, p. 253.

9. The wings that frame the *Deposition* picture the Crowing with Thorns and the Ecce Homo. On Van Adrichem, see M. Thierry de Bye Dólleman, "Aelbrecht Adriaenszoon, de stamvader van het geslacht Van Adrichem van Dorp, en zijn naaste familieleden," *Jaarboek van het Centraal Bureau voor Genealogie* 16 (1962), pp. 147–68. Mochizuki discusses the location of the altarpiece in St. Bavo's before iconoclasm (p. 92 n.62) and gives a ground-breaking account of the visual culture of the church after iconoclasm. Mochizuki, *The Netherlandish Image*.

10. Van Adrichem is alone rather than accompanied by one of his three wives, which suggests the work may have been commissioned while he was a widower. Wilhelmy, *Der altniederländische Realismus*, p. 107; Dólleman, "Aelbrecht Adriaenszoon," pp. 165–68.

11. Bridget of Sweden, *Life and Selected Revelations*, ed. Marguerite Tjader Harris, trans. Albert Ryle Kezel (New York: Paulist Press, 1990), p. 204.

12. Ludolph of Saxony writes: "Grant me the grace to anoint thee with fragrant spices by fervent devotion and useful speech; to wrap thee in a shroud and linens by purity of affection and conscience." Ludolf von Sachsen, *Praying the Life of Christ. First English Translation of the Prayers Concluding the 181 Chapters of the Vita Christi of Ludolphus the Carthusian*, trans. Mary Immaculate Bodenstedt (Salzburg: James Hogg, 1973), p. 160.

13. *Magnificat: Homilies in Praise of the Blessed Virgin Mary by Bernard of Clairvaux and Amadeus of Lausanne*, trans. Marie-Bernard Saïd and Grace Perigo (Kalamazoo: Cistercian Publications Inc., 1978), p. 36.

14. *Magnificat*, p. 39.

15. On the Byzantine topos of the Virgin's flesh as cloth and the incarnation as clothing, see Nicholas P. Constas, "Weaving the Body of God: Proclus of Constantinople, the Theotokos and the Loom of Flesh," *Journal of Early Christian Studies* 3, no. 2 (1995), pp. 169–94; Maria Evangelatou, "The Purple Thread of the Flesh: The Theological Connotations of a Narrative Iconographic Element in Byzantine Images of the Annunciation," in Antony Eastmond and Liz James, eds., *Icon and Word: The Power of Images in Byzantium, Studies Presented to Robin Cormack* (Burlington: Ashgate, 2003), pp. 265–66.

16. On the Virgin of Mercy iconography, see Vera Sussmann, "Maria mit dem

Schutzmantel" (Dissertation, Philipps-Universität zu Marburg, 1929); Thomas Lentes, "Die Gewänder der Heiligen: Ein Diskussionsbeitrag zum Verhältnis von Gebet, Bild und Imagination," in Gottfried Kerscher, ed., *Hagiographie und Kunst: Der Heiligenkult in Schrift, Bild und Architektur* (Berlin: D. Reimer, 1993), pp. 135–41; Belting, *Likeness and Presence*, pp. 354–58.

17. "Ein swester die hiess sant Anne Hettin, die hat ze einer zit vil lidens an dem Herzen und do si eins tages in dem werchhus sass mit ir werch, do erschein ir unser fraw und trug einen gar schönen mantel an; an dem stund mit guldinen buchstaben geschrieben: ave Maria! und nam si unser fraw under ir mandel und trost si und sichert si des ewigen lebens." Anton Birlinger, "Die Nonnen von St. Katharinental bei Dieszenhofen," *Alemannia* 15 (1887), p. 181. Discussed in Sussmann, "Maria mit dem Schutzmantel," p. 23.

18. "Das ist der andächtig gaystlich mantel der barmhertzigkayt und Beschirmung der hochgelobten iunckfrawn und wirdigen mutter gottes marie damit sy bedeckt und beschirmet alle die, die mit andacht und rechter hoffnung zu lauffen." Sussmann, "Maria mit dem Schutzmantel," p. 25. A document from the Unterlinden Cloister of Colmar gives the cost in prayers for the construction of an imaginary gown for the Virgin. See Lentes, "Die Gewänder," p. 139. For the dressing and undressing of statues of the Virgin, Christ, and the saints in reality and the imagination, see Richard C. Trexler, "Dressing and Undressing Images: An Analytic Sketch," in *Religion in Social Context in Europe and America, 1200–1700* (Tempe: Arizona Center for Medieval and Renaissance Studies, 2002), pp. 374–408.

19. *Magnificat*, p. 57.

20. Julian of Norwich, *Revelations of Divine Love*, trans. M. L. Del Mastro (Garden City: Image Books, 1977), p. 110.

21. On Christ as veil, see Kessler, *Spiritual Seeing*, pp. 58–63; Hamburger, "Body vs. Book," pp. 120, 127–28. In many churches, Lenten cloths were ceremonially parted or dropped on the Wednesday before Good Friday during the reading of Luke's account of Christ's crucifixion, where it is written that, at his death, "the curtain of the temple was torn in two" (Luke 23.45). Frere, *The Use of Sarum*, vol. 1, p. 140; Emminghaus, "Fastentuch," p. 830; Weigert, "Velum Templi," pp. 211–12.

22. John Chrysostom, *The Homilies of S. John Chrysostom, Archbishop of Constantinople, on the Epistle of S. Paul the Apostle to the Hebrews* (London: W. Smith, 1883), p. 191.

23. "Quem quaeritis in sepulchro, o christicolae? Jesum Nazarenum, o caelicolae. Non est hic: surrexit, sicut praedixerat. Ite, nuntiate, quia surrexit de sepulchro." The literature on this trope and its dramatic embellishments is too large to do justice to here.

24. "ecce lintheamina et sudarium, et corpus non est in sepulchro inventum." Young, *The Drama*, vol. 1, p. 268.

25. The passage continues: "Seeing this the three shall lay down their thuribles in that same 'sepulchre' and, taking the linen, shall hold it up before the clergy; and, as though showing that the Lord was risen and was no longer wrapped in it, they shall sing this antiphon: *Surrexit Dominus de sepulchro*." *The Monastic Agreement*, p. 50. According to the Gospel account, it is Peter who discovers the linens in the sepulcher: Peter ran to the tomb and saw "the linen cloths by themselves; then he went home, amazed at what had happened" (Luke 24.12). John writes that when Peter visited the tomb after the resurrection, "he saw the linen wrappings lying there" (John 20.6–7). On the importance of the sepulcher cloths in the paraliturgical rites, see Young, *The Drama*, vol. 1, p. 134; Taubert, "Mittelalterliche Kruzifixe (1979)," pp. 44–5; Franz Niehoff, "Das Kölner Ostergrab: Studien zum heiligen Grab im hohen Mittelalter," *Wallraf-Richartz-Jahrbuch* 51 (1990), p. 26.

26. On the missing body and the sepulcher, see Marin, *Opacité de la peinture*, pp. 126–27.

27. Didi-Huberman, *Fra Angelico*, p. 9, see also pp. 50 and 52.

28. Didi-Huberman, *Fra Angelico*, p. 9.

29. On corporals and other cloths for the altar, see Adolph Franz, *Die messe im deutschen Mittelalter: Beiträge zur Geschichte der Liturgie und des religiösen Volkslebens* (Darmstadt: Wissenschaftliche Buchgesellschaft, 1963), pp. 88–92; Kroesen, *The Sepulchrum Domini*, p. 56. On the Eucharistic implications of picturing the shroud, see Belting, *The Image and Its Public*, pp. 65–68, 170–72. On the depiction of the shroud in early Netherlandish paintings and its relation to the paraliturgical rites, see Lane, "'Depositio et Elevatio,'" pp. 25–29; Lane, *The Altar and the Altarpiece*, pp. 95–99.

30. *Devotio Moderna*, p. 220.

31. Julian, *Revelations of Divine Love*, p. 88, see also p. 91. For Catherine of Siena's use of a metaphor involving clothing and grace, see Caroline Walker Bynum, *Wonderful Blood: Theology and Practice in Late Medieval Northern Germany and Beyond* (Philadelphia: University of Pennsylvania Press, 2007), p. 189.

32. Charleton Fairchild Brown, ed., *Religious Lyrics of the XIVth Century* (Oxford: Clarendon Press, 1957), p. 88.

33. Branden W. Joseph, ed., *Robert Rauschenberg* (Cambridge: MIT Press, 2002), pp. 27–28.

34. John Cage, *Silence: Lectures and Writings* (Middletown: Wesleyan University Press, 1961), p. 102. Discussed in Branden W. Joseph, "White on White," *October* 27, no. 1 (2000), p. 97.

35. Cage, *Silence*, p. 108. Discussed in Joseph, "White on White," p. 97.

36. Cage, *Silence*, p. 98.

37. Walter Hopps, *Robert Rauschenberg: The Early 1950s* (Houston: The Menil Collection; Houston Fine Art Press, 1991), p. 66, see also p. 80. And *Robert Rauschenberg* (Washington: National Collection of Fine Arts, Smithsonian Institution, 1976), p. 66.

38. Hopps, *Robert Rauschenberg*, p. 230.

39. Cage, *Silence*, p. 103.

40. See the essays in Joseph, *Robert Rauschenberg*.

41. "There is no doubt about which way is up. In any case our feet are on the ground. Painting's place is on the wall—painting's place, that is, in process." Cage, *Silence*, p. 102. Cage discusses change in Rauschenberg's paintings throughout this essay.

42. Hopps, *Robert Rauschenberg*, p. 230.

CONCLUSION: HANS HOLBEIN'S *DEAD CHRIST IN THE TOMB*

1. For bequests related to the Holy Sepulcher, see Heales, "Easter Sepulchers," pp. 307–308; Bond, *The Chancel*, pp. 232–36; Brooks, "The Sepulchre," p. 72; Duffy, *The Stripping of the Altars*, pp. 33–35; Kroesen, *The Sepulchrum Domini*, pp. 77–81; Maisel, *Sepulchrum Domini*, pp. 88–89.

2. Belting, *The Image and Its Public*, p. 58.

3. Thomas, *Summa Theologiae*, vol. 54, p. 141.

4. Thomas à Kempis, *The Imitation of Christ*, p. 39, see also pp. 38, 59, 88, 113, 144, 150.

5. "This automatic doll can be nothing else than a materialization of Nathaniel's feminine attitude towards his father.... Olympia is, as it were, a dissociated complex of Nathaniel's which confronts him as a person." Sigmund Freud, "The

Uncanny," in James Strachey, ed., *The Standard Edition of the Complete Psychological Works of Sigmund Freud* (London: The Hogarth Press and the Institute of Psycho-analysis, 1953), vol. 17, p. 232 n.1.

6. Just a little further down on the same page, Lacan continues: "The first symbol in which we recognize humanity in its vestiges is the burial (*la sépulture*), and death as a means can be recognized in every relation in which man is born into the life of his history." Lacan, *Écrits*, p. 262.

7. Jacques Lacan, *The Four Fundamental Concepts of Psycho-Analysis*, ed. Jacques-Alain Miller, trans. Alan Sheridan (New York: W. W. Norton & Company, 1981), p. 62. "The repetition of the mother's departure [is] cause of a *Spaltung* (split) in the subject." Lacan, *The Four Fundamental Concepts*, pp. 62–63.

8. Holbein's monogram and the date are fictively inscribed inside the tomb above Christ's feet. On this inscription and the amendments to it, see Sander, *Hans Holbein*, p. 135.

9. For an overview of the literature on the question of function, see Sander, *Hans Holbein*, pp. 136–37.

10. Müller's theory is based in part on the fact that Holbein's panel is exactly as wide as the Amerbach epitaph. Christian Müller, "Holbeins Gemälde 'Der Leichnam Christi im Grabe' und die Grabkapelle der Familie Amerbach in der Basler Kartause," *Zeitschrift für schweizerische Archäologie und Kunstgeschichte* 58, no. 4 (2001), pp. 279–89.

11. For a review of this literature, see Sander, *Hans Holbein*, pp. 139–40. On Dostoyevsky's comments on the painting, see Victor Ieronim Stoichita, "Ein Idiot in der Schweiz: Bildbeschreibung bei Dostojewski," in Gottfried Boehm and Helmut Pfotenhauer, eds., *Beschreibungskunst, Kunstbeschreibung: Ekphrasis von der Antike bis zur Gegenwart* (Munich: W. Fink, 1995), pp. 425–44.

12. He also compares Holbein's panel to fifteenth-century northern Italian paintings modeled on the *epitaphios*. Herbert von Einem, *Holbeins "Christus im Grabe"* (Mainz and Wiesbaden: Akademie der Wissenschaften und der Literatur; F. Steiner, 1960). Around the same time, Überwasser also suggested precedents for Holbein's composition. Walter Überwasser, "Holbeins *Christus in der Grabnische*," in *Studien zur Kunst des Oberrheins: Festschrift für Werner Noack* (Constance: J. Thorbecke, 1959), pp. 126–27. And, following the lead of Wilhelm Stein, Klotz would soon after propose one sculpture in particular in the Cathedral of Freising as a source for Holbein's composition. Heinz Klotz, "Holbeins *Leichnam Christi im*

Grab," *Jahresberichte der Öffentliche Kunstsammlung Basel* (1964–1966), pp. 117–19.

13. On this isolation, see Julia Kristeva, "Holbein's Dead Christ," in Michel Feher, Ramona Naddaff, and Nadia Tazi, eds., *Fragments for a History of the Human Body. Part One* (New York: Zone Books, 1989), pp. 263–65; Sander, *Hans Holbein*, p. 139.

14. "Ein todten Bild H. Holbeins uf holtz mit Ölfarben." Sander, *Hans Holbein*, p. 40.

15. Sander, *Hans Holbein*, p. 40.

16. On the titulus, see Sander, *Hans Holbein*, p. 138; *Hans Holbein the Younger: The Basel Years 1515–1532* (Munich and London: Prestel, 2006), p. 257.

17. As translated in Stone, *A History of the Doctrine*, vol. 1, pp. 248–49. Original in Lanfranc of Bec, "De corpore et sanguine Domini adversus Berengarium Turonensem" in *Patrologia Latina*, vol. 150, pp. 430B–C.

18. John Rastell, *A replie against an answer (falslie intitled) in defence of the truth* (Antwerp: Aegidius Diest, 1565), fol. 197r. Discussed in John E. Booty, *John Jewel as Apologist of the Church of England* (London: S.P.C.K., 1963), p. 154; Gallagher and Greenblatt, *Practicing New Historicism*, p. 225 n.33.

19. Thomas Harding, *A detection of sundrie foule errours, lies, sclaunders, corruptions, and other false dealinges, touching doctrine, and other matters* (Louvain: Apud Ioannem Foulerum, 1568), fol. 350v. Discussed in Booty, *John Jewel as Apologist*, p. 158; Gallagher and Greenblatt, *Practicing New Historicism*, p. 225 n.33.

20. For Eucharistic miracles associated with Jewish Host desecration, see Kolve, *The Play Called Corpus Christi*, p. 47; Bynum, *Holy Feast and Holy Fast*, pp. 63–64; Rubin, *Gentile Tales*, pp. 123, 158, 160 fig. 21, 163, 165, 171; Gallagher and Greenblatt, *Practicing New Historicism*, pp. 99 and 142; Mitchell B. Merback, "Fount of Mercy, City of Blood: Cultic Anti-Judaism and the Pulkau Passion Altarpiece," *The Art Bulletin* 87, no. 4 (2005), pp. 589–642.

21. Rubin, *Gentile Tales*, p. 123.

22. Stone, *A History of the Doctrine*, vol. 1, p. 252. Original in Durand of Troarn, "De corpore et sanguine Christi" in *Patrologia Latina*, vol. 149, p. 1411A. The aniconic opacity of the white wafer made it possible to imagine Christ in the Host in any number of forms. On this ambiguity, see Miri Rubin, "Der Körper der Eucharistie im Mittelalter," in Klaus Schreiner and Norbert Schnitzler, eds., *Gepeinigt, begehrt vergessen: Symbolik und Sozialbezug des Körpers im späten Mittelalter und in der frühen Neuzeit* (Munich: W. Fink, 1992), pp. 34–36.

23. As translated in Piero Camporesi, "The Consecrated Host: A Wondrous Excess," in Feher, Naddaff, and Tazi, *Fragments for a History*, p. 233. Original in Domenico Cavalca, *Le vite dei SS. Padri* (Milan: Instituto Editoriale Italiano, 1926), vol. 2, p. 71.

24. Thomas, *Summa Theologiae*, vol. 54, pp. 149–51.

25. Thomas, *Summa Theologiae*, vol. 54, p. 149.

26. Robert Persons, *The Christian directory (1582): The first books of the Christian exercise, appertayning to resolution*, ed. Victor Houliston (Leiden and Boston: Brill, 1998), p. 234.

27. Christian Müller, *Hans Holbein d. J.: Zeichnungen aus dem Kupferstichkabinett der Öffentlichen Kunstsammlung Basel* (Basel: Kunstmuseum, 1988), pp. 20–23.

28. *Hans Holbein the Younger*, pp. 146–57.

29. During this same period, he also designed stained glass windows and painted organ shutters. Oskar Bätschmann, *Hans Holbein*, trans. Cecilia Hurley and Pascal Griener (Princeton: Princeton University Press, 1997), pp. 97, 112–19.

30. Bätschmann, *Hans Holbein*, p. 97.

31. Already in 1524, Zwingli had put through a resolution to have religious images removed from churches in Zurich and to have the commissioning of new ones outlawed. Sander, *Hans Holbein*, p. 275.

32. Sander, *Hans Holbein*, p. 313; von Greyerz, "Hans Holbein the Younger," pp. 72–75.

33. Sander, *Hans Holbein*, pp. 21–22.

34. Donald Judd, *Donald Judd: Kunstverein St. Gallen*, ed. Roland Wäspe (St. Gallen: Der Kunstverein, 1990), p. 55.

35. Judd, *Donald Judd: Kunstverein St. Gallen*, p. 52.

36. Judd, *Donald Judd: Kunstverein St. Gallen*, p. 52.

37. John Coplans, ed., *Don Judd* (Pasadena: Castle Press, 1971), p. 36. Cf. "I realized I wasn't at all interested in weight and mass. I like volume." Judd, *Donald Judd: Kunstverein St. Gallen*, p. 55. On Judd's use of negative space, see Yve-Alain Bois, "The Inflection," in *Donald Judd: New Sculpture, September 13–October 19, 1991* (New York: Pace Gallery, 1991), n.p.

38. Coplans, *Don Judd*, p. 36, see also p. 44.

39. Robert Smithson, "Donald Judd," in *Donald Judd: Early Fabricated Work* (New York: PaceWildenstein, 1998), p. 15; Rosalind E. Krauss, "The Material Uncanny," in *Donald Judd: Early Fabricated Work*, pp. 7–13.

40. Krauss, "The Material Uncanny," p. 10.

41. Judd, *Donald Judd: Kunstverein St. Gallen*, p. 52. In a related vein, Judd writes: "While the outside is definite and rigorous, the inside is indefinite. The interior appears to be larger than the exterior. The plastic is very slippery in look." Coplans, *Don Judd*, p. 44.

42. "Materials vary greatly and are simply materials—formica, aluminum, cold-rolled steel, plexiglas, red and common brass, and so forth. They are specific. If they are used directly, they are more specific. Also, they are usually aggressive. There is an objectivity to the obdurate identity of a material." Donald Judd, *Complete Writings 1959–1975: Gallery Reviews, Book Reviews, Articles, Letters to the Editor, Reports, Statements, Complaints* (Halifax: Press of the Nova Scotia College of Art and Design, 1975), p. 187.

43. Judd, *Complete Writings 1959–1975*, p. 117.

44. Judd, *Donald Judd: Kunstverein St. Gallen*, p. 55.

45. Smithson, "Donald Judd," p. 15.

46. "Smithson isn't my spokesman," Judd wrote in a letter to the editor of *Arts Magazine* in February 1967, responding to Smithson's "Entropy and the New Monuments." Discussed in Jennifer L. Roberts, *Mirror-Travels: Robert Smithson and History* (New Haven: Yale University Press, 2004), p. 147 n.43. Cf. "For 200 years or so art has been freeing itself from being obliged to say things about the world which are properly in the area of science. Some recent artists, Robert Smithson for one, have revived this dying anthropomorphism by incorporating scientific ideas and terms in their work. This is an anthropomorphic sentimentalism." Donald Judd, *Complete Writings 1975–1986* (Eindhoven: Van Abbemuseum, 1987), p. 32.

47. Donald Judd, *Donald Judd: Staatliche Kunsthalle Baden-Baden*, ed. Jochen Poetter (Stuttgart: Edition Cantz, 1989), p. 92.

48. Smithson, "Donald Judd," p. 15.

49. Smithson, "Donald Judd," p. 15.

50. Fried, for example, would not accept this assertion: "The apparent hollowness of most literalist work—the quality of having an *inside*—is almost blatantly anthropomorphic." Michael Fried, "Art and Objecthood," in Gregory Battcock, ed., *Minimal Art: A Critical Anthology* (Berkeley: University of California Press, 1995), p. 129.

51. Smithson, "Donald Judd," p. 15.

POSTSCRIPT: WHAT BECAME OF THE SEPULCHERS

1. Peacock, *English church furniture*, p. 65. Peacock also mentions sepulchers "taken from the Church by the vicar and remayneth in his house as wee suppose" (p. 52); "sold to Robert Lond and he saith he haith made a presse therof" (p. 108); "sold to wm Badge the said tyme who haithe made necessaries thereof for his house" (p. 117); "burned and defaced and[!] put to prophaine vse" (p. 148). Discussed in Brooks, "The Sepulchre," p. 75. Sometimes the sepulcher was less imaginatively redeployed: "defaced wearof we made a bear (bier) to carie the dead corps and other things." Peacock, *English church furniture*, p. 67.

2. Peacock, *English church furniture*, p. 144.

3. For discussion of the cabinet's altar-like appearance and position in paintings of early modern art collections, see Victor Ieronim Stoichita, *The Self-Aware Image: An Insight into Early Modern Meta-Painting*, trans. Anne-Marie Glasheen (New York: Cambridge University Press, 1997), p. 112.

4. "Nemen [God] aen . . . ende leyden hem . . . in het Cabinet van haer Herte, als haeren besten en kostelijksten Schat." Dionysius Spranckhuysen, *Opuscula practica, ofte alle de stichtelijke werken, die haar strekken tot een waare oefeninge der Godsalicheidt, voor alle oprechte Christenen* (Franeker: Joh. Arcerius, 1658), vol. 8, p. 40b. Luiken also uses the cabinet as a metaphor for the heart: "Die . . . maak een dierbaar Kabinet, Van 't wel, met Deugd vervulde herte." Jan Luiken, *Het leerzaam huisraad: Vertoond in vyftig konstige figuuren, met godlyke spreuken en stichtelyke verzen* (Amsterdam: Pieter Arentz en Kornelis vander Sys, 1711), p. 166. Both are quoted in the entry for "kabinet" in *Het woordenboek der Nederlandsche taal.*

5. Hester C. Dibbits, "Between Society and Family Values: The Linen Cupboard in Early-Modern Households," in Anton Schuurman and Pieter Spierenburg, eds., *Private Domain, Public Inquiry: Families and Life-Styles in the Netherlands and Europe, 1550 to the Present* (Hilversum: Verloren, 1996), esp. p. 130; Hester C. Dibbits, *Vertrouwd bezit: Materiële cultuur in Doesburg en Maassluis 1650-1800* (Nijmegen: SUN, 2001), p. 100.

6. Klaske Muizelaar and Derek Phillips, *Picturing Men and Women in the Dutch Golden Age: Paintings and People in Historical Perspective* (New Haven: Yale University Press, 2003), pp. 43–44.

7. John Loughman and John Michael Montias, *Public and Private Spaces: Works of Art in Seventeenth-Century Dutch Houses* (Zwolle: Waanders, 2000), p. 32.

8. De Man, *The Rhetoric of Romanticism*, p. 256.

9. De Man, *The Resistance to Theory*, p. 69.

10. In this sepulchral architecture occurs "the dismemberment of the aesthetic whole [read: lyric voice] into the unpredictable play of the literary letter." De Man, *The Resistance to Theory*, p. 70.

11. Walter Benjamin, *Selected Writings, Volume 4, 1938-1940*, ed. Marcus Bullock and Michael William Jennings (Cambridge: Belknap Press, 2003), p. 26. See also Benjamin, *The Arcades Project*, pp. 220–21.

12. "Baudelaire's enterprise was to make manifest the peculiar aura of commodities. He sought to humanize the commodity heroically. This endeavor has its counterpart in the concurrent bourgeois attempt to humanize the commodity sentimentally: to give it, like the human being, a home. The means used were the étuis, covers, and cases in which the domestic utensils of the time were sheathed." Benjamin, *Selected Writings, Volume 4*, p. 173.

13. Benjamin, *Selected Writings, Volume 4*, p. 96.

14. "Baudelaire's reception of the dogma of original sin.... The oldest concept seemed to him just proven enough to master a thoroughly new and disconcerting phenomenon." Benjamin, *Selected Writings, Volume 4*, p. 171.

15. Benjamin, *Selected Writings, Volume 4*, p. 183.

16. Benjamin, *Selected Writings, Volume 4*, pp. 183 and 190.

17. Charles Baudelaire, *Les Fleurs du Mal: The Complete Text of The Flowers of Evil*, trans. Richard Howard (Boston: D.R. Godine, 1982), p. 75. "J'ai plus de souvenirs que si j'avais mille ans. / Un gros meuble à tiroirs encombré de bilans, / De vers, de billets doux, de procès, de romances, / Avec de lourds cheveux roulés dans des quittances, / Cache moins de secrets que mon triste cerveau. / C'est une pyramide, un immense caveau, / Qui contient plus de morts que la fosse commune. / —Je suis un cimetière abhorré de la lune, / Où comme des remords se traînent de longs vers / Qui s'acharnent toujours sur mes morts les plus chers. / Je suis un vieux boudoir plein de roses fanées, / Où gît tout un fouillis de modes surannées, / Où les pastels plaintifs et les pâles Boucher / Seuls, respirent l'odeur d'un flacon débouché." Charles Baudelaire, *Œuvres complètes*, ed. Claude Pichois (Paris: Gallimard, 1975), vol. 1, p. 73.

18. De Man, *The Rhetoric of Romanticism*, p. 256.

19. And, further down the page: "endowing static records with dynamic life." Erwin Panofsky, *Meaning in the Visual Arts: Papers in and on Art History* (Garden City: Doubleday, 1955), p. 24. On this passage in Panofsky, see Michael Ann Holly

"Mourning and Method," in Farago and Zwijnenberg, *Compelling Visuality*, pp. 156–57.

20. De Man, *The Rhetoric of Romanticism*, p. 247.

21. Theodor W. Adorno, *Prisms*, trans. Samuel Weber and Sheirry Weber (Cambridge: MIT Press, 1981), p. 177.

22. Adorno, *Prisms*, p. 183.

23. Adorno, *Prisms*, p. 181.

24. Adorno, *Prisms*, p. 185.

Index

Zone Books series design by Bruce Mau
Typesetting by Meighan Gale
Image placement and production by Julie Fry
Printed and bound by Thomson-Shore